# A HISTORY *and* DESCRIPTION *of* ROMAN POLITICAL INSTITUTIONS

# *A* HISTORY *and* DE-SCRIPTION *of* ROMAN POLITICAL INSTITUTIONS

BY

FRANK FROST ABBOTT

THIRD EDITION

Biblo and Tannen

New York

1963

BIBLO and TANNEN
BOOKSELLERS and PUBLISHERS, Inc.
63 Fourth Avenue          New York 3, N. Y.

Library of Congress Catalog Card Number: 63-10766

*Printed in U.S.A. by*
NOBLE OFFSET PRINTERS, INC.
NEW YORK 3, N. Y.

# PREFACE

THIS book is intended to serve as an introduction to the study of Roman political institutions for those who may wish to carry on more extended investigations in that field, and to give a reasonable acquaintance with the subject to the student of Roman life and literature. It may be said with truth that the art and literature of Rome never had a distinctively national character. Both are hybrid products. Her political institutions, however, are essentially her own, and are, one might almost say, the only characteristic product of the Roman genius. We have tacitly recognized how large a place they fill in Roman history, and how valuable an inheritance they have been to modern civilization, but strangely enough we have almost entirely neglected the study of them in this country. This neglect seems the more surprising since, from the disciplinary point of view, perhaps no subject furnishes a better training in practical logic or gives us a clearer insight into the workings of the average human mind. These facts have been mentioned, not for the purpose of offering a plea for the study of Roman political institutions, but rather in explanation of the reasons which led to the writing of this book.

My aim has been to give a connected view of the development of the constitution from the earliest times down through the accession of Diocletian. Each one of the three periods in its history, — the monarchical, the republican, and the imperial, — is presented as a unit, and its institutions are treated first on the historical, then on the descriptive, side. The historical treatment seemed to me necessary because without it one cannot get a conception of the constitution as an organic whole nor can one understand how the relation of the several parts to one another determined in large measure the development of each. On the other hand, few students will get a complete view and a clear idea of any one institution without a separate description of it. The book is so arranged, however, that teachers who wish to do so may use either the historical or the descriptive part separately.

The brevity at which I have aimed has made it necessary at times in discussing controverted questions to content myself with stating what seemed to me the most probable theory. It has possibly at other points led to the omission of certain details whose presentation might modify the reader's conception of the institution in question. If this has given a dogmatic tone to any part of the work, I hope that the defect has been corrected by the fact that reference has been made to the sources for almost every important statement, and that modern literature has been freely cited, so that the reader may form an independent judgment or may acquaint himself with the views held by others on the matter in question.

Of the works which I have found of service in the preparation of this book I would mention my great indebtedness to the treatises on the Roman constitution by Mommsen, Madvig, Herzog, Willems, and Schiller, and to the general histories of Niese, Schiller, and Pelham. A separate treatment of the Roman judicial system did not fall within the scope of this book as originally planned, but in response to the request of teachers who were using the work a supplement upon the Roman courts was added to it in the new edition which was brought out three years ago.

For the new impression which is now being made the two indices of the second edition have been combined and materially enlarged, and to the bibliography at the end of each chapter the titles of some of the most important books which have appeared during the last nine years have been added. I wish to express again my gratitude to Professor F. G. Moore of Columbia University, to Professor Edward Capps of this University, and to Professor E. A. Bechtel of Tulane University, for the many valuable suggestions which they made while the work in its original form was passing through the press; and to Professor Tenny Frank of Bryn Mawr College, to Dr. J. D. Wolcott, and to Dr. W. K. Clement for assistance in verifying the references. I hope that, with the additions and improvements which have been made, the book may deserve still more the friendly reception which it has had in the two previous editions.

FRANK FROST ABBOTT

PRINCETON, December 7, 1910

# CONTENTS

## PART I — MONARCHICAL PERIOD

### Section I — Historical

### Section II — Descriptive

## PART II — REPUBLICAN PERIOD

### Section I — Historical

### Section II — Descriptive

## PART III — IMPERIAL PERIOD

### Section I — Historical

### Section II — Descriptive

# ROMAN
# POLITICAL INSTITUTIONS

## Part I — Monarchical Period

### SECTION I — HISTORICAL

### CHAPTER I

#### ROME UNDER THE KINGS

**1. The Gens.** The basis of political organization among
the early Romans was the *gens* or clan. This unit of organization, which in one form or another is common to the
Indo-European peoples, retained many of its characteristics
and some measure of its social and political importance to
a very late period. Cicero describes the *gentiles* of his day,
or the members of a clan, as those who could trace their
lineage back to a common ancestor, who could claim that
their ancestors had all been freemen, and who were in possession of their full rights. The civil and political rights
of the individual came to him as a member of a family
belonging to a *gens*, and, since membership in a particular
*gens* was indicated by the possession of the *nomen gen-
tilicium*, or clan name, the legal and social importance
which attached to the name is readily understood. In
fact, in the earliest period, even the right to use the land,

which was the property of the clan as a whole, was enjoyed by the individual only by virtue of his membership in one of those organizations.  Attached to the various *gentes*, or to families belonging to the *gentes*, were hereditary dependents called *clientes*, who enjoyed some of the privileges of members of a clan, and in return therefor owed to their *patronus* such services as assisting in the payment of his ransom, if captured in time of war, and contributing to his daughter's dower.  The control of clan affairs rested probably with the members of the clan, or with its representatives.  Had the organization been under the headship of an individual, some traces of such a system would be discernible in historic times.

2. **Pagi and their Confederation.**  The simplest purely political community was formed by the settlement of several clans about an *arx* or fortified point.  These communities, called *pagi*, were, like the *gentes*, either purely democratic, or controlled by the elders.  The union of "hill settlements" adjacent to one another for mutual protection in trade intercourse naturally followed.  Perhaps several of these confederacies were formed in Latium, but of course the confederacy of greatest historic importance is the one having Alba Longa for its common point of meeting.  The choice of that town as the place at which, even in historic times, the members of the confederacy met to offer a joint sacrifice to Jupiter Latiaris, shows plainly enough that Alba Longa was originally at the head of the league, but before the dawn of history Rome had succeeded her in the headship of at least this group of communities.

3. **The Founding of Rome.**  According to the picturesque account which Roman writers have left us in prose and verse of the founding of their native city, Rome was

an offshoot of Alba Longa, since Romulus and Remus were grandsons of Numitor, the last of the line of Alban kings who traced their lineage back to Ascanius, the son of Aeneas. The tradition which traced the beginnings of Rome to a descendant of Aeneas is only one of the many accounts which sought to bring Rome into connection with Greece. The stories of Evander, of Heracles, and of the Pelasgi, as they are recounted, for instance, by Livy, illustrate the same tendency. Greek and Roman writers dated the founding of the city all the way from 753 to 747 B.C. The first mentioned date, which Varro adopted, is perhaps the one most commonly accepted by the ancients. From this time to the establishment of the republic, in 509 B.C., seven kings reigned, by name Romulus, Numa Pompilius, Tullus Hostilius, Ancus Marcius, L. Tarquinius Priscus, Servius Tullius, and L. Tarquinius Superbus.

4. **The Regal Period.** According to tradition, the first king laid the political foundations for the city, by creating the senate, and by dividing the people into *curiae*. He also extended Roman power by successful wars. Numa Pompilius is the antithesis, in many ways, of Romulus. He organized priesthoods, established religious rites, and sought to develop the religious life of the people. It was the main purpose of Tullus Hostilius, as it had been that of Romulus, to extend the material power of Rome. Ancus Marcius, the fourth king, represents in a way the two types in combination. The peaceful development of Rome was furthered in his reign by the founding of Ostia and the bridging of the Tiber, while her prestige in war was maintained with success. To L. Tarquinius, who was a Greek by descent, but came to Rome from Tarquinii in Etruria, many of the great public works of Rome, notably the Circus and the Cloaca Maxima, were attributed. He

distinguished himself likewise in wars against the Latins and Etruscans.

After Romulus, Servius Tullius was regarded as the great political organizer of the Romans. To him tradition ascribed the division of the people into classes and centuries, the introduction of the *tribus* as a local unit of organization, and the completion of the great encircling wall. Tarquinius Superbus is the typical tyrant, and the outrage of Lucretia by his son Sextus marked the climax of the autocratic course pursued by his family, and led to the overthrow of the monarchy.

**5. Sources of the Traditional Account.** As has been stated already, the part which the Greeks played in the creation and elaboration of the story of the founding of Rome, and of its history under the kings, is discernible at many points. More or less cleverly dovetailed into these productions of the Greek fancy, or into the tales borrowed from Greek history, are folklore stories, explanations invented at a comparatively late date to account for the existence of ancient monuments, of old customs and long-established institutions, and some residuum of authentic tradition. These are the main elements in the traditional accounts set down, for instance, by Livy in the first book of his history, and by Cicero in his *de Re Publica*. So far as we know, a literary form was first given to the story by Fabius Pictor in his history of the Punic wars in the third century. Out of this account the finished productions of the late republic and early empire developed, thanks to the additions and embellishments of successive generations.

**6. The Making of Rome.** It would take us too far from our purpose to analyze the traditional accounts of the early history of Rome, and to separate from one another the constituent elements mentioned above. It is important for us, however, to note certain parts of the story which can be established with certainty, or with a high degree of probability. We can, for instance, rely upon the fact that the original settlement out of which the city of Rome developed was made on the left bank of the Tiber, about fifteen miles from the mouth of the river. Some portions of the wall of the old Palatine settlement are still *in situ*, and from them the compass of the early city can be fairly well determined. Independent settlements existed on the Quirinal, the Esquiline, the Capitoline, and the Caelian also. These hills with the citadels upon them were places of refuge also, in case of necessity, for the settlers upon the adjacent plains, and at a very early date all these hill settlements were fused into a single city. The territory of this unified community was first extended, by conquest, to the south of the city, and along the left bank of the Tiber to its mouth. Tradition is undoubtedly right in dating expansion in this direction from the early part of the regal period.

7. **Its Population.** The various traditions connected with the founding of the city agree in stating that the population of Rome was divided into three parts. According to the commonly accepted form of the tradition, these three parts, the Ramnes, Tities, and Luceres, were independent elements of different origin, the Ramnes being the original settlers of *Roma quadrata*, the Tities a Sabine community, while the identity of the Luceres was a matter of as great uncertainty to the ancients as it is to us to-day. Some modern writers are inclined to accept this view of the case. Others find in the division of the community into three " tribes " only an instance of the adoption of a system of political organization which was not unknown to

other Italian communities. The term *tribus* can of course be urged in support of the latter view. The exact truth in the matter will probably never be known. It may be regarded as highly probable, however, that the original Latin community was reinforced by a colony of Sabine invaders, which in course of time was completely fused with the Palatine settlements into a harmonious political organization.

**8. Early Form of Government.** We have already seen reason to believe that the affairs of the clan were managed by the members or by the elders, who represented it. With the founding of the city a new and predominant element was introduced into the political organization. The clans which were fused into a single community agreed in accepting a single political head, called a *rex*, who was to hold his position for life, while the elders or *patres* of the various *gentes* formed the king's council. To this body the control of the state fell on the death of the king.

**9. Treatment of Conquered Peoples.** The history of Rome under the kings falls naturally into two epochs. The second of these two periods covers the reigns of the last three kings, and is characterized by the extension of Rome's territory, by the development of the plebs and their partial incorporation in the body politic, by the appearance on the throne of kings of foreign birth, and by the fact that the monarchy became hereditary. The ambitious policy of conquest which the Tarquins adopted was attended with success, but it brought the Romans face to face with difficult political questions of great importance. What disposition should be made of conquered territory? What standing should conquered peoples have in the state? The first problem was solved in most cases by the permanent occupation of a part of the newly acquired territory

by the Roman state as *ager publicus*, and the assignment
of the rest to the conquered people with the right of use,
under certain conditions, but not of full ownership. A
majority of those who lived in these subjugated districts
probably accepted these conditions and remained upon the
land, but some of them came to Rome and settled there.
In a few cases the most prominent families among the newcomers were admitted to the full rights of citizenship. This
was perhaps the plan adopted in the case of Alba Longa.
According to Livy's narrative, after the destruction of that
city, its leading clans were admitted among the *gentes*,
and their representatives were made *patres*. Such generous treatment of conquered peoples was, however, exceptional. Ordinarily, if we except those who were brought
to Rome as slaves, newcomers, whether they came to the
city after the conquest of their native land, or were attracted
to it by the possibilities of gain which its growth held out,
assumed one of two positions in the community. They
either attached themselves as *clientes* (cf. p. 2) to the
representatives of prominent Roman families and gained
certain rights and privileges through their *patroni*, or, while
maintaining their personal freedom, they were thought of
as bearing to the king a relation similar to that which the
client bore to his patron. This second class of inhabitants
was probably augmented by the gradual release of many
clients from the performance of the duties which they
owed to their patrons. In these two ways a new element
developed in the community, which had no part in the
management of affairs, an element whose very name of
*plebes* indicated its lack of organization.

**10. Plebeians enrolled in the Army.** But this narrow
policy, which not only denied to a large part of the community all political privileges, and civil rights in some measure,

but also exempted the same element from the necessity of performing military service, was entirely out of harmony with the career of conquest on which the Roman state had entered. The farther the limits of the Roman territory were extended, the more pressing became the need of more fighting men to hold in check the newly subdued peoples within its confines, and to ward off the attacks of enemies from without. The king, as chief executive of the state and commander-in-chief of the army, felt the necessity first and most keenly, and tradition is undoubtedly right in stating that on one or two occasions he took the initiative, with more or less success, in admitting some plebeians to the rights of citizenship. The citizens were naturally loath to lose part of their privileges by sharing them with others, but the military necessities of the case forced them to make certain concessions, and under the constitution which is connected with the name of Servius Tullius the plebeians as well as the patricians, the members of the old *gentes*, were enrolled in the army. We cannot say with certainty what concessions on the part of the patricians made the plebeians willing to undergo the hardships and expense of military service, and insured their loyalty to the state. It would seem, however, to have been the concession of the right to the full ownership of land, which had probably been denied to them before. From this time on, the plebeians had a stake in the community, and it was to their interest to maintain order within its limits and to protect it from its enemies. This change in their position was of no immediate political significance. They were still excluded from any share in the management of the state, but the establishment of an organization, of which plebeians as well as patricians were members, even though it was a body of a military character, had political possibilities for the future.

**11. The Results of Rome's Narrow Policy.** It may have been well for the ultimate development of Rome that the members of the old *gentes* adopted the narrow policy of retaining all political power in their own hands. Had they followed the precedent which Tullus Hostilius seems to have set in the case of Alba Longa, and admitted new *gentes* on a par with the old ones, the narrow tribal basis of the state might have lasted for an indefinite time. Under the ungenerous policy which *was* adopted, the right to control the internal and the foreign affairs of the state was the hereditary privilege of a comparatively small body of men. Over against them was a large and rapidly growing element in the community whose intolerable position would force it to break down the opposing barriers, and thus to overthrow the tribal system on which the state was based. In this connection it is significant that the new Servian organization recognized the individual as an individual and not solely as a member of a certain clan, and that the members of the new body were classified on the basis of their property and not of their family connections.

**12. Etruscan Supremacy.** It is very difficult to understand the foreign relations of Rome during the reigns of the last three kings, which we are now considering. According to tradition, the first of the three, Tarquinius Priscus, during the reign of his predecessor, Ancus Marcius, came to Rome from Tarquinii in Etruria, and on the death of the king succeeded to the throne. It has been suspected that under the guise of the Etruscan ancestry of Tarquin the conquest of Rome by the Etruscans has been concealed, and it is true that many changes attributed to the Tarquins may be urged in support of this hypothesis, but this conclusion is at least open to serious doubt. The favorable location of the city and its rapid growth would undoubtedly attract many strangers to the city. These newcomers, as we have already observed, were in some cases admitted to the full rights of citizenship, and it would not have been an extremely difficult thing for one of these naturalized citizens, if he were a leader of skill and ability, to gain the throne. Such a leader the first of the Tarquins seems to have been, and there is no sufficient reason for refusing to accept the tradition of Tarquinius Priscus at its face value.

**13. Political Changes.** The form of government underwent a noteworthy change under the Tarquins in the substitution of an hereditary for an elective monarchy, and in the subordination of the senate to the king. The first of these two changes is indicated plainly enough by the kinship existing between the last three kings, and by the passage of the scepter to Servius Tullius and to Tarquinius Superbus without the observance of the interregnum. The fact just mentioned illustrates also the autocratic attitude which the reigning family assumed toward the senate. On the death of the king under the old régime the *auspicia* reverted to the senate, and that body, through representatives chosen from its own number, exercised the supreme executive power. The assumption of power by Servius Tullius and Tarquinius Superbus, *neque populi iussu neque auctoribus patribus* (Liv. I. 49. 3), made a serious breach in the theory that the senate was the ultimate depositary of supreme power, gave a dangerous continuity to the king's office and prevented the choice by the senate of a monarch satisfactory to it.

The jealousy which the patricians felt at this usurpation of power by the king led to the overthrow of the monarchy. There are some indications of a *rapprochement* between the king and the plebeians, but the plebeians were exhausted and embittered by long-continued service in the army and by forced labor in the construction of public works, so that they either did not come to the defense of Tarquinius Superbus, or helped the patricians to overthrow him.

# SECTION II — DESCRIPTIVE

## CHAPTER II

### MONARCHICAL INSTITUTIONS

**14. Sources of Information.** The same difficulties which beset one's path in seeking to trace the course of political events during the regal period bring to naught in some respects every effort to gain a clear conception of the political institutions of the epoch in question. Our knowledge of these institutions is derived in the main from tradition, from the explanatory statements of Latin writers, and from an investigation of the political institutions of the republican period. Some further light is thrown on early institutions by an investigation of early laws, treaties, legal and religious formulae, and by a study of the fundamental meaning of the titles of the several offices, as in the case of the *quaestores parricidii.*

Let us confine our attention for the present to the three principal sources, noting at the outset some of the points at which these sources must be used with caution. Many of the descriptions which we find in Livy of the Roman constitution under the kings owe their existence to a deliberate attempt at a later date to account for a political term or usage or institution, which in course of time had lost its original meaning. This same inventive tendency vitiates in some measure the explanations made by the later antiquarians, whose views are also more or less colored by their knowledge of the form which an ancient institution had taken in their own day. So, for instance, historians and antiquarians of the first century B.C. may have been led by their knowledge of the constitutional character of the consulship to assume erroneously that certain corresponding constitutional restrictions were put on the power of the king. It is evident that in using the third source of information, that is, in reconstructing the political institutions of the regal period from our knowledge of the forms which they had taken in republican times, we must make due allowance for development or decay, and must not be guilty of the same mistake which the Roman antiquarians made. The way in which the nature of the interregnum is determined illustrates the use which may be made of these different sources of information. First of all, the technical term itself indicates the period elapsing between the death, resignation, or dethronement of one king and the accession of his successor. This general notion is amplified by the traditional account given in more or less detail by Livy, Dionysius, and Cicero of the way in which the affairs of state were conducted after the death of each one of the first four kings; explanatory remarks on the institution have been made by the commentators Asconius and Servius, and these three sources of information have been supplemented by the contemporaneous accounts which Cicero and other writers have left us of the method of procedure during the interregnums of 53 B.C.

15. **The Senate as the Ultimate Source of Authority.** As we have already had occasion to notice (p. 2), in the prehistoric tribal community the control of affairs was largely, if not entirely, vested in the clan elders. On the establishment of the monarchy, the supreme power was transferred to a single individual, to be exercised by him

during his lifetime. At his death the sovereignty naturally reverted to the elders. This view of the situation Livy has expressed, when, after mentioning the death of Tullus Hostilius, he remarks (I. 32. 1), *res, ut institutum iam inde ab initio erat, ad patres rediit.* This view that the senate was the ultimate source of authority was the aristocratic theory of the constitution down to the end of the republican period, and was the cause of violent and protracted struggles, first between patricians and plebeians, and later between the *nobilitas* and the democracy.

**16. Method of Selecting a King.** The supreme executive power, which thus reverted to the senate, and in the later republican period to the patrician senators, was exercised by that body in a peculiar fashion. A member of the senate, bearing the title of *interrex*, and chosen in a way not entirely clear to us, assumed charge of affairs for a period of five days. He nominated a second *interrex*, and this system was continued until a king was selected. The choice was made by the *interrex* in harmony with the wishes of the senate, and was submitted by him for approval to the people assembled by *curiae*. The senate then ratified the selection by passing the *auctoritas patrum*, and the candidate was formally declared king by the *interrex*. The ceremony ended when the newly elected king had taken the auspices and had been vested with the *imperium* by the *lex curiata de imperio*. The selection of a king rested essentially with the senate. His election or confirmation by the people was a matter of form, although, since the king was primarily the leader of the army, the hearty support of the fighting men of the community was a matter of great importance. Since the real selection of the king was made by the senate through one of its own number, the *auctoritas patrum* had a formal significance only, although it was a safeguard which might take on a real meaning in the case of a usurper or a headstrong *interrex*. The passage of the *lex de imperio*, which is not properly a part of the ceremony attending the choice, and the inauguration of the king, were also matters of form in so far as the choice of the king was concerned, since the refusal of the *curiae* to pass the measure is inconceivable.

**17. Powers of the King.** Sallust characterizes the power of the king as an *imperium legitimum*. This can mean little more than that the king was to observe the *mos maiorum*. So, for instance, he was expected, although not required, to consult the senate on important matters. This general limitation on the power of the king found definite expression, perhaps, in the *lex de imperio*, which was probably in the nature of a contract, on the part of the people to render obedience, on the part of the king to observe the practices of the forefathers. Except for the limitations just mentioned, the king was a supreme ruler, — the chief executive, the chief priest, the lawgiver, and the judge of the state. After war had been declared he had sole power to levy and organize troops, to choose leaders, and to conduct the campaign. The property of the state was under his control, and he was authorized to dispose of conquered territory and to take charge of public works. He was the official representative of the community in its relations with the gods, as well as in its dealings with other communities. Changes of a permanent or far-reaching character, however, such as the introduction of new deities, could only be made with the consent of the priests. It would be unwarrantable to import modern notions into our conception of the king's position and to speak of him as legislating for the people, but undoubtedly he formulated and executed such measures as he thought essential to the community, except that matters affecting primarily the *gentes*, and a declaration ·of war, must be referred to the people. The adjudication of all civil and criminal cases was naturally within the scope of his power. It is quite possible that in civil cases, in some instances, the king may have adopted the practice, which the praetor uniformly observed under the republic, of conducting the case in its preliminary stages (*in iure*), and then of referring it to a *iudex* for settlement. Probably criminal cases involving the question of life and death could, with the consent of the king, be appealed to the people for trial.

**18. Assistants and Insignia of the King.** In the absence of the king from the city, the duties of the office were performed by a substitute, called the *praefectus urbi*. The other political officials of the regal commonwealth were two *quaestores parricidi*, or detective officers, the *duumviri perduellionis*, who assisted the king in cases of treason, and the *tribunus celerum*, who commanded the cavalry. These officials were all chosen by the king, and the power which they exercised was delegated to them by him. In time of war the king wore the *trabea*, a purple cloak, in time of peace a purple toga. His seat on formal occasions was the *solium*. He was attended by twelve lictors.

**19. The Senate.** In organizing the primitive Roman senate a representative was chosen from each clan. As the number of clans in the community increased, the number of members in the senate increased correspondingly, until three hundred was fixed as a maximum. This number, on which the various traditions agree, gives a representation of one hundred for each *tribus* and ten for each one of the *curiae*. The choice of senators was made by the king, but in accordance with principles handed down by tradition. The title *patres* may be a mere term of honor, but probably a minimum age limit was fixed for membership in the body. The functions of the senate may be considered from three points of view, viz., as an organization vested under certain circumstances with supreme power, as a legislative body coördinate with the people assembled in the *curiae*, and as the council of the king. We have already noticed the fact (p. 14) that on the death of the king the control of the state reverted to the senate. The fact has also been noted (p. 14) that matters on which the popular assembly acted came before the senate for approval or rejection. Custom made it incumbent on the king to seek the advice of the senate in important matters, but it was left for him to decide whether to bring a subject before the senate or not, and he was free to adopt or reject its advice, as he saw fit. This theory of the relations existing between the senate and the chief executive was maintained down through the republican period even, although in practice the consul rarely failed to follow the instructions of the senate. The senate could meet only when called together by the king, and its meetings were held in a *templum*, or place consecrated by an augur.

20. **Patricii, Clientes, Plebeii.** There were three principal classes in the community, — patricians, clients, and plebeians. The patricians were legitimate sons in families belonging to the *gentes* recognized by the state. Patricians alone had *civitas optimo iure*, *i.e.*, the full rights of citizenship. This included, besides personal freedom, *ius commercii*, the right to hold and exchange property and be protected in its possession; *ius conubii*, the right to intermarry with other members of the *gentes*, and *ius gentilitatis*, the right to a share in the worship of the clan. The main political privileges enjoyed by the patricians were *ius suffragii*, the right to vote, and *ius honorum*, the right to hold

office. The *clientes* were strangers who had come to Rome to better their condition, or the former inhabitants of conquered territory, or freedmen. Not being members of any one of the recognized *gentes*, they gained certain privileges by attaching themselves to the head of a family belonging to a *gens*. Their protector was known as a *patronus*, who represented them before the law. They did not have the full right to own land, but were allowed to hold it on condition of giving a part of the return from it to their *patronus*. Clients, who were artisans, similarly gave to him a part of the profits of their labor. The relation existing between a *cliens* and his *patronus* was an hereditary one. The origin of the plebeians and the relation which they bore to the *clientes* is somewhat obscure, but they were probably strangers who settled in Rome with the king as their *patronus*, or *clientes* whose relation of dependence was brought to an end with the consent of their *patronus*, or through the disappearance of the family to which they were attached. In return for the service which they rendered in the army the Servian reform granted them *ius commercii*. They had the right to marry within their own class, but they were not allowed to marry patricians.

**21. The Curiae.** The fundamental unit in the division of the people for political purposes in the primitive state was the *curia*, whose organization resembled that of the family in that it had common religious rites, common festivals, and a common hearth. The thirty *curiae* included not only the patricians but also the *clientes*, — and probably the plebeians, — although the plebeians and clients had no vote. The *curiae* constituted the *populus Romanus Quiritium*, and the *comitia curiata*, the organization based on them, was the only popular assembly of a political or semi-political character during the regal period.

**22. The Comitia Curiata.** Only the king or *interrex* had the right to call together the people and lay matters before them for consideration (*agere cum populo*). The usual place of meeting was the *comitium*. In all probability the will of the people could ordinarily be indicated well enough by informal signs of approval or disapproval on the part of the multitude, but the systematic division of the people indicates that from the outset, on certain matters at least, a definite system of voting was adopted, perhaps by acclamation, within the separate *curiae*. A majority of the *curiae* determined the vote of the whole assembly. Stated meetings of the *comitia curiata* were held on the Kalends and Nones of the month to hear announcements with reference to the calendar, and on two fixed dates in the spring, primarily to witness wills. Other meetings were held as occasion might require. The matters which came before this assembly may be roughly classified under four heads. The people might be called together to elect a king, to hear an appeal, to listen to announcements, or to vote on *rogationes* or propositions. The first two points have been discussed elsewhere (pp. 14, 16). The announcements which the people were called together to hear were those made at the stated meetings mentioned above. It would be an anachronism to speak of the legislation of the period, but in matters of great importance the king asked for the approval of the people assembled in the *comitia*, and on occasion of assuming the *imperium* (see pp. 14 f.) or declaring an offensive war the consent of the people was necessary. Questions concerning the *gentes* were those most frequently brought before the *comitia curiata*. These were mainly : *adlectio*, the admission of a new *gens* into a *curia;* *restitutio*, the restoration of citizenship ; *adrogatio*, the reduction of a *pater familias* to a dependent position in another

family, and *detestatio sacrorum*, release from the clan *sacra*
Under the republic matters affecting the clans became the
main business of this body.

**23. The Servian Reorganization of the Army.** Under the
early monarchy the prehistoric division of the people into
three tribes served as a basis for the levy of troops; but,
since the plebeians were not included in these three tribes,
the state lost the use of a large number of able-bodied men,
and there was no way in which they could very well be
included in a system based, as the old one seems to have
been, on kinship and vicinage. This state of things led to
the giving up of the old basis of organization, and to the
substitution in its stead of the property system of classification. Under the Servian reform all freemen who had a
certain amount of landed property were enrolled in the
army without regard to their membership in a clan. The
enrollment was apparently based on the possession of landed
property, and comprised all those who had two acres or
more of land. The possession of twenty acres admitted
one to the first class, fifteen acres to the second, ten acres
to the third, five acres to the fourth, and two acres to the
fifth. The classes were divided into centuries, that is, into
subdivisions, which at the outset perhaps actually contained
one hundred men, but in course of time the term can have
scarcely indicated a fixed number. The *iuniores*, those
between seventeen and forty-six years of age, were drafted
for service in the field; the *seniores*, men from forty-six to
sixty years of age, were expected to perform garrison duty
only. Each class contained an equal number of centuries
of *seniores* and *iuniores*. Those enrolled in the five classes
served as infantry. Cavalry service was rendered by
eighteen centuries made up of the richest men in the
community. There were also two centuries of sappers

and two of buglers, and at the outset, or somewhat later, one century of *proletarii*.

The probable details of the organization may be seen from the following table :

| | Landed property in acres. | | Centuries. |
|---|---|---|---|
| Equites . . . . | 20 (100,000 *asses*) | | 18 |
| 1st class . . . . | 20 (100,000 *asses*) | *seniores* | 40 |
| | | *iuniores* | 40 |
| 2d " . . . . | 15 (75,000 *asses*) | *seniores* | 10 |
| | | *iuniores* | 10 |
| 3d " . . . . | 10 (50,000 *asses*) | *seniores* | 10 |
| | | *iuniores* | 10 |
| 4th " . . . . | 5 (25,000 *asses*) | *seniores* | 10 |
| | | *iuniores* | 10 |
| 5th " . . . . | 2 (10,000 *asses*) | *seniores* | 15 |
| | | *iuniores* | 15 |
| Fabri . . . . . . . . . . . . . . . . . . . . . . | | | 2 |
| Cornicines . . . . . . . . . . . . . . . . . . . | | | 2 |
| Proletarii (?) . . . . . . . . . . . . . . . . . | | | 1 |
| Total . . . . . . . . . . . . . . . . . . . | | | 193 |

The citizens were reclassified at regular intervals, and, for convenience in classification, the city was divided territorially into four *tribus*, called respectively Palatina, Suburana, Collina, and Esquilina. Membership in a *tribus* was hereditary.

This entire organization of the people by tribes, classes, and centuries was for military purposes only, and the *comitia centuriata* based upon it had no political functions during the regal period.

## SPECIAL BIBLIOGRAPHY

**Traditional accounts of the regal period**: Livy, Bk. I; Dionysius, Bks. I–IV; Cic. de Re Publ. II. 4–46; Plutarch, Lives of Romulus and Numa; H. Peter, Veterum historicorum Romanorum relliquiae, Vol. I, Leipzig, 1870. — **Discussion of the sources**: C. Peter, Zur Kritik d. Quellen d. älteren röm. Geschichte, Halle, 1879; Schäfer-Nissen, Abriss d. Quellenkunde d. griech. u. röm. Geschichte, 2te Abt., 2te Aufl., Leipzig, 1885; Wachsmuth, Einleitung in das Studium d. alten Geschichte, Leipzig, 1895; Soltau, Livius' Geschichtswerk, Leipzig, 1897. — **Credibility**: Schwegler-Baur, Röm. Geschichte, Tübingen, 1853–8 (Fortsetzung, Clason, 1873–6); Seeley, Livy, Bk. I³, Oxford, 1881; Ihne, Early Rome, 8th ed., New York, 1895. — **The king**: Cuno, Vorgeschichte Roms, Vol. I, Leipzig, 1878; Vol. II, Graudenz, 1888; L. Lange, Das röm. Königtum, Leipzig, 1881; H. Jordan, Die Könige im alten Italien, Berlin, 1887. — **The senate**: Mommsen, Röm. Forschungen, I, 250–268, 2te Aufl., Berlin, 1864; Fr. Hofmann, Der röm. Senat zur Zeit der Republik, 1847; Bloch, Les origines du sénat romain, Paris, 1883. — **The people, curiae, centuriae, etc.**: Em. Hoffmann, Die patriz. u. pleb. Kurien, Vienna, 1879; Pelham, The Roman Curiae (in Journ. of Philol., IX. 266–279); Mommsen, Die röm. Tribus, Altona, 1844; Kubitschek, de Rom. trib. origine ac propagatione, Vienna, 1882; Soltau, Ueber Entstehung u. Zusammensetzung d. altröm. Volksversammlungen, Berlin, 1880; Genz, Das patrizische Rom, Berlin, 1878; M. Zoeller, Latium u. Rom, Leipzig, 1878.

## GENERAL BIBLIOGRAPHY [1]

### (*The Monarchy and the Republic*)

Th. Mommsen, History of Rome, 5 vols. (Eng. trans.). New York, 1894.

W. Ihne, History of Rome, 4 vols. (Eng. trans.). London, 1871–82.

---

[1] Collections of inscriptions, like the Corpus Inscriptionum Latinarum, of documents, like that of Bruns, and treatises on coins, such as Eckhel's *Doctrina Numorum Veterum*, may be consulted to advantage, but do not fall within the scope of this list. Valuable lists of articles on various periods of Roman history, which have appeared during the last fifteen years, may be found in the *Jahresbericht über die Fortschritte der classischen Alterthumswissenschaft*, Bd. xlviii (1886), pp. 211–314; Bd. lvi (1888), pp. 1–30; Bd. lx (1889), pp. 262–408; Bd. lxiv (1890), pp. 114–185, and Bd. xciv (1897), pp. 1–277.

E. Pais, Storia di Roma, Vol. I.   Turin, 1899.

B. G. Niebuhr, History of Rome (Eng. trans.).   London, 1855.

Schwegler-Clason, Römische Geschichte, 4 Bde.   Tübingen, 1853-8;
    Berlin, 1873-6.

C. Peter, Geschichte Roms, 3 Bde.   4te Aufl.   Halle, 1881.

E. W. Fischer, Römische Zeittafeln.   Altona, 1846.

H. F. Clinton, Fasti Hellenici, Vol. III.   Oxford, 1841.

H. F. Clinton, Fasti Romani, 2 vols.   Oxford, 1845-50.

H. Matzat, Römische Zeittafeln für die Jahre 219 bis 1 v. Chr.
    Berlin, 1889.

H. Matzat, Römische Chronologie, 2 Bde.   Berlin, 1883-4.


SUPPLEMENTARY LITERATURE, 1901-1910[1]

Heitland, The Roman Republic, 3 vols.   Cambridge (England), 1909.

Klio (= Beiträge zur alten Geschichte), 1902—— (passim).

De Ruggiero, Dizionario epigrafico di antichità romane (A–Dend,
    F-Gr).   Rome, 1895-1909.

Wachsmuth, Einleitung in das Studium der alten Geschichte.
    Leipzig, 1895.

Meyer, E., Geschichte des Altertums, II, V.   Stuttgart and Berlin,
    1893, 1902.

Wissowa, Religion u. Kultus d. Römer.   Munich, 1902.

Pais, Ancient Italy.   Chicago, 1908.

Modestov, Introduction à l'histoire romaine.   St. Petersburg, 1902.

Comparetti, Iscrizione arcaica del Foro romano edita ed illustrata.
    Rome, 1900.

Peter, Historicorum Romanorum reliquiae, 2 vols.   Leipzig, 1870,
    1906.

---

[1] See also *Jahresbericht über die Fortschritte der classischen Alterthumswissenschaft*, Bd. cxiv (1903), pp. 1-25, 188-217; Bd. cxxvii (1905), pp. 257-368; *Musée Belge*, vii, pp. 420-465; viii, pp. 194-270.

# Part II — Republican Period

## Section I — Historical

### Chapter III

#### THE PATRICIAN CITY

**24. Credibility of Early Republican History.** The traditional story of the kings is in large measure a transparent fiction. After the establishment of the republic the narrative descends into the realm of the possible and credible, but we should be mistaken in accepting the early part of it as trustworthy. Both the external and the internal evidence show it to be otherwise. For the first century or more of the republic contemporary records are completely lacking. Everything of the sort must have been lost when the city was taken by the Gauls in 390. Then, too, an examination of the history of the early period, which ancient writers have left us, reveals the fact that truth and fiction are constantly interwoven, and that the greater part of the account is the production of a later date. The meager records which religious and political officials made in the fourth century B.C., relying on tradition, were supplemented, as time went on, by traditional tales of popular military heroes and political leaders, and successive generations of writers sought to remove inconsistencies, to suggest explanations, and to embellish the narrative by the use of rhetorical

safety and general welfare of the community, or the life of individual citizens, an exclusive body like the curiate *comitia* should give way before an organization made up of all the fighting men of the state. It would be absurd, in fact, to expect the plebeians to serve faithfully under a leader whom they had had no part in choosing, or to fight in a war which had been declared without consulting them. Under these influences the centuriate assembly gradually acquired a large share of the political functions which under the monarchy had been exercised by the curiate *comitia*. In it magistrates were elected, appeals were heard, and measures affecting the whole community, excepting the *lex de imperio*, were considered and acted on. Another factor contributed to its political importance. Under the monarchy, as we have already noticed (p. 16), an appeal to the people in a case of life and death could be had only with the consent of the king. By the *lex Valeria* (Cic. *de Re Publ.* II. 53), which tradition assigns to the year 509, the right to an appeal to the *comitia centuriata* was granted to all citizens, plebeians as well as patricians. This action undoubtedly made frequent meetings of that body necessary. The eighteen centuries of knights acting with the eighty centuries of the first class constituted a majority, and, since most of the rich landholders were probably patricians, the body had a pronounced aristocratic character. For this reason the action of the centuriate *comitia* in electing magistrates, in passing laws, and in deciding appeals was of no great immediate value to the plebs, but the time was likely to come when the plebeians could exert a controlling influence through an increase in the number of rich plebeian landholders. The organization, but not the character, of the *comitia centuriata* was affected by the formation of seventeen *tribus rusticae*, which tradition assigns to the period immediately after the expulsion of the kings.

The king had held his position for life. Class prejudice, therefore, would not count for much in his case. His interests also lay in conciliating the plebeians. The consul, who was chosen from the ranks of the patricians, held office for a year only, and then returned to their number. Consequently his action must have been largely influenced by prejudice in favor of the patricians. We are not surprised, therefore, that the plebeians found their position intolerable under the new chief magistrates. The condition of foreign affairs, however, helped them to wrest from the aristocracy some protection against the patrician consuls. In 494, when Rome was engaged in a fierce struggle with the Aequi and Volsci, the plebeian soldiers refused to march against the enemy, and took up their position on a hill a few miles from the city. The patricians proposed a compromise at once, and the plebeians returned to their duties on condition that they should be allowed to elect annual officials, perhaps five in number, with sufficient power to protect them against the autocratic action of the consuls. The new officials took their title of *tribuni plebis* from the plebeian *tribuni militum* whom the people had chosen as their leaders in the secession. We do not know how the tribunes were chosen at the outset, but probably the plebeians were divided into *curiae*, and the new officials were elected in a loosely organized plebeian curiate assembly. They were to be assisted in the performance of their duties by two *aediles plebei*. From this time forth the plebeians had political leaders of their own, and the great struggle between the orders begins with their appearance, although important political results cannot be seen for a generation or two.

**28. Improvement in the Organization of the Plebeians.**
For a period of fifty years this struggle centers successively about three points. These three points were : the
improvement of the plebeian organization, the more equitable division of the *ager publicus*, and the codification
and publication of the customary law. At the outset, as
has been stated above, the tribunes were apparently elected
in a plebeian curiate assembly roughly modeled after the
patrician *comitia curiata*. To this body all those outside of
the old *gentes* who were not slaves were probably admitted.
In this organization the patricians may well have exerted
a strong influence through their *clientes*. To eliminate
this influence, in 471, in accordance with a law incor-
rectly attributed by tradition to Volero Publilius, the plebeians were organized on the tribal basis, and the election
of tribunes was turned over to the newly constituted plebeian tribal assembly, and to this organization probably
plebeian landowners only were admitted.

**29. Agrarian Agitation.** Under the monarchy the disposal of land gained in war was left to the king (p. 15).
His fairly impartial attitude towards all classes would lead
him to make arrangements at least tolerable for the plebeians. But the patrician senate and consul inherited the
king's power in this matter, and the plebeians gained little
from the new territory which their own valor had helped
to secure. They suffered not only financially, but also
politically, from this state of things. Membership in the
classes, on which the centuriate organization was based,
depended on the ownership of land. Now, if no new
land was thrown open to the plebeians, as they increased
in number from generation to generation, the average holdings of each one of them would decrease, and plebeians
would drop into lower classes, or become landless. This

was the state of things which led Spurius Cassius, himself a patrician, to advocate the assignment of certain conquered territory to the plebeians. His proposition, which tradition assigns to the year 486, brought no immediate results, but, as Livy notices (II. 41. 3), it marks the beginning of an agrarian agitation which went on to the close of the republican period, the first milestone of which was the *lex Icilia*, so called (Liv. III. 31. 1), of 456, which provided for the division among the plebeians of the *ager publicus* on the Aventine.

**30. The Decemvirate.** The third great achievement of the plebs during the period under consideration, the publication of the laws of the twelve tables, was the result of a long and bitter struggle. The first proposition looking to this end is said (Liv. III. 9. 5) to have been made by the tribune C. Terentilius Harsa in 462, and in 451 a compromise between the two parties was arranged, to the effect that the consuls and tribunes should alike give place to a commission of ten men (*decemviri legibus scribundis*), who should not only exercise the functions of chief magistrates, but should be empowered to publish a code of laws binding on the whole community. The commission of the first year drew up ten tables, but left their task unfinished at the end of their term of office. The commission of the second year, so the story goes, took up the work where its predecessor had left off, but its conduct was so overbearing that the plebeians withdrew to the Aventine, and the decemvirs were forced out of office. The real course of events cannot be determined with certainty, but the appearance of plebeian names in the list of decemvirs for the second year makes it probable that a part of the second commission was plebeian, that certain changes were proposed which the patricians would not accept, and that they drove the commission out of office. The withdrawal of the plebeians may be accounted for by their anger at the course which the patricians took, or by the fact that after the overthrow of the decemvirs they were left without any adequate protection, since the tribunate had been suspended or abolished. It is worth noticing incidentally that if this explanation of the matter is correct, the decemvirate was the first important magistracy to which plebeians were admitted. Whatever the truth of the whole matter may have been, we know that the plebs demanded and secured, as the price of their return, the restoration of the tribunate, and the concession of certain rights which the conservative leaders Valerius and Horatius secured for them. Livy characterizes the body of laws which the decemvirs prepared as *fons omnis publici privatique iuris*. In point of fact, however, the primary importance of the whole incident lay in the publication of the method of procedure to be adopted, especially in civil cases. The only laws of constitutional importance which the code seems to have contained were those forbidding *privilegia*, granting the right of appeal in case of a heavy fine (probably a reaffirmation of the *lex Aternia Tarpeia* and the *lex Menenia Sestia* of 454 and 452 respectively), giving to the *comitia centuriata* the sole right of passing sentence in capital cases, and providing that a measure adopted by the *populus* nullified all earlier constitutional or legal provisions in conflict with it.

31. **The Leges Valeriae Horatiae.** The patricians carried out faithfully the promises which had been made in their behalf. In 449 the consuls Valerius and Horatius secured the passage of a law guaranteeing to citizens the right of appeal in cases of life and death. This enactment was in a way a repetition of the *lex Valeria* and of one of the

provisions of the twelve tables, but the suspension of the
right of appeal during the existence of the decemvirate
justified the repetition. The dictatorship must have been
exempted from the action of this law. Another law of the
same year established the tribunate on a surer basis than
ever. A still more important piece of legislation, whose
passage Valerius and Horatius secured, was an enactment
with reference to the validity of *plebiscita*. Livy summa-
rizes (III. 55. 3) its contents in this wise : *quod tributim
plebes iussisset populum teneret.* It is impossible, however,
that the unsupported action of the plebeian tribal assembly
should have been binding on the whole people. The fact
that it was necessary to secure the approval of the senate
in the case of the Licinian laws in 367 (Liv. VI. 42. 9)
points to the probability that, after the passage of the *leges
Valeriae Horatiae*, the action of the plebeian tribal assembly
acquired the force of law, in case the *auctoritas patrum*
was secured. The constitutional importance of this Valerio-
Horatian measure lies in the fact that it gave to the tribune,
the plebeian leader, the right to initiate legislation, and to
plebeian political aspirations the strength which came to
them through their formulation by a legally recognized legislative assembly. It will be seen that this action involves a
complete change in the nature of the tribunate. It gives
a positive character to it for the first time. The importance of the negative functions of that office also was augmented shortly before the establishment of the decemvirate
by the increase of the number of tribunes to ten. This
increase made it possible for them to extend their protec-
tive power over a greater number of plebeians. The great
constitutional gains which the plebeians made during the
period under consideration, from the first to the second
secession, bear a close relation to the fact that Rome was

harassed during this whole time by fierce raids on the part of the Sabines, the Aequi, and the Volsci. The patrician state needed the support of the plebeians, and that could be had only in return for certain political concessions. The stress of these wars also led Rome and the neighboring peoples of the Latins and Hernici to form a league at the beginning of the fifth century which continued in force to 340.

**32. The Comitia Tributa.** It will be remembered that in the regal period the king was assisted in the collection of evidence by the *quaestores parricidii*. The power of appointing these officials, which the king had enjoyed, descended to the consul and was exercised by him up to the year 447, when, as Tacitus tells us (*Ann.* XI. 22), they were for the first time elected by the people. This change was in itself a direct gain for the plebeians, but the method by which the quaestors were elected suggests a far more important indirect advantage to the plebeians. The jurisdiction of the quaestors extended over patricians as well as plebeians, and the only definite reference which we have to the method of electing them (Cic. *ad Fam.* VII. 30. 1) indicates that they were chosen in a tribal assembly presided over by a magistrate. We must consequently infer that patricians as well as plebeians took part in the election. From 447 on, then, there are two tribal assemblies, — one an assembly of the *populus* under the chairmanship of a magistrate, and therefore properly called the *comitia tributa*, the other an assembly of the plebs presided over by a tribune, to which Latin writers now and then refer as the *concilium plebis*.

**33. The Lex Canuleia.** A great social change which led to important political results was effected at about the same time, to be exact in 445, by the passage of the *lex*

*Canuleia de conubio,* which recognized *conubium* between patricians and plebeians.   Mixed marriages between patricians and plebeians had never been considered strictly illegal, but the sons of a patrician who took a plebeian woman in marriage lost the patriciate by virtue of that fact.   The passage of this law or plebiscite was therefore, in a way, to the advantage of the patricians.   Indirectly it furthered the cause of the plebeians and benefited the whole community. It was to the advantage of the entire state, because it served to unify the interests of its citizens.   It helped the plebeians, since through it influential patricians were sometimes led by kinship to support plebeian leaders at critical moments.   This was notably true in the case of Licinius in the year 367.

**34.  Agitation for the Consulship.**   The great majority of the measures whose passage the plebeians had secured since 509 had for their avowed object the restriction of the consul's power.   The plebeians now felt themselves in a position to make a direct assault on the patrician stronghold by demanding a representative in the consulship.   A proposition embodying this demand was made by the tribune Canuleius in 445.   The patricians could not be forced to yield the point in question, but they granted a compromise by providing that each year it should be decided whether the chief magistrates should be consuls or *tribuni militares consulari potestate.*  The *tribuni militum* alternated in command of the legion, and since the office was open to plebeians as well as to patricians, the demands of the plebeians were nominally recognized.   In point of fact the concession was intended to be, and was in large measure, a nominal one.   The patricians hoped to save the consulship by substituting the consular tribunate temporarily in its stead, with the intention of restoring the consulship when they found themselves strong enough to do so. In the interval they felt that they had secured themselves by a number of safeguards. It was, for instance, within the power of the senate to decide each year whether the chief magistrates should be consuls or consular tribunes; the election of consular tribunes by the *comitia centuriata* required the ratification of the patrician senators, and finally, since the number of these officials was not fixed, it was probably possible in some cases to reject successful plebeian candidates on the ground of unfavorable auspices, or for similar technical reasons. These legal restrictions, combined with the superior political ability of the patricians and the prestige which their social position gave them, enabled them to exclude the plebeians entirely from the office up to 400, and after that date the number of plebeian successes was small.

**35. Economic Difficulties.** The political situation, which was already serious, in consequence of the repeated disappointments of the plebeians, was still further complicated by the development of an agrarian difficulty. We have already had occasion to notice (p. 29) the unfair treatment in the division of land to which the plebeians were subject, and the economical and political hardships which resulted from it. The difficulty steadily grew in seriousness. In the first third of the fourth century B.C. there was an almost unbroken series of wars with the Aequi, the Volsci, the Latins, and the people of Veii. During these long campaigns patrician estates could be cultivated by dependents, but the returns from the little holdings of the poor plebeian grew smaller and smaller, and the land itself steadily deteriorated in value. Undoubtedly, also, the peasant proprietor was finding it more and more difficult to compete with the owner of large estates.

**36. The Leges Liciniae Sextiae.** This was the political and economic condition of the plebs which the two tribunes of the year 377, C. Licinius Stolo and L. Sextius, endeavored to relieve. They accomplished their object in 367, after ten years of agitation, by securing the passage of a *lex satura*, or law covering the various matters in dispute. The contents of the law are somewhat in doubt, but, if we may follow Livy and Appian, it included the following points: (1) restoration of the consulship, with the provision that one of the two consuls should always be a plebeian; (2) a provision forbidding an individual to occupy more than five hundred acres of arable land belonging to the state, and to pasture more than one hundred head of cattle and five hundred sheep on the common pasture land; (3) an article fixing the proportional number of free laborers and slaves to be employed on any estate; (4) a clause providing that interest already paid on debts should be deducted from the principal, and that three years should be allowed for the payment of the rest; (5) a provision that the number of priests in charge of the Sibylline books should be increased to ten, and that five of these should be plebeians.

**37. Results of the Struggle.** The first point in these laws marks the beginning of the end of the patricio-plebeian struggle. The other important magistracies to which plebeians had been eligible, viz., the decemvirate and the consular tribunate, were of a temporary character, and, as we have seen, the patricians had easily thwarted their efforts to attain them. From this time on, one of the incumbents of a regular magistracy must be a plebeian, and admission to the consulship foreshadowed admission to the other offices also. The law was observed in the following year by the election of L. Sextius to the consulship.

The second law differs from the *lex Icilia* (p. 30), and from many agrarian laws of a later date, in being an automatic principle of a general character, rather than a measure for a specific case. The third provision was evidently the result of an effort to check the growth of an evil which ultimately drove peasant proprietors and free laborers out of the country districts, and transformed Italy into a land of large estates worked by slaves. The fourth measure is a forerunner of the socialistic legislation of the next century, and foreshadows a re-division of the people into rich and poor, as soon as political equality has been secured. The political significance of the last provision lies in the fact that it made a breach in the integrity of the aristocratic religious system. The plebeians might hope soon to gain admission to the offices of augur and pontiff, and thus wrest from the patricians one of their most effective defensive weapons, the taking of the auspices.

**38. The Establishment of the Offices of Censor, Praetor, and Aedile.** The civil duties of the chief magistracy were increasing so rapidly in consequence of the growth of the city that they could no longer be satisfactorily performed by the two consuls. The difficulty of the situation was increased by the frequent absence of the consuls from the city in the performance of their military duties. This state of things led to the establishment of the censorship in 443 (or possibly in 435), and of the praetorship in 366. A secondary motive for the establishment of the praetorship may be found in the desire of the patricians to keep in their own hands some of the powers of the chief magistracy, for at the outset patricians only were eligible to the office of praetor. The establishment in 366 of the curule aedileship, to which plebeians were not eligible, was also perhaps a part of the bargain on the basis of which the patricians allowed the passage of the Licinian laws of the year before.

**39. The Senate and the Tribune.** The relations which the senate bore to the tribune and to the magistrates underwent an interesting change in the period under consideration, from 445 to 367. The original function of the tribune was to protect citizens against the magistrate by personal interference in specific cases. The increase of the number of tribunes to ten, in the middle of the fifth century, and the bitterness of the long struggle which the plebeians made for the consulship, led to a continual clashing between the tribunes and the magistrates executing the decrees of the senate, and in many cases the working of the governmental machinery was completely suspended. It was felt, therefore, that it would be far better to get the opinion of the tribunes with reference to a bill under consideration in the senate, before action was taken on it. With this purpose in mind they were given seats in the senate, and were allowed to interpose their objections formally at any point in the proceedings. At least no better explanation can be suggested for the new rôle which the tribunes play in the deliberations of the senate in this period.

**40. The Senate and the Magistracy.** On the other hand, the senate gained in power at the expense of the chief magistrate, and perhaps at this time it took the first step toward gaining that controlling influence in the state which it exercised a century or more later. The explanation of the change lies partly in the fact that it rested with the senate each year to decide whether the chief magistrates should be consuls or tribunes with consular power. This fact in a way made the chief magistracy dependent on that body.

**41. Foreign Affairs.** In foreign affairs the period of the consular tribunate is one of conquest. Rome's territory was extended, and her influence over her neighbors was greatly strengthened. These successes were due partly to the rapid growth of Rome and to the improvement in her domestic policy, partly to the weakening of her enemies and rivals. The brilliant victories of M. Camillus over the Volsci and Aequi in 389, followed by successes in subsequent years, broke the power of both peoples, who were already hard pressed by the inroads of the Sabellians. Paradoxical as it may seem, even the invasion of the Kelts, which led to the capture of Rome in 390 (or 387?), was of permanent advantage to the city. The losses which Etruria suffered from the Kelts, following closely, as they did, on the fall of Veii in 396, made it easy for Rome to extend her control over southern Etruria. Rome's old allies, the Latins and Hernici, became jealous of her growing power, and, availing themselves of the confusion which followed the Keltic invasion, Praeneste, Tibur, and other neighboring communities took up arms against her. They were quickly conquered, and in the new treaty, which was made in 358 between the Latin communities and Rome, the former probably lost their position as co-equal members of the confederacy. These successful wars had a direct and an indirect effect on internal politics in many ways. Among the direct effects were the establishment of four new tribes, — the Stellatina, Tromentina, Sabatina, and Arnensis in 387 in southern Etruria, — and, to pass for a moment beyond the period we are considering, the addition of two new tribes, the Publilia and Pomptina, in Volscian territory.

## SELECTIONS FROM THE SOURCES

**The consulship:** Liv. I. 60. 4; II. 1; III. 55. 12; Cic. *de Re Publ.* II. 56; *de Legg.* III. 8. — **Lex Valeria de provocatione:** Cic. *de Re Publ.* II. 53. — **The dictatorship:** Liv. II. 18; Cic. *de Re Publ.* II. 56. — **The first secession:** Liv. II. 32-3. — **The tribune:** Liv. II. 33. 1-3; II. 34-5; II. 58. 1; III. 20. 7; III. 30. 7; Cic. *de Re Publ.* II. 57-9; *de Legg.* III. 9; III. 16-26; Dionysius, VI. 89; IX. 41. — **The concilia plebis:** Liv. II. 56-7; II. 60. 4-5; Dionysius, IX. 41-9. — **The decemvirate:** Liv. III. 33-59; Cic. *de Re Publ.* II. 61-3; Dionysius, X. 55-61; XI. 1-46. — **Leges Valeriae Horatiae:** Liv. III. 55; Dionysius, XI. 45. — **(Patricio-plebeian) comitia tributa:** Liv. IV. 44. 2; Cic. *ad Fam.* VII. 30. 1; Tac. *Ann.* XI. 22. — **The consular tribunate:** Liv. IV. 1. 2; IV. 6. 8; V. 12. 8-12. — **Lex Canuleia:** Liv. IV. 1. 1; IV. 6. 3. — **The censorship:** Liv. IV. 8. 2-7. — **Fall of Veii:** Liv. V. 19-22. — **The Keltic invasion:** Liv. V. 34-49. — **The Volsci and Aequi:** Liv. VI. 2; VI. 32. — **The leges Liciniae Sextiae:** Liv. VI. 35. 4-5; Appian, *B. C.* I. 8; Liv. X. 13. 14; X. 23. 13. — **The praetorship:** Liv. VI. 42. 11; VII. 1. 1-2. — **The curule aedileship:** Liv. VI. 42. 12-14. — **The Sibylline books:** Liv. VI. 42. 2.

## CRITICISM OF THE SOURCES[1]

Bröcker, Untersuchungen über die Glaubwürdigkeit der altrömischen Geschichte.  Basel, 1862.

E. Herzog, Ueber die Glaubwürdigkeit d. aus d. röm. Republik bis zum Jahre 387 d. St. überlieferten Gesetze.  Tübingen, 1881.

Niese, Grundriss d. röm. Geschichte (pp. 7-11).  Munich, 1897.

Pais, Storia di Roma, Vol. I, Pt. II.  Turin, 1899.

C. Peter, Zur Kritik d. Quellen d. älteren röm. Geschichte.  Halle, 1879.

Soltau, Livius' Geschichtswerk (pp. 156-184, and bibliography, pp. 9-14).  Leipzig, 1897.

Thouret, Ueber d. gallischen Brand in Fleckeisens Jahrb. Suppl. (N.F.), XI. 95-188.

Virck, Die Quellen d. Livius u. Dionysius für d. älteste Geschichte d. röm. Republik.  Strassburg, 1877.

---

[1] See also general bibliography on p. 22.

# CHAPTER IV

## THE STRUGGLE BETWEEN THE ORDERS

**42. The Period from 367 to 287.** In the last chapter we traced the course of events from the founding of the republic down to the passage of the Licinio-Sextian laws in 367. The history of the period in question is primarily a history of the early efforts which the plebeians made to gain political equality with the patricians. The passage of the Licinian laws marks their first great success. Their victory was made complete, and the struggle came to an end when the Hortensian law was passed in the year 287, making the assemblies independent legislative bodies. The last-mentioned year, therefore, marks a new dividing line in the development of Roman political institutions, so that it is convenient to treat the history of internal affairs during the years from 367 to 287 as a unit. It is in part a matter of chance only that this period also constitutes a natural epoch in the history of external politics. In 295, at the battle of Sentinum, the Romans were called on to face the combined forces of the Kelts and Samnites, the two peoples who had most fiercely and persistently disputed the supremacy of Rome in Italy. The victory of Rome in that battle, followed by the submission of the Samnites in 290, crushed the Kelts, broke the power of the Samnites forever, and made the Romans the chief people in Italy.

**43. The Magistracies.** The history of the period under consideration may be conveniently considered from the point of view of the magistracies, the senate, the people, and foreign affairs. The magistracies provided for under the constitution in 366 were those of consul, interrex, dictator, censor, praetor, quaestor, and curule aedile. With the magistracies the plebeian tribuneship and aedileship should be mentioned. Notwithstanding the fact that the law of 367 stipulated that one of the two consuls should be a plebeian, on seven occasions in the twenty-five years which followed both consuls were patricians. This state of things may not have been due, however, to the bad faith of the aristocracy. Probably the cleverest statesmen and generals were still those of patrician descent, and the plebeians may well have put patriotism above class prejudice in foregoing their claim to one of the two positions. The right to hold the consulship naturally carried along with it eligibility to the offices of dictator and censor, and it is not surprising that a plebeian filled the former office in 356 and the latter in 351, without waiting for the formality of a law throwing those positions open to his class. However, the plebeians thought it wise to secure the passage of a law in 339, formulating their claim to one of the two censors. They won still another success two years later, when the great plebeian leader, Q. Publilius Philo, was elected to the praetorship, in violation of the bargain in accordance with which the patricians had conceded the consulship. The quaestorship had been thrown open to the plebeians in 421, when the number of quaestors was increased from two to four. By establishing the curule aedileship, which was not open to plebeians, and by granting the incumbents of that office special honors, the patricians hoped to secure an offset to the office of plebeian aedile, but they soon gave up their exclusive claim to the office, and a peculiar arrangement was adopted for it. In

one year it was thrown open to plebeians, in the next
patricians only were eligible. We have already noticed
the fact (p. 37) that the importance of opening one of
the priestly offices to the plebeians lay in the fact that
a precedent was established for the adoption of a similar
provision in the case of the augurate and pontificate.
The hopes of the plebeians in this respect were realized
by the passage of the *plebiscitum Ogulnium* in 300, which
reserved to the plebeians a certain number of places in
each of the colleges mentioned. These changes all benefited the commonwealth and the plebs, in that they unified
the community and gave the plebeians such a representation in the several magistracies as their number and services to the state entitled them to have, but they were
of special importance to those plebeians who were prominent through wealth or ability, for they alone could hope
to secure election to a magistracy.

**44. Reëlection and Plurality of Offices.** The special
interests concerned in the matter are in fact indicated
clearly by two plebiscites attributed to the year 342, one
of which provided that a citizen should not be reëlected
to an office until an interval of ten years had elapsed, while
the other made it unlawful to hold more than one office
at a time. These provisions were not inspired by a fear
of autocracy, but by a desire on the part of rising politicians to keep as many offices open as possible. The
first-mentioned law was not well observed, however, since
T. Manlius Torquatus was consul in 344 and 340, and
M. Valerius Corvus in 343 and 335.

**45. Promagisterial Government and the Prorogatio Im-
perii.** The law which forbade immediate reëlection to
an office made the military situation intolerable. In the
period which we are considering Rome was carrying on

a number of campaigns simultaneously at points remote
from the city.   Several commanders, and a term of service
extending beyond twelve months, were absolutely necessary
to success.   To meet the need of more than two commanding officers, as early as 465, according to tradition, an army
was placed in charge of a certain T. Quinctius, acting *pro
consule*, and in 326 Q. Publilius Philo, the consul of the
previous year, was authorized to remain in charge of his
army *pro consule*, until the campaign was finished.   The
changes in the constitution which developed in after years
out of these two precedents were of tremendous importance.   The first incident led in time to the development
of the whole system of promagisterial government which
was adopted for the provinces.   The extension of an official's term of office (*prorogatio imperii*) beyond one year,
which was first allowed in the case of Publilius, was out of
harmony with a fundamental principle of Roman government, and the frequent adoption of the device accustomed
the Romans to the protracted exercise of supreme power
by an individual, and thus prepared the way for the empire.

46. **The Tribunes and the Senate.**   In our examination
of an earlier period (p. 38) we noticed a *rapprochement*
between the senate and the tribunes.   The case of Publilius in 326 offers another striking instance of the same
tendency, if we may accept the traditional narrative.   The
measure extending Publilius's term of office would seem to
have been laid before the *concilium plebis* by a tribune, at
the request of the senate.   This fact seems to indicate,
not only greater harmony between the two elements in the
community, but also a recognition on the part of the aristocracy of the possibility of using plebeian officials to
accomplish desired objects.

The willingness of the tribune on this occasion, and in

other instances, to carry out the wishes of the senate in the matter of legislation, is a natural return on his part for the permission, which, as we have already seen, the senate had given him to occupy a seat in the senate-house, and to state formally his objection to any action under consideration in that body.    In this period, too, probably the tribune acquired the right, which he exercised freely in later times, of calling meetings of the senate and laying matters before it for consideration.    The friendly relations which were thus developing between the senate and the tribune were fostered by the large measure of success with which the plebeian senators met in securing the tribunate for members of their families, and in making it the stepping-stone to a magistracy.    The result of these changes in the powers and functions of the tribune's office was the gradual assimilation of his duties to those of a magistrate, and, especially after the legislation of 339 and 287, which made the action of the *concilium plebis*, over which the tribune presided, unconditionally binding on all citizens, the tribune may with practical, though not with technical, correctness be called a *magistratus plebeius*.    The plebeian character of the office of course consisted in the fact that its incumbents must be of plebeian descent, and must be elected by an assembly made up solely of plebeians.    The rôle which the tribune played during this period is a characteristic and an important one.    The life-and-death struggle which the Romans were carrying on with the Samnites during these years must have developed the military spirit at home.    The tribune sought to maintain the civil liberty of the citizen against the encroachments of this tendency.    The services which he rendered to the community were valuable, and his attitude was in harmony with the traditions attaching to his office, which made him the

protector of the helpless individual against the tyranny of
autocratic power.

**47. The Senate and the Ovinian Law.**   An examination
of the *plebiscitum Ovinium* takes us naturally from the
magistracies to the senate, since its provisions affected both
the censor and the senate.   Strangely enough, although
this measure was one of great importance, its contents are
not given by any of the historians.   Festus, however, tells
us that senators were chosen by the consuls and consular
tribunes, *donec Ovinia tribunicia intervenit qua sanctum est
ut censores ex omni ordine optimum quemque curiati (iurati?)
in senatum legerent, quo factum est ut qui praeteriti essent et
loco moti haberentur ignominiosi.*   There are two important
points in the law as stated by Festus : the transfer of the
*lectio senatus* from the consul to the censor, and the establishment of the basis on which the choice of senators was to
be made.   The first provision placed the composition of
the senate and the fortunes of individual politicians, to some
extent, in the hands of the censor, and the great prominence of that official during the next century is due in large
measure to the passage of this law.   The term *ordo*, which
Festus uses, is often applied to any " class " of citizens, but
that can hardly be its meaning in the passage before us.
The Romans can scarcely have admitted members of the
*ordo libertinus*, for instance, to the senate at this time.
Furthermore, the census rolls of the period show about
200,000 citizens, and it would have been absurd to stigma-
tize as *ignominiosi* the 199,700 whose names were not
placed on the senate's list.   The term must be applied to
officials, as it is elsewhere at times, and the censor was
instructed to put in the senate all such magistrates or ex-
magistrates as were of approved character.   Probably the
Ovinian law did not introduce an essentially new method

of procedure, but it put into a more definite legal form a principle which the consuls had followed in a general way for many years. From this time forth the senate is a body of ex-magistrates, and very important results followed in the next century in consequence of this change in its composition. The following considerations enable us to fix approximately the date of the Ovinian law. It was a plebiscite, and since by its provisions the right to make out the list of senators was transferred from the consul to the censor, we may be sure that it was not passed until after plebeians were eligible to the censorship, that is, until after 339. The earliest *lectio senatus* by a censor, of which we have any record, dates from 312, so that the law must have been passed between 339 and 312. At the time of its passage plebeians were eligible to all the ordinary political offices, so that under its operation the number of plebeian senators must have increased greatly. In fact, it would be only a question of time when the majority would be plebeian.

**48. The Appearance of the Nobilitas.** Under the new régime the choice of senators was made indirectly by the people in their centuriate and tribal assemblies. A candidate of obscure position, however, had little chance of election. Only unusual ability or a great danger enabled an *ignobilis*, like Marius or Cicero, to secure a political office ; for, since wealth became a more and more influential factor in politics and society, and since the *imagines* of distinguished families appealed in a forcible, concrete way to the Roman's deeply rooted respect for the past, political office, and consequently a seat in the senate, became practically the hereditary privilege of a few rich families, and constituted the basis of a new patricio-plebeian aristocracy, the *nobilitas*, which from this time on took the place in the state and in society which the patricians had formerly held. The exclusive rights of the old aristocracy had rested on the law. By a revision of the law they could be and had been removed. The privileges of the new aristocracy depended, not on the law, but on the organization of society. Nothing but a revolution could, therefore, take them away. In this way the appearance of the *nobilitas* marks a turning point in Roman history, and the whole history of the republic falls into two great epochs. In one the patricians are in the ascendant, in the other the *nobilitas*.

A contest of two hundred years had at last brought the rich plebeians to the goal of their ambition, — political equality with the patricians, — but the position of the poor plebeian had not improved in like measure. In fact, the establishment of the patricio-plebeian *nobilitas* not only brought into more marked contrast the conditions of the rich and the poor, but the fusion of prominent plebeian families with the patricians into a new aristocracy with exclusive privileges, and with common interests hostile to those of the poor plebeians, robbed the latter of the help of their most powerful leaders.

**49. The Distress of the Poor.** Their difficulties were partly economical, partly political. It will be remembered that some attempt had been made in the Licinian laws to relieve the distress of the proletariat, but the measure brought little help. Perhaps a resumption of the *ager publicus* by the state, and its assignment to the needy with the full right of ownership, might have relieved the difficulty for a time, but probably nothing short of revolution or another secession could have forced the rich to make this concession. Resort was, therefore, had to other measures, some of them excellent, some of them absurd. The old laws against usury were enforced with more vigor, and new laws against the same offense were enacted. If tradition can be relied on, even the taking of interest was forbidden. A far more rational measure of relief was the *lex Poetelia* of 326, which alleviated the condition of such debtors as were turned over to their creditors for failure to pay their debts. In 352 an entirely new method of improving the credit system was tried. A state bank was opened, if we may apply so pretentious a term to the institution established in that year under the control of a commission of five. This commission was probably appointed to make state loans, and to secure loans from individuals, on securities not readily negotiable at reasonable rates of interest, but the plan apparently met with very little success. The greatest relief to the proletariat came indirectly as a result of the long series of wars in which Rome was engaged during the period under consideration. It is a significant fact that one of the provisions of the so-called *lex sacrata militaris*, whose passage was forced by a mutiny in the army, directed that no soldier's name should be dropped from the army rolls without his consent. Payment for military service, the prospect of booty, and a share in conquered land had evidently made service in the army a profitable form of employment. The relief which the proletariat derived from the acquisition of new territory can be readily appreciated when we remember that between 367 and 287 twenty-one Latin colonies and six Roman colonies were founded. In some of these cases a large number of colonists was sent out. Thus, for instance, 2500 were sent to Cales in the year 334.

50. **The Lex Publilia and the Lex Hortensia.** The great political movements of this period, in which the mass of the people were concerned, are connected with the passage of the *lex Publilia* in 339, of the *lex Hortensia* in 287, and

with the career of Appius Claudius. It seems hopeless to
try to make out the circumstances under which the Publilian
law was passed. The patrician coloring given to the narrative has wholly obscured the real truth of the case. The
legislation of 287 grew out of economic difficulties, and yet
here, too, the ground is very uncertain, since the eleventh
book of Livy, in which an account of the matter was preserved, is not extant, so that we must rely on the epitome
of that book, and on incidental references in other writers.
This much seems to be clear, however, with reference to
the movement in 287, that the debtors demanded a radical
measure of relief. To this the patricians in the senate, who
belonged in most cases to the creditor class, refused their
consent. Thereupon the needy withdrew to the Janiculum,
but returned to the city on condition of the enactment of
certain favorable legislation. Let us pass now to the laws
themselves, taking up first the *lex Publilia*. If we examine
its contents, we find that besides the clause to which reference has already been made (p. 42), providing that one
of the two censors should be a plebeian, the Publilian law
contained two provisions. One of these directed that a bill
should be approved by the patricians in the senate before
it was acted on by the centuriate *comitia*. Previously
the *auctoritas patrum* had followed the action of the *comitia
centuriata*. It would seem easier to defeat an undesirable
bill in its inchoate state than after the interest of the people
had been aroused and favorable action taken by a popular
assembly. One would, therefore, expect this change to
increase the importance of the *auctoritas patrum*, but such
was not the case. In point of fact, from this time on it
became a meaningless form. The mere fact, however, that
the approval of the patrician senators lost its significance
during this period is not difficult to understand, when we

remember that the whole tendency of constitutional development at this time was to rob the patricians of exclusive political powers, but it is hard to see how the change made in 339 can have helped to accomplish this end.   The principle which the Publilian law applied to legislation was extended by the *lex Maenia*, passed probably in the year 287, to elections also.   By the decadence of the influence of the *auctoritas patrum*, which followed this legislation, the last serious obstacle was removed from the path of the *comitia centuriata* as an elective and a legislative body.   Two clauses of the *lex Publilia* have been discussed. The third clause, according to Livy's narrative, enacted *ut plebiscita omnes Quirites tenerent*.   This part of the Publilian law, at least in the form in which it has come down to us, seems to be identical in force, not only with one of the Valerio-Horatian laws of 449 (p. 32), but also with the *lex Hortensia* of 287, which, according to the elder Pliny, provided *ut plebiscita universum populum tenerent*.   What relation do these three laws bear to one another?   It is almost impossible to say.   We can assume that the law of 449 made enactments of the plebeian assembly unconditionally binding on the whole people, and that the measures of 339 and 287 reaffirmed the principle already established, and sought to strengthen it at weak points; but on the one hand it is incredible that the plebeian assembly was made a supreme legislative body as early as 449, and on the other hand it would be highly improbable to suppose that the plebeians would have needed almost one hundred and seventy-five years to secure the recognition of a principle already formulated into law.   Of one fact we are sure, viz., that after 287 *plebiscita* were unconditionally binding on the whole community.   We seem forced to assume, therefore, that under the Valerio-Horatian law enactments of the plebeian assembly were valid under certain conditions, and that the Publilian and Hortensian laws removed these restrictions. In discussing the Valerio-Horatian law (p. 32) an attempt was made to show that a measure adopted by the *concilium plebis* acquired the force of law, if it was subsequently ratified by the patrician senators. Between 449 and 339, then, in the case of both the *comitia centuriata* and the *concilium plebis*, a bill, in order to become a law, required, first, favorable action by the popular assembly, then the sanction of the patrician senators. In other words, the method of procedure was the same in both cases. Now one clause of the Publilian law, as we have already seen, provided that in the case of the centuriate *comitia* the *auctoritas patrum* should precede the action of the *comitia*. If we assume that the same change was made in the case of the plebeian assembly, and the assumption is not improbable, the relation which the three laws bear to one another is clear. It may be stated as follows: from 449 to 339 a bill became a law if it was favorably acted on by the centuriate *comitia* or by the plebeian tribal assembly, and subsequently approved by the patrician senators; from 339 to 287 the *auctoritas patrum* preceded in both cases; after 287 the preliminary approval of the patrician element in the senate was necessary in the case of the centuriate assembly, but unnecessary for the action of the plebeian tribal assembly. One difficulty in the situation has not yet been spoken of. The fact has already been mentioned (p. 33) that in 447 a patricio-plebeian tribal assembly comes into existence. After that date, then, there are two tribal assemblies, one made up of plebeians, the other of both patricians and plebeians. Ancient writers do not carefully distinguish between these two bodies, so that it is often difficult to say to which one reference is made. However, since in the case of all three of the laws under consideration distinct mention is made of the assembly of the plebs, we seem to be safe in applying the principle to the plebeian tribal assembly.   In fact, the patricio-plebeian tribal assembly seems to have been largely an electoral and judicial and not a legislative body until the close of the fourth century, since the first legislative enactment of the *comitia tributa*, of which we have any record, belongs to the year 357.   If the action of this body required the preliminary approval of the patrician senators, that restriction must have been removed in 287.   In other words, the Hortensian law applied the same principle to both tribal assemblies, as, on general grounds, we should have expected it to do.

One must not assume that the passage of these three laws gave the popular assemblies practical control of legislation and robbed the senate of all its powers in this field of activity, or, to put it in another way, one must not infer that the passage of the *lex Hortensia* marked the final triumph of democracy over aristocracy.   In point of fact, no one but a magistrate could bring a bill before one of the popular assemblies for action, and since, as we shall see later, the senate found means of maintaining its control over the magistrates, very few bills came before the popular assemblies of which the senate did not approve, and a way was generally found to secure the passage of bills which the senate favored.   It was the patrician element in the senate, not the senate itself, which lost power and prestige at this time.   In other words, the Hortensian law robbed the patricians of the last exclusive political power of any importance which they possessed, but the mantle of the old patriciate fell, not on the shoulders of the democracy, but on those of the new *nobilitas*.

**51. The Policy of Appius Claudius Caecus.** Attention has already been called to the fact (p. 48) that the causes of the distress among the lower classes were partly economical, partly political, and we have considered some of the efforts which were made in this period to remove their financial difficulties. These reforms were intended to help poor debtors, and especially, we may suppose, farmers with small holdings. The political movement toward the close of the fourth century B.C., of which Appius Claudius Caecus is the central figure, removed in part the political disabilities of another element in the community, that is, of the freedmen and of freemen with less than two acres of land. Probably neither of these classes was enrolled in the tribes at this time, while the *proletarii*, that is, the citizens who owned no land or had less than two acres, were massed in the centuriate assembly in a single century, which exercised practically no influence in a body containing one hundred and ninety-three centuries.

Appius Claudius, as censor in 312, made a great change, therefore, in the composition of the popular assemblies, when he admitted landless freemen and freedmen to the tribes, and in fact to any tribe which an individual might choose, and when he also enrolled men belonging to these two categories in such "classes" as their property, in whatever form it might be, entitled them to enter. By this procedure wealth in any form was substituted for landed property as the basis of admission to a tribe and of classification in the centuriate assembly. By this change artisans and tradesmen were to be enrolled in the popular assemblies, and those bodies were likely to lose the stability which an organization composed solely of farmers or landowners is likely to have. The admission of freedmen further increased the danger. Appius violated tradition in a still more striking way by putting the names of freedmen's sons in the list of senators, which, under the Ovinian law, it was his duty as censor to draw up. An equally revolutionary proceeding was his conduct in securing the election of Cn. Flavius, the son of a freedman, as curule aedile in 304. We have not space to consider at length the motives of Appius in making these changes. The question is one of high dispute. He was certainly far-sighted, and saw that Rome was soon to be mistress of Italy. He may well have felt that by strengthening the hands of the magistrate he would secure for her that firmness and promptness of action, and that consistency in policy, which would be essential to her in her new rôle. By lowering the prestige of the *nobilitas* in the senate, and of the petty landed aristocracy in the assemblies, as his changes certainly did, he increased the importance of the magistracies, and indirectly accomplished his purpose by essentially the same method as that which Caesar adopted two centuries and a half later. The independent course which he took during his censorship was in harmony with the view which he held with reference to the magistracies. In fact, his policy was reactionary. It involved a return to the magistrate of many of the powers of which two hundred years had robbed him. This is not to say that his motives were purely patriotic, or that he had a single purpose in mind. A fine patrician contempt for the plebeian nobility in the senate and for the *bourgeois* landholders of the assemblies, who had first pushed their way into a position of equality with their betters, and were now themselves following the policy of exclusion toward their less fortunate fellow-townsmen, seems to have played some part in his mind. But the Romans were not yet ready for such revolutionary changes.

A conservative reaction came in 304. Some regard,

however, was paid to the changes made by Appius. Q.
Fabius Rullianus, one of the censors of that year, allowed
landless freemen and freedmen to remain in the tribal
organization, but assigned them to the four city tribes,
which were so large that individual votes were of comparatively little avail.   The sons of freedmen were again treated
as ineligible to the senate or to a magistracy, but in other
respects they enjoyed the political rights of citizens.   As
a result of the whole incident the position of the senate
and of the *nobilitas* was strengthened.   It had proved itself
more powerful than its enemies.   Two achievements of
Appius of a permanent character should be mentioned,
before we leave the discussion of his career, viz., the part
which he played in securing the publication of the calendar
and of the *legis actiones* in 304, and the construction of the
*via Appia* in 312.   Exactly what happened in 304 is not
clear from the words of Livy, — *civile ius repositum in pene-
tralibus pontificum (Cn. Flavius) evulgavit fastosque circa
forum in albo proposuit* (IX. 46. 5).   The general method
of procedure in civil cases and the calendar had both been
given in the laws of the twelve tables.   The service which
Flavius rendered to the people consisted perhaps, as some
writers maintain, in the publication of the pertinent contents of the laws of the twelve tables *in book form*, or he
may have set down for general use a list of court days and
a complete set of the forms which were to be employed
in civil cases.   Whatever the exact truth of the case may
have been, information essential to everyday life, which
had formerly been confined to a few, became the common
property of all.   To Appius, Rome was also indebted for
the first of those great military roads which proved such a
powerful factor in extending Roman commerce and Roman
ideas, and in facilitating the transfer of troops to all parts

of the world. None of his achievements shows more clearly the correctness with which he foresaw the future of Rome and her needs as a world-power.

**52. The Conquest of Central Italy.** The period which is under discussion in this chapter is one of rapid external development. Rome waged war with all the peoples of central Italy. Of them all the Samnites resisted her claim to supremacy with the greatest valor and stubbornness. When the Romans and Samnites were first brought into close relations in the middle of the fourth century, they apparently agreed to a peaceful division among themselves of certain territory belonging to their weaker neighbors. This seems to be the correct explanation of the course of events of the years 343–1, which one tradition exalts into a war. The ambitious spirit of expansion which Rome showed in dealing with smaller states, supported as she was now by Samnium, suggests also a sufficient explanation of the desperate struggle which the Latin communities at once made to break her power. The result of the war, which followed, and lasted from 340 to 338, was most disastrous to the Latins. Although they were assisted by the Campanians and Volscians, they were defeated and lost many of the rights which they had enjoyed since the adoption of the *foedus Cassianum* in 493. Rome made a separate treaty with each one of the Latin communities, with the express purpose of preventing future confederations between them. The terms adopted varied from state to state, but all the members of the old league were apparently deprived of the right to trade with one another and the right to intermarry. Both Rome and Samnium were eagerly seeking to extend their influence in Campanian and Volscian territory. A contest between the two powers was inevitable. The immediate cause of the war between them was the establishment of a colony at Fregellae in a Volscian district claimed by the Samnites, and an attack which the Romans made in 327 on Palaepolis, a little town on the bay of Naples, to punish it for the incursions which its citizens had made into Roman territory in Campania. War was formally declared by Rome in the following year, and was carried on by the two peoples with varying results until 304. The peace which Samnium concluded with Rome in that year was of short duration. A few years later tidings came to the city that the Samnites were bringing Lucania under their control. The Romans protested without effect, and war followed in 299 or 298. This time, although the Samnites were assisted by the Kelts and Etruscans, their spirit was finally broken, and they formed a permanent alliance with Rome in 290. The overthrow of Samnium established the supremacy of Rome in central Italy. Her success in all these wars was due, not simply to the valor and skill with which she carried them on, but also to a variety of external circumstances. Her enemies rarely showed that harmony among themselves and that singleness of purpose which characterized the Romans, and Rome did her best to develop the spirit of discord among them by arraying community against community and the aristocracy against the democracy. An overpowering dread of the Kelts and the Etruscans held many of the smaller states to the side of Rome, while doubtless the comparatively mild treatment which they received at the hands of Rome made her sway seem less objectionable than that of Samnium. Furthermore, her central position, and the construction of a military road into Campania, which was so frequently the seat of war, gave her a great advantage. The terms made with Samnium were alike honorable to her and to the Romans. She was allowed to keep her territory and her independence.

**53. The Treatment of Conquered Territory.** During these wars and at their close Rome devoted herself earnestly to the assimilation of her newly allied and conquered peoples. Her two great agents in this work were the construction of roads and the establishment of colonies. The first of the great roads was built in 312, and their importance has already been noted. The twenty-seven colonies which Rome sent out between 367 and 287 were a still more important factor in Romanizing Italy. They not only served as garrisons in controlling the surrounding country, but they introduced the Latin language, and a knowledge of Roman law and Roman political institutions wherever they were established. The policy which Rome adopted toward the Latin communities after their defeat in 338 was typical of her method of dealing with all the peoples in Italy. In general she isolated each town or tribe from its neighbors and attached it to herself. These communities, according to their political status, were either *municipia* or *civitates foederatae*. The *municipia* were *civitates sine suffragio*, that is, they had only the civil rights of *commercium* and *conubium*. In some cases they were given a local self-government; in other cases they were governed by *praefecti* sent out from Rome. Ultimately they received the full rights of citizenship. The privileges of the *civitates foederatae* depended in each instance on the special treaty made with Rome. They were not allowed to declare war against other communities, nor to make treaties with them, and they were expected to furnish Rome with a certain number of troops in case of need, but within their own borders they were supreme.

**54. The Status of Colonies.** The founding of colonies was one of the functions of the senate, which appointed a commission to carry out its instructions. One third of

the land assigned for the purpose was usually given outright
to the colonists, another third was made *ager publicus*, and
the remainder was used for the construction of temples
and for other public purposes.  The *coloniae Romanae* were
few in number and were located on the seacoast.  The
colonists in these settlements, who rarely numbered more
than three hundred, had full political and civil rights.  The
*coloniae Latinae* held the same relations with Rome as the
Latin cities did after 338.  They were independent within
their own limits, and adopted Roman political institutions
or not, as they saw fit.  To these colonies several thousand
settlers were often sent out.  In time of war they served
as allies of Rome.  In 268 they were deprived of some of
their political and civil rights which were restored to them
in 90 B.C. only as the result of the Social war.

**55. Preparations for Conquest beyond the Sea.**  The organization and equipment of the Roman army were greatly
improved in the period under consideration.  The troops
were now paid, and became accustomed to long periods
of service, and Roman commanding officers acquired the
ability to conduct serious campaigns, and control large
bodies of men.  Rome was in a position to gratify, not
only in southern Italy, but beyond the sea also, that
appetite for conquest which her successes in central Italy
had developed.  Even at this early date there are some
indications of her aspirations to be a sea power.  The
founding of *coloniae maritimae* at Antium, Tarracina, Min-
turnae, Sinuessa, Sena Gallica, Castrum Novum, and on
the island of Pontia, all of which were established between
367 and 287, either shows the existence of a sea-going trade
or foreshadows its early development.  In 311 for the first
time naval officers were chosen with the title of *duoviri
navales*.  The treaty which was made with Carthage in

348, and renewed in 306, is also an indication that foreign trade was developing, and that Roman interests were
extending beyond the limits of Italy.

### Selections from the Sources

**First plebeian dictator**: Liv. VII. 17. 6. — **Laws concerning debt**:
Liv. VII. 21. 5; VII. 27. 3; VII. 42. 1; VIII. 28. — **First plebeian
censor**: Liv. VII. 22. 6-10. — **Treaties with Carthage**: Polybius,
III. 22-7; Diodor. XVI. 69. 1; Liv. VII. 27. 2; IX. 43. 26. —
**First Samnite war (so-called)**: Liv. VII. 29-VIII. 2. — **Laws concerning reëlection and plurality of offices**: Liv. VII. 42. 2. — **Lex
sacrata militaris**: Liv. VII. 41. — **War with Latins**: Liv. VIII.
3-12. — **Peace of 338**: Liv. VIII. 13-14. — **The leges Publiliae Phi-
lonis**: Liv. VIII. 12. 14-16. — **First plebeian praetor**: Liv. VIII.
15. 9. — **Second Samnite war**: Liv. VIII. 22-IX. 45; Diodor.
XIX, XX (passim); Dionysius, XV. 7-10. — **Colony of Fregellae**:
Liv. VIII. 22. 1-2; VIII. 23. 6; Dionysius, XV. 8. 7. — **Attack on
Palaepolis**: Liv. VIII. 22-3; Dionysius, XV. 5-6. — **Caudine Pass**:
Liv. IX. 1-12; Appian, *Samn*. IV. 2-7; Cic. *de Off*. III. 109. —
**Peace with Samnium**: Liv. IX. 45. 1-4. — **Prorogatio imperii**: Liv.
VIII. 23. 12; IX. 42. 1-2; X. 22. 9 (cf. III. 4. 10). — **Plebiscitum
Ovinium**: Festus, p. 246, ed. Müller. — **Censorship of Appius Clau-
dius**: Liv. IX. 29. 6-11; IX. 33-34; IX. 46. 10, 11; Diodor. XX.
36. — **Via Appia**: Liv. IX. 29. 6; Diodor. XX. 36. 2; Frontinus,
*de Aquaeduct*. 5. — **Duoviri navales**: Liv. IX. 30. 4. — **Cn. Flavius**:
Liv. IX. 46; Cic. *de Or*. I. 186; Diodor. XX. 36. 6; Gell. VII.
(VI.) 9. — **Reaction of 304**: Liv. IX. 46. 14-15; XLV. 15; Val.
Max. II. 2. 9. — **Lex Ogulnia**: Liv. X. 6-9. — **Third Samnite war**:
Liv. X. 11-46; *Ep*. XI; Florus, I. 17; Eutropius, II. 9 f.; Dionysius,
XVII (XVIII); Dio Cass. *fr*. 33. 29 f. — **Outbreak of war**: Liv. X.
11-12; Dionysius, XVII (XVIII) 1-3. — **Sentinum**: Liv. X. 27-30;
Polybius, II. 19. — **Peace with Samnium**: Liv. *Ep*. XI; Eutr. II. 9.
— **Sabine war**: Liv. *Ep*. XI. — **Secession of 287**: Liv. *Ep*. XI; Dio,
*fr*. 37. — **Lex Hortensia**: Plin. *H. N*. XVI. 10. 37; Gell XV. 27.
4. — **Lex Maenia**: Cic. *Brut*. 55; Liv. I. 17. 9.

## CRITICISM OF THE SOURCES[1]

Binneboessel, Untersuchungen über Quellen u. Geschichte d. zweiten Samniterkrieges. Halle, 1893.

A. Kiessling, De Dionysii Halicarnassensis antiq. auctt. lat. Bonn, 1858.

B. Niese, Das sogenannte licinisch-sextische Ackergesetz, Hermes XXIII, pp. 410–423.

Schubert, Die Quellen Plutarchs, N. Jahrb. für Philol. (N.F.), Suppl. IX, pp. 647 ff.

Soltau, Livius' Geschichtswerk, pp. 117–140. Leipzig, 1897.


## SUPPLEMENTARY LITERATURE, 1901–1910

Binder, Die Plebs. Leipzig, 1909.

Bloch, Die ständischen u. sozialen Kämpfe in d. römischen Republik. Leipzig, 1900.

Dreyfus, Essai sur les lois agraires sous la république romaine. Paris, 1898.

De Sanctis, Storia dei Romani: La conquista del primato in Italia, 2 vols. Milan, 1907.

Oliver, Roman Economic Conditions to the Close of the Republic. Toronto, 1907.

[1] See also general bibliography on p. 22.

# CHAPTER V

## THE SUPREMACY OF THE NOBILITAS

**56. The Period from 287 to 133.** With the passage of the Hortensian law the great struggle which had gone on for more than two centuries was brought to an end. The efforts of the plebeians to secure their political rights had been crowned with complete success. In fact, in some respects, the plebeians enjoyed a political advantage over the patricians. So, for instance, under the new constitution one of the two consuls *must* be a plebeian, and both of them might be plebeians. The discrimination which the law made in their favor in this matter, and in certain other matters, was only fair from the democratic point of view, since at this time they must have far outnumbered the patricians. Of course the social prestige which an old nobility enjoys, and the solidarity of interests which binds together the members of a close corporation, must have given the patricians a political power which the plebeians did not possess, but the law was powerless to secure equality in this respect. As one might naturally expect, the settlement of the great questions which had divided the Roman people into two parties made the period after 287 one of comparative political inactivity. Not only were the questions at issue settled, but the Romans were occupied in adapting the new institutions to the needs of the community, and their energy was expended in the management of foreign affairs. The wars of the period, in fact, and the results which flowed from them, exerted a

controlling influence on the social and political development
of the community. The wars with Pyrrhus, with Carthage,
with Philip, Antiochus, and Perseus occupied the Romans
sixty-seven years, and three of these contests — that with
Pyrrhus, and the first and second wars with Carthage —
strained the resources of Rome to the utmost. In their
presence all the elements at Rome united in the common
defense, and, for the time, internal differences disappeared
and a remarkable political harmony prevailed. The intense
interest which the Romans felt in military affairs naturally
gave a political prominence to men who had won distinction in the field. Furthermore, the soldiers who came
back to the city did not look on their commander, as
their fathers had done, as a simple fellow-citizen, who had
like themselves been serving the state, and now resumed
his place by their side. Long periods of service abroad,
where the soldier was only one of a great army carrying
out an elaborate plan of campaign under the direction of
one man, had accustomed many of the Romans to follow
implicitly the guidance of an individual. Had Scipio
Africanus been an able and ambitious politician, it would
not have been difficult for him to exercise a paramount
influence in Roman politics. Had that been the case, the
senate would have lost its control, and the tide, which
was setting strongly toward oligarchical government, would
have been checked. But neither he nor any other successful Roman general had the ability to devise a comprehensive political programme, or the ambition to make
himself a popular leader. This is not to say that all the
political leaders of the period were actuated by unselfish
motives. The strenuous efforts which certain noble families
made to use the campaign against Antiochus to further
their own selfish ends is a proof of the opposite state of

affairs. As for the great mass of the people, the immediate effect of the long wars was to bring into relief the same sturdy qualities which they had shown in their struggle with the Samnites. Their indirect result was a complete change in the social and economic condition of the whole Italian people. The political connection of the period from 287 to 133 with that which precedes it lies in the fact that in it the institutions created during the preceding period were gradually developed and adapted to the needs of the people. It is linked to the subsequent period by the fact that in the latter the forces which developed out of the new social and political conditions resulting from the great wars took definite shape, and furnished the basis of a new political reorganization. During these years the state was ruled by the *nobilitas*, a fact which gives the period its political unity. Its end is fixed by the determined stand which the Gracchi took against the oligarchy in the name of the democracy.

**57. The Senate and the Popular Assemblies.** After the passage of the Hortensian law the Roman government was in theory essentially a democracy, in so far as landowners were concerned. Its magistrates were elected by the popular assemblies, and the measures enacted by those bodies were valid without further condition in the case of the tribal assemblies, or required only the formal preliminary approval of the patrician senators in the case of the centuriate *comitia*. In reality, however, the government was in the hands of an oligarchy, and almost all the legislation of the period emanated from the senate. One might almost say that the democracy was satisfied with the possession of power but did not care to exercise it. There is indeed some truth in this way of stating the case. The people recognized the fact that the senate was better able to direct the policy of the state than they were themselves. Now and then they asserted their constitutional rights. This was the case in 232, when the *concilium plebis*, under the leadership of the tribune C. Flaminius, passed a bill, contrary to the wishes of the senate, dividing certain land in Picenum and Gaul. Even in the second Punic war, in the case of Scipio, the senate was forced to yield to the people or to popular sentiment. In general, however, the senate had a free hand in the administration of affairs.

The reasons are not far to seek. The number of voters during this period ranged from 250,000 to 300,000. Many of them lived at a great distance from the place of voting. It was obviously inexpedient to call together such an assembly for the passage of ordinary administrative legislation. Many matters, especially in time of war, require prompt action. This could not be secured through one of the popular assemblies. Furthermore, the questions which came up for consideration were far more difficult to settle than those of earlier years had been. The scene of active operations at present was far from Rome. The average Roman knew little about the conditions abroad, and was not, therefore, in a position to express an intelligent opinion on the majority of the questions at issue. What made matters worse was the fact that adequate discussion in the *contio*, which preceded the casting of the ballots, was impossible. The senate, however, was eminently qualified to meet all the conditions mentioned. It was a body of only three hundred members, so that it could be called together quickly, and could discuss fully any important question laid before it. Its members were men of means who could afford to meet frequently for the transaction of public business. This fact alone would have given the senate precedence over any one of the popular assemblies, for administrative legislation at least. A still greater advantage which the senate had lay in the character of its composition after the passage of the Ovinian law. Under that law it became a body of ex-magistrates, whose experience in administration and knowledge of affairs at home and abroad fitted them in a peculiar way to settle wisely the complicated questions of foreign policy which engaged the attention of the Roman people during this period. One should also bear the fact in mind that the senate had always played a leading part in directing the foreign policy of the state. In managing foreign affairs during the period of the great wars it was, therefore, in large measure following well-established tradition, and as foreign questions completely overshadowed domestic affairs in number and importance, another reason for the ascendency of the senate as a legislative body is apparent. Not only did the qualifications of the senate help it to acquire a supremacy in legislative affairs, but it found means to prevent the popular assemblies from taking the initiative in such matters. A popular assembly could meet only when it was called together by a magistrate or a tribune, and only to discuss such matters as were laid before it by a magistrate or tribune. Now both these classes of officials were under the control of the senate, so that it was practically impossible to get a bill of which the senate did not approve before any one of the assemblies.

58. The Senate and the Magistrates. What has been said will explain in part the influence which the senate exercised over the magistracies. The Ovinian law had made the senate a body of ex-magistrates. All of the senators were men of experience in government. Some of them were ex-consuls who had filled with distinction the same office which their presiding officer was now filling. Some

of them had a greater technical knowledge of the questions at issue than he had himself. Furthermore, strong motives of self-interest bound the members of the senate together in maintaining and extending its prestige. The consul himself came from their number; he was imbued with their ideas of government and at the end of the year he would return to their ranks. It was impossible for him to make a stand against such influences as these. His submission to the senate was inevitable. In the earlier period the list of senators was drawn up by the consul and he probably exercised some discretion in the matter of choice. This duty was now performed by the censor, so that membership in the senate was in no wise dependent on the favor or approval of the consul. In fact, the senate was practically independent of any magistrate in this respect. The Ovinian law had instructed the censor to give preference to ex-magistrates in the selection of senators, and the rather extreme interpretation which was put on this law made its action automatic and practically gave ex-magistrates the *right* to a seat in the senate. The tribune was not much more inclined than the consul to take the initiative in matters of legislation. The influences which controlled the consul affected him also. Furthermore, as we have already noticed (p. 44), the senate had taken pains to cultivate friendly relations with him. His office, too, was a stepping-stone to the magistracies, in candidacy for which the support of the *nobilitas* would be of great importance. The result of all this was that the senate met, not to give the consul advice which he was free to accept or reject, but to take action which he was expected to carry out as its minister.

**59. Benefits and Evils of Senatorial Government.** The system of senatorial government had both its light and its dark side. Technical administrative questions were decided by a body of experienced administrators. A consistency and continuity was given to Roman policy which would hardly have been possible with the free initiative of magistrates holding office for a year only. The element of selfish personal ambition was in large measure eliminated. In fact, the senate checked in its own interest any attempt at self-aggrandizement. However, this necessity of preventing an individual from attaining eminence had its evil side. Great success and the resultant popularity gave rise to distrust in the minds of the oligarchy, so that at a critical moment the state might be robbed of the services of a valuable leader. The senate was undoubtedly actuated by patriotic motives in almost all of its actions, but it was impossible for it, in domestic affairs, to throw off entirely its conservative bias. In foreign affairs the results of a divided, and, therefore, a diminished, responsibility were painfully apparent. The senate often adopted a policy in dealing with another state which individual senators, had they been magistrates vested with supreme power, would have scorned to follow. The harmony which existed between the senate and its commanders in the field during this period is remarkable, and it is surprising that a series of great wars could have been brought to a successful completion under the joint management of a commanding officer in the field and a jealous legislative body of three hundred members at home. It devolved upon the senate not only to maintain a supervision over the military operations carried on simultaneously at different points and to provide money and troops for the various campaigns, but also to assume a general care of newly acquired territory in Italy or abroad. The last-mentioned duty imposed on the senate the responsibility of drawing up a constitution for the community in question, or of ratifying a treaty with it, of taking necessary

measures to protect it and hold it in subjection, of dividing
the provinces among the various classes of officials, and of
receiving foreign ambassadors and deputations.

**60. Magistracies.**  The subordination of the magistrate
to the position of minister of the senate involved a certain
loss of prestige on his part, but it brought partial compensation with it.  The development of the powers of the
senate gave an added value to the magistracies, since election to one of them carried with it admission to the senate.
Indeed, from this time on the importance of a magistracy
consisted largely in this fact.  Furthermore, the immense
gain which the senate made, after the development of an
imperial policy, in the variety and importance of its functions, increased correspondingly the scope of the powers
which the magistrate enjoyed who followed its mandatory
advice.  The determination of the senate to protect itself
against ambitious individuals found expression in various
laws affecting the magistrates which were passed in this
period.  In 180 the tribune L. Villius secured the passage
of a law which fixed, directly or indirectly, the age at which
citizens might become candidates for the more important
offices (*quot annos nati quemque magistratum peterent cape-
rentque*).  By this measure the *cursus honorum* was established.  Its observance would prevent an ambitious politician
from riding into power on a wave of popular enthusiasm.
As early as the fourth century any one who had held a
given magistracy was ineligible for reëlection to the same
office until an interval of ten years had elapsed.  Even this
stringent provision did not satisfy the oligarchy, and toward
the close of the period we are considering, — that is, about
the middle of the second century, — reëlection to the consulship was absolutely forbidden.  In the next century, however, Sulla reverted to the legislation of the earlier period.

**61. Bribery and Ballot Laws.** The laws against bribery and providing for a secret ballot are also to be attributed largely to the desire of the oligarchy to protect itself against ambitious and unscrupulous politicians. A careful study of the legislation against bribery would throw a flood of light on the history of Roman morals during the last century of the republic, and undoubtedly men like Cato, in supporting legislation to check the evil, were actuated mainly by a desire to stem the tide of degeneracy, but the real purpose of the early laws on that subject was political. A new *lex de ambitu* was passed in 181. A second followed in 159. The *lex Gabinia* of 139, which provided for a secret ballot at elections, the *lex Cassia* of 137, and the *lex Papiria* of 131, which made the same provision for meetings of the *comitia*, respectively as a court and as a legislative body, were intended to accomplish essentially the same purpose as the laws against bribery, in a different but perhaps in a more effective way.

**62. Change in the Number and Functions of the Praetors.** The only change of any moment in the magisterial system was the addition of another praetor toward the end of the first Punic war, the increase in the number of these officials from two to four in 227, and to six in 197. The second praetor was chosen to take charge of cases in which foreigners were concerned, and so received the title of *praetor peregrinus*, while his colleague, who presided in matters where only citizens were parties to the suit, was known as the *praetor urbanus* (cf. p. 187). The increase in the number of praetors in 227 and 197 went along with a complete change in the functions of certain members of the college, since the four new praetors were not assigned to essentially judicial duties, but were made governors of the newly acquired provinces of Sicily, Sardinia, Nearer Spain, and Farther Spain.

**63. The Quaestorship and Dictatorship.** The addition of four new quaestors in 267, which raised the number in the college to eight, brought with it no radical change in the duties of those officials. It was a natural consequence of the extension of Roman territory. The new quàestors were the financial representatives of the central government in the various sections of Italy. It is significant of the thoroughness which the senate showed in carrying out its oligarchical policy that dictators for other than such temporary and special purposes as the holding of an election during the absence of both consuls, or the annual driving of a nail in the wall of the temple of Jupiter, were rarely appointed during this period, and, when they were chosen, they deferred, not less than the consuls, to the senate. The choice of a plebeian for the first time as *pontifex maximus* in 253 is little more than an echo from the din of battle of an earlier period.

**64. The Censorship.** The censor's office became one of immense political and moral importance during the period which we are considering. His main constitutional functions consisted in assessing the property of citizens, in preparing a register of them according to tribes, classes, and centuries, in drawing up the list of senators, and in managing the finances of the state. The increased importance of this magistracy was due to a variety of causes. Foremost among these should be mentioned the precedent set by Appius Claudius in his performance of the duties of that office in 312. We have already noticed (p. 54) the autocratic manner in which he changed the composition of the tribes and the centuries. The reaction of 304 was not a protest against the exercise of such powers by the censor, but rather a reversal of the action of one censor by another. The right of the censor to make such radical changes as

Appius had made was, therefore, strengthened and not weakened by the events of 304. In fact, the reform of the centuriate assembly in 241 was probably due in large measure to the efforts of the censor. The immense increase in the income and the expenditure of the government which resulted from the prosecution of a long series of wars and the acquisition of provinces, was a still more potent factor in giving importance to his office. The taxes levied in the new provinces were farmed out to the highest bidders, and the contracts were made by the censor in the name of the state. Besides the income from this source, immense sums of money came into the treasury in the form of booty. Aemilius Paulus, for instance, brought home 300,000,000 sesterces after the war with Perseus.

It is difficult, with the scanty information we have, to account for the development of the right to supervise the morals of the people which the censor exercised in the third century. This is the probable course of events, however : In drawing up a register of a tribe or a class it was necessary for him to inquire closely into such matters as the name, age, residence, family, and property of each citizen (cf. p. 192). It is probable that he gradually extended the range of his inquiry to cover also the manner of life of citizens, without waiting for legislation to authorize him in taking such a course. Such action on his part would find abundant justification in the determined stand which the community was making against the degenerate tendencies of the time. In fact, the functions of the censor made his office the natural agency to employ in the effort to preserve the integrity of the Roman character.

**65. Improvement in the Judicial System.** A development of some importance, which for convenience may be mentioned in this connection, consisted in the improvement of the judicial system, by sending *praefecti iuri dicundo* to various points in Italy to represent the praetor, and by the occasional establishment of judicial commissions to take the place of the popular assemblies in the trial of certain criminal cases. The advantage which a small, select body had over a popular assembly in such cases was so apparent, that by the *lex Calpurnia* of 149 a permanent court was established for the trial of magistrates guilty of peculation in office, the so-called *quaestio* (*perpetua*) *de* (*pecuniis*) *repetundis*. The historical importance of this innovation lies largely in the fact that it was the first step toward the organization which Sulla made in the next century of a fairly complete judicial system. It is interesting to note that the offense, of which the first standing court was to take cognizance, was extortion. Evidently the magistrates had already found it necessary to seek reimbursement in the provinces for the great expenses attendant on an election to office at Rome. The establishment of a court to try those guilty of peculation goes hand in hand with the legislation against bribery. Little immediate gain could be expected from the court, however, because its juries were made up exclusively of senators, and could hardly be trusted to convict senatorial governors.

**66. Reform of the Centuriate Comitia.** The most comprehensive political change of this period which affected the whole people was the reform of the centuriate assembly about 241. That body was completely reorganized on the tribal basis. Each of the tribes was divided into *seniores* and *iuniores;* then the members of each of these two sections were assigned to classes according to their wealth, the members of each class of *seniores* and *iuniores* forming a century. The division of each of the thirty-five tribes into centuries is indicated in the following diagram.

| Seniores | Century of 1st class |
|----------|----------------------|
|          | "      "   2d   "    |
|          | "      "   3d   "    |
|          | "      "   4th  "    |
|          | "      "   5th  "    |

*Tribus*

| Iuniores | Century of 1st class |
|----------|----------------------|
|          | "      "   2d   "    |
|          | "      "   3d   "    |
|          | "      "   4th  "    |
|          | "      "   5th  "    |

To the three hundred and fifty centuries thus formed there should be added eighteen centuries of knights, four supplementary centuries, not definitely enrolled in the classes, and one century of *proletarii*, making a grand total of three hundred and seventy-three. The property qualification for admission to the several classes was henceforth calculated on a money basis, and was probably raised for each class, but of this we cannot be sure. It is clear, at all events, that the new organization was of a far more democratic character than the old one. In the old body the number of centuries in the first class, supplemented by the knights, was greater than that in all the rest put together. The eighteen centuries of knights combined with the eighty centuries of that class constituted a majority. In the reformed organization the number of centuries in each class was the same, so that the only advantage which wealth gave lay in the fact that the centuries of the upper classes were probably smaller than those of the lower classes, and yet had equal weight with them in voting.

In one other respect the organization fell short of being strictly democratic. The *seniores* in a given tribe, that is, the men between forty-six and sixty years of age, made up five centuries, so that they had as great a voting power as the *iuniores*, or men between seventeen and forty-six years of age, although by the natural laws of mortality there cannot have been more than half as many of the former as of the latter in a tribe. Therefore, although the reformed centuriate assembly was essentially democratic, wealth and age enjoyed indirectly some advantages.

**67. The Tribal Assemblies.** Legislation of the fifth century, possibly the *lex Aternia Tarpeia* of the year 454, had allowed magistrates, tribunes, and plebeian aediles to impose fines up to a certain limit. All cases involving a larger amount than the minimum fixed could be appealed to the tribal assembly. The effect of this arrangement was to make the tribal assemblies criminal courts of appeal in all but capital cases. This change had its political side. It enabled the tribune to hold a magistrate responsible for his conduct, but its value in this respect was in large measure offset by the use of the court for partisan purposes. An important step toward robbing the tribal assemblies of their judicial functions altogether was taken toward the close of this period by the establishment, in 149, of the first *quaestio perpetua* (p. 74).

The most important laws of this period were passed in the tribal assembly. For instance, the *leges Villia* (p. 70), *Gabinia* (p. 71), *Cassia* (p. 71), *Calpurnia* (p. 74), and various sumptuary laws, *e.g.*, the *lex Oppia* and the *lex Orchia*, were all *plebiscita*. The tribal assembly met within the city and had a simpler organization than the centuriate assembly. Furthermore, the tribune who presided over the *concilium plebis* represented better than the magistrate the progressive sentiment of the community. The *leges Aelia et Fufia* of about 155 applied the auspices to the tribal assemblies for the first time. The senate secured the passage of this law for the purpose of preventing undesirable action in the tribal assembly, when all other forms of opposition had failed. As a defensive weapon, however, the measure was of little avail.

**68. Growth of the Proletariat.** The economic changes in the condition of the people were far more serious than the political. The immediate result of them was the widening of the gap between the rich and the poor. A number of reasons may be given for the growth of the proletariat on the one hand, and, on the other, for the acquisition of great wealth by the favored few. The long wars had taken the peasant proprietors from home, and their land, left without cultivation, rapidly deteriorated in value. Hannibal's occupation of Italy increased the damage which had resulted from neglect, and at the close of the second Punic war a large part of the land in Italy had passed out of cultivation. This change bore heavily on the free laborer also. The demand for his services was greatly diminished by the transformation of arable into pasture land, and the introduction of a vast number of slaves brought his wages down to a very low point and put a stigma on manual labor. The massing of landed property in the hands of a few and the employment of slave labor made the business of the peasant proprietor unprofitable. Competition with the newly acquired provinces was still more disastrous to him. The ranks of the proletariat, which were reinforced in this way by free laborers out of work and by bankrupt peasant proprietors, were still further swelled by the manumission of slaves. Many of the slaves who had been brought to Rome as captives during the wars outside of Italy were clever artisans or good farmers, and their owners found it more profitable to manumit them, give them a small capital, and share in the profits of the enterprise, than to retain them as slaves.  This condition of things was somewhat relieved in the early part of the period by drawing off large numbers of the *proletarii* to the newly established colonies.  Ten or twelve colonies were founded in the interval between 287 and the close of the second Punic war, and twice as many in the early part of the second century, but after 180 we hear of only one new colony, so that the proletariat lost even this form of relief.

**69. Amassing of Great Fortunes.**  The aggrandizement of the rich kept pace with the impoverishment of the middle classes.  Several states in southern Italy, which had sided with Hannibal, were punished after the close of the second Punic war by being deprived of a large portion of their territory.  The rich men at Rome found little difficulty in getting possession of the greater part of this confiscated land. The acquisition of territory beyond the sea was of immense value to the capitalist and successful politician.  On the one hand, it gave the Roman officials who were sent out to the provinces a good opportunity to amass fortunes at the expense of the provincials.  On the other hand, the conquests in Spain and the East opened new outlets for trade, which the special privileges granted to Roman citizens, and the destruction of Rome's commercial rival, Carthage, threw almost entirely into the hands of the Roman merchant and banker, and Roman capitalists began to reap rich returns for the investment of their money.  Another profitable field for investment was the collection in the new provinces of the taxes which the state let out by contract to private citizens.  Since the provincials were without defense, and the ruling class at Rome winked at the extortionate demands of its representatives abroad, enormous fortunes were made in a short time.  The evils which naturally follow a sudden increase in wealth were aggravated by the fact that the conquest of Magna Graecia and the East brought the Romans into contact with a highly developed civilization to which their previous simple life was in marked contrast.  The development of luxurious tastes and the means of gratifying them came simultaneously, and the rich Roman rushed into reckless expenditure on his household and his retinue with the intemperance which characterizes the parvenu.  The long series of sumptuary laws, which began with the *lex Oppia* of 215, is in itself a striking proof of the tendency of the time.  The attempt to check the growing evil by legislation was of as little effect as such efforts usually are.  In fact, the *lex Oppia* itself was repealed after it had been in force only twenty years.  The severe measures which the censors took to check extravagance were of as little permanent value.

**70. Political Results.**  The immense increase, on the one hand, in the number of freedmen, and of freemen out of work, and, on the other, the acquisition of large fortunes by a few, had a most disastrous effect on Roman politics. A large number of freedmen and of those who had lost their holdings or their occupation in the country districts drifted to Rome and were admitted to the popular assemblies, in so far as their property allowed it.  Their votes were in many cases to be had by the candidate who gave the most for them, or whose games were the most magnificent.  The laws to punish bribery and to provide for a secret ballot, to which reference has already been made (p. 71), furnish an indication of the growing demoralization of the popular assemblies.  The great inequality in wealth had another unfortunate political result. It gave rise to a spirit of dependence among the great mass of the people, in some cases of hostility toward the rich on the part of the poor, which found expression in class legislation of various kinds. Thus, in 217, the democratic leader Flaminius secured the passage of a bill lowering the money standard; in 216 a commission was established to facilitate the negotiation of loans; and in the same decade a law was passed prohibiting senators from owning ships of more than a certain tonnage.

**71. The Conquest of Southern Italy.** The conclusion of the third Samnite war had already made Rome mistress of central Italy. A petty quarrel with Tarentum, in 282, opened the way for her conquest of southern Italy. In the war which followed, the Tarentines and their allies in southern Italy were unable to cope with Rome and sent to Pyrrhus, the king of Epirus, for help. He inflicted a severe defeat on the Romans near Heraclea in 280, and advanced through Samnium and Campania to the borders of Latium; but at that point he turned back. Again, in 279, Pyrrhus was successful at Asculum, and negotiations looking to peace were entered into; but the appearance of a Carthaginian fleet at Ostia offering help induced the Romans to refuse all terms. The urgent requests which the Greeks in Sicily made for help, and his discouragement over the state of affairs in Italy, led Pyrrhus to cross to Sicily in 278. After an unsatisfactory campaign in that island, he returned to Italy in 275, was defeated by the consul M'. Curius at Beneventum, and retired permanently from Italy, leaving Rome free to bring the cities in the lower part of the peninsula completely under her control.

**72. The First Punic War.** The harmonious relations which existed between Carthage and Rome during the war with Pyrrhus were brought to an untoward end by the

course of events in Sicily. Besides her possessions in
Africa, Carthage controlled Sicily, with the exception of
Syracuse and Messana, and also Sardinia, Corsica, the
Balearic islands, and the south coast of Spain. An opportunity presented itself in 264 to make herself mistress of
Messana also, and she eagerly embraced it. One party in
this city, however, appealed to Rome for help, and the
senate was forced by popular clamor to send the consul
Appius Claudius to its assistance. The Romans were successful on land, but they found that such success would
count for little as long as Carthage controlled the sea.
Accordingly they fitted out a fleet in the year 260 which
won a great victory off Mylae, and from this time on the
contest was in large measure a struggle for naval supremacy.
In fact, the defeat of the Carthaginian fleet by Catulus in
241 brought the war to an end. Had it not been for their
new allies, the Romans would have been helpless in such
a struggle, but the seamanship of the Greeks of southern
Italy, and the knowledge which they had of the Sicilian
coast, helped to offset the naval experience of Carthage.
By the terms of peace Carthage gave up Sicily to Rome,
surrendered her prisoners, and agreed to pay a war indemnity of 3200 talents. Three years after the close of the
war, in 238, when she was weakened by a long-continued
mutiny in the army, she was forced to give up Sardinia and
Corsica also.

**73. War with the Kelts and Illyrian Pirates.** In the
years which followed the first Punic war, Rome strengthened
her position in Italy and on the Adriatic. She was startled
in 225, however, by the news of a fresh Keltic invasion on
the part of the Boii and Insubres and Transalpine merce-
naries. Notwithstanding the enrollment of 150,000 men
for the protection of Italy, the invaders advanced as far as

Clusium in Etruria, and defeated a detachment of the Roman army; but the approach of another strong force obliged them to retire, and they were crushed between the two Roman armies at Telamon in Etruria. The submission of the Boii followed in 224; that of the Insubres, who resisted more stubbornly, in 222. The northern frontier of Italy was secured by planting colonies at Mutina, Placentia, and Cremona, and by building a military road, the *via Flaminia*, to Ariminum. The war which broke out against Illyria in 229 had the two practical results of freeing Italian trade in the Adriatic from the depredations of the Illyrian pirates, and of throwing Rome into the cauldron of Greek politics.

**74. The Second Punic War.** The rapid progress which Carthage was making in Spain disturbed the Romans to such an extent that a treaty was made with her, by the terms of which she agreed to limit her acquisitions to the region south of the Ebro. The city of Saguntum lay south of that river, but it was not considered necessary to provide for her independence in the treaty mentioned, because she was in alliance with the Romans. The attack which Hannibal made on that city in 219 was, therefore, a direct affront to Rome. The Carthaginians refused to grant redress, and preparations were at once made in Rome to fit out expeditions against Spain and Africa. But Hannibal, by a rapid march into northern Italy, which he reached with an army reduced to 26,000 men, put the Romans on the defensive, and by brilliant victories on the Ticinus and the Trebia in 218, at the Trasimene lake in 217, and in the following year at Cannae, put the supremacy of Rome in Italy in extreme peril. In fact, the battle of Cannae was a signal for the withdrawal of almost all the cities of southern Italy from their alliance

with Rome.   Only a few seacoast towns remained loyal,
or were held in subjection by garrisons.   In spite of these
great disasters the spirit of the Romans was not broken.
They adopted, however, the policy of avoiding a direct
trial of strength with Hannibal, and devoted their energy
to cutting off all his sources of supply.   With this object in
view they sought to regain the Italian cities which had
allied themselves with Hannibal, or had been conquered
by him.   With the same purpose in mind they carried
on a vigorous campaign against the Carthaginians and
their allies in Spain and Sicily.   The result of this policy
was that Spain, the great center of Carthaginian strength,
was overrun by the Romans, and Hasdrubal, Hannibal's
brother, after coming into Italy in response to Hannibal's
urgent request for reinforcements, was defeated and slain
at the Metaurus in 207, and Hannibal himself stood alone
with his little army in a corner of Italy.   The Romans
were now ready for a bold stroke, and in 204 the senate,
yielding with some hesitation to popular demand, sent over
to Africa young Scipio, who had distinguished himself in
Spain.   The audacity of this step was justified by the
complete victory which the Roman army won at Zama in
202 over Hannibal, whom the Carthaginians had hastily
recalled.   By the terms of the peace, which was concluded
in the following year, Carthage was stripped of all her
foreign territory, and even in Africa Numidia was declared
independent.   She was, furthermore, forbidden to wage war
abroad, and in Africa except with the consent of Rome.
She gave up her fleet also, and agreed to pay an indemnity
of 10,000 talents.

**75.  First Macedonian War.**   The most important result
of the war against the Illyrian pirates, as we have already
noticed, was the fact that Rome's new acquisitions placed

her in a position where she would be easily involved in the
meshes of Greek politics. The inevitable entanglement
came in 214. King Philip of Macedon, with an envious eye
on the Roman possessions on the Illyrian coast, took advantage of Rome's weakness, after the battle of the Trasimene
lake, to form an alliance with Hannibal, promising him help
in Italy in return for the above-mentioned Illyrian towns.
Rome was forced to accept Philip's challenge, but her main
purpose in the war which followed was to prevent him from
giving help to Hannibal, so that she was content, in the
main, with putting herself at the head of the Greek states
opposed to Philip, and not unwillingly made peace with him
in 205 on terms which extended the limits of Macedonian
territory.

76. **Second Macedonian War.** But the successful completion of the second Punic war left Rome free to deal with
the Eastern question, and the development of Philip's
ambitious plans seemed to make interference necessary.
He had formed a plan with Antiochus III of Syria for
the division of Egypt, and while Antiochus occupied himself with the conquest of Coele-Syria, Philip seized Egypt's
possessions on the Aegean. Rhodes came to their relief,
and later joined Athens and Egypt in asking help from
Rome. Philip refused to grant the demands which a
Roman embassy made on him at Abydos in 200 that he
should make peace with the Greeks, give up the territory
which he had taken from Egypt, and submit his quarrel
with Rhodes to arbitration — and war was declared at once.
Rome was assisted by Rhodes and by Attalus, king of Pergamum, and with their help forced Philip to yield after the
battle of Cynoscephalae in 197. Philip gave up his conquests, withdrew from Greece proper, surrendered his fleet,
and paid a war indemnity. The Greeks were declared free,

and Rome's friends and allies in Greece were treated with unparalleled generosity. By adopting this plan, instead of following her usual policy of territorial aggrandizement, Rome furnished a proof of her admiration for the Greek civilization, and avoided rousing the passionate opposition of the whole Greek world. What motive determined her course it is hard to say.

**77. War with Antiochus.** In the meantime Antiochus had completed the conquest of Coele-Syria, and in 197 proceeded to seize the Egyptian possessions on the south coast of Asia Minor. Notwithstanding the urgent appeals of Eumenes of Pergamum and the free Greek cities, Rome could not be induced to interfere with the movements of Antiochus in Asia, but when he crossed the Aegean sea in 192, on the invitation of the Aetolians, an army was sent against him. His utter defeat at Thermopylae in the year 191 drove him out of Europe, and vindicated the main principle for which Rome was contending, that of the non-interference of foreign potentates in European politics ; but the opportunity to break the power of Antiochus was so promising that the Romans followed him into Asia, and inflicted a crushing defeat on him at Magnesia in Lydia in the year 190. Peace was made on condition that he should retire beyond the Taurus, pay 15,000 talents, and limit his fleet to ten ships of war. Rome's allies were flattered by being allowed to take part in the peace negotiations, and were rewarded for their services by valuable gifts of territory.

**78. The Third Macedonian War.** Among others, Philip of Macedon had supported the Romans loyally, and in return he received Demetrias and a certain amount of territory in Thessaly and Aetolia. But, suspicious of his growing influence in Greece, the Romans a few years later took his new possessions from him. Their suspicions were not without justification. Jealousy of Rome's interference in Greek politics was growing rapidly; the national spirit of the Greeks was developing, and Philip cleverly appealed to both these sentiments. His successor, Perseus, strengthened the position of Macedonia by alliances with his neighbors. The attempted assassination of Rome's friend, Eumenes of Pergamum, at Delphi, at the supposed instigation of Perseus, and the support which Rome gave to a petty Thracian prince banished by Perseus, fanned the smouldering embers into flame, and war broke out in 171. Success attended the Macedonians at the outset, and the Romans pretended to consider favorably the proposals of peace. Their real purpose, however, was to crush Macedonia completely, and this object they accomplished by their success at Pydna in 168. The former kingdom of Macedonia was divided into four parts, each independent of the other, and one-half of the tribute formerly paid to the king was turned into the Roman treasury.

79. **Subsequent Changes in Macedonia, Greece, and Spain.** The partition of the country led to endless confusion, and a pretender, named Andriscus, took advantage of this state of things to put himself at the head of reunited Macedonia. He was defeated without much difficulty in 148, and Rome at once made Macedonia a province, adding to it southern Illyria, Epirus, and Thessaly. The settlement of affairs in Greece proved to be equally unsatisfactory. The Greek states were constantly quarreling. The hostility toward Rome was persistent, and the Achaean league was developing strength and confidence in a way which threatened to make it the central point of an uprising. The trouble reached a climax in 147, when the Achaeans declared war against Sparta, in spite of warnings from Rome against the

adoption of such a course.  The Romans put an army in the field at once.  The Achaeans on their side were joined by the Boeotians, Euboeans, Phocians, and Locrians.  The war was of short duration, and after its conclusion the Achaean league was disbanded, Corinth destroyed, and the greater part of Greece was placed under the supervision of the governor of Macedonia.  The policy of Rome in Greece and the Orient was, not to extend her sovereignty, but to weaken the strong powers already existing in those quarters and to prevent the growth of new ones.  In the uncivilized West her purpose was very different.  In Spain she acquired from Carthage, as a result of the second Punic war, only the southern portion of the peninsula.  This territory was divided into two provinces and assigned to praetors.  The unwise and cruel rule of the Roman governors and their subordinates brought on an uprising in 154, which, beginning first with the Lusitanians, spread far and wide, and cost the Romans twenty years of determined effort to crush.  After the fall of Numantia in 133, the last point of resistance, peace reigned in Spain for many years.

**80.  The Third Punic War.**  The Romans looked across the Mediterranean at the regeneration of Carthage after the second Punic war with unmixed anxiety.  Masinissa of Numidia took advantage of their jealous attitude to claim on one pretext or another certain possessions of Carthage, until at last the Carthaginians were driven to the point of making war on him.  This step was in contravention of the treaty of 201, and Rome, therefore, sent a strong army across to Carthage in 149 ; but three years of hard fighting intervened before the city could be taken.  Carthage and the cities faithful to her were destroyed ; a part of the surrounding territory was given to her neighbors, and part was taken by Rome herself.

**81. Development of Imperialism.** The long series of wars which came to an end with the capture of Carthage in 146, left Rome in possession of large tracts of new territory outside of Italy. Sicily, with the islands of Sardinia and Corsica, she felt compelled to hold for the protection of Italy. Spain had shown itself in the second Punic war such a point of vantage for Carthage that it seemed necessary to take it under Roman control. A large party at Rome had come to feel that the safety and growth of their native city required the destruction of Carthage, and, after she had been destroyed, it could be regarded as a matter of duty to give the conquered peoples some form of stable government. In the case of Macedonia, at the end of the first war the form of government was left unchanged, and even after the second war autonomy was granted to the four sections into which the country was divided. A Roman government was imposed on the people only after other plans had failed. In other words, it seems clear that Rome did not deliberately adopt a policy of conquest and territorial aggrandizement outside of Italy, but the protection of her own interests seemed to make an extension of territory necessary in each case. The successful prosecution of these wars, however, developed the thirst for conquest; the legitimate and illegitimate profits from the new territory appealed to the commercial spirit and the greed of the Romans, and the control of Spain, Italy, Sicily, Sardinia, Macedonia, and Africa, which made Rome the strongest power in the Mediterranean, suggested inevitably the rounding out of her possessions by the conquest of Asia and Egypt.

**82. The Model adopted for Provincial Government.** The Romans organized a definite government in Sicily and in Sardinia and Corsica in 227, in the two Spains in 197, **and**

in Macedonia and in Africa in 146.   The earliest form of
provincial government was an adaptation of the system
which had been introduced throughout Italy, with two
important modifications, however.   The relations which
the Italian communities bore to one another were under
the direct supervision of the senate.   Such supervision
would be impossible in most cases for territory outside of
Italy.   Imperial interests were, therefore, placed in the
hands of a Roman governor.   The second important difference consisted in the fact that the provincials were subject
to taxes which were not imposed on the Italians.   This is
not to say that in other respects the provincials were as
well off as the Italians.   In practice their condition was
much worse, partly because they were largely at the mercy
of a governor who was allowed a large liberty in his management of the province, whose transgression of the principles laid down to check his exercise of autocratic power
it was almost impossible to punish.

83. **The Lex Provinciae and the Governor.**   The government of territory outside of Italy was a new problem for
the Romans, so that various experiments were tried with the
earliest provinces before an essentially permanent system
was adopted.   But from 146 down to the later years of the
republic, the senate drew up a set of regulations for each
new province, and sent a commission of ten to the province
to coöperate with the commanding general in putting them
into execution, and in arranging such details as seemed
necessary.   This body of regulations formed the *lex provinciae*, or constitution of the province.   The first period in
the history of the provinces extends to the time of Sulla.
Up to that time provision was made for their government
by an increase in the number of praetors as provinces were
from time to time acquired.   The provincial governor had

the right to collect money and supplies for war, commanded the troops in the province, and exercised jurisdiction in criminal and civil cases. In criminal cases he could even impose a sentence of death, although Roman citizens, after a certain date, had the right of appeal. In his administration of provincial affairs he was bound, at least theoretically, by the *lex provinciae*. Money, troops, and subordinate officials were provided by vote of the senate.

**84. The Status of Communities in a Province.** A uniform system of government was by no means adopted for all the people within the limits of a single province. In fact, the way in which the degree of civil liberty enjoyed by the peoples in different cities under one governor varied is one of the unique features of Roman provincial government. The Romans accepted in most cases the political units which they found already in existence, and treated the different communities generously or harshly, according to their previous attitude toward Rome. Cities which had proved themselves faithful friends were made *civitates liberae*. Those which surrendered became *civitates stipendiariae*, while those which resisted to the end, like Carthage or Numantia, were ordinarily destroyed. *Civitates liberae* were classified as *civitates foederatae* or *civitates sine foedere immunes et liberae*, according to the basis on which their independence rested. The independence of communities of the first class was formally recorded in duplicate on bronze tablets. One of these tablets was preserved on the capitol at Rome, the other in the city concerned. Communities of the second class received their independence by a *lex* or *senatus consultum*. Its permanence was, therefore, conditioned on the favor of the Roman people or senate. The *civitates liberae* were not allowed to deal directly with other states, but they were permitted to coin money and receive exiles, and in domestic affairs they were independent of Rome. The citizens of such a community were tried before their own courts, were left untaxed by Rome, and were subject to no other obligation than that of furnishing such a number of ships or of troops as might be stipulated in the treaty. The constitution of a *civitas stipendiaria* was drawn up by a senatorial commission, or embodied by the provincial governor in an edict. It usually permitted the community to retain its senate, popular assemblies, magistrates, and courts, and to conduct in general the administration of local affairs ; but all this was done under the supervision of Roman officials. Thus the governor supervised the choice of senators, allowed or forbade the holding of the local *comitia*, and examined the city's finances. Upon the land of such a community a fixed tax, or *stipendium*, was laid, or a certain proportion of the annual returns, *i.e.*, a *vectigal*, was paid to the Roman government. As time went on, the Romans more and more rarely granted to a community the rights of a *civitas libera*. In some provinces *municipia* and colonies were established, but their position was the same as that of corresponding communities in Italy, with the important exception that such communities in the provinces were subject to all the regular provincial taxes. The condition of things in one of the earlier provinces may be illustrated by the case of Sicily, in which there were three *civitates foederatae*, five *civitates liberae et immunes*, thirty-four *civitates decumanae*, paying a tenth of the produce from the land, and twenty-six *civitates censoriae*, whose territory was made state land.

## SELECTIONS FROM THE SOURCES

**Outbreak of Tarentine war:** Liv. *Ep.* XII. — **Heraclea:** Liv. *Ep.*
XIII; Plut. *Pyrrh.* 16–17. — Pyrrhus crosses to Sicily: Eutrop.
II. 14. — **Beneventum:** Liv. *Ep.* XIV; Eutrop. II. 14. — **Outbreak
of first Punic war:** Polyb. I. 10–12; Gell. XVII. 21. 40. — **Blockade
of Agrigentum:** Polyb. I. 17. — **Naval victory of Duilius:** Wilm. *Ex.
Inscr.* 609; Polyb. I. 22–3; Eutrop. II. 20; Tac. *Ann.* II. 49. —
**Capture of Regulus:** Polyb. I. 33–5; Liv. *Ep.* XVIII. — **Naval
defeat at Drepana:** Liv. *Ep.* XIX; Eutrop. II. 26; Polyb. I. 49–52.
— **Naval victory of Catulus:** Eutrop. II. 27; Polyb. I. 60–61; Liv. *Ep.*
XIX. — **Peace with Carthage:** Polyb. I. 62–3; Liv. XXX. 44. 1.
— **Acquisition of Sardinia:** Polyb. I. 79 and 88. — **Lex Flaminia
agraria:** Polyb. II. 21; Cic. *de Inv.* II. 52; *de Sen.* 11. — **Illyrian
war:** Polyb. II. 8 ff. — **Increase in number of praetors:** Liv. *Ep.* XX.
— **War with Insubres and Boii:** Polyb. II. 23–34; Liv. *Ep.* XX. —
**Fall of Saguntum (second Punic war):** Polyb. III. 17; Liv. XXI.
14–15. — **Ticinus:** Polyb. III. 65; Liv. XXI. 39. 10; 45–6. — **Trebia:**
Polyb. III. 71–4; Liv. XXI. 52–7. — **Lex Claudia:** Liv. XXI. 63. 3.
— **Trasimene lake:** Polyb. III. 83–4; Liv. XXII. 4–7. — **Cannae:**
Polyb. III. 107–117; Liv. XXII. 43–50. — **Lex Minucia:** Liv. XXIII.
21. 6. — **Treaty between Hannibal and Philip:** Polyb. VII. 9; Liv.
XXIII. 33–4; Eutrop. III. 12. — **First Macedonian war:** Liv. XXIV.
40. — **Capua recaptured:** Polyb. IX. 3–9; Liv. XXVI. 4–16. —
**Treaty with the Aetolians:** Liv. XXVI. 24. — **Events in Spain:** Liv.
XXVI. 41–51. — **Colonies:** Liv. XXVII. 9–10. — **Hasdrubal defeated:**
Polyb. XI. 1–3; Liv. XXVII. 46–9. — **Carthaginians expelled from
Spain:** Liv. XXVIII. 12–37. — **Peace with Philip:** Liv. XXIX. 12.
— **Thirty-five tribes:** Liv. XXIX. 37. 13–14. — **Scipio crosses to
Africa:** Liv. XXIX. 24–7. — **Zama:** Polyb. XV. 5–16; Liv. XXX.
29–35. — **Peace with Carthage:** Polyb. XV. 18; Liv. XXX. 43.
— **Second Macedonian war:** Liv. XXXI. 5 ff. — **Cynoscephalae:**
Polyb. XVIII. 1–10; Liv. XXXIII. 7–10. — **Treaty of peace
made:** Liv. XXXIII. 30. — **Number of praetors increased:** Liv.
XXXII. 27. 6. — **Lex Porcia de provocatione:** Cic. *de Re Publ.* II.
54; *pro Rab. perd. reo,* 12; Gell. X. 3. 13; Liv. X. 9. 4. — **Greece
proclaimed free:** Polyb. XVIII. 27–9; Liv. XXXIII. 32; Plut.
*Flamin.* 10. — **Lex Sempronia de pecunia credita:** Liv. XXXV. 7. —
**War with Antiochus:** Liv. XXXVI. 1 ff. — **Magnesia:** Liv. XXXVII.

37–44. — **Leges sumptuariae**: Liv. XXXIV. 1–8; Gell. II. 24; Macrob. *Saturn*. III. 17. — **Leges de ambitu** and **Leges tabellariae**: Liv. XL. 19. 11; Cic. *de Legg*. III. 35; *Brut*. 106; Liv. *Ep*. XLVII. — **Lex Villia annalis**: Liv. XL. 44. 1; Cic. *Phil*. V. 47. — **Third Macedonian war**: Liv. XLII. 52 ff. — **Pydna**: Liv. XLIV. 40–42; Plut. *Aem*. 18–22. — **Third Punic war**: Appian, *Punic*. VIII. 74 ff.; Liv. *Ep*. XLIX. — **Lex Calpurnia de pecuniis repetundis**: Cic. *Brut*. 106; *de Off*. II. 75. — **Andriscus**: Liv. *Ep*. XLIX. — **Carthage destroyed**: Appian, *Punic*. VIII. 127 ff.; Liv. *Ep*. LI. — **Achaean war**: Liv. *Ep*. LII. — **Numantia taken**: Appian, *Hisp*. VI. 84–98; Liv. *Ep*. LVII.

## CRITICISM OF THE SOURCES [1]

C. Böttcher, Kritische Untersuchungen über d. Quellen d. Livius im 21 u. 22 Buch, Fleckeisen, Jahrb. (N.F.) Suppl. V. 351–442.

Nissen, Kritische Untersuchungen über d. Quellen d. IV. u. V Dekade d. Livius. Berlin, 1863.

Soltau, Livius' Geschichtswerk (pp. 21–84, and bibliography, pp. 9–14). Leipzig, 1897.

Soltau, De fontibus Plutarchi in secundo bello Punico enarrando. Bonn, 1870.

R. B. Smith, Rome and Carthage. London, 1880.

## SUPPLEMENTARY LITERATURE, 1901–1910

Ferrero, The Greatness and Decline of Rome (to close of the reign of Augustus), 5 vols. New York, 1907–1909.

Audollent, Carthage romaine. Paris, 1901.

---

[1] See also general bibliography on p. 22.

# CHAPTER VI

## THE STRUGGLE BETWEEN THE DEMOCRACY AND THE NOBILITAS

**85. Tiberius Gracchus.** An investigation of the preceding period has revealed (pp. 77–80) the serious economic and political changes which followed as a result of the great wars. The republic had been at the outset, and for several centuries afterward, a commonwealth of free land-owners. This great middle class was now swept out of existence, and with it went the foundation on which the state rested. The object of the movement connected with the name of Tiberius Gracchus was to build this class up again. His attention is said to have been called to the wretched condition of affairs in Italy when he was on a visit to Etruria, where the evil had reached its greatest height. He thought relief could be had by assigning state land to citizens, and, with this purpose in mind, he secured an election to the tribunate for the year 133 and at once proposed a reënactment of that clause of the Licinian law which limited the amount of land to be held by an individual to five hundred acres, with the modification that for each of two grown sons two hundred and fifty acres in addition should be allowed. That portion of the *ager publicus*, the control of which the state would resume under the operation of this law, was to be divided among poor citizens on condition of the payment of a yearly tax. Payment for improvements was to be made to those already in possession, but this claim on the Roman treasury was met by the inheritance which Attalus III of Pergamum had lately bequeathed to the Romans. A standing commission of three, whose members were to be chosen annually, *III viri agris iudicandis adsignandis,* was to carry out the provisions of the law. This proposal was essentially different from earlier colonizing projects. It was distinctly socialistic. Earlier colonies had been sent out to points of danger to hold, and to Romanize, newly acquired territory. The protection which they gave the state was a sufficient return for the land which the state gave them. The new colonists were to be settled in peaceful sections of Italy and received land from the government solely by virtue of their poverty. The proposal of Tiberius naturally aroused the violent opposition of the rich, whose profits from the *ager publicus* would be materially diminished by its adoption. It was opposed on the ground that it revived an obsolete provision of a law passed two hundred years before, and probably because it was a piece of class legislation, and because it also diminished the public revenue. Believing that he could not secure the support of the senate, Tiberius submitted his proposal to the people at once. This he had a constitutional right to do under the Hortensian law, but even here he was thwarted by the veto of his colleague Octavius. Up to this point the question at issue had been a social one. It took on a political character when Tiberius secured the removal of Octavius from office by a vote of the people. In fact, his agrarian proposal becomes unimportant in comparison with the constitutional question involved in the removal of Octavius. While the long agitation which culminated in 287 had established the general principle that the will of the people expressed in their assemblies constituted the law of the land, their will had to be ascertained in a certain way, and the expression of it was subject to certain hindrances. One of the limitations, for instance, on the freedom of the action of the people in the *comitia*, consisted in the right of a tribune to interpose his veto. Now, in securing the removal of Octavius from office, Tiberius was acting on the theory that a representative of the people ceases to be such when in a particular matter he acts out of conformity with the wishes of a popular majority. The logical application of this theory in all cases would remove all constitutional limitations upon the expression and execution of the people's will, and would put the state absolutely under the control of a temporary popular majority. The principle was not only out of harmony with the genius of Roman political institutions, but it is subversive of stable government. It found logical expression in the democratic empire of Julius Caesar. The agrarian law of Tiberius was adopted, but he himself was killed while seeking reëlection to the tribunate.

**86. The Years following the Death of Tiberius.** The ten years which followed the tribunate of Gracchus were years of comparative political inactivity. The development of a democratic opposition to the *nobilitas*, however, went on steadily. The passage of the agrarian law, and of other less important measures, in a popular assembly against the wishes of the senate had stimulated the activity of the tribal assembly, and its importance, both as a legislative body and as a center of political agitation, increased rapidly, and an attempt was made to preserve its purity by the *lex tabellaria* of the tribune C. Papirius Carbo, which supplemented the *lex Gabinia* and the *lex Cassia* (p. 71) by providing for a secret ballot, when the *comitia* met as a legislative body. That the agrarian law of Gracchus was actively carried out for some time is indicated by the census, which shows an increase in the number of citizens from 318,000 in 135 to 395,000 in 124. A large majority of these 77,000 new citizens must have gained their citizenship by becoming landowners under the operation of the new law. The death of Tiberius Gracchus, therefore, by no means put an end to the agrarian movement. Another question, of a political character, was brought into the foreground by the agrarian legislation. The position of the Latins and other Italians was already bad enough. The passage of the new law made it worse, since it took from them some of their privileges in the *ager publicus*, and therefore emphasized the disadvantage of their position when compared with that of Roman citizens.

**87. The Legislation of Gaius Gracchus.** Accordingly, the necessity of settling satisfactorily the land question and of admitting the Italians to the rights of Roman citizenship were the two questions which confronted Gaius, the brother of Tiberius Gracchus, on his election to the tribunate in 123. Two motives probably actuated him in the course which he took, — a desire to avenge the death of his brother, as well as to bring to an end the supremacy of the senate. To accomplish the latter purpose he sought to bring to his support the proletariat and the knights, the two non-senatorial elements in the community. He aimed at securing the favor of the former by the passage of a *lex frumentaria*, which put grain at the disposal of the poor at a price lower than the market rate. He favored the knights at the expense of the senate by substituting knights for senators on the juries in the *quaestio de repetundis*. Since the *equites* had very important financial interests in the provinces, while the provincial governors, whose cases were heard in this court, were senators, the change involved a great gain for the former and at the same time put the latter in serious peril. Although a number of laws had confirmed the citizen's right to appeal to the people in cases of life or death, the senate found means of suspending this right, when it wished to get rid of an enemy, by establishing a special judicial commission or by passing a *senatus consultum ultimum*. Both these devices had been used successfully against Tiberius and his followers. A *lex Sempronia* of Gaius forbade the appointment of such commissions, and denied the validity of the interpretation put on the *senatus consultum ultimum*. The agrarian law of Tiberius, which had not been carried out for several years, was reënacted or reaffirmed. The tribal assembly under the leadership of Gaius encroached aggressively on the traditional prerogative of the senate by taking part in the control of foreign affairs, as it did in regulating the tax system in Asia and in founding colonies. Of far-reaching importance was a law which made it incumbent on the senate to decide which provinces should be consular before the new magistrates were chosen (cf. p. 237). Toward the end of his second tribunate Gaius took up the second great political problem, which, as we have seen, confronted him at the beginning of his political career, and proposed to give Roman citizenship to the Latins, and Latin rights to the other Italian allies; but at this point the selfish democracy of Rome deserted him. He became a candidate for the tribunate a third time, was defeated, and, like his brother, met a violent death. The agrarian movement which had been instituted by Tiberius and Gaius was summarily checked by the legislation of 118 and 111, which gave the full rights of ownership to those already occupying state land; but the other legislation of Gaius remained in force. A still more important result of the Gracchan movement was the consciousness which the democracy gained of its own strength and of the weak points in the position of the senate.

**88. Marius and the Wars with Jugurtha and the Cimbri.** In fact, the weakness of the *nobilitas* soon gave the chance of success. In 112 the government was compelled by public sentiment to declare war against Jugurtha, the king of Numidia, who had not only dispossessed of their rights his cousins, Adherbal and Hiempsal, and put them to death, but had treated the protests of the Romans with scorn. In the war which followed, the open purse of Jugurtha on the one hand, and the venality and incapacity of the senatorial leaders on the other, brought disgrace to the Roman name and defeat to the Roman arms. The popular party insisted on a change, and in 107 succeeded in electing to the consulship C. Marius, a man of humble birth who had shown his ability at the siege of Numantia, and to him the control of the forces acting against Jugurtha was committed. Jugurtha was defeated and the war was speedily brought to an end. Marius was still in Africa, arranging the affairs of the province, when he was elected to the consulship for the year 104 and intrusted with a still more serious undertaking. A horde of barbarians, of Germanic origin, from the shores of the North Sea, in search of lands and booty, had swept southward toward Italy, and in 113 defeated a Roman army under the consul Cn. Papirius Carbo at Noreia (the modern Neumarkt). After this victory the Cimbrian invaders were joined by two Helvetian peoples, the Teutones and Tigurini, and in Gaul in 109 inflicted a second defeat on the Romans under M. Junius Silanus. Two years later the Roman consul L. Cassius suffered a still more serious reverse at the hands of the Tigurini, and in 105 at Arausio the combined forces of the barbarians destroyed the two armies which the proconsul Q. Servilius Caepio and the consul Cn. Mallius Maximus commanded, and left 60,000 Romans dead on the field of battle. This was the condition of affairs when Marius entered on his second consulship in 104. Great anxiety prevailed in Italy, and complete distrust of the senatorial régime. The withdrawal of the Cimbri toward Spain and the inactivity of the other barbarians gave Marius an opportunity to reorganize and train his forces, so that later, when the enemy sought to enter Italy at two different points, they were completely annihilated, the Teutones at Aquae Sextiae in 102, and the Cimbri the following year on the Raudine plain.

**89. Saturninus and the Conservative Reaction.** The brilliant successes which the *novus homo* Marius thus won in the Jugurthine and Cimbrian wars, following, as they did, on the disasters which the state had suffered under senatorial leadership, inflicted a severe blow on the prestige of the senate, and the democracy was quick to take advantage of the situation by allying itself directly with Marius. For the year 100 he was elected consul for the sixth time, and liberal assignments of land in Africa were made to his veterans in a measure introduced by the tribune Saturninus; but the radical character of the agrarian bills which Saturninus brought forward in his second tribunate in 100, and the forcible means which he and the praetor Glaucia used to secure their passage, alienated a large part of the people, and drove even Marius over to the opposition. In the reaction which followed, the laws of Saturninus were repealed, and an attempt was made to check hasty legislation in the *comitia* in the future by the *lex Caecilia Didia* of the year 98, which provided that a bill should be published seventeen days before it could be submitted to the people for action (cf. p. 254). This measure also forbade the inclusion of different matters in the same bill.

**90. Drusus and the Italians.** It is a strange illustration of the irony of fate that M. Livius Drusus, the son of the conservative whose clever manoeuvres had brought political disaster and death to the younger Gracchus when he tried to ameliorate the political condition of the Italians, should have been the man who revived the movement to relieve the Italians, thereby losing his life. The ultimate political aim of the younger Drusus, however, differed essentially from that of his predecessor. C. Gracchus had tried to overthrow the senate by combining all the other forces in the state against it. Drusus, on the other hand, sought to strengthen the conservative position by removing the principal causes of discontent, not only in Rome but in all Italy. He sought to conciliate the poor by an agrarian law and a corn law. He tried to reconcile the senate and the knights by a measure which made both senators and *equites* eligible for jury duty, and finally he promised citizenship to the discontented Italian allies. But the selfishness of all the parties concerned brought his efforts to naught. Despairing of the support of the senate, he submitted directly to the popular assembly a bill with clauses embodying his plans with reference to the distribution of grain, the assignment of land, and the composition of the juries. The measure was passed in spite of violent opposition, but his subsequent proposal to give citizenship to the allies alienated the people, who were unwilling to share their privileges with others, and Drusus became a victim of popular passion, as C. Gracchus had been. The senate had by this time mustered courage enough to declare that the laws already passed were in contravention of the *lex Caecilia Didia*, and therefore invalid.

**91. The Social War.** The bill which Drusus submitted in the year 91 was the last of many attempts to better the condition of the Italians by conservative methods. When, like its predecessors, it resulted in failure and was followed by severe repressive measures directed against them, the discontent of the Italians broke out into an open revolt, in which all except the Latins and the aristocratic states of Umbria and Etruria joined. The loosely organized confederacy which they formed had its capital at Corfinium, and imitated the Roman system in having a senate with five hundred members, two consuls, to represent respectively the Oscan and Latin speaking peoples, and twelve praetors. The Italians were as good soldiers as the Romans; they found able leaders, and they were better prepared for war than the Romans. Consequently, the advantage in the early part of the war, which began in 90, rested with them, and when the Umbrians and Etruscans showed signs of joining the confederacy Rome thought it wise to make concessions. Within a year after the outbreak of the war the consul L. Julius Caesar secured the passage of a law granting citizenship to the allies who had remained loyal, and in the early part of the next year, 89, on the proposal of the tribunes M. Plautius Silvanus and C. Papirius Carbo, the *lex Plautia Papiria* was passed, providing that Roman citizenship should be given to the citizens of allied states who should register their names with a Roman praetor inside of sixty days. The *lex Pompeia* of the same year gave Latin rights to the Transpadanes. The newly made citizens were, however, assigned to eight tribes, and this fact limited their influence. These concessions placated a majority of the Italians, and the smouldering embers of revolt among the Bruttii, in Samnium, and in Lucania were stamped out in the following year.

**92. Sulla and the Mithridatic War.** The state of affairs in the East was the immediate cause of the next trial of strength between the two parties at Rome. The Romans had been so engrossed with affairs in Italy that they had not heeded the rapid development of a new power in the Orient. For twenty years or more Mithridates Eupator, the king of Pontus, had extended his power without serious hindrance in Asia Minor and along the north shore of the Euxine. At last he came into conflict with the Romans in Bithynia, and war broke out in 88. The Roman forces in the East proved to be no match for Mithridates, and the conduct of the campaign was intrusted to one of the consuls, L. Cornelius Sulla, who had distinguished himself in the Social war and had some knowledge of the Eastern question.

**93. Sulla, Marius, and Cinna.** Marius, however, coveted the position and formed a compact with the tribune P. Sulpicius Rufus, as he had earlier with Saturninus. Under the leadership of Sulpicius laws were passed giving the Italians access to all the tribes and assigning the command of the forces acting against Mithridates to Marius. Sulla, who had not yet left Italy, returned with his army; Marius fled, and the laws of Sulpicius were repealed. The power of the tribune to do mischief was curtailed by a law which made the preliminary approval of the senate necessary before the *concilium plebis* could act upon a measure, and probably the Servian organization of the *comitia centuriata* was restored. Then Sulla set out for the East, leaving as consuls for 87 the aristocrat Cn. Octavius and the democratic leader L. Cornelius Cinna. Dissensions sprang up between them at once. Cinna was driven out of Rome by Octavius, but, with the assistance of Marius and his veterans, he returned and made himself master of the city. The democratic party was at last installed in power, but the record which it made was not one to be proud of. Its leaders not only violated well-established traditions, as, for instance, in admitting young Marius to the consulship before he had reached his twentieth year, but they also transgressed the essential principles of democracy in advancing men to the magistracies without waiting for a formal election and in substituting magisterial edicts for popular legislation. Furthermore, they had no comprehensive political programme. Sulla concluded a peace with Mithridates in 85. In the spring of 83 he landed in Italy with his troops, and in the autumn of 82 overcoming all resistance captured the city.

**94. The Legislation of Sulla with reference to the Senate.** Sulla had himself made dictator for an indefinite period with the express purpose of reforming the constitution. His tendencies were naturally conservative, and these had been strengthened by his observation of the results which had followed the democratic government of Marius and Cinna. It is not strange, therefore, that his legislation bore a marked reactionary character. His primary purpose, in so far as the home government was concerned, was to strengthen the oligarchy, and especially the senate as the official representative of that element in the community. To increase its power as a law-making body, he reaffirmed the principle that the preliminary approval of the senate was necessary before a measure could be submitted to the plebeian tribal assembly. This change robbed the tribune of his power of initiating legislation and diminished the importance of the senate's greatest legislative rival. He lessened the influence of individual magistrates by increasing materially the number of praetors and quaestors and by encouraging a system of dependence on the senate. Thereby the importance of the senate as an administrative body was correspondingly increased. The same change released it also from the control of the censor. The number of magistrates was henceforth large enough to fill the senate, and the censor no longer drew up the list of senators. Senators were substituted for knights on the juries, and, since the number and competence of the courts were greatly increased (cf. p. 106), the judicial duties of the senators became very important.

**95. The Magistracies.** To protect the oligarchy against the preëminence of any one man, Sulla secured a reaffirmation of the principle that no one could be reëlected to an office until an interval of ten years had elapsed, and established definitely the *cursus honorum*. The number of praetors was increased to eight, and the number of quaestors to twenty. This made the administration of the duties of these offices more efficient, but at the same time decreased their dignity. In the early period it had been customary for magistrates to command the armies of the state during their year of office. From this time on they were rarely sent to a foreign post until their term of office had expired ; that is, they became purely civil magistrates during their first year of office, and provincial governors the second year. In this way the promagisterial system was definitely instituted, although perhaps Sulla did not originate it. It is possible that a practice already followed in many cases was made the regular method of procedure after this time. The importance of the tribunate he lessened by taking from its incumbent the right to initiate legislation (cf. p. 104), and still more effectively by providing that an ex-tribune should be ineligible to any other office in the state ; that is, a citizen by accepting the tribunate lost all chance of further political advancement.

**96. The Courts.** In originality, permanence, and practical value Sulla's reform of the judicial system was perhaps of more importance than any other change made by him. He reorganized the juries, increased the number of permanent courts, and extended the judicial system so as to include many new classes of cases. Since the time of C. Gracchus the juries had been composed exclusively of knights, and, while the *quaestio de repetundis*, in view of its constitution, had exercised a restraining influence on the rapacity of senatorial governors, it had frequently been used by the *equites* to punish upright governors who had checked the extortionate practices of the financial representatives of the knights in the provinces. The Gracchan change in the composition of the juries had been made on purely political grounds. It substituted one bad method for another. When Sulla restored the old practice by putting senators on the juries in place of the knights, he also was actuated by political motives, and the judicial system in this respect was in as bad a plight as it had been before. Justice could hardly be hoped for when one member of a closely knit political and social organization was tried before a jury made up of other members of the same body. In 149, as we have already noticed, a permanent court, the *quaestio (perpetua) de repetundis*, had been established for the trial of magistrates who were charged with accepting bribes or otherwise unlawfully using official positions for their own advantage. Somewhat later another standing court had been established, the *quaestio de sicariis et veneficis*, to take cognizance of attempts on the life of citizens. Following these precedents Sulla provided for criminal courts to inquire into serious attacks on popular freedom, or into conduct prejudicial to the interests of the state (*de maiestate*), forgery (*de falso*), the use of unlawful means by candidates for office (*de ambitu*), and embezzlement of public funds (*de peculatu*). By the increase of the number of praetors to eight, presiding judges were provided for these courts, and their establishment practically brought to an end the criminal jurisdiction of the *comitia*. Henceforth justice was dispensed in a speedier, simpler, and surer way than had been possible before a popular assembly. This change also involved differentiation and classification of criminal offenses, and furnished a scientific basis for the development of a complete criminal code.

**97. The Priesthoods.** In early times new members of the colleges of priests were chosen by coöptation, and this plan was followed up to the year 104. After that time, under the operation of the *lex Domitia*, new members of the more important colleges were elected in a partial assembly of the tribes. Sulla restored the earlier method of selection, but in 63 the *lex Domitia* was put in force again.

**98. Pompey and the War with Sertorius.** In 79 Sulla resigned the dictatorship and retired into private life. He thought that he had established the oligarchy firmly and that he had guarded it at every point, but his own career indicated a fatal weakness in the conservative position. The army was henceforth arbiter of the fortunes of the state. In fact, within ten years after Sulla's death, two of his own lieutenants, Pompey and Crassus, used the prestige which successful campaigns brought them to undo a great part of his work. Pompey's success was achieved in Spain; that of Crassus in Italy itself. During the ascendency of the democratic party in Rome the Marian leader, Q. Sertorius, had been sent out as governor of Nearer Spain, and by his personal qualities, and his ability as a political and military leader, he had succeeded in defeating the various leaders of the senatorial party, and

in making himself master of the greater part of the peninsula.   He even formed an alliance with Mithridates, and
there seemed to be a possibility of his crossing to Italy
and putting the Marian party in power again.   This was
the situation which forced the senate in 77 to give the
title of proconsul to Pompey, and send him out to Spain
with 40,000 troops, although he had not yet held even
the quaestorship.   The war went on with varying success
for several years, but the reinforcements which Pompey
received from Italy and the treachery of the followers of
Sertorius at last turned the tide of battle in Pompey's
favor, and in 71 he was able to return victorious to Italy.

**99. Crassus and the Slave War.**   Just as Pompey was
bringing the war in Spain to an end, Crassus was commissioned to take charge of the campaign against the slaves in
southern Italy.   The escape of a few gladiators from Capua
in 73 seemed an insignificant event; but when in a few
months their number had increased to 70,000, and they had
defeated the praetors Clodius and Varinius, the Romans
were thoroughly frightened.   In 72 both consuls took the
field, but were also defeated.   The destruction of this dangerous force in the following year by the praetor Crassus, in
a brilliant campaign of only six months, was, therefore, an
achievement which might well win for him the gratitude
and admiration of the Roman people.

**100. Pompey, Crassus, and the Democracy.**   Both Pompey
and Crassus now returned to Rome to secure an election to
the consulship for 70 as a reward for their services in the
field.   They found the democratic party fiercely attacking
the reactionary constitution of Sulla.   In fact, as early as
78 the democratic leader Lepidus had tried as consul to
annul some of its provisions.   That party now agreed to
elect Pompey and Crassus to the consulship in return for

the repeal of the most obnoxious Sullan laws ; and, thanks to its support and to the presence of troops outside the gates, their candidacy was successful. The new consuls loyally carried out their part of the compact by removing the restrictions placed on the tribunate, by providing that the juries should be composed of senators, knights, and *tribuni aerarii,* and by restoring the censorship with the right to pass on the qualifications of senators.

**101. The Gabinian and Manilian Laws.** For several years the Cilician pirates had threatened the safety of the coast towns, and had seriously interfered with commerce in the Mediterranean and with the transportation of grain to Rome. To meet the popular demand for a vigorous policy, and to gratify Pompey's ambition for an important command, A. Gabinius, a tribune, proposed in 67 that the forces acting against the pirates should be put in charge of one man, with absolute power extending to a distance of fifty miles from the coast. The bill was carried in spite of the opposition of the conservatives to the extra-constitutional provisions which it contained, and in a second measure Pompey was named as commander. The war with the pirates had scarcely been brought to a successful conclusion, when the recall of Lucullus from the East, and the incompetency of his successor, M'. Acilius Glabrio, gave Pompey's adherents an opportunity to pass the Manilian law, which conferred on him the conduct of the war against Mithridates. The command which he assumed under this law removed Pompey from all direct participation in politics up to the close of the year 62.

**102. The Conspiracy of Catiline.** It is within this period that the Catilinarian conspiracy falls. Looking at the political side of the movement, at the outset it seems to have had for its object the improvement of the condition of certain classes in Rome and throughout Italy by constitutional, or at least by peaceful, methods. The repeated disappointments which its leaders met in the years 66–64 led to the formation of a secret conspiracy, ready to use any means whatsoever for the accomplishment of its purpose. At this point the timid, the judicious, and in large measure the respectable, supporters of the movement fell away, and its further development was left in the hands of moral and financial bankrupts or of honest fanatics and adventurers. So, for instance, Caesar and Crassus supported Catiline and his sympathizers at the outset, just as they supported every promising attack on the oligarchy ; but as the incompetency of the Catilinarian leaders became apparent, and their plans assumed a violent character, they withdrew from a venture which was sure to fail and to wreck the fortunes of those concerned. The Catilinarian movement is similar in its inception, in its development, in the character of its supporters, and in its methods, to the other uprisings of the party of discontent during the first century, for instance, to those under Sulpicius in 88 and under Lepidus in 78. It may be worth while to illustrate this fact from the case of Lepidus, who, like Catiline, was an aristocrat, and had personal qualities remarkably similar to those of Catiline. Like Catiline he had been a follower of Sulla and had taken part in the Sullan proscriptions. Like Catiline he proposed radical and socialistic measures for the benefit of the honest and the dishonest poor. Both men found adherents in Rome among the bankrupt aristocrats, the poor freemen and freedmen, and the democrats, and among the discontented peasant proprietors in the country districts. In both cases the rallying point of the movement outside of Rome was Faesulae, a natural hotbed of agrarian agitation. The leaders in each case were ready, if necessary, to resort to

riot and bloodshed.   The plan of operations was the same
in the case of both movements.   The rural malcontents
were to advance on Rome, and to be seconded by an uprising in the city.   The only essential difference between the
two movements lies in the fact that Lepidus at the head of
his Italian force succeeded in reaching the gates of Rome,
whereas Catiline's armed band was checked and destroyed
before it came to the city.   On the side of the senatorial
party there was the same general alarm, hesitation, and
incompetency shown in both cases.

**103.  Political Effect of the Catilinarian Conspiracy.**  The
revolutionary tendencies of the Catilinarian movement and
its suppression inflicted a severe blow on the democratic
party, because that party had evidently fallen into the hands
of desperadoes.   All the forces which stood for law and order
were united against it, and Cicero might well pride himself
on the fact that the union took place under his leadership.
C. Gracchus had practically detached the knights from the
conservative party by putting the juries in their hands, and
the partisan way in which they conducted the trials of senatorial governors alienated the two factions still further.
By depriving the knights of the privilege which they had
enjoyed for almost fifty years, Sulla widened the breach
between them and the senate.   The bitterness existing
between the two factions can hardly have been lessened by
the hostility which the senate showed to the restoration of
the knights to a place on the juries in 70.   Furthermore,
senatorial governors and the financial representatives of the
knights were continually at odds in the provinces, and the
*equites* were undoubtedly provoked at the opposition of
the senate to the Gabinian law.   Accordingly the harmonious action in 63 of these hitherto discordant elements
was a political event of great importance.

**104. The First Triumvirate.** The senate was, in fact, so elated by its success that, when Pompey returned from Asia toward the close of 62, it failed to confirm his arrangements or to grant suitable rewards to his veterans, and he was powerless to force it to yield. The result was that when Caesar returned from the propraetorship of Spain at the close of the year 61, he found it easy to make a private arrangement with Pompey to their mutual advantage. Crassus, too, with whom Caesar was already on good terms, was induced to cast in his lot with them, and a private compact, commonly known as the first triumvirate, was formed between the three men. In the bargain it was stipulated that Pompey's arrangements in Asia should be ratified, that land should be assigned to his veterans, that Caesar should have the consulship in 59 and a term of five years as governor in Gaul, while to Crassus a future consulship was promised and probably a place on the Pompeian land commission, or else certain tax concessions.

**105. Caesar's First Consulship.** The triumvirs carried out the first item in their programme by electing Caesar to the consulship for 59, but Bibulus, an extreme aristocrat, was his colleague. The senate rejected the agrarian measure which he proposed for Pompey's benefit, but he secured its passage in a more radical form in the *comitia*, overcoming by violent means the obstacles which his colleague threw in his way. Pompey's course in the East was approved, and on the proposal of the tribune P. Vatinius a bill was passed assigning to Caesar, for five years, from March 1, 59, the provinces of Cisalpine Gaul and Illyricum, with an army of three legions, to which the senate, apparently of its own motion, added Transalpine Gaul and a fourth legion, but probably not for a fixed period. It is worth while to notice that Caesar's governorship in Gaul began during his term of office as consul. Perhaps this enabled him to make certain arrangements for his province which could not otherwise have been made.

**106. Humiliation of the Senate.** Caesar did not care to go to his province at the end of his consulship and leave affairs in Rome in the hands of two such unskilful political leaders as Pompey and Crassus, until he had crushed the spirit of the senate and deprived it of its most dangerous leaders, Cato and Cicero. Cato was accordingly sent to Cyprus on a mission which would take him from Rome, and which seemed pretty sure to ruin his reputation, while Clodius, an ex-patrician, who was very bitter against Cicero, was allowed to become tribune for 58. Clodius prepared the way for his attack on Cicero by securing the passage of popular measures, which provided that grain should be given gratis to the poor, that an announcement of unfavorable auspices should not interfere with the meetings of the *concilium plebis*, and that certain clubs of a semi-political character should no longer be unlawful. Then he carried through two bills banishing Cicero on the ground that he had put the Catilinarian conspirators to death without granting them an appeal to the people.

**107. Renewal of the Triumvirate.** But Pompey and Crassus showed themselves incapable of managing affairs at Rome. Clodius terrorized the city with his armed bands, and gratuitously affronted Pompey to such an extent that he forced him to make common cause with the senatorial party to the extent of securing Cicero's recall in the autumn of 57. Cicero's recall was a triumph for the optimates. The political incapacity of Pompey and rumors of disagreement between the triumvirs encouraged them still more, so that in April of the year 56 the senate took under consideration a proposition to repeal the Campanian land-law of 59. This action, which was directed against both Caesar and Pompey, brought about an immediate renewal of the compact between them and Crassus, and in accordance with its terms Pompey and Crassus were elected to the consulship for the following year, and, during their term of office, secured the passage of laws assigning Spain to Pompey, and Syria to Crassus, for five years, and prolonging Caesar's proconsulship for the same period. Crassus set out for the East toward the close of the year, but Pompey remained in Rome.

**108. Estrangement of Pompey and Caesar.** The violence and disorder, with their accompaniment of bribery and political intrigue, which prevailed almost uninterruptedly from midsummer of the year 54, reached its climax in January, 52, in a riotous contest between the followers of Clodius and Milo which resulted in the death of the democratic leader Clodius, and, as a last resort, Pompey was elected sole consul in the intercalary month of this year. This sudden elevation to extraordinary power completed the separation of Pompey and Caesar. Pompey thought himself at last in a position to crush the rival, who alone, since the death of Crassus in the East, stood between him and the realization of his hopes for supreme power.

**109. The Question at Issue between Caesar and the Senate.** After assuming office Pompey secured the passage of laws imposing heavier penalties for bribery and violence, and prolonging his proconsulship of Spain for five years, also of a *lex de iure magistratuum*, providing that candidates for office must appear in person a certain number of days before the election, and that those who had held office in Rome must wait five years before taking the government of a province. Caesar, however, was exempted from the operation of the first clause of the *lex de iure magistratuum*

by a special measure, and also by a provision unconstitu-
tionally appended to the law itself, as an afterthought, by
Pompey. By a *lex Pompeia Licinia* of 55, as we have
already noticed, Caesar's term of office was extended for a
period of five years — probably, therefore, to March 1, 49 —
and special legislation of the year 52 in his favor had allowed
him to sue for the consulship in 49, without personally
attending the canvass. His successor in the provinces
would not naturally begin his term of office until January 1,
48, and, in accordance with the regular practice in such
cases, Caesar might count on holding his provinces until
that time, when he would pass directly from the provincial
government to the consulship at Rome, thus avoiding the
snares which his enemies would otherwise have set for him.
As early as April of the year 51, however, the senate began
to discuss his immediate recall; but the clever and persistent opposition of his representatives in that body,
and the hesitation of Pompey, prevented matters from
reaching a climax until, in December, 50, the consul
M. Marcellus, a bitter opponent of Caesar, went to Naples,
and on his own motion requested Pompey to take charge
of the legions near Luceria and defend the state. This
overt act hastened the course of events. When the senate
met, January 1, 49, Curio, Caesar's agent, presented a formal
ultimatum. Caesar's proposals were not accepted, and a
resolution was passed declaring that he would be acting
*adversus rem publicam* if he did not give up his army
by July 1, 49, while on January 7 the *senatus consultum
ultimum* was passed. Thereupon the tribunes Antonius
and Cassius, as well as Caesar's representatives, Curio and
Caelius, set out for his camp at Ravenna. As soon as he
had learned of the action of the senate, Caesar crossed
the Rubicon into Italy and marched toward Rome. On

January 14 the senate passed the *decretum tumultus*, but
the news of Caesar's rapid advance forced Pompey, the
consuls, and senators to leave the city, and even the forms
of civil government were given up.

**110. The Conquest of the East.** Some of the wars which
fall within the years under consideration in this chapter have
already been mentioned.   Two great military achievements
of this period, however, the conquest of the East and the
extension of Roman power to the west, call for separate
consideration.   For sixty years after the defeat of Antiochus
at Magnesia (p. 85) the Romans took little active interest
in Asiatic politics, but when in 133 Attalus III, king of
Pergamum, bequeathed to them his territory, including
Ionia, Caria, Lydia, and Mysia, and the new province of
Asia was thus established, the possibilities in the East
appealed strongly to their political and commercial ambition.   The weakness of the various Asiatic powers, and the
internal dissensions which prevailed in many states seemed
to hold out to the Romans the promise of an easy extension of territory, but the rapid development of a new power
on the southeastern shore of the Euxine seriously imperiled
their prospects.

**111. The First Mithridatic War.**   In 121 Mithridates
Eupator succeeded his father on the throne of Pontus.
Seven years later he threw off the tutelage of his mother
Laodicê and entered on a career of conquest, for which
his personal qualities and his skill as a soldier and a diplo-
mat eminently fitted him.   In rapid succession he brought
under his control almost all the territory along the north
shore of the Euxine, Colchis and Armenia Minor, and
made alliances with the Scythians, Thracians, and Bastarnae.
Then he turned his attention to Paphlagonia, Cappadocia,
Galatia, and Bithynia.   The Romans opposed his designs in

Cappadocia and Bithynia, and even induced Nicomedes III of Bithynia to invade the territory of Mithridates, whereupon Mithridates declared war against Rome. He rapidly overran Cappadocia, Bithynia, and Asia, instigated an indiscriminate slaughter of Italians in the Greek cities of Asia, and then sent his general, Archelaus, through Thrace into Macedonia. A fleet was also dispatched across the Aegean sea. All Greece, except Aetolia and Thessaly, was quickly subdued, but Sulla's arrival in Greece at the head of five legions quickly changed the aspect of affairs. His victories in 86 at Chaeronea and Orchomenus brought the war in Greece to an end, and his quaestor, L. Licinius Lucullus, collected a fleet and freed the islands in the Aegean the following year. These disasters, followed by disaffection in Asia Minor, induced Mithridates to sue for a peace which Sulla's eagerness to return to Italy to instal his party in power again made him ready to accept. By the terms of the treaty which was finally arranged at Dardanus in 85, Mithridates agreed to give up the acquisitions which he had made since the beginning of the war, viz., Cappadocia, Paphlagonia, Galatia, Bithynia, and Asia, to pay a war indemnity of 2000 talents, and to surrender seventy ships.

112. **The Second and Third Mithridatic Wars.** The peace at Dardanus proved to be little more than a truce. Two years after its conclusion hostilities were resumed between Mithridates and L. Licinius Murena, Sulla's successor in Asia, and, when Nicomedes III of Bithynia died in 75, bequeathing his kingdom to the Roman people, Mithridates, who claimed Bithynia, invaded the territory of that state without hesitation, and war broke out again. On the Roman side, the provinces of Cilicia and Asia and the conduct of the campaign were intrusted to L. Licinius Lucullus, the consul for 74, while Bithynia with command

of the fleet was given to his colleague, M. Aurelius Cotta.
Mithridates easily defeated Cotta near Chalcedon, destroyed
the Roman fleet, and then laid siege to Cyzicus. But
before the city could be taken Lucullus came to its relief,
and Mithridates, after losing many of his troops from famine
and disease, was forced to raise the siege and withdraw into
Pontus. The rapid advance of Lucullus compelled him to
retire from Pontus also, and to take refuge with his son-in-
law, Tigranes, king of Armenia. Lucullus followed up the
campaign with vigor, and, when Tigranes refused to give
up his father-in-law, he entered Armenia, defeated him
near Tigranocerta in 69, and in the following year gained a
signal victory over the combined forces of Mithridates and
Tigranes. But the enemies of Lucullus in Rome, notably
the money-lenders and tax-gatherers, who had been embittered by the strictness with which he had checked their
exorbitant demands in Asia, had for several years been
urging his recall, and on the eve of his final triumph
accomplished their purpose. He was recalled, and, by the
Manilian law of 66, Pompey was sent out to succeed him
as governor of the provinces of Bithynia and Cilicia, with
exceptional powers as commander-in-chief of the forces
in the East. The resources of Mithridates were already
well-nigh exhausted, and the vigorous campaign of Pompey
soon brought the war to an end. A crushing defeat was
inflicted on Mithridates on the banks of the Euphrates in
Lesser Armenia in 66, and, although the king himself
escaped, he was never again able to offer any effective
resistance to Roman arms. Three years later he committed suicide. Tigranes, harassed by troubles at home,
made his peace with Pompey.

**113. The Pirates in the Mediterranean.** Before taking
charge of the forces acting against Mithridates, Pompey had

rendered a valuable service to Rome by ridding the Mediterranean of the pirates who had infested it for many years. The number of these freebooters had been largely augmented by those who fled from Asia to escape the severe measures which Sulla adopted during his campaigns in the East, so that in a short time they were strong enough to terrorize the islands in the Aegean, plunder almost all the sanctuaries in Greece, and establish themselves securely in western Cilicia. P. Servilius Isauricus, who carried on a campaign against them from 78 to 74, and his successors, M. Antonius and Q. Caecilius Metellus, failed to accomplish permanent results, and the boldness of the pirates increased to such an extent that the grain supply of Rome and the safety of Italian coast towns were seriously threatened. The passage of the Gabinian law in 67 was, therefore, in response to the urgent popular demand for the complete suppression of piracy in the Mediterranean. This measure gave Pompey charge of the forces acting against the pirates for a period of three years, and supreme control of territory on the shores of the Mediterranean to a distance of fifty miles from the coast. In forty days he drove the pirates out of the western Mediterranean, and then captured their strongholds in Cilicia. The mild policy which he adopted after their conquest, as well as the vigorous campaign which he had carried on against them, effectually removed this menace to Roman commerce.

114. **The Empire in the East.** In fact, the wisdom which Pompey showed in his dealings with the conquered peoples of the East and the thoroughness of his work of reorganization are as remarkable as his successes in the field. Not only did his conquests extend Roman power to the Euphrates, but the administrative arrangements which he made secured permanent quiet throughout the newly acquired

territory. Roman authority was henceforth recognized
in all parts of Asia Minor and Syria. The provincial status
of Asia had been finally fixed in 129. To Bithynia, which
Nicomedes III bequeathed to the Roman people in 74,
Pompey added western Pontus in 65. Cilicia, which was
made a province in 102, included after 64 Cilicia Campes-
tris, Cilicia Aspera, Pamphylia, Pisidia, Isauria, Lycaonia,
and a part of Phrygia. In Syria, which he made a province
in 64, Pompey established various free cities and principalities under the Roman protectorate, wisely leaving time to
bring about that unity in administration which tradition
and existing political subdivisions made well-nigh impossible at the moment. Cappadocia and Galatia were allowed
to retain a nominal independence under the suzerainty of
Rome. The ill-starred expedition of Crassus in 53 made
no change in the arrangements of Pompey, since the Parthians did not take advantage of their success to invade
the territory of Rome.

**115. The Conquest of Gaul.** Caesar's achievements in
the West between 58 and the outbreak of the Civil war in
49 were as noteworthy as those of Pompey in the East.
When he went north in the spring of 58 to take charge of
his three provinces, Cisalpine Gaul, Illyricum, and Transalpine Gaul, he found two very serious questions facing
him. For nearly three years the Helvetii had been preparing to leave their old home and migrate westward into
Gaul. In the early part of 58 their arrangements were
complete, and the migration began. They had intended
to go through the Roman province, but by a rapid march
northward Caesar closed this route, forced them to pass
through the territory of the Sequani, ultimately inflicted a
crushing defeat on them near Bibracte, and forced the
remainder of the great host to return to its own country.

The other immediate danger threatening Rome and her allies resulted from the ambitious projects of the Germans. In 72 they had been invited by the Sequani to cross the Rhine and assist them against their old enemies, the Aedui. The invitation was accepted. But the coming of the Germans proved to be more of a disaster to the Sequani than to the Aedui, since a large number of them settled in the territory of the Sequani and more were planning to follow. The entreaties of the Aedui and the proximity of the Germans to Farther Gaul induced Caesar to advance against the German king Ariovistus. In a sharp, decisive campaign Ariovistus was defeated and driven back across the Rhine. The campaign of 57 was directed against the Belgae, who were so irritated and alarmed by the presence of Roman troops near their frontier that they declared war and began to mass their forces to oppose the Romans. The Nervii were the only Belgic tribe which made a serious resistance to his progress, however, and they were subdued before autumn, and the entire territory of Belgic Gaul recognized the authority of Rome. In the year 56 Caesar built a fleet, reduced the Veneti at the mouth of the Loire, and subdued the Morini and the Menapii on the North sea, while his lieutenant, P. Crassus, received the submission of the Aquitani. The next two years were signalized by two enterprises more suggestive and dramatic in their character than of immediate practical value. In 55, after driving out two German tribes, the Usipetes and Tencteri, who had come over to the left bank of the river, the Roman army crossed the Rhine for the first time, to deepen the impression already made on the Germans, while in the same year an armed reconnaissance was made into Britain. Neither this expedition into Britain, nor the more carefully planned one of the following year, produced results of value.

Toward the close of the year the revolt of the Treveri, Eburones, and Nervii inflicted serious loss on the Romans, and for a time put Q. Cicero, the brother of the orator, in great peril; but before the close of the year the insurrection was quelled for the moment.    In 53, however, trouble broke out afresh in the same quarter, and the entire summer was needed to restore order again.    Report of a general uprising in the central and southern sections of Gaul obliged Caesar to hurry back from Italy across the Alps in the winter of 53–2.    He found that the leaders in the movement were the Arverni and Carnutes, who had united under the Arvernian chief Vercingetorix.    The attempt of the Gallic forces to prevent Caesar from reaching his army failed, and Vercingetorix was obliged to retire to Alesia and ultimately to surrender, notwithstanding the vigorous efforts made by the Gallic troops, which came to his relief, to force Caesar to withdraw.    After the fall of Alesia, Caesar encountered no more serious resistance during his term of office as governor.    Roman authority was now recognized in Belgica, Gallia Narbonensis, and in the districts known later as Aquitania and Gallia Lugdunensis.    The outbreak of the Civil war, and the shortness of the interval between its conclusion and his death, prevented Caesar from properly organizing the newly acquired territory; but the character and the wisdom of his plans are evident from the fact that he granted Roman citizenship to the Transpadane Gauls in 49, gave Latin rights to many other communities, and that between 46 and the date of his death he sent out five new colonies to points in Gaul.    Everywhere, too, he sought by his policy of moderation to avoid a clash between the old national spirit and traditions and the new civilization.

116. The Condition of the Provinces.    The form of government which Rome gave to her provinces has already

been discussed (pp. 88 ff.), but the condition in which they really were was far different from that which an examination of *leges provinciarum* would lead us to expect. The Roman government and the Roman people looked at a province solely as a possible source of profit to the state and the individual. Care was taken, therefore, to develop the material resources by improving methods of cultivation and by promoting trade and building roads ; but the welfare of the provincial was not a matter of concern, except in so far as his prosperity helped to fill the pockets of government officials, of the *publicani*, and of the *negotiatores*. The former were, indeed, forbidden by the *lex provinciae* to receive presents, engage in trade, or accept favors, but the possibilities were so great, and the needs of the average Roman official so pressing, that few of them resisted the temptation. A special court had been established in Rome for the trial of such offenders, it is true, but the provincials found it almost impossible to secure a conviction. As for the *publicani*, the Roman system of tax farming practically put a premium on extortion, and the moneyed interests at Rome behind the tax-gatherers effectually checked any attempts which a merciful governor might make to protect the provincials, as Lucullus found to his cost. The same may be said of the *negotiatores*, who had come into possession of almost all the landed property and the commercial interests in the provinces, and exacted from needy individuals and communities interest amounting in some cases, as we learn from Cicero's correspondence, to 48 per cent.

**117. General Political Results.** The conquests of Pompey and Caesar, which had brought within the sphere of Roman influence the entire Mediterranean coast with the exception of Egypt and Mauretania, and had extended the Roman frontier to the Euphrates on the east and the Rhine on the north, could not fail to exert a reflex influence on Italy itself. The economic and political changes among the masses, to which earlier extensions of Roman territory had given rise (pp. 77–80), were accelerated by the conquests made between 66 and 49. Furthermore, the general machinery of government had broken down under the strain put upon it by the policy of imperialism. All the great achievements of Caesar and Pompey required a violation of the oligarchic, or republican, tradition. This is notably the case in the matter of the term of office, the special powers, and the great extent of territory granted to both men. The danger to the republican form of government which lay in the disappearance of the middle class, and in the preëminence of individuals, was aggravated by the change in the composition of the army and in its relations to its chief. We have already had occasion to notice the transformation which had taken place in the attitude of the Roman soldier toward his leader (p. 64) as a result of long campaigns abroad. The new spirit of implicit obedience and personal allegiance which he had begun to show, became still stronger in the case of soldiers drawn from the provinces, as were many of Caesar's soldiers, for whom the civil traditions of Rome had no existence. An extended term of office in the provinces had put at the service of Caesar and Pompey resources greater than those which the state could command, and armies which recognized allegiance to their generals rather than to the Roman government. The issue, therefore, lay not between the state and one or the other of these great commanders, but between these leaders themselves.

## Selections from the Sources

Livy, *Epp.* LVIII–CIX; Plutarch, *Lives of Ti. Gracchus, C. Gracchus, Marius, Sulla, Sertorius, Lucullus, Crassus, Pompey, Cicero, Caesar;* Appian, *Iberian, Numidian, Illyrian, Mithridatic, Civil Wars;* Dio Cassius, XXXV–XL; Zonaras, X. 1–8; Diodorus, XXXIV–XL; Velleius Paterculus, II. 2–49; Sallust, *Histories* (fragments), *Jugurthine War, Conspiracy of Catiline;* Cicero, *Letters, Orations;* Asconius, *Commentaries;* Caesar, *Gallic War.*

Lex agraria Ti. Gracchi: Liv. *Ep.* LVIII; Appian, *B. C.* I. 9; Vell. II. 2.3. — Rogatio Fulvia de civitate sociis Italicis danda: Val. Max. IX. 5. 1. — Lex Sempronia frumentaria: Liv. *Ep.* LX; *Schol. Bob. ad Cic. pro Sest.* pp. 300, 303, ed. Or.; Cic. *pro Sest.* 103; *de Off.* II. 72. — Leges Semproniae de provocatione: Cic. *pro Rab. perd.* 12; *in Cat.* IV. 10; *in Verr.* ii. 5. 163; *pro Cluent.* 151; Gell. X. 3; Plut. *C. Gracch.* 4. — Lex Sempronia iudiciaria: Liv. *Ep.* LX; Appian, *B. C.* I. 22; Vell. II. 32. 3; Tac. *Ann.* XII. 60; Cic. *in Verr. Act.* I. 38. — Lex Sempronia de provinciis consularibus: Cic. *de Domo,* 24; Sall. *Iug.* 27. — Death of C. Gracchus: Liv. *Ep.* LXI. — Outbreak of Jugurthine war: Sall. *Iug.* 27 ff.; Liv. *Ep.* LXIV. — Defeat of Postumius: Liv. *Ep.* LXIV; Sall. *Iug.* 38 f. — Close of the Jugurthine war: Liv. *Ep.* LXVI. — Invasion of the Cimbri: Liv. *Ep.* LXIII; Tac. *Germ.* 37; Flor. III. 3. — Defeat of Silanus: Liv. *Ep.* LXV. — Defeat of Cassius: Liv. *Ep.* LXV; Caes. *B. G.* I. 7. — Battle of Arausio: Liv. *Ep.* LXVII; Orosius, V. 16; Sall. *Iug.* 114. — Aquae Sextiae and Campi Raudii: Liv. *Ep.* LXVIII; Vell. II. 12. — Lex Domitia de Sacerdotiis: Cic. *De Leg. Agr.* II. 16–18; Vell. II. 12. 3. — Marius, consul for sixth time: Vell. II. 12. 6; Liv. *Ep.* LXIX. — Lex Apuleia agraria: Appian, *B. C.* I. 29. — Lex Apuleia frumentaria: *Auct. ad Her.* I. 21. — Lex Caecilia Didia: *Schol. Bob. ad Cic. pro Sest.* p. 310, ed. Or.; Cic. *de Domo,* 41. — Condemnation of P. Rutilius Rufus: Liv. *Ep.* LXX; Vell. II. 13. 2. — Leges Liviae Drusi: Appian, *B. C.* I. 35; Vell. II. 13; Liv. *Epp.* LXX–LXXI. — Social war: Liv. *Epp.* LXXII–LXXVI, LXXX; Appian, *B. C.* I. 39–53; Vell. II. 15 ff. — Lex Iulia: Cic. *pro Balbo,* 21; Gell. IV. 4; Appian, *B. C.* I. 49. — Lex Plautia Papiria: Cic. *pro Arch.* 7; *Schol. Bob.* p. 353, ed. Or. — Lex Pompeia: Ascon. *in Cic. Pis.* p. 3, ed. Or. — Outbreak of first Mithridatic war: Liv. *Epp.* LXXVII–LXXVIII; Appian, *Mith.* 17 ff.; Vell. II. 18. — Chaeronea:

Appian, *Mith.* 41 ff.; Plut. *Sulla*, 15 ff.; Eutr. V. 6.— **Orchomenus :**
Appian, *Mith.* 49–50; Plut. *Sulla*, 20–21; Eutr. V. 6.— **Peace of**
**Dardanus :** Plut. *Sulla*, 22; Appian, *Mith.* 54–8; Liv. *Ep.* LXXXIII;
Vell. II. 23.— **Marius and Sulpicius :** Liv. *Ep.* LXXVII; Eutr. V.
4; Plut. *Sulla*, 7–10; *Mar.* 34–5; Appian, *B. C.* I. 55–60; Vell.
II. 18–19.— **Cinna and Marius :** Liv. *Epp.* LXXIX–LXXX; Vell. II.
20 ff.; Plut. *Mar.* 41 ff.; Appian, *B. C.* I. 67 ff.— **Sulla's return :**
Liv. *Epp.* LXXXV–LXXXVIII; Plut. *Sulla*, 27 ff.; Appian, *B. C.*
I. 79 ff.; Vell. II. 24 ff.— **Sulla, dictator :** Appian, *B. C.* I. 98;
Plut. *Sulla*, 33; Liv. *Ep.* LXXXIX.— **Leges Corneliae de magistra-**
**tibus :** Appian, *B. C.* I. 100; Cic. *Phil.* XI. 11; Tac. *Ann.* XI. 22;
Caes. *B. C.* I. 32. 2.— **Lex Cornelia tribunicia :** Appian, *B. C.* I. 100;
Liv. *Ep.* LXXXIX; Cic. *de Legg.* III. 22; Caes. *B. C.* I. 5, 7.—
**Leges Corneliae iudiciariae :** Vell. II. 32; Tac. *Ann.* XI. 22; Cic.
*in Pis.* 50; *pro Cluent.* 148; *in Verr.* ii. 1. 108; Tac. *Ann.* XII. 60;
— **Rogatio Quinctia de abrogandis legibus Corneliis :** Plut. *Luc.* 5.—
**Lex Terentia Cassia frumentaria :** Cic. *in Verr.* ii. 3. 163; ii. 5. 52.—
— **Sertorius murdered :** Liv. *Ep.* XCVI; Oros. V. 23. 13; Plut. *Sert.*
25 ff.— **Spartacus defeated :** Appian, *B. C.* I. 118 ff.; Liv. *Ep.*
XCVII; Eutr. VI. 7.— **Lex Pompeia tribunicia :** Vell. II. 30; Cic.
*in Verr. Act.* I. 43–5; *de Legg.* III. 22, 26.— **Lex Aurelia iudiciaria :**
Ascon. *in Pis.* p. 16; *Schol. Bob.* p. 229. 17.— **Outbreak of third**
**Mithridatic war :** Plut. *Luc.* 7; Appian, *B. C.* I. 111.— **Relief of**
**Cyzicus :** Appian, *Mith.* 72 ff.; Plut. *Luc.* 11.— **Invasion of Pontus :**
Appian, *Mith.* 82 ff.; Plut. *Luc.* 19 ff.— **Tigranocerta :** Plut. *Luc.*
25 ff.; Appian, *Mith.* 84–5.— **Lex Gabinia :** Cic. *de Imp. Cn. Pomp.*
52 f.; Dio, XXXVI. 6–19; Plut. *Pomp.* 25; Vell. II. 31.— **Lex**
**Manilia :** Cic. *de Imp. Cn. Pomp.;* Dio, XXXVI. 25–6; Plut. *Pomp.*
30; Vell. II. 33.— **Defeat of Mithridates :** Dio, XXXVI. 29–33;
Appian, *Mith.* 97–101.— **Catilinarian conspiracy :** Sall. *Coni. Cat.;*
Cic. *Orationes in Cat.;* Dio, XXXVII. 29–42; Plut. *Cic.* 10–22.—
**First triumvirate :** Dio, XXXVII. 54–8; Appian, *B. C.* II. 9; Plut.
*Crass.* 14; *Pomp.* 47; *Caes.* 13.— **Lex Iulia agraria :** Cic. *ad Att.*
II. 18. 2; Suet. *Iul.* 20; Vell. II. 44.— **Lex Vatinia de imperio**
**Caesaris :** Suet. *Iul.* 22; *Schol. Bob. in Vat.* p. 317; Dio, XXXVIII.
8.— **The Helvetii :** Caes. *B. G.* I. 1–30.— **Ariovistus :** Caes. *B. G.*
I. 31–54.— **Belgae :** Caes. *B. G.* II.— **Veneti :** Caes. *B. G.* III.
7–16.— **Aquitani :** Caes. *B. G.* III. 20–27.— **Usipetes and Tencteri :**
Caes. *B. G.* IV. 1–15.— **Second British expedition :** Caes. *B. G.*
V. 2, 5–23.— **Nervii, etc. :** Caes. *B. G.* VI. 1–8.— **Vercingetorix :**

Caes. *B. G.* VII. — Cicero's banishment : Vell. II. 45 ; Cic. *de Domo*,
43–64; *pro Planc.* 86–90, 95–103. — His recall : Dio, XXXIX. 6–11 ;
Plut. *Cic.* 33; Cic. *ad Att.* IV. 1. — Renewal of triumvirate : Plut.
*Caes.* 21 ; *Pomp.* 51 ; Appian, *B. C.* II. 17 ; Suet. *Iul.* 24. — Crassus
killed : Dio. XL. 25–7; Plut. *Crass.* 28–31. — Pompey, sole consul :
Vell. II. 47 ; Dio, XL. 50. — Lex de iure magistratuum : Suet. *Iul.*
28; Cic. *ad Att.* VIII. 3. 3; Cic. *Phil.* II. 24. — First overt act in
civil war : Dio, XL. 64–6 ; Plut. *Pomp.* 58–9. — Negotiations in
senate : Caes. *B. C.* I. 1–6; Cic. *ad Fam.* XVI. 11. — Caesar marches
southward : Caes. *B. C.* I. 8 ff. ; Suet. *Iul.* 32 ff. ; Appian, *B. C.*
II. 35 ff.

### SELECTED BIBLIOGRAPHY [1]

W. Drumann, Geschichte Roms, 6 Bde., Koenigsberg, 1834–44
(Bd. I.[2] Berlin, 1899).

G. Long, The Decline of the Roman Republic, 5 vols. London,
1864–74.

C. Neumann, Geschichte Roms während des Verfalles der Republik, 2 Bde. Breslau, 1881–4.

K. W. Nitzsch, Die Gracchen, etc. Berlin, 1847.

Ed. Meyer, Untersuchungen zur Geschichte der Gracchen. Halle,
1894.

A. H. Beesly, The Gracchi, Marius and Sulla. New York, 1893.

W. Strehl, M. Livius Drusus, Volkstribun 91 v. Chr. Marburg,
1887.

W. Forsyth, Life of M. Tullius Cicero, 2 vols. New York, 1863.

W. W. Fowler, Julius Caesar and the Foundation of the Roman
Imperial System. New York, 1891.

J. A. Froude, Caesar. London, 1886.

Strachan-Davidson, Cicero and the Fall of the Roman Republic.
New York, 1894.

Erich Marcks, Die Ueberlieferung des Bundesgenossenkrieges
91–89 v. Chr. Marburg, 1884.

Th. Reinach, Mithridate Eupator, roi du Pont. Paris, 1890.

Th. Lau, L. Cornelius Sulla. Hamburg, 1855.

E. v. Stern, Catilina u. d. Parteikämpfe in Rom d. Jahre 66–63 v.
Chr. Dorpat, 1883.

E. Beesly, Catiline, Clodius, and Tiberius. London, 1878.

[1] See also general bibliography on p. 22.

Ch. Merivale, The Roman Triumvirates.  New York, 1893.

Th. Mommsen, Die Rechtsfrage zwischen Cäsar u. dem Senat. Breslau, 1857.

O. E. Schmidt, Der Briefwechsel d. M. Tullius Cicero.  Leipzig, 1893.

H. Nissen, Der Ausbruch d. Bürgerkriegs 49 v. Chr., in von Sybel's Hist. Zeitschr. (N.F.) VIII, 409–445, and X, 48–105.

## Supplementary Literature, 1901–1910

Drumann-Groebe, Geschichte Roms, etc., 4 vols.  Berlin, 1899——.

Greenidge and Clay, Sources for Roman History, 133–70 B.C. Oxford, 1903.

Greenidge, A History of Rome during the Later Republic and Early Principate, Vol. I (133–104 B.C.).  New York, 1905.

Callegari, La legislazione sociale di Caio Gracco.  Padua, 1896.

Fowler, Social Life at Rome in the Age of Cicero.  New York, 1909.

Boissier, La conjuration de Catilina.

Salvioli, Le capitalisme dans le monde antique.  Paris, 1906.

Holmes, Caesar's Conquest of Gaul.  New York, 1899.

C. Jullian, Gallia: Tableau sommaire de la Gaule sous la domination romaine.  Paris, 1892.

Barbagallo, Le relazione politiche di Roma con l'Egitto dalle origini al 50 A.C.  Rome, 1901.

# CHAPTER VII

## THE PERIOD OF TRANSITION

**118. The Period from 49 to 29 B.C.** The external history of the Roman Empire from the outbreak of the Civil war in January, 49, to the summer of 29, when Octavius returned to Rome from the battle of Actium, falls into two sharply marked periods. The dividing line is the assassination of Caesar. From the point of view of constitutional development or change there is no such clear division. The same elements in society and in the state which supported the Pompeian cause in the early part of the first period were in the main arrayed against Antony and the triumvirs in 43 and 42. Furthermore, the means which Julius Caesar adopted to hold the power in his hands served the purpose of the triumvirs so well that they did not find it necessary to make many changes in the governmental machinery. So far as the essential character of the government is concerned, it makes little difference whether an autocrat holds the title of dictator, as Caesar did, or of triumvir, as in the case of Octavius. Consequently, from the standpoint of internal history the twenty years in question form a unit. Our interest in them consists largely in the fact that in this period the development of the Roman constitution along certain lines, which it had been following almost imperceptibly for several generations, is now evident and rapid, and that Rome begins to develop out of a city-state with widespread dependencies into the capital of a great empire.

**119. Campaigns in Italy, Spain, and Africa.** Even if Pompey was intending to make a stand in Italy after the precipitate departure of the senate from Rome in January, 49, as many of his party supposed, the rapidity of Caesar's march southward and Caesar's continued success forced him to change his plan at once, and on March 17, scarcely more than two months after Caesar entered Italy, the Pompeian troops hastily embarked for Epirus from the city of Brundisium, to which siege was already being laid. Pompey's departure from Italy was unfortunate from the political point of view, since it left the recognized seat of government and the machinery of the state in the hands of his opponent; but on military grounds it was wise, for his name was a power in the East, while Caesar was unknown, and the postponement of the inevitable conflict gave him the time which he needed to collect and train his newly recruited forces to meet the veteran legions of his enemy. Caesar felt himself unprepared to follow Pompey at once, and, after a few weeks' stay in Italy, crossed over to Spain, which was held for Pompey by his three lieutenants, Petreius, Afranius, and Varro. Petreius and Afranius occupied a well-chosen position at Ilerda, and their forces were equal in number to those of Caesar; but by a clever move on his part they were cut off from their supplies and forced to surrender. Varro's submission soon followed, so that the Spanish campaign was brought to an end within a month and a half after Caesar's arrival in the peninsula. The expedition which his representative, C. Curio, conducted into Africa at the same time did not meet with a like success. The complete destruction of Curio's two legions of raw troops by King Juba, and his subsequent suicide, offset in some measure the Pompeian losses in Spain.

**120. The Campaign in Epirus.** The breathing space which Caesar's campaign gave him Pompey used to great advantage in collecting troops and supplies. In the spring of 48 the army of 30,000 which he had brought over to Epirus had grown to nine legions, supported by a large body of auxiliaries and a strong fleet. To them Caesar could oppose the six legions with which he made a successful landing at Oricum in Epirus in November, 49, and the four legions which M. Antonius brought him in April of the following year by the way of Lissus. Caesar's legions were depleted by sickness and long campaigns, however, so that, although his troops were more experienced than those of Pompey, they were numerically far inferior to the opposing force. Caesar placed his army between Dyrrachium and Pompey's camp, and at once began offensive operations in the hope of shutting Pompey in ; but the Pompeian forces broke through his lines and inflicted upon him so severe a loss that later, when Caesar advanced into Thessaly, Pompey followed him and was induced by his over-confident advisers to risk a battle at Pharsalus on August 9, 48. The battle resulted in a complete defeat for the Pompeians, and Pompey himself, who fled for safety to Egypt, was put to death by the orders of King Ptolemy as he was landing at Pelusium.

**121. Campaigns in Egypt, Asia Minor, and Africa.** In the autumn of 48 Caesar followed Pompey to Egypt, but, on hearing of his death, occupied himself with the settlement of Egyptian affairs. Ptolemy Auletes, the late sovereign, had left the kingdom to his two oldest children, Ptolemy and Cleopatra, but Cleopatra had been dispossessed by her brother. Caesar's rather arrogant attempt to enforce an understanding aroused the anger of the Egyptians, and put him in such a perilous position that only the timely arrival of reinforcements under Mithridates of Pergamum saved his army from destruction. The settlement of political affairs and the charms of Cleopatra held him in Egypt until the late spring of 47, when the defeat in Armenia Minor of his lieutenant, Calvinus, and the rapid development of the ambitious projects of Pharnaces, the son of Mithridates Eupator, made his presence in the East necessary. Pharnaces sought delay, but Caesar forced an engagement at Zela, August 2, and completely defeated him. The disaffection among the troops in Italy who were being levied for a campaign in Africa led Caesar to return to Rome in September. The mutinous soldiers were soon brought under control by his personal influence, and in December he landed with them near Hadrumetum, defeated the Pompeians at Thapsus, April 6, 46, and captured Utica soon after, notwithstanding Cato's vigorous efforts to defend it. Juba was conquered by the old Catilinarian leader, P. Sittius; his kingdom of Numidia was made a Roman province, and the Pompeian power in Africa was completely broken.

**122. Second Spanish Campaign.** On his return to Rome in July he found time at last to put the government of Italy on a more secure basis, and to introduce some much-needed political and economic reforms. In the three years which had elapsed since the battle of Ilerda the Pompeian cause had made great headway in Spain. Their forces had lately been largely increased by the arrival of fugitives from Africa, and Caesar's representative, C. Trebonius, was no match for them. Caesar's plans for making comprehensive changes in the government of Italy were, therefore, cut short by the necessity of recovering the ground which had been lost in Spain. He left Rome in the early part of November for this purpose, and, although he found thirteen Pompeian legions opposed to the eight legions which he had brought with him, he boldly attacked the enemy at Munda, March 17, 45, and inflicted a crushing defeat upon them.

**123. Caesar's Assassination.**   After his return to the city Caesar occupied himself partly with various administrative reforms, but mainly in making preparations for a great expedition against the Parthians.   His plans, however, were brought to a tragic end by his assassination on the Ides of March, 44.   The conspirators were actuated by personal and by political motives.   Many of them were jealous of Caesar, or dissatisfied with the recognition they had received from him.   Many members of the senate (for about sixty senators took part in the conspiracy) were aggrieved at the loss of power and prestige which that body had suffered at his hands.   Their smouldering discontent was kindled into flame by the new powers and honors conferred on Caesar in the early part of 44, and by the rumors, which were current, that he would be made king and would transfer the seat of government to Alexandria.   That the feeling of discontent, out of which the conspiracy sprung, was vague, and that the conspirators lacked a definite plan or purpose is plain from the subsequent course of events.

**124. Caesar's Policy.**   The work which Caesar had set himself to do after the battle of Pharsalus, and which was left unfinished at his death, was threefold.   He wished to suppress within the Roman territory all armed resistance to a central authority, to establish in Rome a permanent government strong enough to carry out a positive policy in spite of all opposition, and finally to knit together all parts of the Roman Empire.   We have already seen the steps which he took to accomplish the first-mentioned object.

To carry out the rest of his plan it was essential that his control of all the functions of government should be undisputed. In 44, after Caesar's death, the dictatorship which he had held for several years was characterized by Cicero as one *quae iam vim regiae potestatis obsederat*, and it is highly probable that during the last years of his life Caesar did take into his hands all those powers which in their natural development gave Augustus and his successors their exalted position. He secured his supremacy in the state partly by increasing his own power, partly by diminishing the influence of other factors in the government. He increased his own power directly by securing for himself important magistracies, often with special prerogatives. He accomplished the same object indirectly by controlling the nomination of candidates, by placing a large number of his own supporters in the senate, and by preventing hostile measures from being brought before the popular assemblies.

**125. His Offices and Titles.** The sources of our information are not precise and detailed enough to enable us to determine the exact position which Caesar held in the state. His constitutional power seems to have depended largely, however, on the fact that he held the dictatorship, tribunate, and, perhaps alternately, the consulship and proconsulship. Shortly after his first victory in Spain he was nominated dictator by the praetor, M. Lepidus, under a special law authorizing the establishment of that magistracy. This position he held for a few days only, but in the autumn of 48 he was again chosen to the same office, apparently for an undefined period. In 46, after the battle of Thapsus, he received the dictatorship for ten years, and in 44 for life. Caesar's position as dictator was probably like that of Sulla, and, therefore, differed in two important particulars from the traditional magistracy. His

functions covered a wider field than those of the historical dictator did, and his term of office was much longer
(cf. pp. 183, 218). In 48 the tribunician power was given
to him for life. From the positive point of view this
enabled him to interpose a veto and to convoke the
plebeian assembly, and made his person inviolable. On
the negative side he hoped that his assumption of this
office, and the control which he exercised over the nomination of other members of the college, would protect him
against serious interference with his plans. This hope was
not always realized. On more than one occasion some
member of the college asserted his independence, and
once Caesar was obliged to resort to the theory of popular
sovereignty which Tiberius Gracchus had applied in the
case of Octavius (cf. pp. 95 f.). The offending tribunes in
this case, C. Epidius Marullus and L. Caesetius Flavus,
were brought before the senate, and on Caesar's complaint
were divested of office. This drastic proceeding probably
checked for the future any hostile action on the part of
members of the college. Caesar did not use the title of
tribune, however, in official documents, as his imperial
successors did. On several occasions he was regularly
elected to the consulship and performed the duties of
that office, and it is quite probable that he was invested
with the pro-consular power, so that, when he was not in
office as consul, he acted *pro consule*. This conclusion has
been drawn, at least, with great plausibility, from the fact
that on an important document he bears the titles *dictator
consul prove consule*. The *praefectura morum*, which he
created and held in 46, was new only in name. Its
functions were similar to those of the earlier censorship.
From the battle of Munda up to the close of his life
honors were heaped on him in profusion. He was given

the titles *parens patriae* and *imperator* for life. The latter ordinarily appears in official documents immediately after his cognomen, and was made an hereditary title. Coins bore his likeness, and the right was probably granted him to express his opinion first in the senate.

**126. Changes in Magisterial Functions.** Some changes were intentionally made in the functions of certain magistrates, or were the result of circumstances. Attention has already been called to the fact that Caesar's dictatorship was not that of the early republic, but was similar to Sulla's; that in 44 he was chosen permanently to this office and given the tribunician power for life, whereas under the old constitution the dictator and tribune had held office for six months and a year respectively. Furthermore, the judicial functions which Caesar exercised in criminal cases, like that of Ligarius, did not belong to the republican dictatorship. The *magister equitum* and *praefectus urbi* play a more important part from 49 to 44 than they do in any other period of Roman history, but their significance comes solely from the fact that the dictator was frequently absent from Italy and his power was exercised by these officials as his representatives. In this connection the law of 46 may be mentioned, which limited the term of office for governors in praetorian provinces to one year, in consular provinces to two years. Caesar's purpose in making this regulation was evidently to guard against a possible rival.

**127. Increase in the Size of Magisterial Colleges.** The increase which he made in the size of certain colleges of magistrates was justified by the need of additional administrative officers. It also gave Caesar an opportunity to reward some of his political followers, and incidentally exalted his own position by decreasing the importance of the individual members of the colleges affected. Thus the

number of praetors was first raised from eight to ten, then
to fourteen, and finally to sixteen, while the number of
quaestors was increased to forty. The establishment of the
office of *aedilis cerialis* with its two incumbents, and the
addition of a member to the college of the *III viri capitales* and the *III viri monetales* were probably dictated by
administrative considerations only.

**128. Method of choosing Magistrates and Terms of Office.**
To protect his interests at Rome during his absence on the
projected Parthian campaign, Caesar secured the passage
of a law which allowed him to name all the magistrates
for 43, as well as the consuls and tribunes for 42. This
measure would make the magistrates for the immediate
future official representatives of the dictator, and would at
the same time lessen the importance of the popular electoral bodies. In the case of the consulship he introduced
an innovation of great importance. In October, 45, he
resigned that office, which he had held without a colleague,
and had two successors elected for the rest of the year. In
taking this step Caesar was restoring the traditional consulship, since the constitution did not recognize a single
consul without a colleague. In a way, however, he was
establishing a precedent for the imperial system of *consules
suffecti*, and six years later, following this precedent, as it
were, the triumvirs, when holding the consular elections for
34–1, had terms of less than a year indicated for the various candidates at the time of the election, and the *Fasti* of
the year 33 give the names of eight consuls.

**129. The Senate and People.** The senate was reduced
in number to such an extent by the Civil war, that immediately after his return to Rome in 47 Caesar made numerous additions to it, and two years later raised the number
of its members to 900. This change robbed the *nobilitas*

in large measure of its prestige and made the senate sub-
servient to his wishes. As for the people, they met as
before in the *comitia*, but the selection of candidates for
office by Caesar, and the fact that he alone was directly or
indirectly the author of all bills laid before them, made the
meeting of the *comitia* largely a matter of form. He sought
to relieve the congested condition of Rome, and to prevent
the idle from flocking thither, by founding colonies, and
by carefully regulating the list of those who received free
supplies of grain. As a result of the census of 46, the
number of these beneficiaries was reduced from 320,000 to
150,000.

**130. Italy and the Provinces.** But the plans of Caesar
were not limited to the city of Rome. They embraced all
Italy and the provinces. A year before his death he drew
up the *lex Iulia municipalis*, a charter for all the Italian
municipalities, which gave them their own popular assemblies, senates, magistrates, and courts. To many cities in
Sicily and Gallia Narbonensis Latin rights were given, and,
what was of still more importance, provincial governors
were appointed by Caesar. Hitherto each one of the
provinces had been practically a principality which the
Roman governor used to fill his pocket or to advance his
political fortunes. The interests of the provincials and of
the home government were alike held in light esteem.
Under Caesar's régime a governor felt his subordination
to a central authority, and knew that he was responsible
to a man who regarded each province as an integral part
of the empire.

**131. Course of Events after Caesar's Death.** After
Caesar's death both his friends and the conspirators waited
in great suspense for some move on the part of the opposing faction, as well as for some indication of the attitude of

the Roman populace.    M. Lepidus, who had been Caesar's *magister equitum*, was the first to adopt a positive course. He moved his troops into the city and thus gave a tactical advantage to the Caesarians.    The consul Antony strengthened their position still further by securing possession of Caesar's papers and of the state treasure in the temple of Ops.    But both parties were ready for the compromise, adopted by the senate March 17, which confirmed the arrangements of Caesar, but provided that no investigation should be made into the circumstances of his death.    On the basis of this action Antony laid directly before the popular assembly a series of bills which he found, or which he claimed to have found, among the papers of Caesar. Furthermore, on the pretext that his safety was endangered by disturbances in the city, he secured a bodyguard of several thousand men.    A systematic effort was made also to win the favor of the veterans living in Italy.    The support of his colleague, Dolabella, was secured by obtaining for him the province of Syria.    He had the province of Macedonia assigned to himself at first, with control of the legions which Caesar had collected for the Parthian war; but, feeling that it would be better for him to be nearer Rome, he had the popular assembly take Cisalpine Gaul from D. Brutus, to whom it had been assigned, and give it to him. Somewhat later the Macedonian legions were also placed under his command.

**132.  Octavius.**    The arrival in Italy of Octavius, Caesar's grand nephew, a young man in his nineteenth year, whom the dictator had adopted and made his heir, seemed likely to give affairs an unexpected turn.    The deferential manner which Octavius assumed toward certain senatorial leaders on the one hand, and on the other hand his generous treatment of Caesar's followers, and the fact that he bore their great leader's name, won for him at the same time the respectful consideration of senators and the enthusiastic support of many Caesarians. Antony appreciated how dangerous a rival he might become and tried to thwart his plans at every point, but Caesar's veterans forced a reconciliation between their two leaders.

**133. The Liberatores.** Meanwhile the *liberatores*, as Cicero styled the conspirators, were without a plan and without leaders. M. Brutus and Cassius thought it wise to withdraw from the city. Cicero despondently set out for Greece, and the other senatorial leaders gave little effective support to the old régime. In September the Macedonian troops arrived in Italy, but Octavius found means to detach so many of them from Antony's service that two months later Antony, for fear of losing the rest, hastily set out for Gallia Cisalpina with his bodyguard and the three legions which remained loyal to him.

**134. The War about Mutina.** With the departure of Antony from Rome the senate began to assert itself once more. Under the leadership of Cicero, who attacked Antony vigorously in his Philippic orations, the senate was induced to invest Octavius with the *imperium*, and to commission him, in coöperation with the consuls of 43, to conduct the war against Antony. Acting under this authority, in the early part of 43 Octavius set out from Rome with Hirtius, one of the consuls, to relieve D. Brutus, while Pansa, the other consul, followed in March with four legions of recruits. After some preliminary skirmishing, in which Antony gained the advantage, a decisive battle was fought near Mutina, April 21, in which his army was completely defeated. But the victory was dearly bought. Hirtius fell on the field of battle and Pansa was mortally wounded, dying two days later. The command of the forces acting against Antony was assigned to D. Brutus. Octavius, who had good reason to feel aggrieved at this slight, withdrew from further participation in the struggle, and marched to Rome at the head of eight legions, demanding the consulship. There was no means at hand to withstand him, and August 19 he was elected consul. Meanwhile, in the North Antony was strengthened by the accession of Lepidus, governor of southern Gaul, of Plancus, who had charge of northern Gaul, and of Pollio, with troops from Spain. D. Brutus was deserted by his troops, and while seeking to escape was murdered at Aquileia.

**135. The Second Triumvirate.** In October Octavius went north, and held a conference with Antony and Lepidus at Bononia, which resulted in the formation of a compact for the adjustment of affairs in Italy and for the prosecution of the war in the East against M. Brutus and Cassius; and in November, by a vote of the tribal assembly, Antony, Lepidus, and Octavius were made *III viri rei publicae constituendae* for a period of five years. The second triumvirate was, therefore, distinguished from the first by the fact that it rested on a legal basis, while the compact which Caesar, Pompey, and Crassus had formed was purely a private arrangement. The triumvirs of 43 adopted the principle of collegiality on its positive but not on its negative side. All three members were at all times vested with the full power of their office, but the possibility of interposing a veto was not recognized. In so far as its exercise of executive and legislative powers was concerned, the second triumvirate differs little from Caesar's dictatorship. The magistracies, the senate, and popular assemblies were all directly or indirectly under the control of the new officials. In Rome and Italy the triumvirs were confronted with the problem of establishing a new regime and of maintaining

order, of punishing certain republican leaders, levying
troops, and apportioning suitable rewards to the veterans.
Outside of Italy there were still more urgent matters,
notably the task of bringing the provinces under their control and of prosecuting the war against M. Brutus and
Cassius.   Their return to Rome was followed by a reign of
terror which rivaled that of Sulla.   Cicero was one of the
early victims of their fury.   In reaching an agreement for
the government of Italy and the provinces no immediate
difficulty was experienced.   The several provinces were
assigned to the individual members of the triumvirate and
their followers, while the administration of affairs in Italy
and the war in the East were left to the joint direction of
all three triumvirs.

   **136.  The Battle of Philippi.**   The situation in the East
called for immediate attention.   In the early part of 43
M. Brutus entered Macedonia and was recognized as its
legal governor by his predecessor, Q. Hortensius.   Cassius
also took possession of his province, Syria.   Both of them
succeeded in levying large bodies of troops, and C. Antonius,
the brother of Marcus, and Dolabella, who had come out
to take possession of Macedonia and Syria respectively, by
virtue of measures whose passage Antony had secured, were
disastrously defeated.   The two republican leaders met at
Sardis, and with nineteen legions of foot soldiers and 20,000
horsemen advanced to Philippi in the autumn of 42.   Over
against them lay the army of the triumvirs, of about the
same size.   Two battles followed.   In the first the forces
under Cassius were defeated by Antony, and Cassius committed suicide.   Brutus, however, gained a victory over
the troops of Octavius.   In the second battle, which his
troops forced him to fight against his judgment, he was
defeated and took his own life.

**137. The Movements of the Triumvirs.** Lepidus was suspected of being disloyal to his colleagues, and, in the division of territory after the battle of Philippi, Spain and Gallia Narbonensis, which had been placed under his control, were taken from him; but later, on grounds of expediency, Octavius thought it wise to allot Africa to him. From this time forth, however, Lepidus played a subordinate part in the triumvirate. Antony remained in the East. At Tarsus he met Cleopatra, who came to explain her conduct during the war, and accompanied her to Egypt. To Octavius in Italy fell the hardest task.

**138. The Perusian War and the Peace of Brundisium.** Nearly 200,000 veterans were demanding the land which had been promised to them. High taxes, the scarcity of food, and the confiscation of land for the soldiers developed a spirit of discontent. L. Antonius the brother, and Fulvia the wife, of the triumvir, put themselves at the head of the disaffected. All efforts at reconciliation proved fruitless, and civil war followed. L. Antonius was soon shut up in Perusia, however, and after a long siege was forced to yield. After the surrender of Perusia, Fulvia hurried to her husband for help. A number of circumstances induced Antony to listen to her appeals and to take an active part in the management of Italy. One thing especially that influenced him to adopt this course was the fact that Octavius had taken possession of Gallia Narbonensis, because of the help which its governor had given L. Antonius. This province had been allotted to Antony, and its acquisition by Octavius made the latter master of the entire West. The time for action seemed a favorable one to Antony, since he had secured the support of Sextus Pompeius, whose fleet controlled the Mediterranean. He appeared before Brundisium, therefore, in the summer of 40, and civil war seemed imminent; but the mediation of Octavius's friends, Cocceius Nerva and Maecenas, and of Asinius Pollio, who represented Antony, as well as the strong stand which the legionaries took in favor of peace, brought about a reconciliation between the rivals. The need which Antony felt of Italian reinforcements for the Parthian war also induced him to listen to proposals of peace.

**139. War with Sextus Pompeius and the Retirement of Lepidus.** As for Octavius, the prospect of carrying on a war against the combined forces of Antony and Sextus Pompeius may well have alarmed him. In fact, Pompeius had made himself master of the Mediterranean, and, by interfering with the transportation of grain, had Rome and Italy in his power, in a measure. It was this state of things which forced Octavius in 39 to recognize formally the demands of Sextus Pompeius. His claim to the islands of Sicily and Sardinia was confirmed; he received compensation for the loss of his father's property, and a consulship in the future was promised to him. But Octavius felt that his own position was a precarious one so long as Sextus Pompeius controlled the Mediterranean. The treachery of Menodorus, one of the fleet commanders of Pompeius, put Sardinia in his power. Thereupon war broke out at once. A misunderstanding with Antony seemed likely to involve Octavius in still greater difficulty, but fortunately a reconciliation was effected at Tarentum in 37 through the mediation of Octavia, the wife of Antony and sister of Octavius, and Antony as well as Lepidus sent a fleet to help Octavius. Sextus Pompeius was defeated at Naulochus in 36, and fled to Asia. His forces surrendered themselves to Lepidus, who thereupon took possession of Sicily, and showed signs of an intention to regain his influence in the triumvirate. His success was short-lived, however.

Octavius won over his troops, and Lepidus was deprived of his provinces and forced into retirement. The result of this war was of immense importance to Octavius. He had rid himself of a rival who threatened his supremacy in the West; he had removed the danger of famine in Italy — a most prolific cause of discontent in the peninsula — and he had made himself master of the provinces and of the forces of Lepidus.

**140. Estrangement of Octavius and Antony.** The enforced retirement of Lepidus from the triumvirate doubtless intensified the rivalry between Octavius and Antony, just as the death of Crassus had made the conflict between Caesar and Pompey inevitable. Antony resented in particular the acquisition by Octavius of Sicily and of the provinces which had belonged to Lepidus. On the other hand, Antony's relations with Cleopatra and his plans in the Orient excited suspicion and hostility at Rome. Egypt, Cyrene, Cyprus, and portions of Crete and Cilicia were placed under her control. Only Asia and Bithynia retained the character of Roman provinces. In fact, there was some reason for believing that Antony was planning the establishment of a great rival power in the East with Alexandria for its capital. The feeling which this suspicion excited was intensified when the contents of Antony's will were revealed by some of his former friends, and it became known that the assignment of territory to Cleopatra was therein confirmed. Antony's neglect of Octavia, and the fact that he divorced her in 32, played no small part in stirring the anger of the people. The policy of Octavius was as well adapted to win the gratitude of the Italians as that of Antony had tended to estrange them. The suppression of the piratical enterprises of Sextus Pompeius in the Mediterranean, the lightening of the taxes, and the

restoration of order in Italy, largely through the efforts of
Maecenas, and the far-reaching improvements which Agrippa
effected in Rome had won for Octavius the sympathy and
support of all classes in the peninsula.

During the years 35–3 Octavius was engaged in a
campaign against the Illyrians, who had taken advantage
of the disturbed condition of Italy to make incursions into
the peninsula.   These peoples, as well as the Dalmatians,
were conquered, and points of great strategical and commercial importance in Pannonia were occupied.   Antony,
in the meantime, was carrying on operations in Armenia
and Media as a sequel to the war which he had been
unsuccessfully waging against the Parthians ever since the
year 40.

**141. Outbreak of the War.**   At the close of the year
33 both of them were free from other complications, and
the election of two of Antony's supporters to the consulship for the following year precipitated the conflict.   The
attacks which the new consuls made on the policy of
Octavius in taking possession of Sicily and Africa were
without effect, and they left the city to go to Antony.
Adopting the policy which his great leader had proposed
in the year 50, Antony offered to give up his exceptional
powers if Octavius would adopt the same course; but
Octavius had forestalled his action by deposing him from
his position as triumvir, and the war which followed was technically waged, not against Antony, but against Cleopatra.

**142. Battle of Actium and Death of Antony.**   During
the year 32 Antony and Cleopatra collected a force of
more than 100,000 men and 500 ships.   The fleet and
army of Octavius crossed from Brundisium in the spring
of 31, and the two armies lay encamped near one another
for several months.   The issue was decided by a naval battle

near Actium, September 2, 31. The fleet of Antony and Cleopatra was deserted by its leaders and forced to surrender, and after the battle the opposing army went over to Octavius. Antony and Cleopatra fled to Egypt. Octavius followed them thither a year later, and when Alexandria had fallen into his hands and they had learned that he would show them no mercy, they both took· their own lives. Egypt came under the personal control of Octavius. The latter returned to Italy in the summer of 29, after settling certain affairs in the Orient, and concluding a peace with the Parthians.

### SELECTIONS FROM THE SOURCES

**Caesar becomes master of Italy:** Caes. *B. C.* I. 7–29; Cic. *ad Att.* Bks. VII–IX; *ad Fam.* Bks. XIV, XVI (passim); Plut. *Caes.* 32–5; *Pomp.* 60–62; Appian, *B. C.* II. 35–8. — **First Spanish campaign:** Caes. *B. C.* I. 37–55, 59–87; II. 17–21; Cic. *ad Att.* X. 1?a. 3. — **Defeat of Curio:** Caes. *B. C.* II. 23–44. — **Pharsalus:** Caes. *B. C.* III. 84–99; Appian, *B. C.* II. 75–82; Plut. *Caes.* 42–6. — **Pompey's death:** Caes. *B. C.* III. 96, 102–4; Appian, *B. C.* II. 81, 83–6; Plut. *Pomp.* 77–80; Dio, XLII. 3–5. — **Events in Egypt:** Caes. *B. C.* III. 106–112; *Bell. Alex.* 1–33; Appian, *B. C.* II. 89–90; Plut. *Caes.* 48–9; Dio, XLII. 7–9, 34–44. — **Zela:** Appian, *B. C.* II. 91; Plut. *Caes.* 50. — **African campaign:** *Bell. Afr.;* Appian, *B. C.* II. 95–100; Plut. *Caes.* 52–4; *Cato,* 56–73; Dio, XLIII. 2–13. — **Second Spanish campaign:** *Bell. Hisp.;* Appian, *B. C.* II. 103–5; Plut. *Caes.* 56; Dio, XLIII. 28–40. — **Caesar's death:** Appian, *B. C.* II. 111–117; Plut. *Caes.* 60–69; *Brut.* 14–17; Suet. *Iul.* 80–89; Vell. II. 56; Dio, XLIV. 9–19. — **Caesar's dictatorships:** Caes. *B. C.* II. 21. 5 (cf. III. 2. 1); Appian, *B. C.* II. 48; Dio, XLII. 20; Plut. *Caes.* 51; Cic. *ad Fam.* IX. 15. 4–5; Dio, XLIII. 14; Suet. *Iul.* 76; Appian, *B. C.* II. 106; Plut. *Caes.* 57; Dio, XLIV. 8; XLVI. 17. — **Caesar's tribunate:** Dio, XLII. 20. — **Title of imperator:** Dio, XLIII. 44; Suet. *Iul.* 76. — **Praefectus morum:** Dio, XLIV. 5; Suet. *Iul.* 76. — **Praetorian governors, 1 yr., consular governors, 2 yrs.:** Cic. *Phil.* I. 19; V. 7; VIII. 28. —

16 praetors, 40 quaestors: Dio, XLIII. 47, 49, 51; Suet. *Iul.* 41. —
**Power to nominate**: Dio, XLIII. 47, 51; Cic. *Phil.* II. 80; Appian,
*B. C.* II. 128; Suet. *Iul.* 76. — 900 **senators**: Dio, XLIII. 47. —
**Bestowal of Latin rights**: Cic. *ad Att.* XIV. 12. 1; Tac. *Ann.* XI. 24.
— **Appointment of provincial governors**: Dio, XLII. 20. — **Consules
suffecti**: Dio, XLIII. 46. — **Seizure of Caesar's papers and treas-**
**ure**: Cic. *Phil.* I. 17; II. 93; Appian, *B. C.* II. 125. — **Meeting of
senate, March 17**: Appian, *B. C.* II. 135-6; Dio, XLIV. 22-34;
Cic. *Phil.* I. 1 f.; I. 31 f.; Vell. II. 58. — **Antony acquires Cis-**
**alpine Gaul**: Cic. *ad Att.* XIV. 14. 4; Appian, *B. C.* III. 27-30;
Vell. II. 60; Appian, *B. C.* III. 55. — **Octavius comes slowly to
Rome**: Cic. *ad Att.* XIV. 5. 3; *ibid.* 10. 3; XV. 2. 3; Appian, *B. C.*
III. 9-23; Dio, XLV. 1-4. — **His relations to Antony**: Appian, *B. C.*
III. 28-45; Dio, XLV. 5-9; *ibid.* 11-15; Suet. *Aug.* 10. — **Antony
marches north**: Cic. *Phil.* III. 1; V. 24; Appian, *B. C.* III. 46. —
**Battle near Mutina**: Appian, *B. C.* III. 66-72; Dio, XLVI. 37. —
**Lepidus joins Antony**: Cic. *ad Fam.* X. 23. 2; Appian, *B. C.* III.
83-4. — **Pollio and Plancus join Antony**: Appian, *B. C.* III. 97; Dio,
XLVI. 53; Vell. II. 63. — **Octavius is elected consul**: Liv. *Ep.*
CXIX; Appian, *B. C.* III. 88-94; Dio, XLVI. 40-45. — **Death of
D. Brutus**: Appian, *B. C.* III. 97-8; Vell. II. 64. — **Second tri-**
**umvirate formed**: Liv. *Ep.* CXX; Appian, *B. C.* IV. 2 ff.; Dio,
XLVI. 54-6; Suet. *Aug.* 27; Plut. *Ant.* 19. — **Lex Titia**: Appian,
*B. C.* IV. 7; Dio, XLVII. 2. — **Death of Cicero**: Plut. *Cic.* 47-8;
Appian, *B. C.* IV. 19-20; Vell. II. 66. — **Macedonia, Illyricum, and
Greece allotted to M. Brutus**: Cic. *Phil.* X. 13-14; Plut. *Brut.* 27;
Dio, XLVII. 22. — **Syria assigned to Cassius**: Cic. *Phil.* XI. 29 ff.;
Dio, XLVII. 28; Vell. II. 62. — **Philippi**: Appian, *B. C.* IV.
109-131; Dio, XLVII. 37-49; Plut. *Brut.* 38-53; Vell. II. 70-72.
— **Division of territory**: Appian, *B. C.* V. 3; Dio, XLVIII. 1-2. —
**Perusian war**: Appian, *B. C.* V. 12-49; Dio, XLVIII. 4-15; Vell.
II. 74. — **Treaty of Brundisium**: Appian, *B. C.* V. 64-5; Dio,
XLVIII. 28-30; Vell. II. 76. — **Concessions to Sex. Pompeius**:
Appian, *B. C.* V. 72; Dio, XLVIII. 36. — **War with Sex. Pom-**
**peius**: Appian, *B. C.* V. 77-122; Dio, XLVIII. 45-XLIX. 10;
Vell. II. 79. — **Treaty of Tarentum**: Dio, XLVIII. 54; Appian,
*B. C.* V. 93-5; Tac. *Ann.* I. 10. — **Retirement of Lepidus**: Liv. *Ep.*
CXXIX; Suet. *Aug.* 16; Appian, *B. C.* V. 122-6; Dio, XLIX.
11-12. — **Parthian campaign of Antony**: Dio, XLVIII. 24-7; *ibid.*
39-41; XLIX. 19 ff.; Plut. *Ant.* 37-52; Vell. II. 82. — **Illyrian**

campaign of Octavius: Dio, XLIX. 34-8; Appian, *Bell. Ill.* 16-28; Liv. *Epp.* CXXXI-CXXXII. — Territory given to Cleopatra: Plut. *Ant.* 54; Dio, XLIX. 32, 41; L. 1, 3. — War declared against Cleopatra: Plut. *Ant.* 60; Dio, L. 4, 6. — Actium: Plut. *Ant.* 64-8; Dio, L. 31-5; Vell. II. 85. — Surrender of Antony's army: Plut. *Ant.* 68. — Death of Antony: Dio, LI. 10; Plut. *Ant.* 76-7. —Death of Cleopatra: Dio, LI. 11-14; Plut. *Ant.* 84-6.

## SELECTED BIBLIOGRAPHY [1]

O. E. Schmidt, Der Briefwechsel des M. Tullius Cicero. Leipzig, 1893.

Tyrrell and Purser, The Correspondence of M. Tullius Cicero, Vols. V and VI. London, 1897-9.

W. Drumann, Geschichte Roms, 6 vols. Koenigsberg, 1834-44.

A. Stoffel, Histoire de Jules César: Guerre Civile, 2 vols. Paris, 1887.

A. v. Goeler, Caesars Gallischer Krieg. Tübingen, 1879.

W. Judeich, Caesar im Orient. Leipzig, 1885.

O. E. Schmidt, Die letzten Kämpfe der röm. Republik (Neue Jahr. f. Philol. u. Paed. XIII, Suppl. pp. 665-722).

A. v. Hagen, De bello Mutinensi quaestiones criticae. Marburg, 1886.

V. Gardthausen, Augustus und seine Zeit (I. 1, 2; II. 1, 2). Leipzig, 1891-6.

Th. Mommsen, Res gestae divi Augusti, 2d ed. Berlin, 1883.

[1] See also general bibliography on p. 22.

# SECTION II — DESCRIPTIVE

## CHAPTER VIII

### THE ATTRIBUTES OF MAGISTRACY

#### (a) *Magistratus, Imperium, Potestas*

**143. Method of Treatment.** Our historical survey of the development of Roman political institutions has shown that the right of initiating action was the peculiar prerogative of the magistrate, and that in the early period he was practically the supreme lawgiver and judge, as well as the executive. To put it in another way, the functions acquired later by other branches of the government were in the early days exercised by the executive. We have traced the process of differentiation. First of all, the senate, which was at the beginning of the republic merely an advisory body, found means to enforce its claim to a share in the control of the state. Later, the popular assemblies developed, and finally a well-organized judicial system was established. A systematic examination of Roman political institutions will, therefore, follow the order of historical development, in taking up first the magistracies, then the senate, the popular assemblies, and finally the courts of law. Our historical investigation has suggested one other important point in the method of treatment. At the beginning of the republican period the magisterial power was vested in a single college of magistrates. The establishment of new magistracies, as time went on, meant simply the assignment of certain specific duties to the new officials. The new magistracies had all the general characteristics of the original magistracy out of which they sprang. Therefore, before passing to an examination of the functions of the individual magistrates, it will be natural and convenient to consider the general attributes of the Roman magistracies taken as a unit.

144. **Definition of Magistratus.** The term *magistratus* was used of the office and of its incumbents. In the concrete sense the *magistratus* was the authorized representative of the people for the conduct of public business of a secular character. His authorization came through an election by the *populus*. The dictator, interrex, and magister equitum, who were appointed by a magistrate, and were, therefore, only indirectly dependent on a popular election, were relics of the monarchical constitution, and not products of the republic at all. The tribunes were chosen in an assembly made up of plebeians only, so that in the strict sense of the word they were not magistrates. Priests do not fall in this category because their duties were of a religious character.

145. **Magistratus Maiores and Minores.** According to the point of view from which they are considered the magistracies may be classified as *magistratus maiores* or *minores, patricii* or *plebeii,* curule or not curule, ordinary or extraordinary, *cum imperio* or *sine imperio*. The Romans themselves differed in their classification of the magistracies as *magistratus maiores* or *minores*. Thus the augur Messala (Gell. XIII. 15. 4) maintained that the interrex, consul, praetor, dictator, censor, magister equitum, and all magistrates or pro-magistrates vested with consular or praetorian power, inasmuch as they had the right to take the *auspicia maxima,* were *magistratus maiores*. The others,

who could take only the *auspicia minora*, were *magistratus minores*. On the other hand, it seems better to draw the line of distinction between these two classes of magistrates below the quaestorship, because the quaestors and aediles with the higher magistrates were admitted to the senate in the later republic by virtue of having held their respective offices, whereas magistrates of a lower rank were not members of that body.

Will. I. 225 f.

**146. Magistratus Patricii and Plebeii.** Up to the middle of the fourth century B.C. the terms *magistratus patricii* and *plebeii* were applied to the magistracies open to patricians and plebeians respectively. After plebeians had been made eligible to all the magistracies the distinction has no technical meaning. The tribunes are sometimes styled *magistratus plebeii*, but inaccurately, because, as we have seen, the tribunes were strictly speaking not magistrates at all.

**147. Curule and non-Curule Magistracies.** The right to use the curule chair was a privilege belonging especially to magistrates who had the *imperium*. When the curule aedileship was established, however, the *sella curulis* was made one of the insignia of the office, although the incumbent of the office did not have the *imperium*. The magistrates (not including plebeian officials) above the quaestor were *magistratus curules*.

St. R. I. 401 f.

**148. Magistratus Ordinarii and Extraordinarii.** Ordinary magistrates were those who were chosen at fixed intervals, like the consul or censor. Those who were elected for an exceptional purpose were called *magistratus extraordinarii*. Some of the magistracies of the latter class, as, for instance, the dictatorship, formed a regular part of the Roman administrative system, while others, like the decemvirate or the consular tribunate, were extra-constitutional.

**149. Magistratus cum Imperio and sine Imperio.** The consul, praetor, dictator, and magister equitum had the *imperium*. The censor, aedile, quaestor, and of course the plebeian officials, were *sine imperio*. The *imperium* represents the supreme authority of the community in its dealings with the individual. It is not strictly opposed to *potestas*, which is a generic term to indicate the power with which a magistrate was vested for the discharge of his duties. Under the republic the exercise of the *imperium* within the city was limited, especially by the right of appeal. It was still enjoyed by the magistrate abroad, however, and the term was practically restricted in its application to the absolute power exercised by him.

Festus, v. cum imperio, p. 50, ed. M.

**150. Maior Potestas.** The various magistrates exercised functions of so different a character that the members of the several colleges had the right of initiative, and within their own sphere of duties were practically free from outside influence. However, to avoid the danger of conflict and the consequent stoppage of the machinery of government, in matters like the summoning of the senate or the comitia, where the abstract right to take the contemplated action was vested in more than one magistracy, the *maior potestas* of one college over against another was recognized by the constitution. On this basis the offices were arranged in the order of dictator, consul, praetor, aedile, and quaestor. No one of the magistrates mentioned had the *maior potestas* over the censor, but he enjoyed that right over the quaestor and aedile, whose duties were in some respects akin to his. In the exercise of his *maior potestas* a higher magistrate could either forbid a lower magistrate to take action in a specific case, or suspend him from office altogether.

Lex Salpensana, chap. 27.

Gell. 13. 16. 1; Liv. 3. 29. 2–3; 8. 36. 1.

We have seen (p. 25) that the republican chief-magistrate, when compared with his monarchical predecessor, was placed under two important limitations. He shared his office with a colleague, who had the right to veto his action, and he held office for a limited period. The system of collegiality was one of the most peculiar features of the Roman constitution. It promoted efficiency, in that the functions of an office could be exercised simultaneously by the several members of a college. This was not the real purpose of the arrangement, however. It was rather devised to protect the citizen from the arbitrary action of a single magistrate.

**151. Par Potestas and the Veto Power.** Each member of a college was at all times vested with the full power of his magistracy, and his negative right to prevent the completion of a given undertaking took precedence of his colleague's positive right to take the step in question. The technical term for this exercise of the *par potestas*, which existed between the members of a college, was *intercessio*. The exercise of this negative power was subject to three conditions. The protest must be made by a magistrate in person; it must be made against a magistrate, and directed against a matter already partially advanced toward completion. The first limitation made an oral exercise of the right necessary. The second one theoretically exempted action taken by the *comitia* from the scope of the *intercessio*. Even this limitation, however, left it within the power of a magistrate to interfere with the action of a colleague presiding over a popular assembly up to the point where the people declared their will with reference to a proposition.

The *par potestas* was, therefore, more restricted in its application than the *maior potestas*, since the latter allowed a higher magistrate not only to exercise the right of *intercessio*, as just indicated, but also to forbid a lower

Gell. 13. 12. 9;
Caes. B. C.
3. 20. 1.

magistrate to make a proposed arrangement, before any preliminary steps looking to its establishment had been taken, or to declare invalid such an arrangement when perfected by him. A member of a magisterial college, however, in the exercise of his *par potestas*, could interpose his veto only when his colleague had made some progress toward the accomplishment of his purpose. The veto power was not often used by a magistrate against a colleague. It was of little effect, because the magistrate who disregarded it could not be called to account until his term of office had expired. The tribune, however, could veto the action of any regular magistrate, and could impose an immediate penalty for the non-observance of the veto, and since, as we have already seen (p. 45), at an early period the tribune became the recognized representative of the rights of the individual, as opposed to the claims of the community, his veto power superseded that of the magistrate, and put an effective limitation on the magisterial prerogative. In point of fact conflicts between members of a college were generally avoided by taking joint action in a specific case, by adopting the principle of alternation, by assigning functions on the basis of seniority or by lot, or by giving different *provinciae* to the several members of a college. Thus, in the early period, the consuls, although both were in full possession of the consular power throughout the year, in practice alternated from month to month in the active exercise of that power within the city. When they were in joint command of an army in Italy they commonly alternated day by day. The possession of the *fasces* passed from one to the other to indicate the change. In the case of most magistracies, however, *provinciae*, or distinct spheres of action, were assigned to the several members of a college, so that there

Cic. de Re Publ. 2. 55; Liv. 2. 8. 6; 22. 27. 10; 35. 20. 2.

Liv. 4. 46. 5 22. 41. 3.

was scarcely a possibility of conflict. This was true, for instance, of the praetorship and the aedileship. In such cases the system of collegiality dropped away altogether.

## (b) Term of Office

**152. Limited Term of Office and the Prorogatio Imperii.** The second limitation put on the republican magistracies was of still greater importance than the one just discussed, and perhaps no political change contributed more to the downfall of the republic than the failure to observe it. All magistrates held office for a fixed and brief period, and the more exceptional the power of an official was, the briefer his term of office was. Thus the consul and most of the regular magistrates held office for one year, while the dictator's term was not to exceed six months. Two contingencies might arise which would lead to a violation of this practice. Exceptional circumstances might necessitate a *prorogatio imperii*, or extension of the term of office beyond the fixed period, or magistracies might become vacant before the expiration of the legal term. The first contingency arose now and then in case of an important war. In 326, at the end of the consular year, the consul Q. Publilius Philo, who had charge of the forces acting against the Samnites, was instructed to retain command of the army until the war was brought to an end (cf. p. 44). He was said to act *pro consule*, but his power was less than that of a consul, since it could be exercised for a specific purpose only and only within a limited territory. The precedent which was set in this case was not infrequently followed later, but the *prorogatio imperii* was usually for a year or even for a shorter time. However, when the era of territorial aggrandizement outside cf

Cic. de Legg. 3. 9.

Liv. 8. 23. 12.

Liv. 9. 42. 2.

Italy began, toward the close of the third century B.C., this occasional expedient became an integral part of the Roman administrative system. Instead of directly choosing officials to act as provincial governors, these positions were filled by extending the term of office of magistrates who had served for a year at Rome, and the governors in the various provinces acted *pro consule* or *pro praetore*, as the case might be, and in course of time the maximum limit of one year set for such an extension of the term of office was no longer observed.

**153. Filling of Vacancies.** On the other hand, a magistracy might become vacant before the expiration of the legal term. Such a contingency might arise, for instance, from the death or resignation of one consul or of both. If there was one vacancy in a college, it was filled by the election of a new member to hold office for the rest of the term. If both places were vacant, two new members were chosen to hold office for a full year from the date of their inauguration. Consequently in the early period the official year does not begin at any fixed date in the calendar; but from 217 the beginning of the official year was fixed at March 15. This continued to be the accepted date until 154. From that time on, the consuls regularly entered on their offices January 1.

Herz. I. 611.

St. R. I. 597 f.

Herz. I. 614.

### (c) Constitutional Powers of the Magistrate

**154. The Constitutional Powers of Magistrates.** A magistrate having the *imperium* represented the community in all its dealings with gods and men. The *imperium* included the power (1) to take the auspices and to supervise certain other religious matters which had a bearing on political action, (2) to represent the state in its dealings with individuals and with other communities, (3) to command the army and navy, (4) to punish those who withstood constituted authority, (5) to exercise civil and criminal jurisdiction, (6) to issue proclamations and edicts, (7) to summon the senate and popular assemblies for deliberation and action on affairs of state, (8) to supervise administrative matters affecting the welfare of the community or of individual citizens.

**155. The Taking of Auspices.** As we have already noticed (p. 26), after the establishment of the consulship, the control of strictly religious affairs, whether of a general or a particular character, rested with the priests; but religious matters having a political significance were left to the magistrate, and the priests participated in such cases only to the extent of assisting or giving technical advice. The Romans believed that the pleasure of the gods in a particular case could be learned by adopting the proper means, and that it was desirable to govern one's action by it. In particular it was necessary to consult the gods by taking auspices before the election of a magistrate, before his assumption of office, before a meeting of the *comitia* as a legislative body, and before a magistrate set out on a campaign. In the first three cases the auspices must be taken on the day and on the spot of the proposed action. If unfavorable omens preceded or accompanied the election of a magistrate, or the passage of a law, there existed a legal defect (*vitium*), which in the one case made it incumbent on the magistrate to lay down his office, and in the other case necessitated the reënactment of the bill by the *comitia*. In the last century of the republic, however, if a measure with a technical defect of this sort was taken up later by the senate and favorably acted on, it became valid. In all cases political action of which the gods

Cic. de Div. 1. 3; Liv. 3. 20. 6; 21. 63. 7–9.

Gell. 3. 2. 10; Censorinus, 23. 4.

Cic. ad Att. 4. 9. 1; Phil. 2. 80; de Legg. 2. 31; de Div. 2. 42; in Vat. 20; Liv. 4. 7. 3; 8. 15. 6.

disapproved could be taken on a subsequent occasion, if the auspices were favorable. No legal penalty attached to the non-observance of unfavorable omens. Thus Crassus did not expose himself to a penalty at the hands of man when he disregarded unfavorable auspices in crossing the Euphrates, but the disaster which befell his Parthian expedition vindicated sufficiently the dignity of the gods.

**156. Auguria Oblativa and Auspicia Impetrativa.** The gods were supposed to indicate their will through unsought manifestations (*auguria oblativa* or *dirae*), or by means of *auspicia impetrativa*, i.e., in answer to inquiries properly made. The first class of warnings came, for instance, in the form of a flash of lightning before a meeting of the *comitia*, or took the shape of a case of epilepsy among the voters. Officiating magistrates, or augurs commissioned by them, obtained *auspicia* by watching for signs (*spectio*). They were of three classes: *signa ex avibus, signa ex quadrupedibus*, and *signa caelestia*. Omens of the first two sorts were to be had by marking off a square (*templum*) on the ground, or on the sky by drawing imaginary lines, and by watching the progress across it of four-footed beasts or birds, as the case might be. *Signa caelestia* were obtained by noting the direction of flashes of lightning through a previously determined part of the heavens. In the field *auspicia pullaria* were commonly taken from the behavior of chickens while eating.

**157. Regulations governing the Auspices.** The officiating magistrate could theoretically heed or disregard the announcement (*obnuntiatio*) of unfavorable auspices by another official. In case conflicting omens were observed by different magistrates, the preference was given to those of the magistrate who had the *maior potestas*. Ultimately, however, the higher magistrates avoided such conflicts by

Festus, v. prohibere, p. 234, ed. M

Servius on Aen. 1. 92 and 6. 197; Festus, v. minora templa and sinistrae aves, pp. 157, 339, ed. M.

Cic. de Div. 2. 82.

Liv 10.40.2f.

Gell. 13. 15. 1.

forbidding the lower magistrates to take the auspices on a given day. The practice of taking the auspices was a part of the old patrician régime, so that for several centuries the tribunes did not exercise the right, and omens played no part in the meetings of the plebeian assembly; but by the *lex Aelia Fufia*, of about 155, they were applied to the plebeian assembly, and could be taken by the tribunes, and were also used by the magistrates against the tribunes. The use of auspices afforded such a convenient means of interfering with meetings of the popular assemblies that the mere announcement of a magistrate's intention to take them on a certain day was sufficient to cause a postponement of the *comitia*. Consequently, by the *lex Clodia* of 58, *obnuntiatio* was forbidden. Besides the taking of the auspices, other religious matters, which rested with the magistrate, sometimes with the coöperation of the senate or the *comitia*, were the reception of new forms of worship, the establishment of new priesthoods, the building of temples, and the authorization of holy days.

St. R. I. 113.

Cic. pro Sest. 33.

**158. Power to represent the State.** As the authorized representative of the state, the magistrate in time of war could declare a truce with the enemy, and he could conclude peace with a hostile state, subject to the approval of the people. Disposal of the spoils of war and control of the state land had been part of the royal prerogative, but under the republic the senate and the people took these matters into their own hands. However, all current business connected with conquered territory and the *ager publicus*, such as the rental of state lands, was in the hands of the magistrates.

Liv. 9. 5. 1; 21. 19. 3.

**159. Rights as Commander-in-Chief.** The centuriate *comitia* alone had the right to declare war, but the prosecution of it was left to the chief-magistrate. As commander-in-chief of the forces of the state he was empowered to levy and organize troops, to conduct a campaign, and to conclude a provisional treaty of peace with the enemy. A strict line of distinction was drawn between the powers of a magistrate at home (*domi*) and abroad (*militiae*). Up to the first milestone outside the city the magisterial power was limited by the right of appeal and by the tribunician veto. Beyond that point the magistrate, in whose favor the *lex curiata de imperio* had been passed, acquired the unlimited power of the *imperium*. The civil magistrate, as well as the general in time of war, therefore, had the power beyond the limit mentioned of inflicting the death sentence ; but, sometime between the second Punic war and the period of the Gracchi, the *leges Porciae* gave citizens, wherever they might be, the right of appeal in a question of life or death. A Roman general, however, retained the right to inflict death as a military penalty, although in such a case a man could not be flogged to death. The possession of the full power of the *imperium* was indicated to the eye by the fact that beyond the first milestone the bundle of *fasces* borne by the lictors included the ax (*securis*). On the other hand, the magistrate lost the *imperium* and the insignia indicating it, except in case of a triumph, when he entered the city. The right to a triumph was implied in the possession of the military authority which the *imperium* conferred, but was conditional on winning a decisive battle in which the enemy lost 5000 men. The war must also have been carried on against a foreign foe, and must have led to an extension of the limits of Roman authority. The honor could be claimed only by dictators, consuls, or praetors, or by pro-magistrates acting with the authority of the two last-mentioned officials. In the last years of the republic the senate used its power of granting or refusing a triumph to express its approval or disapproval of the

Liv. 22. 38.
2-3; 39. 20. 4

Herz. I.
645, n. 2.

Cic. de Re
Publ. 2. 54;
pro Rab.
perd. 12;
in Verr.
ii. 5. 163;
Liv. 10. 9. 4

St. R. I.
67, 379 f.

Liv. 10. 37. 8
28. 9. 7 f.;
28. 38. 4;
31. 20. 3;
Val. Max. 2.
8. 1.

conduct of a campaign, without strictly observing the legal

Cic. Phil.
14. 37.

requirements in the case.    A *supplicatio* was also sometimes granted by the senate, and a successful general might

Liv. 27. 19. 4;
Cic. Phil. 14.
12; Tac. Ann.
3. 74.

receive the title of *imperator* from the senate, or on the field of battle by acclamation.

**160. Disciplinary Power of the Magistrate.** The Roman magistrate had the power to punish the disobedient or those who interfered with him in the discharge of his duty. His exercise of this disciplinary power is to be distinguished from his judicial functions.    In the latter case offenses were carefully defined and classified by law; the facts were elicited in accordance with a prescribed method of procedure, and the penalty was also prescribed.    In disciplinary actions conducted by an executive officer the nature of the offense and of the penalty were determined by the magistrate, largely in accordance with his own discretion. This disciplinary power belonged originally only to the *magistratus cum imperio*, but was subsequently conferred upon the censors, aediles, and even the tribunes.    The

Cic. de Legg.
3. 6.

common penalties inflicted were fines, corporal punishment, imprisonment, and death.    Within the city in the course of time magistrates were forbidden to inflict corporal punishment on citizens, and cases involving the death sentence were tried before the centuriate *comitia*.    After the passage

Cic. de Re
Publ. 2. 60;
Festus,
p. 237, ed. M.;
Gell. 11. 1. 2.

of the *lex Aeternia Tarpeia* (cf. p. 76) all cases in which the fine exceeded 3020 *asses* could be appealed to the tribal assembly.

**161. Civil Jurisdiction of the Magistrate.** The civil jurisdiction of the magistrate might be *inter privatos* or *inter populum et privatos*.    In the early republican period cases of both kinds were heard by the consul.    In course of time, however, the exercise of judicial functions became the exclusive prerogative of certain magistrates chosen solely or partly for that purpose.   Thus, in the year 366, praetors were elected for the first time to relieve the consul of his judicial duties (p. 37) in civil suits in which both parties were private individuals.   In Italy, outside of Rome, similar functions were performed by circuit judges, known as *praefecti iuri dicundo* (cf. p. 74).   In the provinces the governor administered justice.   The collection of the taxes and of rental from the state land gave rise to many civil suits to which the state was a party.   Such cases were heard by censors, quaestors, and aediles, within whose province the management of public finances fell.   This method of procedure was manifestly unfair to the individual.   Under it the magistrate who brought or defended the suit in the name of the state also acted as the judge, from whose decision no appeal could be taken.

**162. Criminal Jurisdiction of the Magistrate.**   The exercise of the magistrate's judicial functions, as well as his disciplinary power, was limited by the right which citizens had of appealing to the popular assembly when a magistrate imposed the death sentence or a fine of more than 3020 *asses*.   The establishment of *quaestiones perpetuae*, or standing courts, in the second century (cf. p. 74), and the development which the system underwent during Sulla's dictatorship (cf. p. 106), led to very important changes in the criminal jurisdiction of the magistrate.   Most of the newly established courts were under the presidency of the praetor, whose duty it was to conduct the preliminaries to the trial, to preside during the trial proper, and to announce the innocence of the accused person, or fix the penalty, in accordance with the decision of the jury.

**163. The Right to issue Proclamations.**   The right to enforce obedience carries with it the right to announce publicly regulations which shall be binding on the community.

In Rome proclamations took the form of *edicta*, or magisterial announcements affecting the entire community or whole classes of citizens, or of *decreta* concerning individuals. The proclamation of a magistrate naturally dealt with matters over which he had special jurisdiction. It was valid only during the term of office of the magistrate who issued it. In this respect it differed from a law. It acquired the practical force of a law, however, in the case of the *edictum tralaticium*, *i.e.*, when successive magistrates adopted and announced the same body of regulations which their predecessors had issued.

**164. The Right to preside over Legislative and Electoral Bodies.** Public meetings for the discussion of political questions had an official character, since they could be called by officials only. Such gatherings, called *contiones*, were under the presidency of an official, and no one could address them without his consent. They usually preceded the *comitia*, or assemblies held for electoral or legislative purposes. The higher magistrates had the *ius agendi cum populo*, or the right to summon the *comitia* and preside over them. Limitations put on certain magistrates in specific cases will be noted later. The plebeian officials had only the *ius agendi cum plebe*. The tribune, as well as the higher magistrates, had the right to call the senate together (*ius agendi cum patribus*), lay matters before it, and ask for a vote upon such motions as might be made.

**165. General Powers as an Executive.** It may go without saying that to the magistrate, who represented the legislative branch of the government, fell the superintendence of administrative business and the execution of judicial decisions. He had charge of such matters, therefore, as the erection of public buildings, the receipt and payment of public moneys, and the maintenance of order.

Cic. de Legg. 3. 10.

Gell. 14. 7. 4-5.

**166. The Consilium.** In the performance of important duties he was assisted by a *consilium*, or board of technical advisers. Such a board assisted the censor, for instance, and the praetor in rendering their decisions in certain judicial matters. The theoretical relation also which the senate bore to the consul was that of a *consilium*.

St. R. II. 465

### (d) Emoluments, Insignia, Attendants

**167. Emoluments of Office.** A Roman magistracy under the republic was regarded as an *honos* pure and simple, so that no salary was paid to any official. For this reason only the well-to-do could hold office, and, during the last century of the republic, when success in the elections depended on extravagance shown in the games, candidacy must have been confined to the rich — or at least to those whose credit was good. The magistrate received compensation out of the state treasury, however, for any money which he might be required to pay out in the performance of his duty. In some cases the compensation fell far short of the sum which he was required by necessity or tradition to spend. This was true, for instance, of the outlay which the aedile made for the public games. On the other hand, the requisitions which commissioners and provincial governors could make for the suitable maintenance of themselves and their retinues became a source of great profit.

Liv. 29. 11. 4
44. 22. 13;
Cic. de Leg.
Agr. 2. 32;
in Verr.
(passim).

**168. Insignia of Office.** The magisterial dignity was indicated to the eye by insignia and by attendants. The most characteristic mark of office was the *toga praetexta*, which all magistrates from the consul to the aedile wore within the city. When abroad, the consul put on the *paludamentum*, a short red cloak. On occasion of a triumph a

Plut. Q. R. 81

Festus, v. pa
ludati, p. 253
ed. M.

successful general wore the *toga purpurea*. On formal
occasions, as when administering justice, dictators, consuls,
censors, praetors, and curule aediles sat on a *sella curulis*,
placed on a *tribunal*. In early times the magistrate also had
the right to ride in a vehicle within the city limits. Perhaps
no external mark of office was more highly prized and of
more practical importance than the *ius imaginum*. Every
family which included a curule magistrate in its number had
the right after his death to keep in the *atrium* a painted
waxen mask in his likeness with an inscription (*libellus*)
beneath it setting forth his offices and achievements.
These *imagines* constituted the patent of nobility for that
patricio-plebeian aristocracy which ruled the state for three
centuries.

169. **Lictors.** The higher magistrates were attended in
public by lictors, who protected them and cleared a way
for their passage. The lictors bore over their left shoulder a
bundle of rods, called the *fasces*, which symbolized the magistrate's right to enforce obedience. The ax (*securis*), placed
within the bundle and carried outside the city, indicated
his power of life and death. The number of lictors in
attendance varied according to the rank of the magistrate.
Twenty-four attended a dictator, and twelve a consul. The
*praetor urbanus* had two, while the praetor or propraetor
in a province was accompanied by six. Censors, and
magistrates from the aedile downwards, had no lictors. In
the provinces the lictors inflicted corporal punishment and
the punishment of death, when ordered to do so by the
magistrate.

170. **Scribae, etc.** The *scribae* held the most important
position among the subordinates of the several magistrates.
They were assigned to magistrates by lot, and from them
received the titles of *scribae quaestorii, aedilicii*, etc., as the

Liv. 40. 45. 8;
Gell. 3. 18. 4;
7. 9. 6.

Cic. ad Fam.
9. 21. 2;
in Verr.
ii. 5. 36;
Liv. 10. 7. 11;
Plin. N. H.
35. 6.

Polyb. 3. 87.
7; Censo-
rinus, 24. 3;
Cic. in Verr.
ii. 5. 142.

Wilm. Ex.
Inscr. 1302.

case might be. *Viatores* acted as messengers, and *praecones* announced a meeting of the senate or the people, and summoned individuals to court. *Accensi* were personal attendants of a magistrate, who were usually chosen from his own household, and had, therefore, only a quasi-official status. Most of these positions were held by freedmen or the sons of freedmen, and the principles of civil service reform were observed to such an extent that an *apparitor* was not only reasonably sure of retaining his office during good behavior, but could usually transmit it to his son, or sell it, provided, of course, that the new incumbent was regarded as a suitable person for the position.

Festus, p. 371, ed. M.; Varro, L. L. 6. 86–91.

Cic. ad Q. fr. 1. 1. 13.

### (e) Conditions of Eligibility

**171. General and Special Conditions of Eligibility.** In early times, of course patricians only were eligible to the magistracies, but after the middle of the fourth century class distinctions counted for nothing, in so far as eligibility to political office was concerned, except that patricians could not be elected to plebeian offices, nor to certain places in the magisterial colleges reserved for plebeians. In Cicero's time it was required of all candidates for office that they should be citizens, and that they should have a respectable standing in the community. Furthermore, they were not eligible to reëlection until an interval of ten years had elapsed (p. 70), nor could a person hold two offices at the same time. Freedmen and their sons were in general not eligible. Some of these points were not strictly observed during periods of political disturbance. The magistrates who conducted the election passed on the eligibility of all candidates. Special conditions of candidacy were fixed for particular offices, notably the higher

St. R. I. 488

ones.   The most important of these were the attainment
of a certain age and the observance of the *certus ordo
magistratuum.*

**172. The Certus Ordo.**   From a comparatively early
period the tradition had grown up that certain offices must
be held before one could be elected to certain other
offices.   This condition was given a legal form by the
*lex Villia* of 180 (cf. p. 70), and by one of the *leges
Corneliae* of 81 (cf. p. 105).   These laws required one to

St. R. I.
538 ff.

hold the quaestorship before assuming the praetorship, and
the praetorship before the consulship.   Further than this
republican legislation does not seem to have gone, but
custom had set the quaestorship before the curule aedileship, and the duties of the curule and plebeian aediles
were so similar that they both fell into the same place
in the series.   The tribunate was so closely connected with
the plebeian aedileship that it was placed next in order
below it.   However, since plebeian offices could not be
held by patricians, it was not necessary that a candidate
for a higher magistracy should hold them.   Membership
in one of the colleges making up the *XXVI viri,* and
the office of *tribunus militum,* preceded the quaestorship.

St. R. I. 548.

Finally it was customary to choose ex-consuls only to the
dictatorship and censorship, so that the *certus ordo,* established partly by law and partly by custom, in the way

St. R. I.
561 f.

indicated above, was: *dictator, consul, interrex, praetor,
magister equitum, censor, aedile, tribunus plebis, quaestor,*
one of the *viginti sex viri, tribunus militum.*   Perhaps the
censorship was assigned in this official *gradus honorum* to
the position which it holds, below the consulship and praetorship, because the censor was not attended by lictors.

**173. Age Requirement.**   In the early period of the
republic there was no minimum age requirement fixed for

candidates for the various offices. The matter was left wholly to the discretion of the magistrate who conducted the election. It was, however, covered in part by the *lex Villia* and by legislation of 81, but the provisions of these two laws are not known with certainty. It is probable, however, that after the time of Sulla thirty-one years was the minimum age for the quaestorship, and forty years for the praetorship, and that an interval of at least two years was required between the end of a term of office and the assumption of the magistracy next above it. Indirectly these two provisions also made forty-three the minimum age for the consulship.

Will. Dr. 242, n. 2; Herz. I. 668, n. 1; St. R. I. 568 ff.

## (*f*) *Candidacy, Election, Resignation, Responsibility*

**174. Professio.** Candidates were not formally nominated for office by their supporters, as is the case in this country, but they announced their own candidacy, as in England those who wish to be elected to membership in the House of Commons usually do; although, if we may make an inference from the political posters found in Pompeii, this personal announcement was often prompted by the privately or publicly expressed desire of personal friends or political supporters. Since the official who presided at an election exercised his discretion in passing on the eligibility of a candidate, it was desirable to get his opinion on that point before the election took place. For this reason candidates came to adopt the practice of formally notifying the prospective chairman of their intention to stand for a certain office. Thereupon the official formally announced his acceptance or rejection of their candidacy, although this did not prevent him from reconsidering his decision at the time of the election. This

Liv. 7. 22. 8; 26. 18. 5; Vell. 2. 92. 3-4.

practice of making a *professio*, or preliminary announcement of one's candidacy, was crystallized, probably in 98,
into a law, which provided that the *professio* should be
made seventeen days before the election took place. This
law, as we have already noticed (p. 114), played an
important part in the quarrel between Caesar and the
senate.

**175. Petitio.**    In the interval between the *professio* and
the election came the *petitio*, although in point of fact in
the last years of the republic the political canvass began at
least a year before the election.    Candidates for office
appeared in the forum clad in a newly whitened toga.

Cic. ad Att.
I. I. I;
Liv. 4. 25. 13;
7. 15. 12–13.

They shook hands with voters, and took care to have a
well-attended *salutatio*, and to be accompanied by large
escorts in going to and fro.    They sometimes gave largesses, contributed money out of their own pockets for the
public games, and aimed at securing the support of guilds
and political clubs.    Of course success in a foreign war
gave a candidate prestige, and full use was made of this
fact.    As the right of citizenship was extended beyond

Cic. ad Att.
I. I. 2.

the limits of Rome, electioneering tours were undertaken
throughout Italy.    General public meetings to promote the
interests of a particular person do not seem to have been
held, but candidates probably had an opportunity to set
forth their political " platforms," and to criticise their
opponents at *contiones* called by friendly magistrates to
discuss public measures, and doubtless certain clubs and
guilds held meetings of a political character.    That candidates for office were not contented with the use of legitimate political methods is shown by the passage of numerous
bribery laws from the early part of the second century
onwards (cf. p. 71), and by legislation against the *sodalicia*,
or political clubs.

**176. Elections.** All elective magistrates were chosen by the *populus*, *i.e.*, in the *comitia centuriata* or the patricio-plebeian *comitia tributa*. In the former the consuls, praetors, and censors were elected. Curule aediles and quaestors were chosen in the *comitia tributa*. Tribunes and plebeian aediles were elected in the *concilium plebis*. For the centuriate *comitia*, meeting as an electoral body, the presiding officer was the dictator, consul, or interrex; for the tribal *comitia*, the dictator, consul, or praetor; for the *concilium plebis*, the tribune. After Sulla's time elections took place usually in the latter part of July. The exact date was fixed by the magistrate. A postponement was not uncommon in the later years of the republic. Thus, in 59, the elections were not held until October, while bribery and violence prevented them from being held at all in 54. Even after a majority of the votes had been cast for a candidate his election did not become valid until a formal announcement (*renuntiatio*) of the result had been made by the presiding officer, and cases were by no means unknown where the chairman had refused to declare a certain person elected.

Gell. 13. 15. 4

Tac. Ann. 11. 22; Liv. 9. 46. 1 f.

Cic. ad Att. 9. 9. 3.

St. R. I. 584, n. 5.

Cic. ad Att. 2. 20. 6.

Cic. ad Q. fr. 2. 16. 3; Dio, 40. 17.

Vell. 2. 92. 3-4; Val. Max. 3. 8. 3.

**177. Entrance on Office and Retirement from It.** In Cicero's day the quaestors assumed office December 5, the tribunes December 10, the consuls and all the other magistrates January 1. Early in the morning of the first of January one of the newly elected consuls took the auspices, went to the capitol, attended by senators, and made a sacrifice to Jupiter. Later in the day he called a meeting of the senate, which was attended by the other magistrates, to consider public questions of a general character. Within five days after taking office, magistrates were expected to take an oath to support the laws (*iurare in leges*). Those magistrates who were to hold the *imperium*

Cic. in Verr. Act. i. 30; C. I. L. I. 202

Ov. Fast. I. 79 ff.; Suet. Aug. 26; Liv. 26. 26. 5

Gell. 13. 15. 4;
Cic. de Leg.
Agr. 2. 26 ff.
were required to secure the passage of the *lex curiata
de imperio*. Some fictitious importance was given to this
formal act in the later years of the republic by the opposition of the tribunes. A magistrate could resign before
his term of office had expired, and, in case of criminal conduct, moral pressure could be brought to bear upon him
to induce him to resign, as was done in 63 in the case of

Cic. in Cat.
3. 15.
St. R. I. 628 f.
Lentulus. He could be removed from office, however, only
by the people who had elected him, but this radical step was
rarely taken in times of peace (cf. pp. 95, 135).

**178. Responsibility of Magistrates.** Theoretically, magistrates, like private citizens, were amenable to the laws, and
civil or criminal action could be brought against them
either during their term of office or after its expiration.
However, certain considerations of a theoretical and practical nature put a check on the application of this principle
in its extreme form. Thus action could not be brought
against a magistrate in office unless the judge before whom

Suet. Iul. 17;
Digest, 4. 8. 4.
the case came had the *maior potestas*. The consul was,
therefore, exempt from trial during his term of office,
because no magistrate had the *maior potestas* over him.
Furthermore, the danger of interfering with the transaction of public business usually checked any attempts to
hold even a lower magistrate responsible in the courts,
until his term had expired. The dictator could not be
called to account in any case, and, although the censor
does not seem to have been exempted by law from
responsibility for his conduct, the proper performance of
his duties involved the exercise of so much discretion
that no successful action ever appears to have been
brought against him. The development of one phase of
the tribune's functions deserves special notice in this
connection. From the outset he was vested with the right

to inflict a summary punishment on any one who violated the sanctity of his person, or disregarded his veto power. As we have already noticed (p. 76), the irregularity of this procedure, and the theory that a failure to recognize the rights of the representative of the plebs was an offense against the dignity of the whole order, led to the practice of bringing such cases, especially if magistrates were offenders, before the *concilium plebis*. Before this court ex-magistrates were freely held responsible for malfeasance in office, embezzlement of public funds, and for other offenses of a more or less political character. After the establishment of the *quaestiones de repetundis, de ambitu*, and *de maiestate* (cf. p. 106), offending magistrates, especially provincial governors, at the end of their term of office were brought before these courts. The purpose of these actions was often, not to secure justice, but to win an advantage by discrediting a political opponent.

## SELECTED BIBLIOGRAPHY[1]

Mommsen, Röm. Staatsrecht, 3 vols.  (Vols. I and II in 3d ed.) Leipzig, 1887.  (Cited in reference, *St. R.*)

Herzog, Geschichte u. System d. röm. Staatsverfassung, 2 vols. Leipzig, 1884-7.  (Cited in reference, *Herz.*)

Bouché-Leclercq, Manuel des institutions Romaines.  Paris, 1886. (Cited in reference, *B.-L.*)

Madvig, Verfassung u. Verwaltung d. röm. Staates, 2 vols.  Leipzig, 1881-2.  (Cited in reference, *Madv.*)

Schiller, Staats- und Rechtsaltertümer in Müller's Handbuch, Bd. IV.[2]  Munich, 1893.  (Cited in reference, *Sch.*)

---

[1] General works of reference like the Dictionaries of Classical Antiquities by Seyffert (revised by Nettleship and Sandys), by Smith (revised by Wayte and Marindin), by Daremberg and Saglio, and by Peck, and Pauly's Real-Encyclopädie (4 vols. now published, revised by Wissowa) may also be consulted with profit in connection with this chapter and with those which follow.

Lange, Römische Alterthümer, 3 vols.  Berlin, 1876–9.

Mispoulet, Les institutions politiques des Romains, 2 vols.   Paris, 1882.

Ad. Nissen, Das Iustitium.  Leipzig, 1877.   (Cited in reference, *Nissen, Iust.*)

Mommsen, Die Rechtsfrage zwischen Cäsar u. dem Senat.  Breslau, 1857.

Karlowa, Römische Rechtsgeschichte, Vol. I.  Leipzig, 1885.

H. Nissen, Das Templum.  Berlin, 1869.

Bruns, Fontes iuris Romani antiqui, ed. VI. cura Theodori Mommseni et Ottonis Gradenwitz.  Lipsiae, 1893.   (Cited in reference, *Bruns.*)

Willems, Le droit public Romain, 6th ed.  Louvain, 1888.   (Cited in reference, *Will. Dr.*)

## SUPPLEMENTARY LITERATURE, 1901–1910

De Ruggiero, Il consolato e i poteri pubblici in Roma.  Rome, 1900.

Le Jeune, L'imperium des magistrats de Rome sous la république.  Rennes, 1889.

# CHAPTER IX

## THE SEVERAL MAGISTRACIES

### (a) *The Consul*

**179. The Consul's Alternative Titles.** At the beginning of the republican period the two chief magistrates were called *praetores, iudices,* or *consules*. The significance of the first two titles is correctly explained in Cic. *de Legg.* III. 8: *regio imperio duo sunto, iique praeeundo, iudicando, consulendo, praetores, iudices, consules appellamino*. Perhaps it was because the functions of the chief-magistrate as commander-in-chief of the army surpassed his civil duties in importance and dignity that he was commonly styled *praetor* in the early period. Perhaps *praetor* indicated his military, and *iudex* his civil functions. At all events, after 367, when the jurisdiction of the chief-magistrate in civil cases was transferred to the incumbent of the newly established magistracy, the former is regularly called consul. Cicero's explanation of the word *consul* is not correct. The title indicates rather that the supreme power was held by more than one person. In this respect of course the position of the republican chief-magistrate was distinguished from that of the king.

Legg. XII.<br>Tab.;<br>Liv. 3. 55. 12

**180. Collegiality.** What has been said (pp. 167–172) in a previous chapter, dealing with the magistrates in general, with reference to eligibility for office, method of nomination, candidacy, elections, entrance on office, and retirement from it, is peculiarly applicable to the consulship.

Both members of this college were at all times vested with the full power of their office. To avoid a conflict of authority, so far as it was possible to avoid it under this system, in the early period, as we have already noticed (p. 155), the consuls took turns month by the month in exercising the right of the initiative, the older of the two enjoying this privilege for the first month of the official year. The consul who was thus honored during a given month was sometimes called *consul maior*. This method of alternation, however, was probably given up before Cicero's time, although it was restored by Caesar. The other methods of avoiding a conflict which have been mentioned, were freely used. In time of war both consuls took the field in the early period, but, after Sulla's reform of the constitution (cf. p. 105), they rarely left the city and, therefore, rarely exercised the military *imperium*.

Cic. de Re
Publ. 2. 55;
Liv. 3. 36. 3;
Gell. 2. 15. 4.

Festus,
p. 161, ed. M.
Suet. Iul. 20.

**181. Ius cum Populo Patribusque Agendi.** The consul was vested with all the powers which belonged to the magistracy (pp. 157 f.). The functions peculiar to his office may be conveniently considered from the point of view of home politics and foreign politics. In the field of domestic affairs his most important powers were those which he exercised as chairman of the senate and of the assemblies of the *populus*. He alone of the regular magistrates could preside over the centuriate *comitia* called for the election of magistrates. The nomination of a dictator was also intrusted to him. Furthermore, custom had conferred on him alone the right to bring important bills before the *comitia centuriata* or the *comitia tributa*. His relations with the senate are more difficult to define. It was his duty to consult that body in important matters, but the law laid down no provisions to govern his action in specific cases, so that the question was left to his own discretion. He could even propose a measure in the popular assembly without securing the *auctoritas senatus*, or previous approval of the senate. This was the course which Caesar adopted in 59 in securing the passage of his agrarian bill. But the senate could usually bring such an attempt to naught by interposing religious diffi- culties, or by persuading a tribune to interpose his veto. In fact, Caesar's course in 59 was regarded as almost revo- lutionary. No satisfactory line of distinction can be drawn between the kind of legislation which the consul secured and that which was proposed by the tribune, except that the latter usually had a more partisan bias. Liv. Ep. 103

**182. Judicial Functions.** The establishment of the prae- torship in 367 took almost entirely from the consul his juris- diction in civil cases (*iurisdictio inter privatos*). Later only friendly transactions which needed the confirmation of the state's authority, like the manumission of a slave, or the emancipation of a son from the *patria potestas*, came under his jurisdiction. The laws establishing the right of appeal, the assumption of judicial powers by the *concilium plebis* (p. 76), and the establishment of the *quaestiones perpetuae* under the presidency of the praetors (p. 106), robbed the consul of his functions as a criminal judge, so far as citizens were concerned. Important criminal proceedings against foreigners and against slaves were, however, still left in his charge.

**183. Religious Duties.** The revolution of 509 trans- ferred the religious functions of the chief-magistrate to the priests. The consul, however, still had certain religious duties to perform, such as taking the auspices (p. 158), making sacrifices, pronouncing and performing vows in the name of the state, dedicating temples, and supervising certain public games. Liv. 9. 46. 6 21. 63. 7; 45. 1. 6.

**184. Financial Duties.** The control which the king, and the consul in the early republican period, had had over the finances of the state, was in later days exercised on the one hand by the senate and the people, on the other by the censor and the quaestor. The right to enact and repeal revenue laws was from the outset intrusted to the senate. In the later period the consuls also adopted the practice of consulting the senate with reference to the expenditure of public funds, until in course of time that body acquired in large measure the control of the public treasury. The financial powers of the consul were still further limited by the establishment of the censorship, and by the elevation of the quaestorship to an independent elective office. The quaestor alone could authorize the payment of public moneys, and the censor, during his term of office at least, had exclusive charge of the *ager publicus*, the farming of the taxes, and the construction of public buildings and public works. However, the consul took charge of most matters of this sort during the last three and a half years of a *lustrum* after the censor had gone out of office.

Liv. 2. 9. 6;
23. 31. 1.

Liv. 44.16.1 f.;
Cic. in Vat.
36.

**185. Functions of the Consul outside the City.** As we have already noticed (p. 161), a sharp line of distinction was drawn between the powers which a magistrate could exercise at home (*domi*) and abroad (*militiae*). Up to this point we have considered the consul's powers and duties in the city. Outside the city his functions consisted mainly in conducting campaigns, and in representing the home government in its dealings with Italy, the provinces, and with independent states.

**186. The Consul as Commander-in-Chief.** A declaration of war always required the favorable action of the centuriate *comitia*. The consul, however, retained the right to call the citizens to arms in case of an emergency, but, as the military operations of Rome increased in importance, and more than two generals in the field were required, the whole question of the levy and the organization of the army was submitted to the senate for its consideration. After 207 also the choice of the *tribuni militum* for the four legions of the regular levy was taken out of the hands of the consul and made by popular election. When military operations were carried on at a single point, the consuls had the supreme command on alternate days. When two campaigns were being carried on at the same time, the senate was often asked to assign the two consuls to their respective fields, and in this way that body made its influence felt still further in the management of military affairs. In the general conduct of a campaign the consul was given a free hand, although at its close he might be held responsible before the *concilium plebis* (pp. 172–3) for such military offenses as cowardice or ill-treatment of prisoners. In the early period apparently the chief-magistrate could conclude a valid treaty of peace with an enemy, but in later times, perhaps after the humiliating treaty of the Caudine Forks in 321, the right to conclude a permanent treaty of peace was taken by the people as its exclusive prerogative. The magisterial right to sue for a triumph, for the title of *imperator*, and for a *supplicatio* has already been discussed (pp. 161 f.).

Liv. 27. 36. 14

Liv. 22. 45. 4–5.

Liv. 9. 5. 1

**187. The Consul's Duties in Italy.** The control which the consul had over Italy outside of Rome and that which he exercised over the provinces differed essentially, for two reasons. In the first place, the provincials were not citizens, while in the first century the Italians had the rights of citizenship in full, or to a limited extent. Furthermore, each province was a political unit subject to its governor, while in Italy affairs other than those of a purely local, fiscal, or judicial character were directed from Rome. The relations which the Italian communities bore to the central government were determined by treaties (cf. p. 59), and one of the principal duties of the consul was to secure the observance of these treaty relations, and, with the coöperation of the senate (cf. p. 236), to suppress conspiracies and put down serious uprisings. In his military capacity he took charge of the contingents of troops furnished by the Italian allies, and protected Italy from inroads from across the frontier.

Liv. 10. 1. 3.

188. **The Consul in the Provinces.** In the early period, foreign campaigns, as well as those in Italy, were conducted by the consul. In case a praetor was already in charge of the province where the war was being carried on, he assumed the same relation to the consul which he would have held to him if both magistrates had been in Rome. If the province was not under a praetorian governor, the consul took upon himself all civil and military duties. Sulla's legislation extended to all the provinces the practice of sending out ex-magistrates as governors at the end of their term of office at Rome, so that after his dictatorship the consul had no occasion to go into a province during his term of office. Sulla's arrangement was slightly modified by the law of 52 which fixed an interval of five years between the incumbency of a magistracy at Rome and the assumption of a provincial governorship.

Dio, 40. 56;
Caes. B. C.
1. 85. 9.

Through the consul also negotiations were carried on with other states. He received embassies, introduced them to the senate, when he saw fit to do so, referred questions of international politics to that body for discussion, and laid before the popular assembly the recommendations of the senate with reference to an offensive war or a treaty of peace.

**189. The Quaestio Extraordinaria, Senatus Consultum Ultimum, and Iustitium.** Certain exceptional powers given to the consul, or assumed by him on his own responsibility in an emergency, are on the border line between his powers *domi* and *militiae*. These extraordinary powers came to him in one of three ways : through the establishment of a *quaestio extraordinaria*, the passage of a *senatus consultum ultimum*, or the announcement of a *iustitium*. When crimes of a political character had been committed by private citizens or by magistrates, for the adjudication of which the ordinary courts seemed unsuitable, the investigation of the accused persons, and their punishment, if found guilty, were sometimes intrusted to special courts under the presidency of the consuls and the other higher magistrates. In such cases the right of appeal was suspended. When a conspiracy, an insurrection, or a revolution threatened public security, or the integrity of the state, the senate at times, instead of instructing the consul to appoint a dictator, passed the *senatus consultum ultimum*, so called, which, under the interpretation put on it for many years, suspended the right of appeal and the tribunician veto power. A *iustitium* could probably be declared by the consul on his own responsibility, but this was so extreme a step to take, that the senate was usually consulted beforehand. The *iustitium* involved the suspension of public business, in particular of fiscal and judicial business, and the closing of the shops.

Liv. 42. 21. 5;
Cic. de Fin.
2. 54.

Liv. 3. 4. 9;
Sall. Cat. 29;
Caes. B. C.
1. 5. 3.
Cic. de Har.
Resp. 55;
Phil. 5. 31;
Liv. 3. 27. 2

### (b) *The Dictator and Magister Equitum*

**190. Appointment of a Dictator.** The consul, as we have already noticed (pp. 25 f.), inherited the political powers of the king, except that he was subject, either at the outset or at an early period, to the checks put on him by the principle of collegiality, the right of appeal, the tribunician veto, and the possibility of being held accountable for his conduct. From all these limitations the dictator in the early period was relieved. A dictator was appointed when the integrity of the commonwealth was threatened by wars without or by dissensions within the borders of the state.

The power to appoint was vested in the consuls. Sometimes the two consuls acted together in making the choice. At other times one of them was chosen by lot to select the dictator. The veto of a colleague or of a tribune was not recognized. Constitutionally the senate had no voice in the matter, but, during the period of its supremacy, that body usually passed on the advisability of choosing a dicta-

tor, and secured the appointment of the individual favored by it. An important change in the method of appointment was made during the second Punic war after the disastrous defeat at Lake Trasimenus. The necessity of choosing a dictator was recognized by every one, and, as if by common consent, an act authorizing the appointment was passed

by one of the popular assemblies. This irregular method of procedure was followed on one or two subsequent occasions also. The choice was usually limited to ex-consuls, but there does not seem to have been any legal restriction covering this point.

**191. His Powers and Duties.** The consuls and other magistrates continued in office after the appointment of

a dictator, but he exercised the right of *maius imperium* (p. 153) over them. He could, however, if he pleased, force them to resign. Inasmuch as his duties involved mainly the preservation of order or its restoration, the exercise of his functions rarely brought him into conflict with the praetor, censor, or aedile, so that the business of those officials was carried on without interruption during a dictatorship. He was attended by twenty-four lictors, who carried axes even within the city. The appointment of a dictator curtailed the rights of the individual citizen. He was in a way also a representative of the conservative party. It is not strange, therefore, that the party of progress fiercely attacked the institution, and as that party grew in power it succeeded in making good the right of appeal, perhaps in 300, and the right of a tribune to interpose his veto — a right which was gained toward the close of the third century. The dictator was never held responsible for his conduct, however, and there is only one recorded instance where a colleague was chosen. Still the two changes mentioned above robbed the dictatorship of its importance in large measure, and the last incumbent of the office was chosen in 202. Dictators were appointed not only *seditionis sedandae causa*, but also to perform certain political or religious acts which could not well be performed by the regular magistrates. Thus they were chosen *comitiorum habendorum*, *feriarum constituendarum*, and *clavi figendi causa*.

**192. Term of Office.** The dictator was expected to lay down his office when the business for which he had been chosen had been brought to an end. The maximum term was six months. The dictatorship of Sulla (p. 104) and of Caesar (pp. 134 f.) in the first century B.C. was, therefore, essentially different in this respect from those of the early period. Sulla assumed the office for an indefinite period, and Caesar for life. Some of the other points in which this new magistracy differed from the old one are noted elsewhere (pp. 135, 218). On the motion of Antony the dictatorship was abolished after Caesar's death.

**193. The Magister Equitum.** At the outset the dictator was called *magister populi*, a term which throws some light

Polyb. 3. 87. 7; Liv. 2. 18. 8.

Liv. 27. 6. 5; Festus, p. 198, ed. M

Liv. 22. 25.

Liv. 7. 22. 10; 9. 34. 12; 27. 33. 6.

Cic. Phil. I. 32.

Cic. de Re Publ. 1. 63.

on the relation which his subordinate, the *magister equitum*, bore to him. The dictatorship was primarily a military office, and its incumbent commanded the infantry, while the *magister equitum* had charge of the cavalry. If we think of the dictator as vested for a short time with the powers of the king, which is essentially true for the early period, the *magister equitum* corresponds to the king's chief military subordinate, the *tribunus celerum* (p. 16). He was appointed by the dictator, was the dictator's immediate subordinate, and during the absence of that official received his exceptional powers. He went out of office with his superior. He was attended by six lictors, wore the *praetexta*, and probably used the curule chair on official occasions. He ranked just below the praetor (p. 168). The office became extinct when the dictatorship was given up, but was revived by Caesar.

*Cic. de Legg. 3. 9; Varro, L. L. 5. 82.*

*Liv. 9. 38. 14 f.*

*Dio, 42. 27.*

### (c) The Consular Tribune

**194. Origin of the Consular Tribunate.** Roman historians give as one reason for the establishment of the consular tribunate the development of military operations and the need of more than two generals in the field. This may have been a subsidiary motive, but the real explanation of the change is probably the one given in a previous chapter (p. 34). From the earliest times the armed force of the community had been commanded by *tribuni militum*. These were at first three in number, then six, and, when more than one legion was levied, six for each legion. The establishment of the office of *tribuni militum consulari potestate* meant simply the investiture of a certain number of these purely military officials with the political powers of the consul. This was accomplished by an election in

*Liv. 4. 7. 2.*

the centuriate *comitia*. All citizens served in the army Liv. 5. 52. 16. and were eligible to the office of *tribunus militum*, so that the substitution of consular tribunes for consuls involved the admission of plebeians to the chief magistracy, Liv. 4. 6. 8. and satisfied their demands in part, while at the same time, as we have already noticed (p. 34), the patricians left a way open to restore to their own class its exclusive political privileges, when a favorable opportunity presented itself.

**195. Number of the Consular Tribunes and their Powers.** The normal number six was suggested by the number of military tribunes in charge of each legion. The numbers three and four, which are not uncommon in the college, may be due to the fact that they adapted themselves readily to the system of monthly sequence during the year. As their title indicates, these officials had all the Liv. 4. 7. 2. powers and insignia of the consul, even the right to take the auspices and to name a dictator. The only particulars in which the power and dignity of the office were inferior to those of the consul seem to have been that the consular tribunes could not delegate their authority, could Liv. 4. 45. 7 f.;<br>St. R. II. 190. not triumph at the close of their term of office, and did not enjoy the privileges which ex-consuls had. The last distinction is of both political and social importance. Those who had been consular tribunes did not have the right of priority in speaking and voting in the senate, which was one of the privileges of ex-consuls. In fact, plebeians who had filled the office were probably not allowed to take part in the debate at all. This limitation St. R. III.<br>962. more than any other must have made the plebeians dissatisfied with the compromise. Furthermore, ex-consular tribunes did not have the *ius imaginum* (p. 166).

**196. Disappearance of the Office.** The office lasted from 444 to 367. It was abolished by the Licinian law. Liv. 6. 35. 5.

During the period of its continuance there were fifty-one
colleges of consular tribunes and twenty-two of consuls, and
for four years, from 375 to 371, there were no curule magistrates. In the year 53 it was proposed to reëstablish the
consular tribunate, in order to satisfy the rival candidates for
the chief-magistracy by increasing the number of positions
available, but the plan was not carried out.

St. R. II. 191.

### (d) The Praetor

**197. Relation of the Praetor to the Consul.** The circumstances under which the praetorship was established have
been noticed elsewhere (p. 37). The new magistrate was
regarded as the *collega consulum*, and in the early period
ex-consuls were not infrequently elected to the office.
Certain important duties which had belonged to the consul
were taken from him and assigned to the praetor. It was
very natural, therefore, to regard the praetor as equal in
dignity to the consul. In point of fact the sphere within
which he exercised his regular functions was so sharply
defined, and he was made so complete a master of it, that
there was little danger of conflict between him and the
consul. When such conflict came, however, the principle
of *maius imperium* was recognized, and the praetor was
forced to yield. His inferior position was indicated to
the eye by the fact that he was attended by only six
lictors, and in the later period he was accompanied by
only two when performing his judicial duties in the city.

Gell. 13. 15. 4;
Cic. ad Att.
9. 9. 3;
Liv. 7. 1. 6.

Liv. 6. 42. 11

Gell. 13. 15. 4.

Appian,
Syr. 15.

**198. Method of Election; Title.** Certain practices observed in electing praetors bring out in a concrete way
the relation which the consul and the praetor bore to each
other. As Aulus Gellius says (*N. A.* XIII. 15. 4): *praetor,
etsi conlega consulis est, neque praetorem neque consulem iure*

*rogare potest, . . . quia imperium minus praetor, maius habet consul, et a minore imperio maius aut maior conlega rogari iure non potest.* Patricians only were eligible to the office at first, but within thirty years of its establishment it was thrown open to the plebeians also (p. 42), whether by law or otherwise is not clear. The chief-magistrate lost the title of praetor and it was given to the new official (p. 175), although it did not suggest his duties as well as *iudex* would have done.

**199. Three Periods of the Praetorship.** The history of the praetorship, from the point of view of the functions which the incumbents of the office exercised, falls into three periods — from 367 to 227, from 227 to 81, and from 81 down into the empire. In the first period the special duties of the praetor were judicial. In the second period the college of praetors was divided into two sections. The members of one section were judges; those of the other were provincial governors. In the third period, under the republic, all of the praetors were judges at Rome, during their first year of office, and provincial governors the following year.

**200. Development of the Praetorship.** There was only one praetor at the outset. This fact distinguishes the praetorship from all the other magistracies. From the theoretical point of view, however, as we have seen, the praetor was regarded as the colleague of the two consuls, and, therefore, in a vague way may have been at first thought of as a member of the college to which the consuls belonged. The judicial duties of the praetor confined him to the city, while the consuls, his two colleagues, if we may so call them, were frequently engaged in carrying on wars abroad. In consequence of this difference he was styled *praetor urbanus.* The duties of the new magistracy increased to such an extent that in 242 it was found necessary to choose

Liv. Ep. 19.

a second praetor. The *praetor urbanus* assumed charge of all civil suits in which citizens only were interested, while the new magistrate officiated when one party or

Liv. 22. 35. 5.

both parties were *peregrini*. It was from this fact that he received his distinguishing title of *praetor peregrinus.* Along with the increase in the size of the college of

Liv. 22. 35. 6;
32. 27. 6.

praetors in 227 to four, and in 197 to six, went a change in the functions of certain of the incumbents of the office, for, as we have already noticed (p. 71), the four new praetors were added to take charge of the four newly acquired provinces. To meet the increasing demand for provincial governors, and to provide for the transaction of judicial business in the city, the Romans were obliged to

St. R. II.
198 ff.

resort frequently to the *prorogatio imperii.* The adoption of this device in the case of the praetor made his office practically one of two years. So far as the term of office was concerned, it was not a radical change which Sulla made, therefore, in formally assigning to every praetor one year in Rome and one year in a province. The importance of the change consisted in the fact that from this time to the fall of the republic the functions of all the praetors were essentially the same, and that all of them

St. R. II.
200 ff.

assumed judicial duties for a year and undertook the government of a province for the following year. The number of praetors, which Sulla raised to eight, was increased by

Dio, 42. 51;
43. 47; 43. 49.

Caesar to ten, then to fourteen, and ultimately to sixteen.

**201. Division of Duties.** From the time when more than one praetor was chosen, the principle of collegiality, and

Cic. in Verr.
ii. 1. 119.

the consequent possibility of exercising the veto power, was recognized; but it did not have much meaning for the praetor's office, because the duties of the several praetors were quite distinct from one another. It occasionally found expression in a positive way in the joint action of two or more praetors in a matter concerning them all. The *praetor urbanus* took precedence of all his colleagues, and assumed the chief-magistracy during the absence of both the consuls. The assignment of each praetor to his *provincia*, or sphere of duties, was made by lot. From Sulla's time the casting of lots took place after the election to determine the praetor's functions for the first year, and during the first year of office to decide which provinces should be governed by the several praetors during the second year.

Liv. 24 9 5

**202. Powers of the Praetor.** The praetor's powers were of three different sorts. He acted as a judge, as a provincial governor, and as an administrative officer. The details of judicial procedure and the duties of a provincial governor are given elsewhere, but one or two facts of a general character bearing on his judicial duties may be stated here.

**203. The Praetor as a Criminal Judge.** To the constitutional changes already mentioned in the functions of the praetor, which divide the history of his office into three periods, may be added the change which resulted from the establishment of the *quaestiones perpetuae* (cf. pp. 74, 106). These courts were put under the presidency of the praetor. Up to the time of their establishment he had been solely a civil judge, but henceforth he conducted criminal cases also. The development of the praetor's criminal jurisdiction out of the civil is not hard to understand. The earliest *quaestio perpetua*, that to try governors charged with extortion, was from one point of view a civil court, in which those who had suffered had the right of complaint. From another point of view the proceeding assumed the character of a criminal action, since the offense had been committed by a state official and was to the detriment of the state.

**204. The Edictum Praetorium.** Of the magisterial powers mentioned above (pp. 157 ff.) the *ius edicendi* assumed the greatest importance at the hands of the praetor. On taking office he published the maxims of law and the forms of procedure (*formulae*) by which he would be governed throughout the year of his office. This edict was properly called, therefore, an *edictum perpetuum*. A praetor commonly adopted the edict of his predecessor, making such additions and changes as seemed to him and his advisers desirable, and in this way a large part of the Roman civil and criminal law was developed. The edicts of the *praetor peregrinus* formed in a similar way the basis of the *ius gentium*.

Ascon. in Cornel., p. 58, ed. Or.

**205. The Praetor as an Administrative Officer.** Administrative action was taken by the praetor, either in his capacity as an independent magistrate, or as the representative of the consul. Action in the first case was usually taken under the authorization of the senate, and covered such matters as presiding over the *comitia* when laws were being passed or inferior magistrates elected. Furthermore, he conducted civil and military affairs under the direction of the consul, and, as noted above, in the absence of the consuls the *praetor urbanus* became with certain limitations the chief-magistrate.

Cic. pro Balbo, 55; Liv. 8. 17. 12; 27. 5. 16.

## (e) *The Censor*

**206. Collegiality.** The censorship was established in 443 or 435 (cf. p. 37). In the case of this office the collegiate principle was carried out in its extreme form. A majority of the centuries must cast their votes for both members of the college at the same meeting to make an election valid. If one censor retired from office, his

Liv. 5. 31. 6; 9. 34. 25; 45. 15. 8.

colleague must also withdraw, and joint action was necessary in all important matters. This requirement of joint action furnished the principal safeguard of the citizen against the arbitrary action of one member of the college, since the censors were practically unaccountable for their official actions.

**207. Election of Censors ; Term of Office.** At the outset patricians only were eligible. The first plebeian was elected to the office in 351, and a few years later the principle governing eligibility to the consulship was applied to the censorship also. One censor must be plebeian ; both might be. Censors were elected in the centuriate *comitia* under the presidency of the consul, and entered on their offices immediately after their election. New censors were chosen at intervals of four or five years, and held office for a year and a half. The business left unfinished at the end of their term of office was turned over mainly to the consuls and aediles. Technically the censorship stood below the praetorship (p. 168), but in practical importance and in public esteem it was rated much higher. In fact, during the first half of the second century it surpassed all the other magistracies in dignity and influence. Consuls and praetors did not have the right to veto the action of the censor, and the tribune rarely exercised it. The censor sat in the curule chair on formal occasions, and, when inaugurated, wore the purple toga. On the other hand, he was not vested with the *imperium*, and consequently was not attended by lictors (cf. p. 166). He did not have the right to convoke the senate or the *comitia*.

Liv. 10. 8. 8.

Liv. 8. 12. 16.

Liv. 32. 7. 1; Gell. 13. 15. 4.

Varro, L. L. 6. 11; Censorinus, 18. 13; Herz. I. 759, n. 3; St. R. II. 332 ff.

Liv. 40. 45. 8 Polyb. 6. 53. 7.

**208. The Duties of the Censor.** The administrative duties of the office consisted (1) in assessing the property of citizens and arranging them in tribes, classes, and centuries, (2) in revising the lists of knights and senators,

(3) in managing the finances of the state. In their performance of these duties the censors exercised a general supervision over the morals of the community.

**209. Preliminaries to the Census.** The first step in the assessment of property was to summon all citizens to a *contio* in the Campus Martius, where the *formula census* which stated the principles to be followed in making the assessment and the lists was announced. Those summoned were *omnes Quirites*, [*equites*] *pedites*, *armati privatique*, *curatores omnium tribuum*, *si quis pro se sive pro altero rationem dare volet* (Varro, *L. L.* VI. 86). It will be noted that those who were exempt from military service on the score of age or physical disability, as well as those who were subject to it, were required to present themselves. Boys who were not under the *patria potestas* and women who were not under the legal control of either father or husband were required to appear, and were registered in a special list. Those who failed to be registered, the *incensi*, were liable to the loss of personal freedom and property, but in the later period the assessment of their property was made without their assistance, and they escaped the penalty. The censors were assisted by the *curatores tribuum*, or administrative representatives of the several tribes, and by a *concilium* made up of officials and expert advisers.

**210. The Census and the Nota.** Every citizen was required to give his name, age, domicile, the name of his father or former owner, his tribe, his family circumstances, the number of years of military service which he had rendered, and the amount of his taxable property. On the basis of the information thus obtained the censors determined the taxes and drew up the lists of citizens according to tribes, classes, and centuries. The basis of classification

Lex Iul.
Munic.
ll. 145 ff.

is discussed elsewhere (pp. 250–251). Law or custom had laid upon them, in the performance of this duty, the obligation of inquiring into the manner of life (*mores*) of every citizen, and in particular of finding out the way in which each one had performed his duty to the state. The commission of a crime like theft, an objectionable mode of life, cowardice in the presence of the enemy, malfeasance in office, and similar matters might lead the censors to assign a citizen to a large tribe (*tribu movere*) and thus diminish the value of his vote, or to deprive him of his centuriate vote (*inter aerarios referre*), to take from a knight his horse (*adimere equum*), or to remove a name from the list of senators (*senatu movere*). The infliction of this punishment was indicated by placing a *nota* after a citizen's name in the list. The effect of the punishment lasted until a new census was made. It was within the censor's power also to issue proclamations forbidding extravagance and scandalous methods of living.

*Liv. 4. 8. 2; 39. 44; Cic. de Legg. 3. 7*

*Gell. 4. 20. 6; 17. 21. 39; Cic. de Re Publ. 4. 10; de Or. 2. 272.*

**211. The Recognitio Equitum.** Admission to knighthood depended mainly on the possession of a certain amount of property. In the late republic and early empire the minimum required was 400,000 sesterces. The general assessment of citizens in the Campus would, therefore, enable the censor to draw up the list of knights, but in the case of the *equites equo publico* a special ceremony took place in the forum. Each knight whose equipment was furnished by the state was required to bring his horse for inspection by the censors. If the state of his equipment and his previous record were satisfactory, he received the order, *traduc equum;* otherwise, *vende equum.* Rewards for distinguished service were also granted at this time.

*Hor. Epist. 1. 1. 58; Plin. N. H 33. 32.*

*Liv. 29. 37 9–10.*

**212. The Lectio Senatus.** The duty of revising the list of senators was assigned to the censor by the Ovinian law (cf. pp. 46 f.) toward the close of the fourth century, and contributed largely to the importance of that magistrate's office. He enjoyed, and, during the period of the censorship's greatest influence, exercised freely the right to drop men from the senate and to fill vacancies. The reform of Sulla took this power from him (p. 105), and, even after the repeal of a large part of Sulla's legislation, the censor did not regain the right to add names to the list of senators. He recovered, however, the power of removal.

**213. Management of Public Finances.** To the censor fell the collection of revenue (*vectigalia*) and the expenditure of public moneys (*ultro tributa*). The most important matters under the first head consisted in farming out the taxes to the highest bidder (*maximis pretiis*), in selling or renting public land, and in granting for a fixed sum certain privileges controlled by the state. The most important expenditure which came under the control of the censor was that entailed by the construction or repair of public buildings, roads, bridges, and aqueducts. The range of his duties in this respect, however, did not often extend beyond Rome and the Italian roads. The work was commonly done by contractors (*conductores*), and paid for out of funds placed at the disposal of the censors by the senate. A record of the contracts made by them (*leges censoriae*) was kept in the *aerarium*. Questions of taxation at issue between the state and individual citizens, and matters in dispute between the state and *publicani* or *conductores*, were submitted to the censor for settlement (cf. p. 163), and this phase of his official duties must have been very important.

Liv. 1. 28. 1;
1. 44. 1-2;
29. 37. 1 f.;
Suet. Aug
97; Serv. on
Aen. 8. 183.

**214. Completion of the Lustrum.** The conclusion of the census was marked by a *sacrificium lustrale*, or offering of a boar, a ram, and a bull (*suovetaurilia*), in the Campus.

After that the censor led the assembled army to the city gate, dismissed it, drove a nail in the wall of a certain temple, deposited the list of citizens in the *aerarium*, and laid down his office. Unfinished business, and new business which might arise before new censors were chosen, were managed by the consuls, aediles, and quaestors.

**215. Census outside of Rome.** By the *lex Iulia municipalis* (cf. ll. 1, 42 ff.) of the year 45, arrangements were made for taking the census in the *municipia* throughout Italy, and for reporting the results at Rome sixty days before the completion of the Roman census.

**216. Decline of the Censorship.** The reasons for the decline and disappearance of the censorship are not far to seek. With the rapid increase of the population, and of the financial interests of the state, the censors were unable to perform within the specified time the duty assigned to them. Toward the close of the second century, and in the early part of the first century, their work was either left undone or done in an unsatisfactory manner. Furthermore, the method which Sulla introduced of filling the senate (cf. p. 105), robbed the censor of one of his most important duties. In fact, there were no censors between 80 and 70. A third agency which contributed to the downfall of the censorship was the fact that with the growth of the city the censors were unable to maintain their control over the morals of the community, and that to make matters worse the *nota* came to be used as a political weapon, so that the right to affix it was curtailed by law in 58. Although the law was repealed six years later, this function of the censor's office never regained its significance.

Herz. I. 796 f

Ascon., p. 9, ed. Or.; Cic pro Sest. 55

## (f) The Tribune

**217. Election, Number, Insignia, Assistants.** The tribune never became a magistrate in the strict sense of the
word (cf. p. 151), but, inasmuch as his functions in the
later years of the republic closely resembled those of a
magistrate, the office may be conveniently discussed at
this point. The law always required a candidate for the
tribunate to be a plebeian. From 494 to 471, tribunes were
probably elected in a plebeian curiate assembly (cf. p. 29).
After the latter date they were chosen in the plebeian
tribal assembly, presided over by a tribune. The number
of tribunes at the outset is uncertain. Perhaps there were
five, one representing each class. In 457 the number was
increased to ten, and this continued afterwards to be the
size of the college. The tribunes had no insignia of office.
In fact, the democratic character of the position was indicated by the simple *subsellia* on which they sat when
performing their official duties. At the outset the plebeian
aediles served as their assistants, but, as the importance and
also the duties of the aedile increased, the two offices drew
apart, and *viatores* were assigned to the tribune to help
him in the performance of his duties.

**218. Fundamental Power of the Tribune.** The tribunate
was established for one specific purpose, viz., to protect the
individual citizen, and especially the plebeian, from arbitrary
action on the part of a magistrate. His effective exercise
of this right was assured to him by two things. In the
first place, he could inflict punishment, even the punishment of death, on the magistrate who persisted in taking
a step which he had forbidden. In the second place, he
himself was sacrosanct, and any one could be put to death
with impunity, and without process of law, who violated

Herz. I. 152,
n. 3.

Liv. 42. 33. 1.

Liv. 2. 56. 13.

Gell. 13. 12. 9;
Cic. pro Tull.
47; Plut. Ti.
Gr. 10.

Val. Max.
9. 5. 2.

the sanctity of his person.   The prohibition of the tribune must, however, be delivered in person, and at the moment Gell. 13. 12. 6 when the contemplated action was being taken.   This fact accounts for the early increase of the number to ten, and Liv. 3. 30 7 for the establishment of the tradition that the tribune must not be absent from home for a night, and must leave his door open.   The principle underlying these arrangements explains also why the action forbidden by the tribune could be taken later, and become valid, unless again vetoed by him.   This power (*ius auxilii*) could be exercised only inside the first milestone.   Even the *ius cum plebe agendi* was possessed by the tribune before 449 only to the extent of convoking the plebs to elect his successor.

**219.  Why the Tribune's Power increased.**   Three factors united to bring about a rapid and far-reaching development of the tribune's powers.   One of these was the political tendency during the early centuries of republican history.   The other two were the inviolability of the tribune's person, and his power of inflicting punishment. From the establishment of the republic down to the middle of the fourth century there was a steady movement toward the equalization of the political rights of the plebeians and patricians.   The tribunes were the natural leaders of the plebeians in this movement, and an increase in their powers was a natural concomitant of the growth of the political rights of the plebeians.   However, without the protection which was given him by the sacrosanct character of his person, and by his right to impose an immediate penalty, he would have found it well-nigh impossible to make good his claims to new power or to overthrow the existing order of things.   With these powers he was almost invincible.   No system of government could permanently resist the *ius auxilii*, safeguarded as it was by the two privileges just mentioned. It is not easy to follow in the traditional account the development of the tribune's authority, but its course can be inferred with a high degree of probability.

**220. Powers of the Latest Tribunate.** In the later years of the republic these powers in the main were : (1) the *ius auxilii*, extended into the *ius intercedendi ;* (2) the *ius coercitionis*, with the complementary right of conducting criminal trials ; (3) the *ius cum plebe agendi ;* (4) the *ius cum patribus agendi ;* and (5) certain general administrative powers.

**221. The Intercessio.** The *intercessio* carried with it the right to thwart any official act of administration. It was directed against the magistrate and not, like the veto of a president, governor, or mayor, against a measure. In the case of the senate, the tribune had the right to impose his veto on the magistrate at any stage in the proceedings ; for instance, when a matter was being laid before the senate for consideration, when the senators were asked their opinions, or when the vote was ordered. In a similar way, when the *comitia* met for legislative or judicial purposes, the *intercessio* was admissible at any point, until the decision of the people had been finally announced. At first sight this extraordinary power seems to have little in common with the *latio auxilii*, which could only take place when a specific thing was being done to an individual by a magistrate, and when that individual called on the tribune for help. The greater power may well have developed out of the less, however, in this way : When the magistrate was instructed by the senate, for instance, to adopt a certain course affecting a large number of citizens, before the measure was carried into effect, the tribune may have announced his intention to protect any citizen against

Cic. ad Fam. 8. 8. 6; Tac. Hist. 4. 9; Liv. 9. 8. 13.

Ascon., p. 70, ed. Or.; Liv. 45. 21. 6.

whom the magistrate should try to carry out the senate's decree. The obvious result of such a declaration would be to make the measure of no effect, and we may well believe that a practical people like the Romans would consider it far better to get the opinion of the tribune, when a measure was under consideration, and to secure his approval, if possible, than to run the risk of passing an ineffective law. Furthermore, peaceable opposition to a bill under discussion was preferable to forcible opposition to an enacted law (cf. p. 38). The *intercessio* of the tribune did not prevent a magistrate from submitting a measure a second time to the senate or *comitia*, however, and if the tribune interposed no objection on the second occasion the bill became a law. The tribune could exercise a modified form of his veto, however, by asking for a night to consider the matter, instead of definitively prohibiting it. Occasionally the senate sought to prevent a tribune from interposing his veto by incorporating in a proposed measure a statement that if any tribune vetoed it he would be acting *contra rem publicam*, but this device does not seem to have been of much avail. The tribunician veto against a measure dealing with the consular provinces was not admissible (unless this restriction was removed in 52), nor could the tribune prevent the election of a magistrate. It is not clear what restrictions Sulla laid on the veto power of the tribune, but they do not seem to have been of a permanent character.

Cic. ad Fam. 8. 8. 6.

Cic. de Prov. Cons. 17.

Cic. de Legg. 3. 22; Caes. B. C. 1. 5. 1; 1. 7. 3.

**222. Criminal Jurisdiction of the Tribune.** As we have already noticed, the *lex sacrata* of 494 empowered the tribune to punish the magistrate who persisted in a course which he had forbidden, or who violated the sanctity of his person. This power was given to him because he represented in his person the rights of the plebeians. It

Cic. pro Tull. 47.

was exercised by him when the magistrate had transgressed in a specific case; but the whole policy of a magistrate might be prejudicial to the interests of the plebeians, and it was a natural development of the tribune's power to hold such a magistrate responsible for his conduct. A summary punishment inflicted by the tribune in such a case would hardly be appropriate, and, furthermore, the objectionable acts might have been committed away from Rome, or some time before. The practice, therefore, grew up of allowing the tribune to prosecute such offending magistrates before the plebeian assembly. But conduct prejudicial to the best interests of the plebeians was prejudicial to the whole state, for the patricians in the later period constituted an element numerically almost negligible in the community; or, to put it in another way, the community was practically a plebeian community, and offenses against the state could, without a serious violation of equity, be tried before the plebeian assembly. In this way the tribune became a public prosecutor, and the *concilium plebis* developed into a court for the trial of magistrates accused of such offenses as cowardice, appropriation of public funds, or illegal retention of office. This method of judicial procedure was gradually given up after the establishment of the *quaestiones perpetuae.*

223. **The Ius cum Plebe Agendi.** Down to 449 the *concilium plebis* met to elect tribunes and aediles, and perhaps also to adopt resolutions. The Valerio-Horatian laws of the year mentioned gave it the power to legislate for the whole community under certain conditions, and the legislation of 339 and 287 removed even these restrictions (pp. 49 ff.). Some of the effects of these changes on the tribune's position have already been noted (p. 45). Sulla limited the legislative competence of the tribune by making

the preliminary approval of the patrician members of the senate necessary to secure the validity of a plebiscitum, but this restriction was removed in the year 70.

**224. The Ius cum Patribus Agendi.** In the early period of the tribunate, the tribunes, as classical writers tell us, sat outside the doors of the senate and waited for the passage of bills by that body. The circumstances under which they were admitted to the senate-house and allowed to state their objections there have already been noticed (p. 38). This change would not have required the passage of a law. The right which the tribune acquired, perhaps in connection with the passage of the Hortensian law, to convoke the senate and lay matters before it for consideration, was also a sign of the *rapprochement* between the tribune and the senate. The Hortensian law took the *concilium plebis* out from under the control of the senate, but the senate may well have hoped that, by allowing the tribune to bring matters directly before it, he would be led to submit bills to it for its consideration before presenting them to the plebeian assembly for action.

**225. Administrative Duties.** Occasionally matters of an administrative character, like the dedication of a temple, or the supervision of the coinage, fell to the charge of the tribune, but duties of this sort never assumed much importance under the republic.

**226. The Tribune as a Political Leader.** The part which the tribune played as a political leader has been noticed here and there in the historical part of this book. A simple solution of the question at issue between the plebeians and patricians in 494 could have been secured by giving the plebeians full political rights, but the patricians were not willing to grant them, and the plebeians were not strong enough to force them to take that step.

In the period from 494 to 337 the plebeians gained their object, however, under the leadership of the tribune, and the tribunate of the first 150 years finds its real political significance in the achievement of this result. In the second period, after 337, when the plebeians had at last gained admission to every magistracy, the tribune is practically no longer a representative of a class, but he stands for the rights of the individual over against the rights, or claims, of the community or of the state.

### (g) The Aedile (Plebeian and Curule)

**227. Relations of the two Colleges.** These two colleges of officials may properly be considered together, and under the head of the magistracies, for, although the plebeian aediles were not technically magistrates, their duties came to be essentially the same as those of the curule aediles, who were magistrates, and the two colleges are closely allied to one another historically.

**228. The Early Plebeian Aedileship.** The plebeian aediles, whose office dates back to the beginning of the republic (cf. p. 28), were two in number, and were always elected by the *concilium plebis*. Only plebeians were eligible to the office, and, like the tribunes, they were sacrosanct. Their main business consisted in helping the tribunes in the performance of their duties, and in preserving plebiscites and decrees of the senate in the temple of Ceres. From the outset, as their title *aediles* indicates, they seem to have supervised to some extent the construction of public buildings. They had, also, a limited criminal jurisdiction.

Festus, v. sacrosanctum, p. 318, ed. M.

Dionys. 6. 90; 6. 95; Liv. 3. 55. 13.

Dionys. 6. 90.

**229. Development of the Office.** Perhaps there is no office which in its history better illustrates the practical

nature of the Romans and their tendency to adapt existing
institutions to new situations than the aedileship does, and
there is no case in which the successive steps by which
this adaptation took place are shown more clearly.   Furthermore, the history of the aedileship presents in a concrete way the process by which the two distinct elements,
which originally made up the Roman community, were
merged into one body.   As the city grew, the necessity for
a more efficient police service developed, and the duties
which the aediles performed in assisting the tribunes made
it natural to employ them in this service.   As early as the
middle of the fifth century they were apparently called on
to protect the city in moments of danger, and to see that Liv. 3. 6. 9.
grain was sold at a low price.   Duties of this sort affected
patricians as well as plebeians.

**230. Establishment of the Curule Aedileship.**   At the
same time their connection with the tribune's office became
looser, and *viatores* were appointed in their stead to assist
the tribunes (cf. p. 196).   In fact, they were rapidly
acquiring the positive functions of magistrates.   Yet the
patricians had no voice in their election, although their
power extended over the patricians.   It was under these
circumstances that the curule aedileship was established
in 366 (cf. p. 42), as an offset to the plebeian aedileship ;
for patricians only were eligible to the new office.   These
modifications in the character of the aedileship evidently
had their origin, partly in a tendency to assimilate the
plebs to the rest of the people, by eliminating the distinctive character of their representatives, and partly in
the need of officials for the performance of new duties.

**231. Differences between the two Colleges.**   The curule
and plebeian aedileships were at first very different from
one another in respect of technical character and official

dignity. The curule aediles were elected by the *populus*
meeting in the *comitia tributa* under the presidency of a
magistrate. They acquired the right to a seat in the senate
after the passage of the Ovinian law (pp. 46 ff.). They had
the *ius imaginum*, and on formal occasions wore the *toga
praetexta* and sat in the curule chair. From this last mark
of office they derived the distinguishing part of their title.
The plebeian aediles, on the other hand, were elected by
the *concilium plebis* under the presidency of a plebeian
official, and lacked all of the distinguishing marks of office
just mentioned. The exclusive right of the patricians to
the curule aedileship was given up in a very few years after
the establishment of the office, and the two positions in the
college were filled by plebeians in alternate years. The
two colleges were also brought nearer together by the
relinquishment on the part of the plebeian aediles of their
sacrosanct character, and by their acquisition in course of
time of a right to a seat in the senate.

**232. Powers of the Aedile.** The members of the two
colleges had essentially the same powers. They had the
supervision of public places (*cura urbis*); they had charge
of the corn supply and of commercial transactions (*cura
annonae*); they superintended the public games; and they
had certain judicial powers.

**233. The Cura Urbis.** The *cura urbis* was a natural
outgrowth of the police functions which the aediles had
first exercised as assistants of the tribunes. They had
charge especially of the streets, baths, temples, and other
public works. It was their duty, for instance, to see
that order was preserved in public places, and that the
regulations governing obstruction of the streets and the
cleaning of them were observed. The construction of
public works was in charge of the censor or consul, but

Cic. pro
Planc. 49;
Liv. 6. 42. 14.

Liv. 7. 1. 5–6;
9. 46. 9;
Cic. in Verr.
ii. 5. 36.

St. R. II.
472, n. 1.

Liv. 7. 1. 6.

St. R. II.
486, n. 2.

Lex Iul.
Munic.
ll. 20–55;
ll. 69 f.

when they were completed the aedile assumed the responsibility of keeping them in repair. Being charged with the maintenance of order in public places, and having a supervision over the public games, as we shall presently see, it was very natural that they should be held responsible for the maintenance of good order, when public gatherings of a secular or religious character, such as *contiones*, processions, or games, were held.

**234. The Cura Annonae.** One of the most important of their duties consisted in supplying the city with grain. After the acquisition of rich provinces to the south and east, and when agriculture in Italy had declined, this function was a matter of great moment, and increased steadily in importance as the city grew. Since it was their primary purpose to have food sold at a low price, the aediles had the right to carry out the laws which fixed the price of grain, to inspect weights and measures, and to exercise a general supervision of mercantile transactions, especially of the sale of articles of food. In the performance of these duties they exercised judicial power, and issued edicts with reference to matters coming under their administrative supervision. In this way they developed a code of commercial law, largely through the influence of the *praetor peregrinus*, who, in the adjudication of cases coming before him, necessarily considered the laws of other commercial peoples.

Liv. 10. 11. 9;
23. 41. 7;
30. 26. 6.

C. I. L. X.
8067. 1;
Pers. 1. 130.

**235. The Cura Ludorum.** The *ludi plebeii* were, perhaps from the first, in charge of the plebeian aediles. These officials also assisted the magistrates in the general public celebrations. Out of these two facts naturally developed the practice of giving the aediles supervision of any newly established games, so that in Cicero's time, for instance, the curule aediles were in charge of the *ludi Romani*, the

Liv. 23. 30. 17

St. R. II.
517 f.

*Floralia,* and the *Megalensia,* while the plebeian aediles conducted the *ludi plebeii* and the *Ceriales.*

**236. Judicial Functions.**  The power of the aedile to act as a public prosecutor, and to summon those who Liv. 7. 28. 9;
10. 23. 11 f.;
25. 2. 9. were charged with usury and certain other offenses before the *comitia tributa,* was never of great importance, and lost its significance in large measure after the establishment of the *quaestiones perpetuae.*

**237. Limits of Jurisdiction and Division of Duties.**  The duties of the aediles were evidently of an urban character. Furthermore, the historical relation which the plebeian aedile bore to the tribune naturally limited the former official too in the exercise of his power to the space within the *pomoerium.*  To this restriction the curule aediles also conformed.  As for the division of duties between the two colleges, so far as concerns police supervision, it was Lex. Iul.
Munic. ll. 25 f. local.  The city was divided into four quarters, and each one of these quarters was placed under the control of an aedile.  In other matters the assignment of duties was determined by tradition or convenience.  Each of the four aediles had the right of veto against his colleague in the same college, but not over a member of the other college.

### (h)  The Quaestor

**238. History of the Quaestorship.**  As we have already seen (p. 16), there were *quaestores parricidii* under the monarchy.  Some light is thrown on the nature of their duties by the definition which Festus gives of *parricida.* He remarks, *nam parricida non utique is, qui parentem occidisset, dicebatur, sed qualemcumque hominem indemnatum.*  The office continued in the republican period, but underwent an important change in its character.  Beginning

with the establishment of the republic, the quaestor is
not only the representative of the state in criminal cases of
a non-political character, but he becomes the keeper of the
state funds.   Under the monarchy the incumbents of the
office were appointed by the king, and the right of appointment was inherited by the consul, and exercised by him
until 447, when the office was made elective, and its
incumbents were chosen in the *comitia tributa* (p. 33).
Perhaps this change in the method of choosing the quaestors came about in the following way :   One of the most
important duties of the quaestor must have consisted in
conducting cases of appeal before the popular assembly.
As long as the quaestor was appointed, he acted, not by
virtue of the power vested in his own office, but solely as
the representative of the chief-magistrate.   The establishment, however, of the right of appeal made the quaestorship
a necessary part of a judicial system which was entirely
independent of the chief-magistrate.   It was natural, therefore, that the office should become independent, that is,
that it should be made elective.   The ancient historians
have very little to say about the judicial functions of the
quaestors under the republic.   They must still, however,
have performed the duties mentioned above, until, with
the establishment of the *quaestiones perpetuae*, such matters
passed altogether out of their hands.   The increase in the
number of the quaestors, to four in 421, to eight in 267
(p. 72), to twenty under Sulla (p. 105), and to forty in the
year 45 (p. 137), involved no essential change in the character of the office.   The size of the college was increased to
provide for the provinces and for the financial administration of Italy, and the functions of the office may be conveniently considered from the point of view of the *quaestore
urbani*, the *quaestores militares*, and the Italian quaestors.

**239. The Quaestores Urbani.** The two principal duties of the *quaestores urbani* have already been mentioned. So little information can be had from the ancient sources with reference to the quaestor's exercise of criminal jurisdiction, that it is impossible to find out exactly what his functions were in this respect, or to determine his relation to certain other officials, such as the *II viri perduellionis*. His financial duties are better known. He received all money due

Cic. ad Fam. 2. 17. 4; pro Flacco, 44; Liv. 33. 42. 4; 42. 6. 11.

to the state, kept an account of the condition of the state treasury, and made such payments from the public funds as he was empowered to make by special law or by the proper magistrate. He represented the state, too, in the

Liv. 4. 15. 8.

smaller matters involved in the execution of contracts. The care of the public records was also intrusted to him. In this last matter the duties of the quaestor and of the plebeian aedile were similar (cf. p. 202), except that the aediles took charge of certain documents only, while the quaestor kept all records. Two special points of weakness in the management of the finances by the quaestors may be noticed. They were simply receiving agents and paymasters for the state. They had no initiative in financial affairs, and could exercise their discretion in minor matters only. Furthermore, they held office for a year only, and in so short a time could not make themselves familiar with all the affairs of their department, so that the honesty with which accounts were kept depended largely on the integrity of their trained assistants, the *scribae*, whose tenure of office was permanent. The records and the accounts of the quaestor were kept in the *aerarium* in the temple of Saturn.

**240. The Quaestores Militares and Provincial Quaestors.** The increase in the number of quaestors from two to four, which took place in 421, was to provide a financial

officer for each of the consuls when in command of an
army. Money intended for a campaign was delivered to
them. They paid the soldiers, took charge of the spoils,
and exercised the same general functions in the field which
the *quaestor urbanus* exercised at Rome. This plan was
adopted for the provinces also, although, in the case of a
province, the quaestor held a somewhat more important
position than the *quaestor militaris* did, since he was next
in rank to the governor, and acted in his stead in case of
his absence or death.

Liv. 35. 1. 12;
Cic. in Verr.
ii. 1. 40;
ii. 3. 177.

Cic. ad Fam.
2. 15. 4.

**241. The Italian Quaestors.** In 267, as we have already
noticed, four new quaestors were appointed. They were
apparently assigned to duty in Italy, but the nature of
their functions is not perfectly clear. Their principal duty
seems to have been to look after the financial interests of
the federal government in Italy. Their headquarters were
in Cispadane Gaul, perhaps at Ariminum, at Ostia, and
possibly at Cales. It is not known where the fourth Italian
quaestor was stationed. The quaestor at Ostia had charge
of the grain supply.

Cic. pro Sest.
39.

### (i) The Viginti Sex Viri

**242. The XXVI Viri in General.** Although the six colleges of magistrates below the quaestorship were independent of one another, they formed a single group, so
far as the *ordo magistratuum* was concerned, and were
known as the *XXVI viri*. This group included the *X viri
stlitibus iudicandis*, the *IIII praefecti Capuam Cumas, etc.*,
the *III viri capitales*, the *III viri monetales*, the *IIII viri
viis in urbe purgandis*, and the *II viri viis extra urbem purgandis*. Several, if not all, of these offices were appointive,
when they were first established, but after a time they all

became elective.   The incumbents were chosen in the
*comitia tributa.*   Besides the specific functions mentioned
below, special duties were often intrusted to the several
colleges by the senate.   The *viginti sex viri* had no insignia
of office.

Cic. de Legg.
3. 6.

**243.  The Several Colleges.**   The oldest of these minor
magistrates were the *X viri stlitibus iudicandis.*   They are
mentioned in the *lex Valeria Horatia*, and, therefore, go
back to at least the middle of the fifth century.   They are
spoken of in the connection mentioned as sacrosanct, and
are associated with the tribunes and aediles, so that the
office was probably established to protect the plebeians.
Very likely they passed on questions involving the right to
citizenship — a matter in which the plebeians would be
vitally interested.   At least in Cicero's time questions of
that sort would seem to have come before them.   Probably
at first plebeians only were eligible to the office, but in later
days that restriction was abandoned.   The *praefecti Capuam
Cumas* were the judicial representatives of the praetor in
Campania, and at first were probably appointed by him.
They took their title from the two principal points within
their district.   The college of *III viri capitales* was established soon after 290, and appointments to it were at first
made by the praetor, but, some time within the next one
hundred and seventy-five years, the office became elective.
These officials were police magistrates, whose duty it was,
under the supervision of the aediles, to preserve order in
the city, to arrest criminals, to sit in judgment on them and
punish them if they were strangers or slaves, and to obtain
evidence against persons under indictment.   Caesar increased the number in this college to four (p. 137).   Little
more is known of the *III viri monetales* or *III viri aere
argento auro flando feriundo*, as they are sometimes called,

Liv. 3. 55. 7.

Cic. pro Caec.
97; de Domo,
78.

Liv. 9. 20. 5;
26. 16. 9 f.

Liv. Ep. 11.

Sall. Cat. 55.
1; Cic. pro
Cluent. 38;
Gell. 3. 3. 15;
Liv. 25. 1. 10.

than is indicated by their title.   The duties performed by
them were for a long time in charge of special commissions,
and the establishment of the magistracy comes at a comparatively late date.   Caesar added a new member to this
college (cf. p. 137).   The *IIII viri viis in urbe purgandis*    Lex Iul.
and the *II viri viis extra urbem purgandis*, as the names of    Munic.
these offices indicate, were charged with the duty of seeing    ll. 50, 69.
that the streets and roads were kept clean.

## (j) Magistrates to fill Vacancies

**244. Delegation of the Imperium.**   The Romans provided for the vacancy which resulted from the death or the
absence of a magistrate in a variety of ways.   No serious
difficulties arose in the case of the lower magistracies,
because of the size of the colleges.   In the case of the
censorship, the duties of the office during the last three
and a half years of a *lustrum* were performed by the consul and aedile (p. 195).   Real difficulty arose, however,
from the death or the absence of both consuls from the
city, from the withdrawal of a governor from his province,
and from the occasional necessity of providing more commanding officers in the field than the higher magistracies
furnished.

**245. The Interrex.**   Provision was made to cover a
vacancy in the consulship by the institution known as the
*interregnum*.   This institution goes back to the monarchy,
and the functions of the *interrex* during that period have
already been noticed (p. 14).   Under the early republic,
when the armies were always commanded by the consuls,
the death of both chief-magistrates occurred in several    Will. II. 10-
instances.   In such cases the method of procedure was    12.
essentially the same as that which was followed on the

Liv. 1. 17. 5 f.  death of the king, except that under the republic the new chief-magistrates were elected in the centuriate *comitia*, summoned for that purpose by the *interrex* and presided over by him.    In fact, the *interrex* was appointed mainly to hold the elections, and the *interregnum* ceased as soon as the new consuls were chosen.    At the same time, how-

St. R. I. 660 f.  ever, he was vested with all the powers and privileges of the consul, but, as the term of office of each *interrex* lasted

Cic. ad Fam. 7. 11. 1.  only five days, it was impossible for him to carry on public business in an orderly way.    The last *interregnum* occurred in the year 53–52.

**246. Praefectus Urbi and pro Praetore.**    When both consuls were obliged to leave the city, the last to depart

Liv. 3. 3. 6; 3. 8. 7.  appointed a *praefectus urbi* to represent him during his absence.    The prefect was vested with all the powers of the consul.    After 366, however, the *praetor urbanus* became chief-magistrate in case both consuls were absent from the city (cf. p. 189), and from that date down to Caesar's time (cf. p. 136), the city prefect was chosen only at the time of the *feriae Latinae*, when all the regular magistrates were absent from the city in attendance on that festival.    In a somewhat similar way, when a consular governor left his province before his successor arrived, he dele-

Cic. ad Fam. 2. 15. 4.  gated the *imperium* to his quaestor, who governed the province with the title of *quaestor pro praetore*.

**247. Privati cum Imperio.**    This practice of conferring on a lower magistrate, or even on a private citizen, the powers and privileges of a higher magistracy was occasionally adopted in times of danger even by the home government.    It amounted to a virtual increase in the size of the magisterial college affected.    The individuals upon whom the *imperium* was conferred received usually the pro-magisterial title.    Thus in 211 the tribunes were

instructed by the senate to secure the passage of a law
authorizing the appointment of some one as commanding
officer in Spain. The law was passed, and P. Scipio, at
that time an ex-aedile, was made governor of the province
with the title *pro consule*. In the same year a *senatus consultum* conferred the *imperium* on all the ex-dictators, ex-
consuls, and ex-censors for the defense of the city against
Hannibal. This practice was carried to a still greater
length in 77, when Pompey, who had held no magistracy
at all, was made commander of the forces in Spain with
the title of proconsul. The *senatus consultum ultimum*
and the *prorogatio imperii* have been mentioned elsewhere
(pp. 156, 181), and do not properly come into consideration
here.

*Liv. 26. 2. 5;*
*26. 18. 4 f.*

*Liv. 26. 10. 9.*

*Liv. Ep. 91;*
*Plut. Pomp.*
*17.*

## (k) Elective Military Officers and Judges

**248. Elective Military Officers.** There were two colleges
of officials, that of the *tribuni militum* and of the *II viri
navales*, whose members, like the magistrates, were elected
by the people, but they differed from the magistrates in
that they had no civil functions.

**249. Tribuni Militum.** Down to 362 the *tribuni militum* had been appointed by the consuls, but in that year for
the first time six of them were elected in the *comitia tributa*.
In 311 the people were allowed to elect sixteen, and after
207 they elected twenty-four. As six were required for a
legion, this last change provided for the usual levy of four
legions. If more than twenty-four tribunes were needed,
the additional appointments were made by the consuls. It
is a significant fact that the date of the election of the first
military tribunes coincides so nearly with the date of the
Licinian law. That law put an end to the consular tribunate by substituting the consulship for it. Now the consular

*Liv. 7. 5. 9;*
*9. 30. 3;*
*27. 36. 14.*

tribunes were merely military tribunes vested with political power (p. 184). The abolition of the consular tribunate meant a certain loss to the democracy. The concession made in 362 was, therefore, by way of compensation for that loss. The tribunes elected by the people were known as *tribuni militum a populo*. Their duties were of a purely military character, and differed in nowise from those of the tribunes appointed by the commanding officer.

**250. The II Viri Navales.** The *II viri navales* held essentially the same position in the fleet which the *tribuni militum* held in the army. The office was at first an appointive one, like that of military tribune, but in 311, when the number of elected tribunes was raised to sixteen, the *II viri navales* were for the first time chosen by the people. They were not elected annually, but as circumstances required, since under the republic there was no permanent fleet, and, therefore, naval commanders were not always needed. The holding of the election was authorized by the senate. Nothing is heard of the office in the later republic.

Liv. 9. 30. 4.

**251. Elective Judges.** Since the number of praetors was not large enough to provide presiding judges for all the *quaestiones perpetuae*, at intervals a *iudex quaestionis* was chosen from the ex-aediles by popular election. In dignity, then, the office stood between the aedileship and the praetorship. The *iudex quaestionis* had charge of the *quaestio de sicariis et veneficis*. The nature of the cases brought before this court made the position of its presiding judge an important one. The first mention of this *iudex* is in 98, but the epoch of greatest importance for the office is from Sulla's dictatorship down to the time of Augustus, when it disappears. The incumbents of the office had no political functions.

Madv. I. 389 f.: St. R. II. 586 ff.; Herz. I. 845, a. 1.

## (*l*) *Extraordinary Officials*

**252. Two Classes of Extraordinary Officials.** All the magistracies and offices which have been considered up to this point formed for a longer or shorter period a regular part of the Roman administrative system, but emergencies arose when the regular officials did not seem capable of dealing with the situation. Under such circumstances extraordinary offices were created by special laws, or special officials were chosen to carry out a particular undertaking. It may be convenient to classify these extraordinary officials in two categories, according as they were placed under constitutional restrictions, or were above the constitution. The principal officials of the first class were the *II viri perduellionis*, the commissioners *agris dandis adsignandis* and *coloniae deducendae*, the commissioners appointed to dedicate public buildings, or carry out some financial undertaking, and the *legati*. The most celebrated officials coming under the second head were the *X viri consulari imperio legibus scribendis*, the *dictator legibus scribendis et rei publicae constituendae*, and the *III viri rei publicae constituendae*.

**253. The II Viri Perduellionis.** The college of *II viri perduellionis*, which passed judgment on those charged with treason, and represented the state in such cases before the centuriate *comitia*, if appeal was taken, has little meaning for the republican period. There are only two known instances after 509 when *II viri perduellionis* were appointed, and in the second case, that of Rabirius in 63, the institution was called into life for political purposes only. The power attaching to the office was too great to be granted to two men, while, on the other hand, the centuriate *comitia*, to which appeal from their decision was

Liv. 6. 20. 12; Cic. pro Rab perd. 12.

carried, was too unwieldy a body to settle judicial matters. The *II viri perduellionis*, therefore, gave way to the *quaestiones*.

**254. Special Commissions.** The duties of land commissioners consisted in dividing and assigning the land chosen for allotments, and, in case a colony was to be established, in drawing up a charter and in providing for the immediate government of the community. The number of members serving on these commissions ran all the way from three to twenty. The commission expired when the work for which it had been established was finished. The size of the allotments and the methods and conditions of assignment were fixed in the law creating the commission. From a very early period the principle was recognized that state land could be given away only with the consent of the people. When a temple or other public building was to be constructed, the power to use public land for the purpose in question was granted by law and *II viri aedi locandae* were chosen. The dedication of a temple often fell to the lot of one of the higher magistrates, but not infrequently the matter was intrusted to *II viri aedi dedicandae*. The execution of economic measures, especially those of a novel character, was sometimes intrusted to a commission rather than to a magistrate. A case in point was furnished by the *V viri mensarii*, or commission appointed in 351 to assist individuals in securing loans (cf. p. 49).

*Cic. de Leg. Agr. 2. 96.*

*Liv. 10. 21. 7–9; 31. 4. 1–2; 31. 49. 5.*

**255. Legati.** In its management of foreign affairs the senate from time to time sent out *legati*. They were appointed by the magistrate or commanding officer at the instance of the senate. They may be divided into two classes according to the duties assigned to them. Those of one class were sent to independent states to deliver a

*Liv. 43. 1. 10.*

message from the senate or to carry on diplomatic negotiations. *Legati* of the other class were sent to assist
generals in the field. As we have already seen (p. 69),
campaigns were carried on under the joint direction of the
senate and of the officer commanding the forces. The
*legati* attached to the staff of the general in command
were, therefore, the representatives of the senate, and, as
such, took part in the councils of war and held important
commands. This right of the senate to send out commissions was much abused in the later years of the republic.
The practice developed of granting to senators a *legatio
libera*, which allowed them to travel through the provinces
on their private business and enjoy all the privileges and
honors of accredited commissioners. Midway between the
two classes of *legati* which have been mentioned were the
commissioners sent out by the senate to draw up, with
the help of the general in the field, the *lex provinciae*
(cf. pp. 89–90) for the people of a newly acquired territory. Senatorial commissions varied in number from two
to ten. The commission appointed to draw up a provincial
constitution always numbered ten. Members of senatorial
commissions were almost always senators.

Liv. 8. 35. 1c;
25. 34. 8.

Cic. ad Fam.
12. 21; pro
Flacco, 86.

Liv. 29. 11. 3;
31. 11. 18;
37. 55. 4.

**256. The X Viri Legibus Scribendis.** The cases in which
the Romans under the republic chose extraordinary officials
to revise the fundamental law of the state, and released
them from restrictions ordinarily laid on magistrates, are
few in number. The decemvirate of 451 (cf. pp. 30 f.) is,
however, an instance in point. That commission was
chosen to revise, or codify, and to publish the law of the
land. Its members were elected in the popular assembly,
and, like other magistrates, they were liable to a veto from
other members of the college. On the other hand, they
were not subject to the tribunician veto. In fact, the

tribunate was suspended or abolished for the time. The
term of office for the first decemviral college was a year.
The second was apparently to continue in office until its
task was complete. The Valerio-Horatian law of appeal
forbade the establishment of such a magistracy in the
future.

Liv. 3. 32. 6.

Liv. 3. 55. 5;
Cic. de Re
Publ. 2. 54.

**257. The Later Dictatorship.** Some of the points of
difference between the dictatorship of Sulla and the traditional dictatorship have already been noticed (pp. 134 f.).
The *lex Valeria* of 82, which conferred this position on Sulla,
authorized him to undertake a thorough revision of the
constitution, as the title of the office shows, viz., *dictatura
legibus scribendis et rei publicae constituendae*. The unlimited power of the office is indicated not only by Cicero's
characterization of it as an office of such a sort *ut omnia,
quaecumque ille* (i.e., *Sulla*) *fecisset, essent rata*, but also by
the use which Sulla made of it. Caesar's dictatorship was of
the same sort. Sulla's term of office as dictator was probably unlimited. As for Caesar, we have already noticed
that in 48 the dictatorship was apparently given to him for
an undefined period, in 46 for ten years, and in 44 for life.
Some of the important powers exercised by Sulla and Caesar
by virtue of their dictatorship were: the right to name the
magistrates (cf. pp. 137 f.) and to add members to the
senate, to name magistrates in the *municipia*, to impose
penalties without submitting to the right of appeal, and to
control the *ager publicus*.

Appian, B. C.
1. 99;
Cic. de Leg.
Agr. 3. 5.

Suet. Iul. 41;
Cic. de Div.
2. 23;
pro Lig. 12.

**258. The Triumvirate.** The triumvirate to which Lepidus, Antony, and Octavius were appointed held a position in the state similar to that which Caesar had held
during his dictatorship. The office was established by the
*lex Titia* of 43 (cf. p. 141) for a period of five years.

St. R. II. 707.

In 38 it was renewed. As we have already noticed, the members of the triumvirate adopted the principle of collegiality on its positive side. Like Caesar, they exercised the right to name the magistrates for Rome and for the *municipia*, to punish without appeal, and to manage state land.

## SELECTED BIBLIOGRAPHY [1]

**The dictator**: A. Dupond, De dictatura et de magisterio equitum, Paris, 1875; E. Servais, La dictature, Paris, 1886; F. Haverfield, The abolition of the dictatorship, Class. Rev. III. 77. — **The consular tribune**: Heinze, De tribunis militum cons. pot., Stettin, 1861. — **The praetor**: F. Faure, Essai historique sur le préteur romain, Paris, 1878; O. Lenel, Das Edictum perpetuum, Leipzig, 1883. — **The censor**: Servais, La censure, Luxemburg, 1880; Willems, Le sénat de la république romaine, I. pp. 239–625, Louvain, 1883; A. W. Zumpt, Die Lustra der Römer, Rhein. Mus. XXV. 465 ff.; XXVI. 1 ff. — **The tribune of the plebs**: Soldan, De origine, causis et primo tribunorum plebis numero, Hanau, 1825; W. Ihne, Rhein. Mus. XXI. 161 ff.; Bélot, De trib. pleb., Paris, 1872; P. Wehrmann, Zur Geschichte des röm. Volkstribunats, Stettin, 1887. — **The aedile**: E. Moll, Ueber d. röm. Aedilität in ältester Zeit, Philol. XLVI. 98 ff.; Fr. Hofmann, De aedilibus romanis, Berlin, 1842. — **The quaestor**: Wagner, De quaestoribus pop. romani, Marburg, 1848; Döllen, De quaest. rom., Berlin, 1847. — **The interrex**: E. Herzog, Das Institut des Interregnums, Philol. XXXIV. 497 ff.; Willems, II. 7 ff. — **The city prefect**: Franke, De praefectura urbis, Berlin, 1851. — **The tribunus militum**: Geppert, De trib. mil. legionum rom., Berlin, 1872. — **The legati**: O. Adamek, Die Senatsboten d. rom. Republik, Graz, 1883; Willems, II. 491 ff. — **The decemvirs**: E. Schmidt, Ueber d. röm. Decemvirat, Halberstadt, 1871.

[1] See also p. 173.

# CHAPTER X

## THE SENATE

### (a) Composition of the Senate and Senatorial Privileges

**259. Method of choosing Senators.** The right which the king had enjoyed of making out the list of senators (p. 16) was inherited by his successor, the consul. This power had both a negative and a positive side. In his exercise of it the chief-magistrate could strike names from the list, or make such additions as would bring the number up to the normal point. Since the right to exercise this power probably belonged to each college of consuls, the roll of senators was subject to revision each year. Towards the close of the fourth century the *plebiscitum Ovinium* (pp. 46 f.) transferred this power to the censor. It was exercised by him under the restrictions imposed by tradition and by the Ovinian law up to the dictatorship of Sulla, when the censorship was allowed to lapse. The office was reëstablished in 70, but, although he recovered the right to remove men from the senate, the censor did not regain the power to make additions to that body (cf. p. 194). Sulla and Caesar named senators in an exceptional way by virtue of the dictatorship which they held.

**260. Number in the Senate.** Before the downfall of the monarchy the normal number in the senate was fixed at three hundred (p. 16), and according to tradition one of the
Liv. 2. 1. 10. first things done by the patrician consuls after the expulsion

of the kings was to fill up the depleted list of the senate.
Sulla raised the number to six hundred, and this continued
to be the normal size of the body, although it was temporarily raised to nine hundred by Caesar.

Appian, B. C.
I. 59; I. 100;
Suet. Iul.
41, 80.

**261. Composition of the Senate.** So far as the composition of the senate is concerned, its history falls into
four periods. The first extends to 509; the second to the
close of the fourth century; the third to Sulla's dictatorship;
and the fourth to the downfall of the republic. In the first
period, patricians only were eligible. According to tradition,
however, the establishment of the republic brought with it
the admission of plebeians into the senate. This change
is somewhat out of harmony with the aristocratic character
of the revolution of 509, but it may have been inspired by
a desire to secure the support of the influential plebeians in
the movement against the monarchy. At all events the evidence justifies us in believing that plebeians were admitted
at a very early date. The new senators were called *adlecti*
or *conscripti* to distinguish them from the *patres*. As Festus
says (p. 7, ed. M.): *nam patres dicuntur qui sunt patricii generis, conscripti qui in senatu sunt scriptis adnotati.* In the
third period, from the close of the fourth century to the
time of Sulla, the senate was largely made up of ex-magistrates. The change did not come abruptly, however. The
*plebiscitum Ovinium*, which instructed the censors to give
the preference to ex-magistrates in drawing up the list of
senators (pp. 46–7), probably only gave a legal sanction
to a practice which had been developing for some time.
Under the legislation of Sulla the senate became exclusively
a body of ex-magistrates.

Liv. 2. I. 10;
Festus,
p. 254, ed. M

Will. I. 35–
48, B.-L. 93.

**262. Conditions of Eligibility.** There were three principal conditions of eligibility to the senate in Cicero's time.
It was necessary that a senator should be a freeman and a

citizen, that he should have held one of the *magistratus maiores*, and that he should not be engaged in any one of certain specified occupations.

**263. Citizen and Freeman.** Conformity to the first condition implied that a candidate for senatorial honors should have reached his majority, and that he should be in possession of the full political rights of a Roman citizen. Furthermore, the sons of freedmen, as well as freedmen themselves, were ordinarily considered ineligible by the censors, although probably the former were not excluded from the senate by law.

**264. A Senator must be an ex-Magistrate.** The Ovinian law did not make the holding of a magistracy a necessary condition of eligibility to the senate, but preference was given to ex-magistrates. The increase which Sulla made in the size of the magisterial colleges (p. 105), however, provided a sufficient number of ex-magistrates to keep the number of senators up to the normal point, so that, after his dictatorship, no one was eligible to the senate unless he had held a magistracy. In the latter half of the first century the tribune and aedile of the plebs, as well as the magistrates down to and including the quaestor, had a right to a seat in the senate. When this right was conferred on the plebeian aediles it is impossible to say. At least it would seem to have been granted to them before 122. The plebeian tribunes acquired the right to a seat in the senate under the *plebiscitum Atinium*, which was probably passed toward the close of the second century. The quaestor gained the same privilege in the year 81.

Liv. 23. 23.
5 f.

Will. I. 231.

Will. I.
225 ff.;
I. 689 ff.

**265. A Senator must abstain from Certain Occupations.** The Romans felt that certain occupations put a moral stigma on an individual, that others were incompatible with the dignity of a senator, that others prevented him from performing his duties as senator in a satisfactory way, and that still others unfitted him for passing on public questions in a disinterested manner. All these occupations, then, made a citizen temporarily or permanently ineligible to the senate. To the first class, for instance, belonged the professions of the *lanista*, the gladiator, and the actor. To receive wages or a salary for one's services did not comport with the dignity of a senator, so that the occupation of a *praeco* or a *scriba* excluded the individual in question from the senate. In fact, if a citizen gained his livelihood in any business which required his constant personal attention, that fact made it impossible for him to perform satisfactorily the duties of a senator. As soon, however, as he gave up the occupation in question, he became technically eligible. Finally, since the senate managed the finances of the state in large measure, men who had taken public contracts could not be allowed to sit in that body.

*Lex Iul. Munic. ll. 108 ff.*

*Gell. 7. 9. 2 f.; Lex Iul. Munic. ll. 94 ff.*

**266. Property and Age Requirement.** Under the republic probably there was no property qualification for admission to the senate, but, since no salary was paid to a senator, the position could be held only by men of means. Furthermore, a reasonable fortune was required to maintain the senatorial dignity. The censors must have taken these facts into consideration in drawing up their lists. No age requirement was definitely established by law or custom, but the Ovinian law, when supplemented by the *lex Villia annalis*, prevented any one from becoming a senator until he had reached the age required for the quaestorship (cf. p. 169). In fact, it may be said in general that obstacles which prevented a person from becoming a magistrate prevented him from becoming a senator also.

**267. Classes of Senators.** We have already had occasion to notice that plebeians were admitted to the senate at a very

early date (cf. p. 221).   A plebeian senator never acquired,
however, two rights which his patrician colleague enjoyed,
viz., the right to act as an *interrex*, and the right to vote on
the passage of the *patrum auctoritas*.   For a long time a
distinction was made also between the senators who had
the *ius sententiae dicendae* and the *pedarii*, who voted on
a motion already made, but were not called on to speak or
make a motion themselves.   The composition of these two

Herz. I.
887 f.;
Will. I. 137 f.;
St. R. III.
962; III. 982.

classes is a matter of high dispute.   As we shall presently
see, the presiding officer asked senators their opinions in
the order of their rank, and it was within his power to
terminate the discussion before all the members of the
senate had stated their views.   Senators of inferior rank,
therefore, took part only in the *discessio*, and were called
on, as the Romans put it, only *pedibus in alienam sententiam ire*.   From this fact they derived their name *pedarii*.
Where the line of distinction was drawn between the *pedarii*
and their more fortunate colleagues is as unsettled to-day
as it was in the time of Aulus Gellius, who mentions (*N. A.*

Will. I. 143 f.;
St. R. III.
871 f.

III. 18) several different explanations of the term.   It seems
probable, however, that the *pedarii* were plebeian senators
who had never held a curule office.   It is also probable
that the *conscripti* of the early period were restricted in
their exercise of senatorial rights in the same way as the
*pedarii* were in the period following the Ovinian law.

Herz.
I. 888, n.

For the time of Cicero the term *pedarii* has no technical
meaning.   As already intimated, senators were classed as
*consulares, praetorii, aedilicii, tribunicii*, and *quaestorii*, and
their opinions were asked in the order indicated.   From
perhaps the third century down to the time of Sulla a patrician senator of the rank of censor usually stood at the head

Will. I. 111 f.

of the list.   He was called the *princeps senatus*, and his
opinion was asked first.

**268. Insignia and Privileges.** Members of the senate in Cicero's day were distinguished by certain insignia, indicating their position. These *ornamenta senatoria*, as they were called, were the *calceus senatorius*, the *tunica laticlavia*, and the *anulus aureus*, although the gold ring was not the peculiar mark of senatorial rank, but was worn by knights also. Senators who had held a curule office wore a special shoe called the *mulleus*. Certain special privileges were also granted to senators. After 194 seats were reserved for them at the public games. At dramatic performances too the orchestra was set apart for them, and a not unimportant privilege was the *ius legationis liberae* (cf. p. 217). They enjoyed, except for a period of about fifty years (cf. pp. 97, 106, 109), the right of sitting on the jury. Corresponding to these privileges were certain restrictions which we have already considered.

Cic. Phil. 13. 28; Hor. Sat. 1. 6. 27 f.; Festus, v. mulleos, p. 142, ed. M.; Suet. Iul. 45; Plin. N. H. 33. 11 f. Liv. 34. 54. 4; Cic. de Har. Resp. 24; Plut. Cat. Mai. 17.

## (b) Meetings of the Senate

**269. The Presidency of the Senate.** The right to call the senate and preside over it, the *ius agendi cum patribus*, was enjoyed by the dictator, consul, praetor, interrex, city prefect, master of the horse, and, after the middle of the fourth century, by the plebeian tribune. Up to the time of Sulla the consuls were absent from the city a great part of the year, so that, strangely enough, the presiding officer in the senate must usually have been, not the chief-magistrate, but his representative, the *praetor urbanus*. In the early period, in case both consuls were in the city, the presidency of the senate fell to the consul who had the *fasces* (cf. p. 155). Later it is impossible to tell how the matter was decided. Each consul had the right to convoke the senate, and he could not be prevented from doing so by

Gell. 14. 7. 4; Cic. de Legg. 3. 10.

the veto of his colleague. In the later years of the republic, therefore, when the two consuls not infrequently belonged to different political parties, cases of conflict must have

Suet Iul. 20. occurred. In one instance, at least, the weaker of the two abstained altogether from political action. After the senate had finished the business which the chief-magistrate had to lay before it, it was competent for any other magistrate, having the *ius referendi*, to lay questions before it, unless such action was forbidden by the chief-magistrate. Consequently, the business which the tribune had to bring before the senate was usually laid before it in that way. The cases in which the tribune convoked the senate were very few. It is evident that the three officials who presided over the senate most frequently were the consuls, praetors, and tribunes. Accordingly, official communications were ordinarily addressed to them (e.g., *M. Tullius M. f. Cicero procos. s. d. cos. pr. tr. pl. senatui*, Cic. ad *Fam.* XV. 1), and to them the senate intrusted the welfare of the state in the *senatus consultum ultimum*. The *ius referendi* carried with it, not only the right to convoke the senate, to lay matters before it for consideration, and secure legal action upon them, but also to determine the order of business.

**270. Place and Time of Meeting.** The senate was

Liv. 3. 38. 8. called together by a *praeco* or by a proclamation. The usual place of meeting was the *curia Hostilia*, at the northeast corner of the forum. There were no days fixed by law for the meeting of the senate. On the other hand,

Will. II. 149 ff. in the later years of the republic, perhaps after 61, it could not be called on certain *dies comitiales*. A session ordinarily began early in the morning and ended before sunset.

Gell. 14. 7. 8. In fact, the legality of a *senatus consultum* passed at a night session was questioned. The public were not admitted to the senate chamber, but the doors were left open, so that it was possible for them to follow the discussion, and their expressions of approval and disapproval often interfered with the orderly transaction of business.    On rare occasions the senate went into executive session.    In such a case the doors were closed, and the lictors and *viatores*, who acted as sergeants-at-arms, were excluded.    In the senate chamber each member chose the place on the *subsellia* which suited his fancy.    The magistrates were on a raised dais, the consuls and praetors seated in their curule chairs, and the tribunes on a *longum subsellium*.    Members rose when addressing the senate and when the magistrates entered and retired.

Cic. ad Q. fr 2. 10 (12). 1.

Liv. 42. 14. 1

Cic. in Cat. 1. 16; 2. 12; ad Fam. 3. 9. 2.

**271. Quorum.**    A quorum does not seem to have been necessary for the transaction of ordinary business, but action on certain matters required the attendance of a specified number.    In particular toward the end of the republic a quorum was necessary when *senatus consulta* were passed with reference to the assignment of the consular provinces. The presiding magistrate could enforce the attendance of members who were absent without sufficient reason, but recourse was rarely had to such extreme action.

C. I. L. I. 196, ll. 8 f.; Ascon. p. 58, ed. Or.; Cic. ad Fam. 8. 9. 2.

Cic. Phil. 1. 11 f.; Gell. 14. 7. 10.

**272. Procedure during the Debate.**    The magistrate who was to preside made an offering and took the auspices before the meeting.    At the beginning of the session dispatches were ordinarily read, and statements were made by the presiding officer, or by others who were authorized by him to speak.    Business was definitely brought before the senate by the *relatio* of the presiding officer, whose remarks began with the formula : *quod bonum felixque sit populo Romano Quiritium, referimus ad vos, patres conscripti* . . . .    The committee system was employed on rare occasions.    The presiding officer could make a simple

Cic. ad Fam. 10. 12. 3; Gell. 14. 7. 9

statement of the facts, or he could advocate a certain course.

Cic. Phil. 1. 3. In rare cases he laid a definite motion before the house. After having stated the case, he could call for a vote at once. This plan was seldom adopted, except when a matter was unimportant, or when the support of the majority to a given proposition was assured beforehand. The demand of a senator for an opportunity to debate a question (*consule*) would scarcely be disregarded. Ordinarily, then, after the business before the senate had been stated, the presiding officer, following the order of rank, proceeded *sententias rogare*. The order was that already indicated (p. 224), except that, after the middle of the

Cic. Phil.<br>5. 35;<br>Sall. Cat.<br>50. 4;<br>Appian, B. C.<br>2. 5. second century, the consuls-elect were first asked their opinions. In a similar way the *praetores designati* took precedence of the *praetorii*. Preference was shown for the opinion of the magistrates-elect, because they were likely to be called on to carry out the measure under consideration. The senators, as they were called on in turn, could either address the house on the question at issue, closing their remarks with a motion, or they could indicate their agreement with a motion already made. In responding to the request of the presiding officer for his opinion, a senator was not required to confine his remarks to the question before the house, but he could, if he wished, speak on

Cic. ad Fam.<br>10. 28. 2;<br>ad Att.<br>1. 16. 9. matters entirely foreign to it, and could request the presiding officer to bring these matters before the senate. This privilege was a very important one, and made up in large measure for the lack of the right of initiative, which right technically the presiding officer alone had. Senators spoke on a question as long as they saw fit, so that the opponent of a measure could prevent action on it by talking until sunset. The chairman had the right to stop a member adopting such a course by ordering a *viator* to take him into custody, but there is only one known instance where a presiding officer made such an attempt, and his efforts ended in a practical failure. Speeches were often violent and personal, and were frequently interrupted by cries of approval and disapproval on the part of the senate. The presiding officer brought the discussions to an end when he saw fit. Probably many of the senators were given no opportunity to speak. Magistrates in office, who sat in the senate, were not asked their opinions.

**273. Method of Voting.** If, during the debate, only one motion had been made, the presiding officer, in case he accepted it, put it to vote. If several propositions had been made, he had the right to reject those which were unacceptable to him, and to put the others to vote in any order which he preferred. The first motion to receive the support of a majority constituted the action of the senate. If a motion comprised several different propositions, a division of the question could be called for, but the presiding officer was not obliged to grant the request. At the request, *qui hoc censetis, illuc transite; qui alia omnia, in hanc partem*, the supporters of a measure passed to one side of the house to be counted, the opponents to the other. Magistrates in office did not vote. The result was announced by the presiding officer.

**274. The Intercessio in the Senate.** The *par potestas* (p. 154) conferred on the colleague of the presiding officer the right to interpose his veto. In point of fact, however, the veto power was rarely exercised by any other official than the tribune, but, as we have already seen (pp. 198 f.), he could exercise that power at any point in the proceedings. An action of the senate which no official had vetoed was called a *senatus consultum*. In case of an *intercessio*, the action of the senate had no legal value, but, inasmuch as it

Gell. 4. 10. 8.

Cic. ad Q. fr. 2. 1. 3; 3. 2. 2; Sall. Cat. 53. 1.

Caes. B. C. 1. 2. 5; Cic. Phil. 14. 22; ad Fam. 10. 12. 3.

Cic. ad Fam. 1. 2. 1.

represented the opinion of a majority of the senate, it had moral force, and was set down in writing and preserved, constituting what was known as a *senatus auctoritas*, to be distinguished, of course, from an *auctoritas patrum* (p. 50).

**275. Formulation and Publication of a Senatus Consultum.** The propositions appended to the third, eighth, and ninth of Cicero's Philippic orations give one an idea of the form of the motions on which the senate voted. A motion was set down in writing in its final form after a meeting by a committee chosen by the chairman. This committee was usually made up of those who had supported the measure. There were two essential parts in such a document: the preamble, or *praescriptio*, and the action proper. The preamble gave ordinarily the name of the presiding officer, the place and time of meeting, and the names of the members of the committee chosen to put the measure in its final form (*adesse scribendo*). Then came a statement of the question on which action had been taken, usually introduced by such a phrase as, *quod M. Marcellus cos. v(erba) f(ecit) de*, etc., followed by the action itself. At the end of the document, in the case of a *senatus consultum*, stood the word *c(ensuere)*; in the case of a *senatus auctoritas*, the name of the magistrate or magistrates who had interposed a veto. It was incumbent on the presiding officer to see that the action of the senate was communicated to those concerned, and to deposit the official copy of a motion in the *aerarium* (cf. p. 208). One of the laws of Caesar of the year 59 provided that official reports of the proceedings of the senate should be made and published.

**276. The Roman Senate and Modern Legislative Bodies.** The method of transacting business followed in the Roman senate was in many respects in marked contrast to that of

C. I. L. I. 196; I. 201; Cic. ad Fam. 8. 8. 5; Gell. 4. 6. 2; Bruns, pp. 160 ff.

Suet. Iul. 20.

modern legislative bodies.   In modern legislative assemblies
a large amount of the work is done by standing or special
committees, which carry on extended investigations, and,
on the basis of the information thus obtained, recommend
certain action to the main body which they represent.
The Romans made practically no use of the committee system.   The fact that in our modern legislative bodies there
are important committees, and that the presiding officer
in most cases determines their personnel, gives him great
influence in controlling members and in directing legislation.   The presiding officer in the Roman senate had
no such means of controlling that body.   Furthermore,
there were no well-organized parties in Rome, nor was the
presiding officer in the senate a party leader to the same
extent that the Speaker, for instance, of our House of Representatives is.   Party government, with all that it implies
in the way of a definite programme, of caucuses, and of
concerted action, was practically unknown.

The senate was distinguished from most modern parlia-
ments in that it could meet only when it was convoked by
a magistrate.   This state of things was consistent with the
theory that the senate was not a legislative body, but an
advisory council.   It rested, of course, with the magistrate to
decide when he needed advice.   The plan did not work in-
conveniently, since the members of the senate were within
call of the senate-house.   In harmony with this theory of the
functions of the senate was the further fact that the order
of business was in the hands of the presiding officer, and
was not determined, as with us, by the house itself.   This
theory also accounts for the fact that senators did not have
the right of initiating legislation, that they could not even
speak until they were called on, that the presiding officer
could stop a debate when he saw fit, and that he could

refuse to put a motion unacceptable to him. As we have seen, however, most of these limitations had little practical meaning. The senate, for instance, had such effective means of forcing a magistrate to convoke it, that no magistrate ever succeeded in ruling without asking its coöperation, and the right to initiate legislation, although theoretically denied, was practically exercised in a roundabout way. It is a matter of surprise that the Roman senate was able to transact complicated business in a wise and orderly way under the loose system which it followed. We have already noticed that business was not prepared for it by committees, but almost all sorts of intricate matters were taken up for the first time on the floor of the house. Furthermore, a comparatively short time was given to the settlement of important questions. There was little of that parliamentary machinery which we think so essential to the orderly transaction of public affairs. There was apparently no fixed order of business. A quorum was not ordinarily necessary. A dozen motions might be under consideration at the same time, and what must have made the situation still worse is the fact that the consul could not prevent members from discussing matters entirely foreign to the subject which he had brought up for consideration. Motions were rarely written down, and, in fact, no official minutes were kept of a meeting, but the senate relied on the memory of the presiding officer or on notes taken by individual senators. Finally, any one of the ten tribunes could interpose his veto and make the action of the senate invalid. These weak points in its method of doing business were offset by its frequent meetings, by the fact that its members were almost all experienced administrative officers, by its willingness to profit by its own long experience and by the wisdom of those best qualified to advise it.

## (c) The Powers of the Senate

**277. Exclusive Rights of Patrician Senators.** The special rights which the patrician members of the senate always retained have already been noticed (p. 224). Of these the right to vote the *auctoritas patrum* was robbed of all significance by the Publilian law of 339 (pp. 50 f.). The right to choose an *interrex* from their own number was very likely a political privilege of some value during the stormy years of the late republic. At all events, the institution served to give continuity to the government.

**278. Relations of the Senate to the Magistrate and the Comitia.** As for the senate taken as a whole, we have already had occasion to notice (pp. 65 ff.) that the relations which it bore to the magistrate and to the popular assemblies gradually underwent a radical change. In the period of its ascendency the magistrate was little more than its presiding officer and minister, while a great part of the business of legislation came before the senate, not before the *comitia*, and even the matters on which the popular assembly ultimately took action were discussed and put in final form for submission to it by the senate. Traditional usage always determined under the republic, however, the relation which its action bore to that of the popular assemblies. A *senatus consultum* never stood on the same plane as a *lex*. It could not annul a *lex*, nor was it valid if its provisions violated those of a *lex*. It could, however, interpret enactments of the popular assembly. It could provide for matters not already covered by them, even when in so doing it seemed to usurp the constitutional rights of the *comitia*, because in so doing, if the tribune did not interpose his veto, it could be assumed that its action was acceptable to the *populus*.

**279. Authority in Religious Matters.** The three fields in which its activity was greatest were those of religion, finance, and foreign politics. The ordinary management of religious matters was intrusted to the *pontifex maximus* and the special colleges of priests. Certain regularly recurring events of a religious character, like the celebration of the games, were in charge of the magistrates; but the welfare of the state depended on the favor of the gods, and, therefore, when the gods indicated their will in some extraordinary fashion, or when an important change in the established religious order was contemplated, the fact became one of great political concern, and it was important to get the advice of the senate. For this reason, the senate was consulted when prodigies had occurred, when new rites were to be introduced, or religious ceremonies to be regulated. Ordinarily these matters were laid before the senate by the magistrates, and that body instructed the proper religious authorities to make investigations, on which appropriate action could be based. This action consisted, in the case of *prodigia*, in the removal of the cause of offense, in making offerings, and appointing festivals. The senate, by its control of appropriations, also exercised some authority even over the ordinary management of religious affairs.

Gell. 4. 6. 1 f.;
Liv. 25. 12.
2 ff.; 32. 1.
10 ff.

**280. Control of Public Finances.** It has been well said that the control of public finances under the republic was an administrative rather than a constitutional question. The right which the chief-magistrate originally had to receive and to pay out public moneys passed over in part to the senate; in large measure because the magistrate often voluntarily referred such matters to it, for the sake of getting its advice and moral support. In short, the same influences (cf. pp. 67 f.) which helped the senate to encroach on the traditional prerogative of the magistrate in other matters were at work in this case also. A magistrate with a brief tenure of office could not maintain his power over against a permanent assembly, whose members held their position for life. In the case of the finances the encroachment of the senate was encouraged by two special facts. At a comparatively early date the supervision of the treasury was taken from the consul and given to an inferior official, the quaestor (p. 207), whose position made him even more amenable to the senate than the consul might have been. Furthermore, a large share of the consul's financial business was transferred to the censor (p. 194) after the middle of the fifth century. Notwithstanding these changes, the consul still retained some freedom of action, inasmuch as appropriations were made not in an itemized form, but in lump sums, and the magistrate was not required to give the senate an itemized account of the receipts of the treasury. In other words, the control which the senate had over the finances of the state was far less complete and definite than that exercised by a modern parliament. The senate appropriated money for the army, for the public games, and for the construction and maintenance of public works. It authorized the imposition of the *tributum*, and fixed the tribute to be paid by the provinces. The control of state land was always in dispute between the senate and the popular assemblies, and the influence of the latter varied according to the democratic or oligarchic tendency of the times.

Liv. 24. 11. 7 ff.; 25. 12. 12.

Liv. 23. 31. 1 f.; Cic. de Off. 3. 87.

**281. Concluding Treaties, Declaring and Carrying on War.** The ultimate right to declare war and to conclude a treaty of peace rested with the people. In practice, however, both questions were really settled by the senate. In the first place, a consul would never take the responsibility

Polyb. 6. 14; Sall. Iug. 39. 3.

of bringing such important matters before the *comitia* without previously consulting the senate (cf. pp. 176 f.). In the second place, the senate actually conducted all the diplomatic negotiations which resulted in a treaty or a declaration of war. These negotiations were usually carried on, in the one case, between the senate and ambassadors representing the power concerned, in the other case, between a senatorial commission and the government of the people concerned. Only when a definite conclusion had been reached was the result submitted to the people for action. In the early period, when wars were carried on near Rome, the senate exercised a great influence over their conduct. When, in the later period, the scene of war was farther removed, the detailed control of a campaign by it was, of course, impossible. However, commanding generals still deferred to its wishes, and reports of military movements were regularly sent to it. The senate found an effective means of controlling generals in the field in the fact that with it rested the right to appropriate money for a campaign, to provide reinforcements, and to grant a triumph or a *supplicatio* in case of a success.

282. **Administration of Italy.** Every extension of Roman citizenship required the consent of the people, so that in founding a Roman colony a *lex* was necessary. A Latin colony, however, could be established by virtue of a *senatus consultum*, which could also determine the number of colonists, and the amount of land to be assigned to each of them (cf. pp. 59 f.). The general control of affairs in Italy was divided between the consul and the senate. The consul was charged with the protection of Italy from incursions, and the maintenance of peace within its borders (cf. pp. 179 f.). It was the duty of the senate to guard the interests of the central government, and to provide for the

Liv. 8. 2;
21. 6; 21. 9 f.;
36. 27. 7;
38. 45. 5–6.

Liv. 9. 5. 1;
21. 17. 4;
37. 55. 1–3.

Cic. ad Fam.
15. 1; 15. 2.

Liv. 23. 21.
1 ff.; 23. 34.
10 f.;
Cic. ad Fam.
15. 4. 13.

Liv. 6. 16. 6.

administration of justice in certain cases. To cope with
cases of treason, conspiracy, riot, or insurrection, a magistrate with the *imperium* was sent by the senate to conduct
an investigation and inflict punishment. Epidemics of
crime, which the local authorities did not seem able to
control, were dealt with in the same way. When two
communities fell into a dispute the senate appointed a
commission from its own number with power to settle the
difficulty. Communities which seemed to have failed in
their duties to Rome were required to send representatives
to the city to explain the situation. If their explanations
were not satisfactory, the towns in question were punished.

Liv. 9. 16.
2–10;
10. 1. 3.

Liv. 39. 41 ff

Liv. 45. 13.
10 f.;
Cic. ad Att.
4. 15. 5.

Liv. 27. 38.
3–5; 29. 15.

**283. The Senate and the Provinces.** The important
part which the senate played in the organization of a
province has been considered in another connection (pp.
89 ff.), but its control had by no means come to an end,
when the provincial charter had been drawn up. Usually
at the beginning of the year it decided which provinces
should be consular, and which praetorian. Thereupon the
consuls and praetors cast lots for their respective provinces,
or came to a friendly agreement on the subject. Sometimes the decision was made after the election, but before
the end of the year. The *lex Sempronia de provinciis* of
123 effected an important change in this arrangement by
requiring the senate to designate the consular provinces
before the election of the consuls to whom they would be
assigned. This prevented it from favoring political friends
or punishing political opponents. The praetorian provinces
were still designated after the elections had been held.
The *lex Cornelia* of 81 definitely instituted the promagisterial system for the provinces (cf. p. 105), but made no
important change in the part which the senate played in
the appointment of provincial governors. The *lex Pompeia*

Liv. 24. 43. 9;
26. 1. 1;
26. 28. 3 ff.;
42. 10. 11 ff.
Liv. 38. 35. 9;
42. 31. 1.

Cic. de Prov.
Cons. 3;
Sall. Iug.
27. 3–4.

Dio, 40 56.

*ae provinciis* of the year 52, which provided that an interval of five years should elapse between the time when one held the cónsulship or praetorship at Rome and took the government of a province, also directed that the designation of the provinces as consular or praetorian in a given case should be made just before the governors went out to their provinces, that is, about four years after their term of office in Rome had come to an end.   After the allotments had

Liv. 33. 43.
3 ff.;
Sall. Iug.
27. 5.

been made, *senatus consulta de provinciis ornandis* were passed, assigning troops and appropriating money for the several provinces.   Complaints made by the inhabitants of a province were addressed to the senate, and, although it rarely interfered in the management of a province, when it did consider favorably a provincial appeal, its action prevailed over the edict of the governor.

**284. The Senate and Foreign Affairs.**   The conclusion of a treaty with a people which had been at war with Rome required, as we have seen (p. 235), the sanction of the people, but the senate on its own motion was competent

Liv. 27. 4.
5 ff.;
29. 10. 4 ff.;
31. 11. 14 ff.;
39. 54.

to enter into a friendly alliance with a foreign nation in the name of the Roman people, to assume the protectorate of a territory, or to confer the title of king or friend of the Roman people on a foreign potentate.   To it also foreign nations addressed their complaints against Rome or Roman officials.   Similarly, demands or requests addressed to foreign countries were sent by the senate.   Embassies from hostile or friendly nations came to it.   The representatives of friendly powers were received into the city and entertained at public expense.   If the senate wished to hear the state-

Liv. 30. 21.
12; 37. 1. 6

ments of an embassy from a hostile people, a meeting was held outside the city; otherwise the ambassadors were ordered to leave Italy at once.   On the day when the members of a friendly embassy were to be heard by the senate they were taken to the *Graecostasis*, a structure near the *curia*, set apart for ambassadors, and later conducted into the senate by the magistrate, and allowed to make a statement in the Latin language. After a certain date the use of Greek was permissible. Then they were questioned by members of the senate, retired during its deliberations, but returned to hear the decision which had been reached. In some cases the senate appointed a committee to confer with the ambassadors and to make a report to it. The sending of embassies to foreign states was authorized by the senate, and all the members, usually three in number, of such embassies were senators. Two circumstances in particular robbed the senate in the first century of its influence in foreign affairs. In the first place, almost all the peoples with whom the Romans had in the early period carried on diplomatic relations were now subject to Rome, and were therefore governed by Roman officials. In the second place, campaigns were carried on at such a distance from Rome that it was usually impracticable for the senate to dictate the terms of a treaty, and commanding officers found it easy to carry on the negotiations without paying it much attention. Furthermore, the extraordinary powers which were granted to generals in the field, as to Sulla, Pompey, and Caesar, or the powers which circumstances allowed them to assume, contributed to the same result.

285. **Measures of Public Safety.** In another connection (pp. 181 f.) reference has been made to the various extraordinary measures which the senate took at moments of great public danger. These measures included the declaration of a *tumultus* or a *iustitium*, the appointment of a dictator, and the passage of the *senatus consultum ultimum*.

Varro, L. L. 5.155–6; Liv. 26. 31 f.; 30. 22. 5; 34. 57. 1–3; Val. Max. 2. 2. 3.

Liv. 34. 59. 8.

**286. The Tumultus and Iustitium.** The dictator could
declare a *tumultus* or a *iustitium* without waiting for any
action on the part of the senate, but if a dictator was not
in office, the declaration was made by the senate. When
a *tumultus* had been proclaimed, the city was occupied with
troops, the citizens put on the *sagum*, and all exemptions
from military service were canceled. The declaration of
a *iustitium* involved the suspension of all business not
required by the exigencies of the case. After the period
of the Gracchi, both these measures were taken to supplement the *senatus consultum ultimum*, but only when a
citizen had put himself at the head of an armed force,
and had been declared an *hostis rei publicae*.

**287. Appointment of a Dictator and Passage of the
Senatus Consultum Ultimum.** A dictator was named by
the consul, at the bidding of the senate, when the integrity of the commonwealth was threatened by wars without,
or by disorders within the confines of the state (cf. p. 181).
A dictator was appointed for the last time in 202. Three
facts explain the disappearance of the office. It had been
used as a weapon by the patricians in their struggle with
the plebeians, but the assumption by the people in the year
217 of the right to pass the enabling act took the office out
of the hands of the senate and made it useless to it. In the
second place, the dictatorship had been gradually stripped
of the exceptional powers which differentiated it from the
consulship (cf. p. 183). Furthermore, during the first
seventy years of the second century, no critical situation
developed in Italy, and the ascendency of the senate was
unquestioned, so that it felt no need of passing exceptional
measures. But the agitations of the Gracchi arrayed the
democracy against the *nobilitas*, and the senate cast about
for means to hold the opposition in check. Now the

Liv. 3. 27. 2.

Liv. 10. 21. 3;
34. 56. 11;
Cic. Phil. 8. 3.

Liv. 3. 5. 4;
Cic. Phil.
14. 1.

Liv.
22. 8. 5–6.

appointment of a dictator meant the investiture of an
extraordinary magistrate with extraordinary powers, but
the right to make such an appointment was no longer
the exclusive prerogative of the senate. The same object
could be attained, however, by conferring extraordinary
powers on a regular magistrate. This step it took in 132 by
granting to the consuls of that year the right to judge and
condemn to death those found guilty of taking part in the
revolutionary proceedings of Tiberius Gracchus. This led
to the passage of the Sempronian law in 123 (cf. p. 98),
which forbade the execution of any citizen until he had
been heard by the people. Two years later, however, the
senate voted *uti L. Opimius consul rem publicam defenderet*,
and, under the authority of this action, the consul attacked
the Gracchan party, which had seized the Aventine hill
and killed C. Gracchus and several of his followers. In
the year 100, during the agitation of the tribune Saturninus
(cf. p. 100), the consuls, with the help of the tribunes
and praetors, were directed to see to it *ut imperium populi
Romani maiestasque conservaretur.* Somewhat similar action
was taken in the years 88, 83, 77, 63, 62, 52, 49, 48, 47,
and 43. The special power exercised by the magistrate
under this decree of the senate was that of putting citizens
to death without granting them the privilege of appealing
to the people. This proceeding was, of course, in direct
contravention of the *lex Sempronia* of the year 123, and
the popular party never recognized the constitutionality of
it. The modification which Cicero introduced in the plan
followed by earlier magistrates, of asking for a specific vote
by the senate on the disposition of the accused persons,
does not make his course more or less constitutional than
that of his predecessors; for if the senate was competent to
act as a court of last resort, and to condemn citizens to

Plut. Ti.
Gr. 20;
Val. Max.
4. 7. 1.

Cic. Phil.
8. 14.

Cic. pro Rab.
perd. 20.

death, it was competent to empower the consuls to impose
the death penalty through the *s. c. ultimum*, and specific
action was unnecessary. If it was not competent in the
first instance, it could not itself impose the penalty. The
whole question of the constitutionality of the *s. c. ultimum* is
a matter of high dispute. In point of fact, the question
seems to bring into conflict two irreconcilable theories of
government, each of which prevailed to a greater or less
degree at different periods. The senate maintained, as
Cicero put it, *salus populi suprema lex est*. Furthermore,
it claimed to have the right to decide when the safety of
the state required the assumption on its part of extra-constitutional powers, and it claimed to be the ultimate depositary of supreme power. The first one of these propositions
will scarcely be questioned. Various historical considerations support the senate's contention on the other two
points. As we have seen (p. 10), when the chief-magistracy
became vacant through death or otherwise, the sovereignty
returned to the *patres*. Furthermore, up to the year 217,
the senate exercised not infrequently the right to decide
when the public safety required the suspension of the constitutional rights of the citizens, and in accordance with its
judgment instructed the consul to appoint a dictator. Its
failure to exercise that power for the next century or more
did not imply the loss of it. Opposed to this view of the
situation, on which the senate could rest its claim, was the
democratic theory that the will of the people is the law of
the land, and the successive achievements of the popular
party mark the advance made from time to time in forcing
the acceptance of that theory. The full recognition of
it, with a somewhat narrow interpretation of the word
"people" (cf. p. 51), was secured in 287. The failure of
the people to make full use of their power does not imply an

Cic. de Legg.
3. 8.

abandonment of the principle.   Indeed, the fact was freely
recognized that a decree of the senate could not stand
against the action of the popular assembly (cf. p. 233).
The position of the popular party was, therefore, a strong
one when it maintained that no *senatus consultum* could
suspend the action of the *lex Sempronia de provocatione.*
The special plea which was made on certain occasions by
the advocates of the senatorial prerogative, that the individuals concerned had become enemies of the state and,
therefore, had forfeited the rights of citizenship, is a piece
of sophistry, because to concede to the senate the right on
its own authority of declaring that a citizen who had not
openly taken up arms against the government was an *hostis
rei publicae* was to grant it indirectly the power of suspending the action of a *lex.*   The question is, therefore, like the
old problem of free will and necessity, and it will probably
be decided by different students according to the theory
of ideal government held by each of them.   In this connection we may mention the action of the senate declaring
that certain individuals were acting, or would act in a given
case, *contra rem publicam.*   Such a motion on the part of
the senate, usually directed against magistrates, often preceded the passage of a *s. c. ultimum,* and indicated the
intention of the senate to pass that measure, if the persons
concerned persisted in the course which they had taken.

*[margin: Cic. in Cat. 4. 10.]*

*[margin: Cic. ad Att. 1. 16. 12; 2. 24. 3; ad Fam. 8. 8. 6; Caes. B. C. 1. 2. 6.]*

### SELECTED BIBLIOGRAPHY[1]

**Composition of the senate and senatorial privileges:** Willems, Le
sénat de la république romaine, Vol. I, Louvain, 1883 ; Th. Mommsen, Römische Forschungen, I.[2] 218–284 ; G. Bloch, Les origines
du sénat romain, Paris, 1883 ; Fr. Hofmann, Der röm. Senat zur
Zeit der Republik, Berlin, 1847 ; Lange, De plebiscitis Ovinio et Atinio

[1] See also pp. 22, 173, 219.

disputatio, Leipzig, 1878 ; Monro, On the pedarii, Journ. of Phil.
IV. (1872) 113–119. — **Meetings of the senate :** C. Bardt, Die Senats-
sitzungstage der späteren Republik (in Hermes, VII. 14 ff.) ; Zur
lex Caecilia Didia (*ibid.* IX. 305 ff.) ; Lange, Die lex Pupia (in
Rhein. Mus. (N. F.), XXIX. 321–336, and XXX. 350–397) ; Lanciani,
L'aula e gli uffici del senato romano (Mem. dell' Accad. dei Lincei,
XI) ; Mispoulet, La vie parlementaire à Rome sous la république,
Paris, 1899 ; B. Pick, De senatus consultis Romanorum, Part I,
Berlin, 1884 ; Hübner, De senatus populique actis, Leipzig, 1859 ;
Willems, Vol. II. — **Powers of the senate :** H. Genz, Das patri-
zische Rom, Berlin, 1878 ; Soltau, Altrömische Volksversammlungen
(109–226), Berlin, 1880 ; Nissen, Das Iustitium, Leipzig, 1877;
Willems, Vol. II.

## Supplementary Literature, 1901–1910

Barbagallo, Una misura eccezionale dei Romani : Il senatus consultum ultimum. Rome, 1900.

Delaunay, Les relations des magistrats et du sénat sous la république. Rennes, 1896.

P. Willems et J. Willems, Le senat romain en 65 de notre ère.
Louvain, 1902.

Sands, The Client Princes of the Roman Empire under the Republic. Cambridge (England), 1906.

# CHAPTER XI

## THE PEOPLE

### (a) *Citizens and their Rights*

**288. How Citizenship could be Acquired.** The rights
of citizenship could be acquired by birth, by naturaliza-
tion, or by manumission. They belonged, therefore, to the
issue of a legal marriage (*iustum matrimonium*), contracted
between those who had the *ius conubii*. Before 445 the
*ius conubii* was enjoyed by the patricians only, but in
that year it was given to the plebeians also (cf. pp. 33 f.).
Foreigners could gain the rights of Roman citizenship only
through action of the popular assembly, although, in the
later years of the republic, generals in the field seem to
have usurped this prerogative of the people in a few cases.
Special facilities were granted to the Latins and the allies
in acquiring citizenship, as we shall presently see. The
formal announcement of a slave's freedom by his master
made him a citizen. This announcement could be made
in the presence of a magistrate, or in a will, or the master
could confer freedom and citizenship on him at the same
time by having his name enrolled in the censor's list.

Liv. 4. 4. 7.
Cic. pro Arch
24; pro
Balbo, 19.

**289. How it could be Lost.** Roman citizenship implied
personal liberty. Consequently, any one who was captured
in war, turned over to the enemy, or sold into slavery, lost
it completely. This complete forfeiture of civic and family
rights, as well as of freedom, was known as the *capitis
deminutio maxima*. Captives who returned to the city

could regain their rights. The *capitis deminutio media* implied the loss of all civic and family rights, but not of personal liberty. Those who had become citizens in another state, who had gone into voluntary exile, or had been banished, suffered this penalty. *Capitis deminutio minima* took place in case of adoption. The adopted person lost the family rights which he had formerly enjoyed, but he acquired the rights of the family into which he was adopted.

**290. Three Classes of Freemen.** There were three classes of freemen under the republic : (I) those who had the full right of Roman citizenship ; (II) those who enjoyed it only in part or when they had conformed to certain conditions ; and (III) those who in their own persons had no rights before the law.

**291. Equalization of the Rights of Citizenship.** Under the monarchy patricians alone had the full rights of Roman citizenship. What these rights were, and what the position of the plebeians was, we have already had occasion to notice (pp. 17 f.). The remodeling of the army by Servius Tullius (p. 20), and the development of the new organization into a political body under the republic (pp. 26 f.) brought important civil and political rights to the plebeians. Henceforth they participated in the meetings of the centuriate *comitia* for the enactment of laws and the election of magistrates. The *lex Valeria* allowed them to appeal to the popular assembly in case the death penalty had been imposed by a magistrate (p. 27). The establishment of the tribunate in 494 gave them greater protection against patrician magistrates (p. 28), and at the same time secured to them a political institution in which the patricians had no part. By the *lex Canuleia* of 445 they gained the *ius conubii* between themselves and the patricians. The political agitation of the fourth century secured them admission to the magistracies and to certain priesthoods. The passage of the Valerio-Horatian, Publilian, and Hortensian laws technically freed the popular assemblies, and in particular the plebeian tribal assembly, from the control of the patrician element in the senate (pp. 49 f.).

(I) **Content of the Civitas Romana.** Henceforth citizenship meant practically the same for patricians and plebeians. It included the *iura commercii, conubii, provocationis, legis actionis, suffragii,* and the *ius honorum.* The privileges retained by the patrician consisted in the right to hold the priestly offices of *flamen* and of *rex sacrorum,* and to be one of the *fratres Arvales, Salii,* and *Luperci,* to take part in the passage of the *auctoritas patrum,* to act as an *interrex,* and to be a member of a *gens,* and, consequently, of the *comitia curiata* (cf., however, p. 252). On his side the plebeian alone was eligible to the tribunate, and none but plebeians could participate in the meetings of the *concilium plebis.*

(II) **Restricted Citizenship.** 1. *Freedmen.* A second class of freemen enjoyed the rights of Roman citizenship only in part, or when they had satisfied certain conditions. In this category were the freedmen. They never gained the right to sit in the senate, and, up to the time of Appius Claudius, they were not enrolled in the tribes. The radical improvement which he made in their position (cf. pp. 54 ff.) was partly lost in the reaction of 304, which restricted them to the four city tribes (cf. p. 56). Numerous attempts were made by democratic leaders in the first century to secure them admission to other tribes, but without permanent success. The concession which was ultimately made to them with reference to admission to the senate has been noted in another connection. They had the *ius commercii* and technically the *ius conubii.*

Herz. I. 996.

As we have already seen, certain offenses, or a reprehensible mode of living, might take from a citizen his right to a vote, or might deprive him of its full value, and the magistrate presiding at an election could refuse to consider the claims of an objectionable candidate (p. 169). This, of course, amounted to a loss of the *ius suffragii* or the *ius honorum*, as the case might be.

2. *Latini.* Under the *foedus Cassianum*, which tradition assigns to the year 493, the members of the Latin league enjoyed the *ius commercii*, and probably also the *ius conubii*. The war of 338 broke the power of the league and enabled Rome to make with each one of its members (cf. p. 57) separate arrangements, in all of which the *ius commercii* was seriously restricted. From that time the rights of these communities depended entirely on their treaties with Rome and differed in different cases. The Latin colonies which the Romans began to found in the fourth century held nearly the same relation to Rome as the communities just mentioned, and a statement of the rights which the settlers in these colonies enjoyed will apply also to the members of the Latin communities allied with Rome. They had the *ius commercii* and perhaps the *ius conubii*. In Rome they were allowed to vote in a tribe determined by lot. Furthermore, a Latin could exercise the rights of Roman citizenship in Rome, provided he had left a son at home. In the colonies founded after 268 this privilege was restricted to those who had held a magistracy and, from the year mentioned, the *ius conubii* was no longer given to new colonies. The *civitas Romana* was probably granted to all communities in Latium in the early part of the second century, and, as a result of the Social war, all cities in Italy of the class under consideration acquired the rights of Roman citizenship (cf. pp. 101 f.).

St. R. III. 623 f.; Herz. I. 1005 f.; Madv. 1. 58 f.

Liv. 25. 3. 16.

Liv. 41. 8. 9.

Appian, B. C. 2. 26; Cic. pro Caec. 102.

3. *Cives sine suffragio.* About 353 the Romans established, in the case of Caere in Etruria, the first of a new
class of communities known as *municipia sine suffragio.*
The people in these communities had the private rights of
Roman citizens, but they could not be enrolled in a tribe,
and, therefore, could not vote. The *lex Iulia* and the *lex
Plautia Papiria* of 90–89 did away with all communities
of this class in Italy.

Liv. 7. 20. 8;
Gell. 16. 13. 7.

(III) **Peregrini, etc.** In the eyes of the law every freeman who was not a Roman citizen was a *peregrinus.* Strictly
speaking, therefore, those who had only the *ius Latii* came
under this head, but the term *peregrini* was commonly
applied to the citizens of independent states or of dependent communities which did not have the rights of Roman
citizenship in whole or in part. Such a freeman, when at
Rome, secured protection either through a treaty made by
his state with Rome, through the offices of the *praetor peregrinus*, who administered the *ius gentium*, or by an *hospitium
privatum* arranged with a Roman citizen, who was thus put
under moral obligation to protect him to the extent of his
power. Furthermore, women, minors, and those of unsound
mind had no political rights, and secured their civil rights
only through the kindly offices of a representative who was a
citizen. Slaves were regarded simply as chattels, for whom
their masters were responsible.

Will. Dr.
346 f.;
Cic. Div. in
Caec. 67.

## (b) Divisions of the People for Political Purposes

**292. The Curiae.** The division of the people under the
monarchy into *curiae*, tribes, classes, and centuries has
already been considered (cf. pp. 18, 20–21). The *curiae*
were in their origin local subdivisions for political purposes.
The local character of their origin seems to be indicated by

such names as Foriensis and Veliensis.   Membership in a
*curia* was handed down from father to son without regard
to change of residence.

**293. The Tribes.**  We have already had occasion to
notice (pp. 5 f., 21) that the term *tribus* has two, perhaps
three, different meanings.  The four Servian tribes were
Suburana, Esquilina, Collina, and Palatina.  The seventeen
tribes added in the early years of the republic (cf. p. 27)
were Aemilia, Camilia, Claudia, Cornelia, Crustumina, Fabia,
Galeria, Horatia, Lemonia, Menenia, Papiria, Pollia, Pupinia,
Romilia, Sergia, Voltinia, and Voturia.  All of these names
with the exception of Crustumina, which is of local origin,
are the names of patrician clans.  To this number four new
tribes (Arnensis, Sabatina, Stellatina, and Tromentina) were
added in 387, two (Pomptina and Poplilia) in 358, two
(Maecia and Scaptia) in 332, two (Falerna and Oufentina)
in 318, two (Aniensis and Teretina) in 300, and two (Qui-
rina and Velina) in 241.  The number never passed beyond
this maximum of thirty-five.  That no additions were made
subsequent to 241 is probably due to the fact that about
this time the tribal organization was adopted as the basis of
the reformed centuriate assembly (cf. p. 74).  After the date
mentioned, newly made citizens were apportioned among
the old tribes.  The importance of the tribe as a political
unit depended, of course, on the fact that the three great
popular assemblies were based on it.  Membership in a
tribe was the mark of citizenship, and was indicated in the
legal name, e.g., *C. Lucilius C. f. Pup(inia tribu) Hirrus*.
We have already considered (pp. 247 f.) the restrictions laid
upon certain classes of citizens with reference to their tribal
relations.  Membership was determined at first by residence
or the ownership of land.  A change of residence did not
entail a change of tribe, but a citizen could pass into a new

tribe in case he settled in a colony, or he could be assigned to a new tribe by the censors. Mention is made of two classes of tribal officials under the republic, the *curatores tribuum* and the *tribuni aerarii*, but their functions are obscure. Perhaps the former had to do with the elections and the census. Possibly the office of *tribuni aerarii* was established when Rome began to raise the *tributum*. At all events, for some time these officials seem to have been financial officers representing the several tribes. After the *tributum* was given up, their position was one of honor only.

**294. The Classes and Centuries.** The basis on which the people were divided into classes and centuries has already been touched on (cf. pp. 20 f., 54 f., 74 f.), and will be considered further when we come to discuss the centuriate *comitia*. A new assignment was made by each college of censors.

### (c) *Popular Assemblies*

**295. Comitia.** There were three classes of popular assemblies among the Romans, viz., *comitia*, *concilia*, and *contiones*. *Comitia* were assemblies of all the citizens, *i.e.*, of the *populus Romanus*, called for the purpose of taking action on matters submitted to them by duly authorized officials. There were three of these assemblies, the *comitia curiata*, *centuriata*, and *tributa*, and they came into existence in the order indicated.

**296. Concilia.** *Concilia*, in the political sense of the word, were formal assemblies of a part of the people. Thus a *concilium plebis* was a legislative or electoral assembly of the plebeians. The distinction between *comitia* and *concilium* has been well indicated by Laelius Felix (Gell. *N. A.* XV. 27. 4) : *is qui non universum populum, sed partem aliquam adesse iubet, non " comitia," sed " concilium " edicere iubet.*

**297. Contiones.** *Contiones* differed from *comitia* and *concilia* mainly in three particulars. The people came together as individuals, and not as members of certain political organizations, like the *curia*, century, or tribe. Hence a strict test of citizenship was not applied. In the second place, these gatherings were solely for the purpose of receiving communications, and no action could be taken. Finally, private citizens, with the consent of the presiding magistrate, could address the assembly. *Contiones* resembled the *comitia* and the *concilia* in that they could be called by magistrates only, and that the procedure in them was directed by the presiding magistrate. A *contio* was usually held before the *comitia* or *concilium* met, to hear a statement and a discussion of the questions which were to be acted on later in the more formal body. They were not a necessary part of the machinery of state, but they exerted an important political influence, especially since political meetings could not be called by private individuals.

### (d) The Comitia Curiata

**298. Admission of Plebeians.** The organization and functions of the *comitia curiata* under the monarchy have been considered in another part of this book (cf. pp. 19 f.).

St. R. III. 92 f.; Herz. I. 1014; Will. Dr. 49 f.; Soltau, 67 f.

Whether the plebeians were admitted is a matter of great doubt. The statements of ancient writers, the fact that plebeians were eligible to the office of *curio maximus* and took part in certain curial religious rites, seem to indicate that they were admitted to the curiate assembly. They

Will. Dr. 51, nn. 1, 2.

probably did not gain the right to vote, however, until midway in the republican period.

**299. Formalities attending a Meeting.** After the passage of the *lex Caecilia Didia* (p. 100), announcement probably had to be made seventeen days before the assembly met. The ordinary place of meeting was the *comitium*. The presiding officer, when the *lex curiata de imperio* was presented for action, was a magistrate. On other occasions the *pontifex maximus* presided. Formal actions of the assembly did not become valid until they had received the *patrum auctoritas*. The importance of this body disappeared to such an extent that in the later years of the republic the *curiae* were at times represented by thirty lictors and three augurs. The semi-political functions which the curiate *comitia* had exercised under the monarchy (pp. 14, 19 f.) fell to the centuriate assembly, and the older body kept its jurisdiction over clan affairs only.

Varro, L. L. 5. 155.

Cic. de Re Publ. 2. 56; Liv. 6. 41. 10 Cic. de Leg. Agr. 2. 31.

## (e) The Comitia Centuriata

**300. Composition of the Comitia Centuriata.** The composition of the centuriate *comitia* has already been sufficiently described (pp. 20 f., 74 f.). In 88 B.C. Sulla restored the Servian organization of the assembly, but the reformed system was speedily reinstated again.

Appian, B. C. 1. 59.

**301. Presiding Officer.** The centuriate *comitia* was in its origin a military body. It could, therefore, be called together only by magistrates who had the *imperium*, or by lower officials commissioned or allowed by higher magistrates to issue a summons. The right which the censor exercised to call a meeting of the people by centuries in taking the census was only an apparent exception to this principle. No vote was taken in the assembly called by him, so that the meeting was not properly a meeting of the *comitia centuriata*. When the assembly met to elect consuls, censors, or praetors, of the regular magistrates only the consul could preside (p. 176).

Varro, L. L. 6. 88; 6. 93.

**302. Dies Comitiales.** The days on which the assembly could meet (*dies comitiales*) numbered one hundred and ninety in the early imperial period, and were indicated in the calendar by the letter *C*. Assemblies could not be held on holidays (*dies nefasti*), nor on days set apart for meetings of the courts (*dies fasti*). The regular place of meeting was the Campus Martius.

C. I. L. I.
pp. 368 f.;
Varr. L. L.
6. 29.

Gell. 15. 27. 5.

**303. Announcement of Meetings.** After the passage of the *lex Caecilia Didia* (p. 100), announcement had to be made for a period of seventeen days before the date of the proposed meeting. The announcement took the form of a magisterial edict giving the date and purpose of the meeting. This edict included the text of the proposed bill, the list of candidates, or the names of persons accused, with a statement of the charges made against them, according as the *comitia* met as a legislative, electoral, or judicial assembly.

**304. The Auspices.** Shortly after midnight on the day of the proposed meeting the prospective presiding officer, accompanied by an augur, took the auspices. If the interpretation of them by the augur was unfavorable, the meeting was postponed to another day. Even if the auspices were favorable, two religious difficulties might lead to a postponement, viz., the announcement of another magistrate that he had seen unfavorable omens, or the occurrence of *dirae* at the time of the meeting. The plan which the Romans finally adopted in dealing with cases of this sort, and the responsibility of the presiding magistrate, have already been considered (cf. pp. 158–160).

Liv. 1. 36. 6;
Varro, L. L.
6. 91; 6. 95;
Cic. de Legg.
3. 11.

**305. Other Formalities.** In case he found no obstacles in the way of holding the meeting, on the spot where he had taken the auspices, the magistrate, through an assistant, proceeded to summon the citizens to a meeting (*vocare* *inlicium Quirites*). The summons was repeated by a trumpeter on the walls and on the Arx, and a red flag was raised on the Arx. Immediately before the holding of the *comitia*, a *contio* was called at which the magistrate who had summoned the *comitia* presided. After a sacrifice had been made, and prayer had been offered, the business to come before the *comitia* was stated and discussed (cf. p. 252). After the *contio* the magistrate summoned the people to assemble by centuries in the *comitia* with the words *impero qua convenit ad comitia centuriata*. Thereupon those who did not have the right to vote retired, and the citizens arranged themselves in centuries under their respective *centuriones*.

Varro, L. L. 6. 88–90; 6. 92–95; Liv. 39. 15. 11.

Varro, L. L. 6. 88; 6. 90; 6. 94.

Liv. 39. 15. 1; Cic. pro Mur. 1.

Liv. 2. 56. 10.

**306. Method of Voting.** Before the reform of 241 the eighteen centuries of knights voted first, all the centuries voting simultaneously, and the result of their vote was announced; then came the centuries of the first and of the second class, and so on, until a majority of the centuries had voted in favor of a certain proposition. In point of fact the knights and the *pedites* of the first class usually voted in the same way. If that proved to be the case, it was not necessary to continue voting after the centuries of the first class had cast their ballots, as their eighty centuries with the eighteen equestrian centuries constituted a majority of the assembly. Under the reform legislation of 241 the knights lost their privilege of voting first. The order of the classes was still observed, however, and a century was chosen by lot (*centuria praerogativa*) from the first class, whose privilege it was to vote and have its vote announced before the ballots of the other centuries were cast. A large enclosure, called the *saepta* or *ovile*, was set apart for the voters, with small sections for the members of each century, and as the voters went out of these enclosures through the

Liv. 1. 43. 11.

Liv. 24. 7. 12; 27. 6. 3; Cic. Phil. 2. 82.

Herz. I. 1123, n. 3; Lange, II. 487 f.

narrow passages (*pontes*), they cast their ballots. During the early republican period, citizens gave their votes *viva voce*, but after the passage of the *leges tabellariae* (cf. p. 71), toward the end of the second century, balloting was secret. At legislative meetings each voter received an affirmative ballot bearing the letters *U. R.* (i.e., *uti rogas*), and a negative ballot marked *A.* (i.e., *antiquo*). At meetings to elect magistrates each voter received a blank *tabella*, on which he wrote the name of the candidate of his choice. When the *comitia* met as a judicial assembly, he received two tablets, one marked *L.* (i.e., *libero*) and the other *D.* (i.e., *damno*). The proper ballot was placed by the voter in the *cista*, which was guarded by the *rogatores* or *diribitores*. A majority of the votes in the century determined the vote of the century, and a majority of the centuries decided the vote of the whole assembly. Announcement of the result (*renuntiatio*) was made by the presiding officer, who had a certain amount of discretionary power in the case of the elections. It was necessary for the *comitia* to adjourn before sunset.

**307. The Centuriate Comitia as an Electoral Body.** The centuriate *comitia* met for three different purposes, viz., to elect the higher magistrates, to enact laws, and to hear appeals in cases involving the death penalty. Of the regular magistrates, it chose the consuls, the censors, and the praetors; of the extraordinary magistrates, the *decemviri legibus scribundis* and the consular tribunes. At the outset it probably had the right only to accept or reject a nomination made by the presiding officer, but, at a comparatively early period, it acquired the power of choosing between several candidates, although the presiding magistrate could always exercise some discretion with reference to the eligibility of the candidates (cf. pp. 169, 171).

*Margin notes:*
Cic. ad Att. I. 14. 5; de Legg. 3. 38. Plut. Cat. Min. 46.

Cic. in Pis. 36.

Lex Malacitana, c. 57.

Before the passage of the *lex Maenia* in 287 (cf. p. 51) an election needed the ratification of the patrician senators, expressed in the *patrum auctoritas*. After that date the *patrum auctoritas* preceded the election and became a mere matter of form.

**308. The Centuriate Comitia as a Legislative Assembly.** At the outset, in the field of legislation, the centuriate *comitia* exercised only the right to declare an offensive war, a right which was transferred to it from the curiate assembly. Soon after the republic was established, however, it acquired the power of legislating, under certain conditions, on any subject (cf. p. 27). After 449 it shared this privilege with the *concilium plebis* (cf. p. 32), and after 447 also with the patricio-plebeian tribal assembly (cf. p. 33). The restrictions laid on both these bodies enabled it to retain its supremacy, however, until 287. From that time on, since they were as free as the centuriate *comitia*, or freer than it, and since their method of procedure was simpler than that of the centuriate *comitia*, their place of meeting more convenient, and their composition more democratic, the importance of the centuriate *comitia* declined rapidly. No sure line of distinction can be drawn between the legislation which the centuriate *comitia* could enact and that which the two tribal assemblies could pass, except that the centuriate assembly retained its exclusive right to declare an offensive war, and to pass an act, modeled on the *lex de imperio* of the curiate assembly, conferring plenary power on the censor, an act known as the *lex de potestate censoria*. The ordinary method of procedure in securing the passage of a *lex* in the centuriate *comitia* was as follows : the consul laid a subject before the senate for consideration ; its action, if not vetoed, was known as a *senatus consultum*, and took the form of advice, or of a request that the magistrate should lay a certain proposition before the popular assembly for its favorable consideration. Announcement of the bill (*promulgatio legis*) had to be made by the magistrate seventeen days before the assembly could vote on it. In this interval probably the *patrum auctoritas* was secured. On the appointed day the bill was read and discussed in a *contio*, and the people voted on it immediately afterward in the *comitia*. As we have already noticed (p. 177), the consul was not required to consult the senate beforehand, nor was he theoretically obliged to bring a proposition recommended by the senate before the *comitia*, or if he did propose the measure, he could oppose its passage, but, for reasons already given, magistrates rarely exercised these constitutional rights.

**309. The Centuriate Comitia as a Court of Appeal.** The right to inflict capital punishment was included under the *imperium*, but, from an early period, citizens in the city who were condemned to death by a magistrate were allowed to appeal to the people. This privilege was extended and confirmed by the *lex Valeria*, the *lex Valeria Horatia* (p. 31), the *leges Porciae*, and the *lex Sempronia*. The appeal was heard by the centuriate *comitia*. The quaestors, *II viri perduellionis*, or tribunes in charge of the matter, appointed a day (*diem dicere*) for the first hearing. This was known as the *prima accusatio*. In this meeting the charge and defense were heard, and arrangements were made for another hearing, known as the *secunda accusatio*, when the investigation, with the taking of testimony, was continued. After the third *contio* (*tertia accusatio*) the magistrate gave his decision, and announced the penalty, upon which the accused, if he wished, could appeal to the centuriate assembly. That assembly voted on the simple

Liv. 10. 9.
3 ff.;
Cic. pro Rab.
perd. 12;
Herz.
I. 1081 f.

Liv. 3. 11. 9;
3. 13. 4 ff.;
3. 24. 3;
26. 3. 5 ff.;
Cic. de Domo,
45.

question of guilt or innocence. It could not modify in any way the proposed sentence. After a date, which we cannot fix, the accused was allowed to go into voluntary exile at any time before the vote was taken in the *comitia*. The two classes of cases which were most commonly carried before the centuriate assembly were those of murder (*parricidium*) and treason (*perduellio*). The proceedings in non-political cases were usually conducted by the quaestor, in political cases by the tribune, under the presidency of the praetor. The establishment of *quaestiones extraordinariae* took many cases out of the hands of the quaestor and the centuriate assembly. The *lex Sempronia* of the year 123 (p. 98) was intended to correct this practice, and in some measure it restored the importance of the *comitia centuriata* as a court of appeal. That body lost its judicial functions entirely, however, after the establishment by Sulla of a complete system of permanent courts. Criminal trials were conducted in them in a simpler and more satisfactory way, and since the severest penalty which they imposed was that of banishment, there were no appeals to be taken to the *comitia centuriata*.

### (f) The Comitia Tributa

**310. The Existence of a Patricio-Plebeian Tribal Assembly.** No ancient historian mentions the establishment of a tribal assembly including patricians as well as plebeians, nor is any distinction drawn between the *comitia tributa* and the *concilium plebis*. In fact, in one case at least, the plebeian tribal assembly is spoken of as the *comitia tributa*. This state of things has led some modern scholars to maintain that there was only one tribal assembly, from whose meetings the patricians were excluded, an assembly

Liv. 2. 56. 2.

Madv. I. 235;
Ihne, Rhein.
Mus.
28. 367 f.

indifferently called the *comitia tributa* or the *concilium plebis*. However, the people meeting in the *comitia tributa* are designated by the term *populus*, which in the republican period can properly be applied only to a body made up of all citizens, patricians as well as plebeians. Furthermore, in a tribal assembly, presided over by a magistrate, as we shall presently see, certain officials were elected to whom the term *magistratus* in its technical sense (cf. pp. 151, 171) was applied. Their election and the fact that a magistrate presided presuppose an assembly containing both patricians and plebeians. On the whole, then, the existence of a patricio-plebeian tribal assembly is highly probable. The assembly came into existence in the middle of the fifth century (cf. p. 33), immediately after the organization of the plebeian tribal assembly.

Herz.
I. 1129, n. 7.

**311. Composition.** We have no direct evidence bearing on the composition of the *comitia tributa*, but it may be safely assumed that all patricians and plebeians belonging to the thirty-five tribes voted in the assembly.

**312. Meetings.** The *comitia tributa* were presided over by a magistrate. It was necessary to take the auspices before a meeting was held. The usual place of meeting was the forum. The method of voting was that followed in the centuriate *comitia*. After the passage of the Hortensian law the action of the assembly did not need the *patrum auctoritas* to be valid.

**313. The Comitia Tributa as an Electoral, Legislative, and Judicial Body.** When the quaestorship became an elective office its incumbents were chosen in this assembly (p. 33), and this became the regular method of electing them. Later the curule aediles were chosen in it, and in fact all the lower magistrates, as well as the members of certain special commissions (cf. pp. 204, 210, 216). The tribal *comitia* could legislate apparently on any subject, and, as we have already seen (p. 257), it is impossible to distinguish between the three popular assemblies with respect to the character of the subjects on which they took action. Certain judicial cases, conducted by the curule aedile, were heard before it (cf. p. 206).

**314. The Modified Comitia Tributa.** A modified form of the *comitia tributa* was adopted at an unknown date for the choice of the *pontifex maximus*. Seventeen of the thirty-five tribes were chosen by lot, and summoned to a meeting for the election of this official from among the pontiffs. The arrangement was a compromise. It gave a popular character to the choice and yet retained in part the religious principle of coöptation. In the same assembly, and by a somewhat similar method, the *pontifices, augures, XV viri*, and *VII viri epulones* were chosen after the passage of the *lex Domitia* in 104 (cf. p. 107).

## (g) The Concilium Plebis

**315. Composition and Presiding Officer.** We have had occasion to notice the fact that the earliest plebeian, like the patrician, assembly was probably organized on the curiate basis. The controlling influence which the patricians were able to exercise over this assembly through their clients (p. 29) may well have led to the adoption of the tribal system in 471. Only plebeians could vote in this new body, and no change was ever made in this regulation. Down to 312 this privilege was enjoyed by plebeian landowners only. The right was extended to landless plebeians in 312, but after the reaction of 304 they, as well as freedmen, were restricted to the four city tribes (cf. pp. 54, 56, 247). The Latins had the right also to vote in one

Will. Dr. 280, n. 4.

Liv. 2. 56. 2 f. 2. 60. 4 f.

tribe determined by lot (cf. p. 248). The meetings of this body were technically *concilia plebis* (cf. p. 251), and not *comitia*. Since the assembly was strictly plebeian, the presiding officer was always a plebeian official — either a tribune or an aedile.

**316. Place and Time of Meeting.** The authority of the tribune did not extend beyond the *pomoerium*, so that the *concilium plebis* met within the city, usually in the *comitium*, occasionally, however, on the Capitol. There were no specified *dies comitiales*, as in the case of the centuriate *comitia* (cf. p. 254). Meetings were commonly held on market days, when large numbers of people were likely to come into the city. The time and place and the business which was to be taken up were announced some days before the meeting was held. In fact, from a comparatively early period the practice grew up of announcing on a market day a meeting to be held a *trinum nundinum*, or seventeen days, later. On the first and second market days, as well as on the market day when the voting took place, there were usually *contiones*.

**317. Auspices and Other Formalities.** The *lex Aelia Fufia* of the year 155 (cf. p. 160) seems to have subjected the *concilium plebis* to the same religious regulations which applied to the centuriate *comitia*. After its passage it was necessary for the tribune to take the *auspicia pullaria* before calling the assembly together, and the meeting was liable to the same kind of interference on religious grounds as the other popular assemblies.

Lange, II. 474 f.

Before the *concilium* a *contio* met in the *comitium* or *forum*, and was addressed from the *rostra* by the presiding officer, or by speakers whom he allowed to address the meeting.

**318. Voting.** At the close of the *contio* the people assembled by tribes, for the purpose of voting, in sections marked off for the reception of the several tribes. A lot was first cast to decide in which tribe the Latins were to vote; then one of the thirty-five tribes was chosen by lot to cast its vote first (*principium*), and as soon as its vote was announced the others voted simultaneously. The method of voting was the same as in the centuriate assembly (cf. pp. 255 f.). The assembly was essentially a democratic body. Certain considerations, however, tended to increase or diminish the value of an individual vote. The larger the tribe was to which a citizen belonged, so much the less influence his vote had. Now the four city tribes were much larger than the country tribes created before 387, and the tribes added after 387 were also larger than the early country tribes, because of the additions which were made to the list of citizens by conquest and by the grant of citizenship. Those who belonged to the city tribes or to the new rural tribes were, therefore, at a disadvantage when compared with the members of the old rural tribes. One factor tended to diminish still more the value of a vote in one of the new country tribes, but to increase the importance of an urban vote. It was easy for those who lived in the city to attend a *concilium*, but difficult for those at a distance.

**319. The Concilium Plebis as an Electoral Body.** The *concilium plebis* was established primarily for the purpose of electing the tribunes, and those officials were always chosen by it. The plebeian aediles were chosen in the same assembly. An interesting extension of the electoral rights of the body was made during the Gracchan period when commissioners were elected in the *concilium plebis* for the division of state land. This precedent proved to be of great importance later, since the Gabinian and Manilian laws, which conferred extraordinary powers on Pompey, were passed in this body.

**320. As a Legislative Body.** The combined effect of the Valerio-Horatian law of 449, the Publilian of 339, and the Hortensian of 287, was to make the *concilium plebis* an independent legislative body (pp. 49 ff.). After 287 the approval of the patrician element in the senate became unnecessary, but the senate was still able to control legislation in large measure (cf. pp. 65 ff.). The plebeian assembly seems to have been competent in Cicero's time to legislate on any subject, except the declaration of an offensive war, and such administrative questions as the assignment of state land to individuals, the appointment of commissions, and the *prorogatio imperii*, were brought up in the tribal assemblies, preferably in the *concilium plebis*, rather than in the centuriate *comitia*. In the later period the plebeian assembly even annulled contracts made by the censor and in this way encroached on the rights of the magistrate and the senate. Its enactments were called *plebiscita*. The three laws just mentioned, however, gave such measures the force of *leges*, so that the action of the assembly is not infrequently termed *lex plebeivescitum*.

**321. As a Judicial Body.** The circumstances under which the criminal jurisdiction of the tribune developed have already been mentioned (pp 199 f.). One class of cases, however, deserves special notice. The *lex Aternia Tarpeia* of 454 would seem to have conferred on all magistrates the right of imposing a fine not to exceed two sheep and thirty oxen, or, according to the money valuation of a later day, 3020 *asses*. An appeal taken from the decision of a magistrate was carried to the *comitia tributa*, but an appeal from a fine imposed by a tribune or a plebeian aedile was heard by the *concilium plebis*. The institution of the *quaestiones perpetuae* did away, however, with the judicial functions of the latter body.

## Selected Bibliography[1]

Citizens and their rights: M. Voigt, Ueber d. Klientel u. Libertinität, Ber. d. k. sächs. Ges. d. Wiss., Philol. hist. Kl., 1878, 1 Abt. 146–219; F. Lindet, De l'acquisition et de la perte du droit de cité romaine, Paris, 1880; L. Pinvert, Du droit de cité, Paris, 1885; A. Josson, Condition juridique des affranchis en droit rom., Douai, 1879; L. Pardon, De aerariis, Berlin, 1853. — Division of the people for political purposes: Pelham, The Roman curiae, Journ. of Phil. IX. 266–279; Soltau, Entstehung der altrömischen Volksversammlungen, Berlin, 1881; Kubitschek, De rom. trib. origine ac propagatione, Vienna, 1882; Plüss, Die Entwicklung d. Centurienverf., Leipzig, 1870. — Popular assemblies: Soltau, Altr. Volksversammlungen; Ullrich, Die Centuriatkomitien, Landshut, 1873; Genz, Die Centuriatkomitien nach der Reform, Freienwalde, 1882; C. Berns, De comitiorum tributorum et conciliorum plebis discrimine, Wetzlar, 1875; Soltau, Die Gültigkeit der Plebiscite, Berlin, 1884; Ihne, Die Entwickelung d. Tributkomitien, Rhein. Mus. (N.F.), XXVIII (1873), 353 ff.; Lange, Die promulgatio trinum nundinum, Rhein. Mus. (N.F.), XXX (1875), 350 ff.; E. Morlot, Les comices électoraux sous la république romaine, Paris, 1884; Ch. Borgeaud, Histoire du plébiscite, Paris, 1887; K. W. Ruppel, Die Teilnahme der Patricier an den Tributkomitien, Heidelberg, 1887.

## Supplementary Literature, 1901–1910

Botsford, The Roman Assemblies. New York, 1909.
Soltau, Gültigkeit der Plebiscite. Berliner Studien, II (1885), 1–176.
Greenidge, The Authenticity of the Twelve Tables. Eng. Hist. Review, XX (1905), 1–21.
Lambert, L'histoire traditionelle des XII Tables. Mélanges Ch. Appleton. Paris, 1903.

---

[1] See also pp. 22, 173, 219, 243.

# Part III — Imperial Period

## SECTION I — HISTORICAL

### CHAPTER XII

#### THE ESTABLISHMENT OF THE EMPIRE

**322. Restoration of Order in Italy.** When Octavius returned to Italy in the summer of 29, he was confronted by a state of things not unlike that which faced him after the battle of Philippi (cf. p. 143). It was necessary to relieve the poverty-stricken people of Italy at once, to provide lands for the veterans, and to decide upon a policy with reference to the soldiers of Antony. The prudence and moderation which he had shown on the previous occasion encouraged friend and foe alike to look for a wise policy now. This expectation was not disappointed. His very arrival in Italy inspired that confidence in the future which is the precursor of prosperity, while immediate financial difficulties were relieved by a liberal use of the treasures of Egypt. One hundred and twenty thousand veterans were provided with land, not by confiscation, but by purchase at a total cost of 600,000,000 sesterces, as Octavius himself tells us in the Monumentum Ancyranum, and in pursuance of the same wise policy a general amnesty was granted to the followers of Antony and Sextus Pompeius. The beneficial results of this course were apparent at once in the rise of the price of land and in the revival of trade, and Octavius received immediate recognition of his services in restoring prosperity in the extraordinary popularity which he enjoyed, — a factor that helped him in no small degree in making the great political changes which he had in mind.

**323. Constitutional Position of Octavius from 32 to 27.** It does not seem to be possible to make out with certainty the authority by virtue of which he made his preliminary arrangements. In the year 32, when he deposed Antony (cf. p. 146), he probably resigned his own position as triumvir, but he would seem to have been vested at once with extraordinary powers similar to those which he gave up. This was the basis of his authority down to 29 B.C., when another change took place of which we know as little. It seems rather probable, however, that in the year 29 the consular *imperium* was conferred on him, together with the control of the army and the provinces, and the right to hold the census.

**324. The Change made in 27 B.C.** The problem which he set himself to solve was to retain his position as master of the state, yet at the same time to keep intact the old forms of the constitution. Various methods of accomplishing this object seem to have occurred to him, and to have been tried, before he established his authority on the basis on which it finally rested. Two of these attempts have been mentioned in the preceding paragraph. A third essay was made in 27 B.C. At a meeting of the senate, held on the 13th of January in that year, he transferred the control of the state to the senate and people. As he himself puts it in the Monumentum Ancyranum, *rem publicam ex mea potestate in senat[us populique Romani a]rbitrium transtuli.* This transfer of authority was only a temporary one, and ancient (*e.g.*, Dio, LIII. 3–11) as well as modern historians have not hesitated to characterize it as a political manœuvre, since he retained the consulship and the tribunician power, and the senate immediately conferred on him the *imperium proconsulare* for a period of ten years, and the title of *Augustus*. It is quite possible that he wished to make the Roman people feel the need of his directing hand by bringing them face to face with the possibility of his withdrawal from public life, and to make the extraordinary powers which he received afresh from them seem their free gift to him.

Modern historians have called attention to the fact, however, that there is an essential constitutional difference between his new and his old powers. His old position was monarchical in some respects. His new authority was not essentially out of harmony with republican tradition, and this change was undoubtedly in his mind a great gain. It was a step also in harmony with his carefully observed policy. His proconsular power was not radically different from that which had been exercised at various times under the republic. Furthermore, it was granted for a limited period, of ten years, and was exercised only over the border provinces, where troops were still necessary. The management of the older provinces was intrusted to the senate, and the control of Italy was vested in the senate and the magistrates, as it had been under the republic. As consul, and in his exercise of the *potestas tribunicia*, which had been conferred on him in the year 36, the principle of collegiality was observed, and his incumbency of the consulship, like that of his colleagues in the office, depended upon an election in the popular assembly. It is evident that the forms of the old constitution had been preserved with great success. At the same time Augustus had secured the supreme power which he wished. The proconsular *imperium* over the unsettled provinces gave him command of the army and navy, and the power of appointing indirectly all the governors in the provinces where legions were stationed. Henceforth, too, he would have no occasion to fear a rival. In his exercise of the tribunician or consular power he was associated with colleagues of nominally equal rank, but he was raised so far above them in the eyes of the people, that independent action on their part was scarcely conceivable.

**325. The Titles of Augustus and Princeps.** The title *Augustus* had no direct political meaning, but, like the laurels which were placed on the doorposts of Octavius' house on the Palatine, it distinguished him from other citizens, and was a mark of the preëminence which was freely conceded to him. This preëminence was also well expressed in the title *princeps*. It has sometimes been maintained that this title was first applied to Octavius in the senate in the restrictive and traditional sense of *princeps senatus*, and came in time to characterize him as the first citizen in the commonwealth, the *princeps civitatis;* but it is more probable that the title never had this restricted meaning, and that from the outset it indicated the relation which the new ruler bore to the whole body of citizens — that it marked him out, in fact, as the foremost citizen of the state.

**326. Final Modifications of the Year 23.** It is not perfectly clear why Augustus introduced into his system the changes which he made in the year 23. Very likely the four years' test which he had given to the new constitution had brought out its weakness at certain points, and the illness which threatened his life in the year mentioned made him feel the necessity of strengthening it at once.

His objection to the old system probably lay in two facts. In the first place, he shared the administration of Rome and Italy with his colleagues in the consulship, and, although his prestige removed in large measure the danger of opposition from them, that danger existed in theory, and might at a critical moment become a serious matter in reality. At all events, the traditional etiquette existing between the two members of the consular college may well have hampered him in carrying out his plans. To have himself made sole consul would have been too violent a departure from tradition to be politic. He, therefore, gave up his practice of holding the consulship every year, and cast about him for a solution which would better meet the needs of the case. Such a solution he found by modifying and extending his proconsular *imperium*, and by giving importance to the tribunician power. Not all the points in which the proconsular *imperium* was extended by Augustus and his successors are clear. However, the extant fragment of the *lex de imperio Vespasiani*, the statements of Dio Cassius, and an examination of the functions actually exercised by the emperor, make it plain that, although he held his *imperium* as a proconsul, a series of measures passed in the year 23 and in subsequent years allowed him to retain it within the city, and gave him a position equal in rank and authority to that of the consul.

In giving a prominent place to the tribunician power, he hit upon a happy idea. The associations connected with the tribunate made it a popular office. In its early history it had been the organ of the plebeians in their struggle for civil and political rights. In its later history it had protected the individual against the encroachments of the state. Furthermore, the tribune had acquired positive and negative powers touching almost every field of

administrative activity.  He could summon the senate or
the popular assemblies for the transaction of business, and
he could veto the action of almost any magistrate.  We
have seen one reason why Augustus turned from the consulship to the tribunate.  Another may perhaps be found
in the fact that the duties of the consul were exercised
within a certain sphere limited by tradition.  The tribunate,
on the other hand, from its very nature and history, was
capable of indefinite extension in all directions.  Poten-
tially Augustus had held the tribunician power ever since
the year 36.  From this time, however, as an indication
of the new importance attaching to it, although he took
the title for life, he assumed it anew each year, and, after
23 B.C., in official documents indicated the year by setting
down the number of times he had held the tribunician
power.  This practice his successors followed.  The significance attaching to this power is also indicated by the fact
that the assignment of it was accepted as marking out a
successor in the principate.

The system of Augustus was now essentially complete.
He accepted no other permanent extraordinary office, even
at the solicitation of the people.  The proconsular *imperium* gave him command of the legions, and his supremacy
in civil administration rested securely on his right to exercise the *imperium* within the city and on his possession of
the *potestas tribunicia*.  The few emergencies of a later
date which required the exercise for a brief time of powers
which he did not have were provided for by special legislation, or by the natural extension of his tribunician or proconsular authority ; and when the ten years of his proconsular *imperium* expired, he secured a formal renewal of the
power for another period.  The position of Augustus in
religious matters was almost as preëminent as it was in

political affairs.  He was made a member of the four great priesthoods, and in the year 12, after the death of Lepidus, he was elected *pontifex maximus*.

**327. The Question of the Succession.**  It remained for Augustus to complete his work by securing the succession to the man of his choice.  The question presented itself in a definite form at the time of his severe illness in the year 23.  At that time he wisely passed over his only male relative, Marcellus, the son of his sister Octavia, because he felt that the young man was not old enough for such a responsible position, and, by giving his signet-ring to Agrippa, indirectly designated him as his successor.  Although he turned to Marcellus on his recovery, the death of Marcellus caused him to revert to his former plan, and in 21 B.C. he married Agrippa to his daughter Julia, the widow of Marcellus, and three years later had the tribunician power conferred on him for a period of five years.  The method which Augustus had found for settling the question of the succession was clear at once.  His own powers were given to him for a fixed term of years or for life.  He could not transmit them, therefore, to any one else at his death.  He could, however, during his own lifetime invest the man of his choice with powers independent of his own and thus do much toward securing the succession for him.  This was the plan which he adopted in the case of Agrippa.  The birth of two children to Julia from her marriage with Agrippa involved a slight modification in the plan of Augustus.  He designated these two grandsons, Gaius and Lucius Caesar, as his heirs, and made Agrippa their guardian.  Upon the death of the latter in 12 B.C. this guardianship was transferred to Tiberius, the stepson of Augustus, and in 6 B.C. the tribunician power was conferred on him for a period of five years.  But Tiberius was aggrieved at his failure to be designated as the successor of Augustus, and retired to the island of Rhodes. To the bitter disappointment of Augustus both of his grandsons died, and he was at last forced to recognize the eminent ability of Tiberius, and his services to the state, by adopting him as his heir and by conferring on him again the tribunician power. The question of the succession was finally settled in A.D. 13 beyond the possibility of change by the passage of a *lex consularis* associating Tiberius with Augustus in the government of the provinces. Henceforth his authority was independent of that of Augustus, and also rested on a legal basis. Augustus died the year after this arrangement was made.

**328. Social Reforms.** Nothing has been said up to this point about the social and financial reforms of Augustus. They were almost as far-reaching as his political changes. His most important legislation on these matters was intended to restore the integrity of the marriage relation and to prevent a decrease of the native population. The influx of foreigners, the development of luxurious tastes, the long-continued civil wars, the public games, and a host of similar influences had undermined public morality and subverted the old idea of the family. Adultery and divorce were not uncommon, and the number of the unmarried and of childless married couples had increased in an alarming way. A series of laws was directed against these evils. The *lex de adulteriis* imposed severe penalties on those convicted of adultery, while, under the *lex de maritandis ordinibus*, restrictions were put on divorce, and the unmarried and childless married were placed under disabilities in the matter of inheriting property and suing for office.

This method of attacking the evil failing of effect, Augustus approached the subject from the other direction. The celebrated *lex Papia Poppaea*, instead of laying penalties on the unmarried and childless, encouraged child-bearing by granting sums of money or privileges in canvassing for office to the father, and certain exceptional property rights to the mother of a family. An attempt was made to check the growth of extravagant tastes, which kept many from marriage, by the passage of sumptuary laws. The demoralizing influence of the public games was somewhat lessened by placing restrictions on the attendance of women. In particular the emperor strove to restore the Roman religion to its old position of dignity by rebuilding the temples, by celebrating religious festivals with great pomp, and by taking certain priestly offices himself, and in no one of his social reforms were the results of a more permanent character.

**329. Financial Reforms.** The restoration of peace, the suppression of piracy, and a more equitable and intelligent government of the provinces did much to restore prosperity to Italy and the provinces. These beneficent reforms were, however, supplemented by a systematic revision of the financial system. The provinces profited in particular by this change. The personal acquaintance which he made with the condition of the provinces in the period from 27 to 24 B.C., and the census which he took in several of them gave Augustus trustworthy information on which to base his financial reforms. In place of the extortionate requisitions made by provincial governors and the taxes, many in number and oppressive in character, of the republican régime, he substituted a land tax and a personal tax. Trade was relieved from harassing restrictions, and public improvements were made. The burden of the provinces was still further lightened by the imposition in Italy of a legacy duty and a tax on the sale of slaves.

**330. The Princeps and the Other Branches of Government.** In our discussion of the political institutions of previous periods it has been found convenient to consider them from the point of view of the magistracies, the senate, and the people. That division of the subject will be adopted now, although it has less significance for the period under consideration, since, in consequence of the subordination of the magistrates, the senate, and the popular assemblies to the will of the *princeps*, their separate activities become matters of less moment, and it is difficult to draw a definite line between them. The constitutional basis on which the authority of the *princeps* rested has already been discussed. It is a more difficult matter to state the theoretical relation which his office bore to the other branches of government. The care which Augustus took to cloak his extraordinary powers in traditional terms, and to reserve for the old institutions the nominal exercise of their old functions, is, of course, the cause of this difficulty. Perhaps it may be safe to say that the functions of the *princeps* were thought of as filling a gap, as supplementing those of the magistrates and senate, rather than as encroaching upon them.

**331. The Magistracies.** In the readjustment of affairs perhaps the executive suffered a greater loss of importance than any other branch of government. The method of electing the magistrates, the prestige of Augustus, and his encroachment on their traditional functions, all contributed to bring about this result. It will be remembered that candidates were required to notify the magistrate, who was to preside at the electoral meeting, of their intention to stand for office (p. 169). Augustus was consul from 27 to 23 B.C., and during this period the announcement was properly made to him. Even after this period, when he no longer held the consulship, candidates made their *professio* to him as well as to the consul. We may feel sure that his acceptance of their candidacy practically settled the question of their eligibility. Election to office was made still more dependent on the favor of Augustus, after he had adopted the practice of recommending certain candidates. His *commendatio* must have insured an election. This practice was not extended to the consulship, however, by Augustus. After election, even in matters where the legal powers of the two were equal, it was impossible for a magistrate to maintain his position over against the *princeps* whose prestige was so much greater, and whose long terms of office relieved him from the danger of being held responsible for his conduct.

There were few if any important executive functions which the *princeps* was not authorized to perform. He, as well as the consul, could convoke the senate and the popular assemblies, for instance, and the consul would hardly venture to take this important step without his approval. In this way the magistrates lost their right of initiative in almost all important matters. Certain powers were also formally taken from the magistrates and given to the *princeps*. Thus, for instance, the consuls probably lost the supervision of the roads in Italy, the *cura annonae* was taken from the aediles, and the *ius intercessionis* of the tribune did not avail against the emperor. The significance which the magistracies still had was derived in fact from the social distinction attaching to them, from the fact that magistrates were colleagues of the *princeps*, and that election to a magistracy secured one admission to the senate and an opportunity to hold an office in the provinces. No important changes were made in the number of the magistracies or in the size of the colleges. The number of praetors was, however, raised to sixteen, while the college of quaestors was reduced to twenty. The censorship disappeared, and various new offices, whose incumbents were subordinates of the *princeps*, were established in the provinces. Certain changes made in the functions of a few of the magistrates may be considered more conveniently in another connection.

**332. The Senate.** The membership of the senate was reduced from 900 to 600. Members were admitted, as under the republic, by virtue of having filled certain magistracies, but since the emperor's right of *nominatio* and *commendatio* gave him a great influence over the selection of magistrates, the rolls of the senate were in large measure indirectly under his control. As we have already had occasion to notice, the senate was in its origin an advisory body ; but it gradually acquired important powers, especially in the matter of administrative legislation, and reduced the magistrate to the position of its minister (pp. 67 f., 233). All this was changed by Augustus. The senate could not successfully assert, in dealing with him, the claims which it had made good against an annually elected magistrate of much less prestige and legal power. Furthermore, the republican practice of submitting all important matters to the senate for its consideration fell into comparative disuse. Finally, the *consilium* which Augustus established in 27 B.C., and reorganized in A.D. 12, must have taken from the importance of the senate. The *consilium*, as finally constituted, contained the *princeps* and certain members of his household, the consuls, the consuls-elect, and a committee of senators. This body, which must be distinguished from the judicial *consilium* of a later period (cf. p. 331), was allowed to pass measures, and these measures had the validity of *senatus consulta*. In one respect the competence of the senate was extended. It was given jurisdiction over important political cases.

**333. The Popular Assemblies.** Under Augustus magistrates were still elected in the popular assemblies, but the *nominatio* and *commendatio* of the *princeps* made the elections largely a matter of form. Augustus called not infrequent meetings of the popular assemblies to act on important measures, but since almost all bills were drawn up by the emperor, or with his approval, the meetings of the *comitia* for legislative purposes did little more than give the form of law to his wishes. This decadence of the assemblies was not, however, a great loss to the cause of popular government. An assembly made up of the rabble of Rome, not only ignorant of the merits of the great questions laid before them, but also ready to sell their votes to the highest bidder, was as far from representing the Roman empire as any assembly could be. It is significant that the decline of the *comitia*, which represented even more definitely than the senate the narrow conception of the city-state, is coincident with the growth of the feeling that there was a community of interests throughout the Roman world, and the development of this idea brought with it, of course, a more intelligent, uniform, and equitable system of government for the provinces. The settlement of important questions in secret was, however, a great loss to the cause of popular government. Even when the senatorial régime was at the height of its power, all phases of serious political questions were fully and freely discussed. Now matters were settled by Augustus in private conference with his ministers. The discussions in the senate were in large measure perfunctory and superficial.

**334. The New Senatorial Aristocracy.** Augustus seems to have consciously adopted the policy of creating social classes, whose position depended upon his favor and whose interests were, therefore, identical with his. At all events, this was the result of certain social and political changes which he made. Under the republic the prestige of having held a curule office was so great that candidates for a magistracy who did not have the *ius imaginum* had little chance of success (cf. pp. 47, 166). Election to any one of the higher magistracies secured for one admission to the senate. This was the basis on which the *nobilitas* rested. In the new aristocracy, created by Augustus, the order was reversed. Only those who had the *latus clavus* were eligible to the quaestorship, and since only those of senatorial rank had the right to the *latus clavus* (p. 225), the sons of senators and no others were eligible to the magistracies. It was necessary to hold a magistracy before sitting in the senate. Consequently, only the sons of senators and those whom the emperor might honor with the *latus clavus* could become magistrates, or members of the senate. Since election to a magistracy depended largely on the favor of Augustus, the new aristocracy owed its privileges entirely to him, and he could count on it for support.

**335. The Knights.** The great middle class was attached to his interests in a similar way. The legislation of C. Gracchus, which turned the juries over to the knights, first gave legal recognition to this class; but its social and political privileges had never been so clearly defined as those of the senatorial order had been. Augustus gave definiteness and importance to this social class by having lists of its members, which he revised, drawn up at regular intervals. With the knights he filled the important financial and administrative offices in Italy and in the provinces which were under his control.

**336. The Augustales.** An aristocracy was also created among the freedmen. Each year the *decuriones* in the municipal towns chose six rich freedmen as *seviri Augustales*.

This board contributed money for some local improvement or for the proper maintenance of the public games. No political functions attached to the position, but the social prestige which it conferred and the privilege which went with it of wearing the *praetexta* and of being attended by lictors probably made it eagerly sought for. Inasmuch as the order was in some way connected with the cult of the emperor, he could rely upon its support.

**337. The City of Rome.** The legislation of Augustus which affected the welfare of the whole people has been considered above. It may not be out of place here to consider certain administrative changes which concerned the several parts of the empire, in particular the city of Rome, Italy, and the provinces. We have already had occasion to notice the incapacity which the republic showed in governing the provinces. That fact is not strange. It was a natural result of the selfishness and indifference of the Romans toward the provincials. However, the thoroughly unsatisfactory character of the government of the city of Rome seems at first hard to account for. In point of fact, Rome had rapidly grown out of a village into a great city, but the development of public improvements and of municipal government had not kept pace with the growth of its population. Augustus set himself to remedy this state of things.

**338. Public Improvements and Municipal Government.** The supplement to the Monumentum Ancyranum gives us a long list of the new buildings which he constructed, and of the old ones which he repaired or rebuilt. The general supervision of public works was put in charge of two *curatores operum publicorum*. Many new aqueducts were brought into the city, and the care of the water supply and of the Tiber was intrusted to imperial commissioners.

All of these officials were of senatorial rank. A still more important matter was the *cura annonae*, which was intrusted to an imperial *praefectus* of equestrian rank. It was the duty of this official to see that Rome was supplied with grain, to superintend its distribution to poor people, and to control the price of it. All these municipal affairs had previously been managed by the aediles and censors, so that the establishment of these imperial offices abridged their powers correspondingly.

**339. Improvements in Municipal Government.** The city was lamentably in need of suitable arrangements for extinguishing fires and maintaining order. A long step toward the accomplishment of these two objects was taken by the organization of a fire and police department of 7000 or 8000 men in A.D. 6. For convenience in administration the city had been divided into fourteen *regiones*, and each one of the seven detachments, into which this force was divided, was called on to protect two of these. The brigade was in charge of a *praefectus*, appointed by Augustus. This official had a limited criminal jurisdiction somewhat like that of the *III viri capitales* (cf. p. 210). To maintain order during his absences from the city, the emperor appointed a *praefectus urbi* (cf. p. 212). It was left for his successor, however, to make this office permanent.

**340. Condition of Italy.** One of the greatest blessings which Augustus conferred on Italy consisted in the encouragement of local self-government along the lines laid down by Julius Caesar in his *lex Iulia municipalis*. The roads were also kept in good condition, and order was maintained. Very few of the Italians from this time on served in the army, but in a way they paid for their exemption from military service by a five per cent tax on legacies and a four per cent tax on the sale of slaves.

**341. The Frontier Policy of Augustus.** In dealing with Roman territory outside of Italy, Augustus directed his attention to the settlement of two important questions — the establishment of a natural and secure frontier and the reorganization of provincial government. In both directions his efforts were crowned with success. In the East, at the beginning of his reign, the Parthian question was still unsettled. The Roman standards and the Roman captives, taken at Carrhae in 53 B.C., were still in the possession of Parthia, while the failure of Antony's campaigns in the years 40 to 36 (cf. p. 146) had increased the feeling of insecurity in the eastern provinces. This situation was very happily relieved by the development of a dynastic quarrel in Parthia in 20 B.C. Augustus took advantage of this quarrel to secure the return of the standards, and King Phraates was even induced to send four of his sons to Rome as hostages. At the same time the Euphrates was made the eastern frontier of the empire.

To the south the great desert of Africa formed a natural boundary, and the provinces in that quarter of the world were safe, except from the occasional incursions of nomad tribes. On the west was the Atlantic. To the north the problem was a more complicated one, and the frontier policy of Augustus was, at the outset, less clearly determined. For a time the Romans seem to have intended making the Elbe the line between them and the Germans, but after the defeat of Varus, in A.D. 9, they withdrew to the west and south of the Rhine and adopted that river, with the Danube, as the northern frontier of their territory. Raetia was organized as a province in 15 B.C., Noricum in the same year, and Moesia in A.D. 6, so that by the reduction of Pannonia to the form of a province in A.D. 10, Rome controlled all the country bordered on the north by the rivers Rhine and Danube from the North sea to the Black sea.

**342. Imperial and Senatorial Provinces.** As we have already noticed (p. 268), in the division of provinces between Augustus and the senate, those in which a military force was needed were assigned to the emperor. After the division in 27 B.C. some transfers were made, but at the death of Augustus the list of imperial provinces included Sardinia and Corsica, Hither Spain, Lusitania, " the three Gauls " (Aquitania, Lugdunensis, Belgica), Pannonia, Dalmatia, Moesia, Galatia and Pontus Polemoniacus, Cilicia, Cyprus, Egypt, Syria, Raetia, and Noricum. The senate controlled Baetica, Gallia Narbonensis, Macedonia, Achaea and Epirus, Asia, Bithynia, Crete and Cyrene, Africa, Sicily, and Cyprus. Cisalpine Gaul had ceased to be a province in 42 B.C., when the limits of Italy had been extended to the Alps.

**343. Improvements in Provincial Government.** To no part of the Roman Empire did the reforms of Augustus bring greater relief than to the provinces. The financial improvement which they experienced has already been noticed (p. 274). The gain which they made in other respects was equally great. This was particularly true of the imperial provinces, for the governors of these provinces were chosen, not by lot, but on the score of honesty and fitness, and were personally responsible to Augustus, who had an intimate acquaintance with the condition of the several provinces and kept a watchful eye on their progress.

One of the defects of the republican system lay in the fact that a provincial governor held office usually for only one year, so that he could scarcely learn the needs of his province before he would be recalled. The evils of the republican system are laid bare by Cicero's letters from

Cilicia in 51–50 B.C.  In the imperial provinces the term of office was invariably of considerable length.  Under the republic governors filled their pockets by requisitions, which demoralized the government and crippled the resources of the provinces.  Under Augustus provincial governors received a generous fixed salary, and service in the provinces became an honorable and attractive profession, with prospect of steady advancement for those who showed themselves capable and honest.  The senatorial provinces still labored under many of the evils of the old system, but even over them Augustus exercised some supervision, and the excellence of the government in the imperial provinces could not fail to exert a beneficial influence.

**344.  System of Provincial Government.**  Augustus directed the government of the provinces by virtue of his proconsular *imperium*, and governors in imperial provinces, who were all appointed by him, acted *pro praetore* regardless of the office which they had previously held in Rome, and were called *legati Augusti pro praetore*.  The governors of senatorial provinces, on the other hand, all had a proconsular title without regard to the magistracy which they had held in Rome.  Only ex-consuls, however, were sent to Asia and Africa.  The higher title which the senatorial governors had did not make their position equal in dignity to that of the imperial governors, however, because the latter had charge of an army, while the senatorial governors did not.

Provincial governors supervised the administrative affairs of their provinces, and had jurisdiction in civil cases, and in criminal cases where *peregrini* only were concerned.  The imperial governor had a military command also.  In imperial provinces an appeal could be taken from the governor's sentence to the emperor; in senatorial provinces, to the

senate or the emperor. The financial interests of an imperial province were in the hands of an official called a
*procurator*, chosen by Augustus himself. Imperial procurators also coöperated with the proconsuls in managing
the finances of senatorial provinces. In military and judicial matters the imperial governor was assisted by *legati
Augusti legionum* and by *legati Augusti iuridici*. In provinces like Egypt or Judaea, where the emperor was regarded
as the legal successor of the previous ruler, a *praefectus*
or a *procurator* was placed in charge. Governors were
assigned to the senatorial provinces by lot, and held office
for a year. The law of 52 B.C., which required an interval
of five years between a magistracy at Rome and a governorship in a province, was still in force. The senatorial governors of consular rank were assisted by three *legati* and a
quaestor. Those of praetorian rank had one *legatus* and a
quaestor. The *legati* were appointed by the governor himself, but his appointments were subject to the approval of
the emperor.

**345. Reforms in the Military System.** The assignment
to Augustus of the provinces where troops were needed not
only gave to him the control of the army, but by implica-
tion took away from the senate the right of levying troops
for its own provinces. When disturbances arose in a senatorial province the emperor took charge of matters. The
necessity of protecting distant frontiers had made it impossible even under the republic to adhere to the traditional
practice of discharging the soldiers each year and levying
and organizing a new force. However, the fiction was
conscientiously observed of reënlisting all the troops at the
end of the year. It was, therefore, a theoretical, not a
practical change in the military system which Augustus
made in 13 B.C., by enlisting troops for a fixed term of

years.   The term was at first made one of sixteen years for
the legionaries and twelve years for the guards, but in
A.D. 5 it was lengthened to twenty and sixteen years
respectively.   A second important change which he made
in the military system consisted in the larger use of auxiliary
troops.   The use of these troops, and the resulting dis-
taste of the Italians for military service, led to a decline
of the martial spirit in Italy, and made the peninsula incapable of resisting a possible invasion; but the strong line
of border provinces which Augustus established prevented
this danger from becoming a real one for many years.

## SELECTIONS FROM THE SOURCES

Livy, *Epp.*, CXXXIV–CXLII; *Res gestae divi Augusti* (or the
*Monumentum Ancyranum*); Velleius Paterculus, II. 89–123; Sue-
tonius, *Augustus;* Dio Cassius, LI. 19–LVI; Florus, II. 22–34;
Eutropius, VII. 8–10; Tacitus, *Ann.* I. 1–5.

Octavius returns to Rome in 29 B.C.: Dio, LI. 21; *C. I. L.* I.[1]
p. 399.— Extraordinary powers granted to him in 29 B.C. : Dio,
LII. 41; Suet. *Aug.* 27.— Gratuities to soldiers: *Res gestae*, ed.
Momm. III. 17.—Takes census: *Res gest.* II. 2–5 and pp. 36–8.—
Revises list of senators: *Res gest.* II. 1–2 and pp. 35–6; Dio,
LII. 42.— Princeps senatus: Dio, LIII. 1.— Meeting of senate,
January 13, 27 B.C.: Dio, LIII. 3–11; *Res gest.* VI. 13–15 and
pp. 145–8.— Proconsular imperium for ten years: Dio, LIII. 13.—
Division of the provinces: Dio, LIII. 12.— Title of Augustus and
other honors: *Res gest.* VI. 16 f.; Suet. *Aug.* 7; *C. I. L.* I.[1] p. 384;
Dio, LIII. 16.— Goes to Gaul and Spain for three years: Dio, LIII. 22.
— Praefectus urbi (25 B.C.): Tac. *Ann.* VI. 11.— Galatia, province:
Dio, LIII. 26.— Augustus returns to Rome: Dio, LIII. 28.— Signet
ring to Agrippa (23 B.C.): Dio, LIII. 30.— New powers granted in
23 B.C. : Dio, LIII. 32.— Marcellus's death: Dio, LIII. 30.— Ten
praetors: Dio, LIII. 32.— Augustus assumes cura annonae (22 B.C.):
*Res gest.* I. 33–5 and pp. 24–7; Dio, LIV. 1.— Refuses dictatorship,
censorship, and consulship for life (22 B.C.): *Res gest.* I. 31–6; Dio,
LIV. 1–2.— Cura ludorum from aediles to praetors: Dio, LIV. 2. —

Sumptuary law (22 B.C.): Dio, LIV. 2. — Conspiracy of Murena and Caepio (22 B.C.): Dio, LIV. 3; Vell. II. 91. — Spends three years in Oriental provinces (22 B.C.): Dio, LIV. 6 ff. — Standards returned by Parthia (20 B.C.): *Res gest.* V. 40–43 and pp. 124–8; Dio, LIV. 8. — Curatores viarum (20 B.C.): Dio, LIV. 8. — Names Q. Lucretius consul (19 B.C.): Dio, LIV. 10. — Returns to Rome (19 B.C.): Dio, LIV. 10. — Charge of provinces and armies ten years more (18 B.C.): Dio, LIV. 12. — Agrippa, tribunician power for five years: Dio, LIV. 12. — Senate, 600 members: Dio, LIV. 13–14. — Lex de adulteriis (18 B.C.): Suet. *Aug.* 34. — Lex de maritandis ordinibus (18 B.C.): Suet. *Aug.* 34; Dio, LIV. 16; Gaius, I. 178. — T. Statilius Taurus, praefectus urbi: Dio, LIV. 19. — Defeat of Lollius by the Germans (16 B.C.): Dio, LIV. 20; Vell. II. 97; Suet. *Aug.* 23. — Augustus goes to Gaul (16 B.C.): Dio, LIV. 19. — Returns from Gaul (13 B.C.): Dio, LIV. 25. — Reorganization of the XX viri (13 B.C.): Dio, LIV. 26. — Agrippa's tribunician power renewed for five years (13 B.C.): Dio, LIV. 28. — Augustus, pontifex maximus (12 B.C.): Dio, LIV. 27; Suet. *Aug.* 31; *Res gest.* II. 23 f. and p. 45. — Agrippa dies (12 B.C.): Dio, LIV. 28; Plin. *N. H.* VII. 8. — Campaigns of Drusus and Tiberius: Dio, LIV. 31 ff.; LV. 1, 29 ff.; LVI. 12 ff.; Vell. II. 110–115; Suet. *Tib.* 16 f. — Tiberius marries Julia (11 B.C.): Dio, LIV. 35. — Cura aquarum (11 B.C.): Frontin. *de Aquaed.* 99 ff. — Quaestors take charge of archives (11 B.C.): Dio, LIV. 36. — Death of Drusus (9 B.C.): Dio, LV. 1. Augustus's charge of armies and provinces renewed for ten years (8 B.C.): Dio, LV. 6. — Tiberius receives tribunician power for five years (6 B.C.): Dio, LV. 9. — Augustus receives title of pater patriae (2 B.C.): Suet. *Aug.* 58. — Lucius and Gaius Caesar receive title of princeps iuventutis (2 B.C.): *Res gest.* III. 4–6 and pp. 52–8. — Tiberius returns from voluntary exile (A.D. 2): Vell. II. 103. 1; Suet. *Tib.* 13. — Augustus's charge of armies and provinces renewed for ten years (A.D. 3): Dio, LV. 12. — C. Caesar dies (A.D. 4): *C. I. L.* XI. 1421 (cf. Clinton, *Fast. Hell.* III. p. 264). — Augustus adopts Tiberius (A.D. 4): Vell. II. 103; Dio, LV. 13; Tac. *Ann.* I. 3, 10; IV. 57. — Tiberius receives tribunician power for ten years (A.D. 4): Dio, LV. 13; Vell. II. 103. — Army reforms (A.D. 5): Dio, LV. 23; Tac. *Ann.* I. 17. — Praefectus vigilum (A.D. 6): Dio, LV. 26. — Tax on sale of slaves (A.D. 7): Dio, LV. 31. — Modification of the commendatio (A.D. 8): Dio, LV. 34. — Defeat of Varus (A.D. 9?): Vell. II. 117–120; Dio, LVI. 18 ff.; Suet. *Aug.* 23; *Tib.* 17. — Lex Papia Poppaea

(A.D. 9); Dio, LVI. 10. — Augustus receives armies and provinces
for ten years (A.D. 13): Dio, LVI. 28. — Tiberius receives tribunician power for indefinite period (A.D. 13): Dio, LVI. 28. — Legislative
committee with powers (A.D. 13): Dio, LVI. 28. — Augustus dies
(A.D. 14): Dio, LVI. 29 f.; Suet. *Aug.* 99–100; Tac. *Ann.* I. 5.

## SELECTED BIBLIOGRAPHY

### A. *The Empire in General*

L. de Tillemont, Histoire des empereurs, etc., 5 vols.   Venice, 1732.

Ch. Merivale, History of the Romans under the Empire, 7 vols.   New
    York, 1862.

H. Schiller, Geschichte der römischen Kaiserzeit, 2 vols.   Gotha,
    1882–7.

Edw. Gibbon, The History of the Decline and Fall of the Roman
    Empire, revised by J. B. Bury.   London, 1900.

L. Friedländer, Darstellungen aus der Sittengeschichte Roms, etc.,
    3 vols., 6th ed.   Leipzig, 1888.

Th. Mommsen, The Provinces of the Roman Empire, 2 vols.   New
    York, 1886.

Th. Mommsen, Römisches Staatsrecht (Vol. II).   Leipzig, 1887.

H. Peter, Die geschichtliche Litteratur über die römische Kaiserzeit,
    etc., 2 vols.   Leipzig, 1897.

G. Goyau, Chronologie de l'empire romain.   Paris, 1891.

Prosopographia imperii romani saec. I, II, III, 3 parts.   Berlin,
    1897–.

### B. *The Reign of Augustus*

V. Gardthausen, Augustus und seine Zeit (I. 1, 2 ; II. 1, 2).   Leipzig,
    1891–6.

W. W. Capes, The Early Roman Empire.   London, 1876.

## SUPPLEMENTARY LITERATURE, 1901–1910

Shuckburgh, Augustus.   London, 1903.

Domaszewski, Geschichte d. römischen Kaiser, 2 vols.   Leipzig,
    1909.

# CHAPTER XIII

## FROM TIBERIUS TO NERO

**346. Tiberius becomes Emperor.** With the death of Augustus the principate legally came to an end. He had made Tiberius his associate in the government (cf. p. 273), but he could not confer upon him nor bequeath to him his powers as *princeps*. Tiberius was placed in such a preëminent position, however, that it was difficult to thwart his ambition, and he understood how to make good use of his opportunity. He felt that the support of the army was the essential thing, and that the acquiescence of the senate and people would follow as a matter of course. He at once, therefore, assumed charge of the praetorian guard, and had the armies take the oath of allegiance. Their example was quickly followed by the magistrates and the senate. This method of procedure forestalled any possible opposition. In fact, when the senate met to confer on him the powers of his predecessor, Tiberius was able to make his acceptance of them appear a concession to its entreaties.

**347. The two Periods of his Reign.** The change which took place in the character of Tiberius under the influence of L. Aelius Sejanus is well known. The same influence brought about a marked change in the character of his government also. Sejanus became prefect of the praetorian guard in the year 16, and greatly strengthened his influence seven years later by bringing all the sections of that force together into one station. However, even this exceptional position did not count for so much as did the perfect

confidence which Tiberius placed in him, and the fact that
Sejanus became his sole confidant.  It is unnecessary for
our purpose to estimate the character of Tiberius, which
assumes such different aspects in the historical works of
Tacitus and Velleius Paterculus.  Each account probably
presents one side of the truth.  In the same way the period
before Sejanus acquired his influence over Tiberius, and the
subsequent period, reflect respectively the good and the
evil elements in the character of the emperor.  When he
ascended the throne there was much to inspire the Romans
with confidence in his wisdom and justice.  He was a man
of affairs; he was simple in his personal tastes; he had a
respect for tradition and a peculiar reverence for the policy
of his predecessor.  Furthermore, he had a wide knowledge
of the condition of the empire, acquired by numerous campaigns and by years of residence in the provinces, and the
early years of his reign seemed to justify the hope which
the possession of these qualities held out.  But with the
ascendency of Sejanus, and the retirement of Tiberius from
Rome in the year 26, the aspect of things changed.  The
results of the baneful influence of Sejanus were aggravated
by the death in A.D. 19 of Germanicus, the nephew of
Tiberius, and, in the year 23, of Drusus, his son.  Both of
these young men enjoyed a popularity, perhaps undeserved,
which made it important for the emperor to keep the good-
will of the people.  With their death this incentive disappeared.  The death of these two men also stimulated
the ambitious designs of Agrippina, the widow of Germanicus, in behalf of her sons, and Tiberius had some
reason to fear cabals among the senators in their behalf.
The two weapons which he used against these senators,
and against others whom he suspected of ambitious designs,
were the processes *de maiestate* and *de repetundis.*

**348. Trials for Treason and Misgovernment.** The conception of *minuta maiestas* was a development of *perduellio*, and in the late republic covered such offenses as attacks on the freedom and sovereignty of the people or the safety of the state, and neglect of important official duties. The change involved in the actions brought during the second part of Tiberius's reign lay in the substitution of the *maiestas principis* for the *maiestas populi*. Any acts which were interpreted as prejudicial to the emperor's welfare or dignity made the person committing them liable to the charge of *minuta maiestas*. Trivial charges also were taken into consideration; the ordinary rules governing criminal procedure were not observed, and the severity of the penalties imposed was out of proportion to the offenses committed.

The equitable treatment of the provinces is one of the things which may be set down to the credit of Tiberius. The most effective means which he found to hold provincial governors to their duty was the institution of actions *de repetundis* against them; but it was very difficult for a governor in the performance of duties which required the exercise of discretion not to lay himself open to a technical charge on this score. The evil features of the situation were aggravated by the machinations of professional informers, and by the fact that trials on both the above-mentioned charges were held before the senate. Tiberius himself would have hesitated to condemn on his own responsibility men for whose condemnation this servile body, with its divided responsibility and its dread of the emperor, cast its vote.

**349. Constitutional and Administrative Changes.** The most important constitutional change made by Tiberius was the transfer of the elections from the people to the senate. Henceforth the popular assemblies met in their

electoral capacity only to hear an announcement of the
results of the elections in the senate. The change was
essentially only a formal one, since popular elections had
already lost their significance. This method of choosing
magistrates was in some respects a reversion to the system
in vogue under the monarchy (cf. p. 14), and, since ex-magistrates were given seats in the senate, that body, nominally at least, chose its own members. It should be noticed,
too, that the new functions which Tiberius and his predecessor assigned to the senate made it not only a legislative but also a judicial and an electoral body. The most
important changes in the magistracies consisted in making
the *praefectus urbi* a permanent official, and in putting
a single prefect at the head of the praetorian cohorts,
although some of the successors of Tiberius reverted to
the Augustan system and appointed two *praefecti praetorio*.
Some temporary importance was also given to the consul's
office by the prolonged absence of Tiberius from the city.

**350. The Reign of Gaius.** Upon the death of Tiberius
in A.D. 37 Gaius Caesar, the son of Germanicus, the adopted
son of Tiberius, who was supported by Macro, the praetorian prefect, was proclaimed emperor by the senate. The
first measures of Gaius seemed to indicate that the enthusiasm with which the death of Tiberius and the accession
of a son of the popular leader Germanicus were greeted
was justified. Actions for *maiestas* were suspended. Professional informers were suppressed, and the elections were
turned over to the popular assemblies again ; but in each
one of these cases Gaius returned in a very short time to
the practices of Tiberius. Throughout his reign, in fact,
he was the creature of caprice, the victim of megalomania,
and represented absolutism in its crudest form. In an in-
credibly short time he had spent upon extravagant projects

of all sorts the sum of 700,000,000 sesterces, which his economical predecessor had saved, and proceeded to meet the resulting deficit by confiscation and oppressive taxation. The only constitutional change of any importance made during his reign was the addition of a fifth decury of jurymen, which brought the number of *iudices* up to about 5000. The wrath of the people groaning under this tyrannous government found expression in one conspiracy after another, until finally in the year 41 Gaius was murdered by the officers of his own guard.

**351. The Reign of Claudius.** By his death the government was left without a head once more, and for two days the senate considered the advisability of restoring the republic ; but the clamor of the populace and the intervention of the soldiers decided the matter in favor of Claudius, the nephew of Tiberius and uncle of Gaius. Claudius had lived up to this time in retirement. In fact, the soldiers found him hiding in the palace for fear of his life. A natural weakness of character and bodily defects had kept him out of public life, and the contempt of those about him, and the ill-treatment which he had received at their hands, had made him distrustful of himself. His life had been given up largely to antiquarian pursuits. These facts determined in large measure the character of his reign. His lack of self-confidence made him lean helplessly on others, while the interest which he had felt in the minutiae of grammatical study incapacitated him for developing comprehensive plans of government. As a result he was easily managed by the members of his household, and the inner history of his reign is a continuous story of intrigue by the women and the freedmen about him, first by his freedman Narcissus and his wife Messalina, and, after her death, by Narcissus and his second wife Agrippina, with the support of Pallas, and of Burrus, whom she had elevated to the position of prefect of the praetorian guard. This transfer of the real authority to men who were virtually imperial ministers — for this was what the new system really amounted to — had its advantages as well as its disadvantages. Narcissus in particular, who played so important a rôle during the greater part of Claudius's reign, had a decided talent for public affairs, and the administration of the government profited accordingly. Thus, for instance, not only were public finances placed on a sound basis once more, but public improvements of great importance were made, such as the extension of the aqueduct system, and the improvement of the harbor at Ostia. The antiquarian tastes of Claudius were not wholly detrimental to the public interests. They encouraged a regard for tradition and for old institutions; the senate in particular was treated with respect. It became once more a deliberative body, and acquired some part of its old-time independence. Although the natural bent of Claudius and his early life had robbed him in a measure of the power of taking the initiative in important matters, it had developed in him an infinite patience in perfecting a system already in existence. To this characteristic is due largely the improvements in the judicial system and in the police and water departments of the city.

**352. Accession of Nero.** In her struggle with Narcissus, Agrippina's first object was to secure the succession for Nero, her son by Cn. Domitius Ahenobarbus. She prevailed at last upon Claudius to adopt him, and, taking advantage of the illness and absence of Narcissus in the year 54, cleared the way for her son by having Claudius poisoned. Her faithful supporter, Burrus, brought Nero before the troops, and he was saluted emperor.

**353. Court Intrigue under Nero.** His reign was like that of his immediate predecessor in two respects. It was full of intrigue, and the control of public affairs was left largely in the hands of advisers and favorites. The character of the government depended on the character and ability of those under whose influence Nero fell. When Agrippina first formed her ambitious plans for her son, she placed him under the tutelage of the philosopher Seneca and the protection of the prefect Burrus. As soon as he ascended the throne, the new emperor showed that he cared only for the pleasures and the distinction which his position gave him, and was content to leave the affairs of state in the hands of his mother and her two advisers; but the outcome did not please Agrippina. She was by no means satisfied with the small share in the government which she soon found that Seneca and Burrus were willing to allow her, and she cast about for means to force Nero to recognize her authority. Her efforts were fruitless, and it is a remarkable illustration of the irony of fate that her downfall was finally brought about by the same means which had raised her to power. Just as her personal charms had been used to encompass the ruin of Messalina, so the beauty of Poppaea Sabina, the wife of M. Salvius Otho, caused the downfall of Agrippina. Ultimately she, as well as Britannicus and Octavia, Nero's wife, fell a victim to the jealous suspicions of the emperor. The death of Burrus three years later, in 62, the appointment of Tigellinus as one of the prefects of the praetorian guard, and the forced retirement of Seneca, left Rome at the mercy of Nero's passions, stimulated as they were by Tigellinus and the freedmen of the court.

**354. Administration of Public Affairs under Nero.** The character of Nero's administration differed greatly in these two periods. Under the ministerial rule of Seneca the senate was associated in the government, as it had been in the time of Claudius (cf. p. 294), and, thanks to the creative ability of Seneca and the patience and energy of Burrus, many important administrative reforms were introduced. The legislation of the years 56–62 touching wills, adoption, and certain abuses in the courts, as *praevaricatio* and *tergiversatio*, was especially salutary. The finances were managed with such wisdom that 60,000,000 sesterces were annually turned into the state treasury. The second period of the reign shows a far different state of affairs. Life and liberty were held in light esteem, and the finances of the state fell into a deplorable condition. The financial difficulties of the empire were due in part to the great fire of the year 64 and to the expenditure of large sums in carrying on foreign campaigns; but only in part, since the extravagance of the court in building palaces and baths and in giving public games was largely responsible for this state of affairs; and, to make matters worse, in meeting this difficulty, the government resorted to the dangerous expedient of debasing the coinage.

**355. Galba, Otho, and Vitellius.** The discontent to which Nero's misgovernment gave rise found expression in numerous conspiracies supported by the aristocracy and members of the senate. But Nero had little to fear from this source. The danger lay in another quarter. The establishment of a standing army by Augustus, with a long, fixed term of service (cf. pp. 285 f.), and the assignment of legions for an indefinite period to a particular province, where allegiance to the emperor was forgotten in devotion to their commander, had divided the empire into a group of inchoate principalities, in each of which the soldiers and inhabitants had begun to feel the community of their interests. In fact, the tendency which was developing in the provinces in the middle of the first century of our era, unless it had been summarily checked, might have led to the immediate disintegration of the Roman Empire. The first clear indication of this nationalist movement appeared in Gaul in 68, but the defeat of the leader of the movement, C. Julius Vindex, by L. Verginius Rufus, the governor of Upper Germany, crushed it out. Rufus himself, however, was proclaimed *imperator* by his troops. He declined the offer, it is true, but not so much because of his loyalty to Nero or the central government as on account of his own low origin, which would probably have frustrated any designs on the throne. No such difficulty stood in the way of Ser. Sulpicius Galba, the governor of Hispania Tarraconensis, who belonged to an old and influential family. He was proclaimed emperor by his own troops, was supported by the German legions, when their commander, Rufus, had positively refused to accept the position, and through the efforts of Numpidius Sabinus, the prefect of the praetorian guard, secured the adherence of that force. Nero, finding himself deserted by every one, took his own life June 9, 68. The policy of Galba did not prove to be a wise one. He punished the disaffected soldiers of the German legions. He removed their popular leader, Rufus, and estranged the praetorian guard by not fulfilling the promises which Numpidius had made in his name. The legions in Lower Germany retaliated by naming their commander, A. Vitellius, emperor, while the praetorian guard in Rome proclaimed M. Salvius Otho. Galba was assassinated in January, 69; the senate confirmed the choice of Otho, and the new emperor set out for the North to check the advance of his rival. Otho was defeated at Cremona, and later at Bedriacum, and left

Italy and his Italian supporters a prey to the wrath and the greed of the German legions by taking his own life in April, 69. Vitellius was at once recognized as emperor by the senate, and began his reign by adopting a conciliatory policy toward the senate and the members of the opposite faction.

**356. Extinction of the Julian Line.** Naturally very little of constitutional or administrative significance was done during this year of confusion. The most important result of the death of Nero was the disappearance of the partially recognized hereditary principle. The recognition of this principle had tended to give continuity to the government. At least, the next of kin to a deceased emperor, if supported by the praetorian guard, was reasonably sure of the succession. The extinction of the Julian line, however, opened the door to any successful commander, and the armies in the provinces became the effective electoral bodies. The necessity of securing the confirmation of the senate was recognized, but the acquiescence of that body was naturally a matter of form.

**357. The Frontier Policy from A.D. 14 to 68.** The successors of Augustus from A.D. 14 to 68 followed out the frontier policy which he had indicated. They strengthened the frontiers of the empire, but made no serious efforts to push them forward, except in the case of Britain. In the East, the reduction of Cappadocia to the form of a province in A.D. 17 helped to protect Roman territory, and, after a long dispute over Armenia, a *modus vivendi* with Parthia was reached in the year 63, under which Tiridates, the brother of the Parthian king, received the Armenian crown in Rome from the hands of Nero. Under Claudius the southern frontier was fortified, and the two Mauretanian provinces, which had been established in 40, were

completely pacified two years later.   In the North no
determined effort was made to force the peoples beyond
the Rhine to recognize Roman authority, but the frontier
line along that river was protected, and the Germans were
encouraged to waste their strength in internecine warfare.
Disturbances in Thrace led to its annexation as a province in 46, and thus the Danube continued the line of
the empire to the Black sea.   In the West only an important increase of territory was made by the conquest of
southern Britain and its erection into a province in the
year 43.

358. **Municipal Government in Italy.**   One of the most
noteworthy constitutional changes under the early empire
consisted in the development of municipal government in
Italy and the provinces, and in the tendency to secure
uniformity, at least within a given area.   The prevailing
system adopted for the *municipia* in Italy was similar to
that in force in Rome.   It comprised magistrates, a senate,
and a popular assembly.   The magistrates were known as
*IV viri*, formed two colleges, and were commonly called
*II viri iure dicundo* and *II viri aedilicia potestate*.   They
were chosen in the popular assembly, although elections
were later transferred to the senate.   The *II viri iure dicundo* had the right to convoke and preside over the local
senate and popular assembly, to exercise jurisdiction in civil
and criminal cases under certain restrictions, and in coöperation with the senate they had charge of the finances
and of the local military contingent.   The *II viri aedilicia
potestate* had charge primarily of the police and of the
public games.   In some communities quaestors were also
chosen.   Otherwise minor financial duties were performed
by the aediles.   All these officials were chosen annually,
and had insignia not unlike those of the magistrates at

Rome. Every five years *II viri quinquennales censoria potestate* were elected to take the census. The senate (*ordo decurionum* or *senatus*) usually comprised 100 members. A senator held his position for life, subject to the discretion of the censors, who made out the list of senators on the same principle which the censors at Rome followed. The relations which a municipal senate bore to the local magistrates and popular assemblies were almost exactly the same as those which the Roman senate bore to the Roman magistrates and to the *comitia*. The inhabitants of the municipalities fell into two classes, *cives* and *incolae*. *Cives* were those who had the rights of citizenship by birth or by special concession. *Incolae* were those who had taken up their domicile in a town without severing their relations with the community from which they had come. Both classes were liable to military service and to the other *munera* imposed by the community, but the *cives* only, under the early empire, were eligible to office. The unit in the popular assembly was the *curia* or the *tribus*, and the method of voting was identical with that in force at Rome.

**359. Local Government in the Provinces.** The unit of government in the newly acquired provinces of the West was the municipality, and to most of these municipalities, as they gave evidence of becoming Romanized, the *ius Latii* was granted. Those who had held magistracies or a seat in the local senate received the full rights of citizenship, and the adoption of this policy did much toward attaching the leading families to the Roman régime. In Germany and the other less civilized provinces to the north, the cantonal or some similar unit of government was adopted. The policy which Rome followed in the older provinces of the East has already been discussed (cf.

pp. 88 ff.). Some modifications of it had been introduced in the later republican period, but in most cases the
old systems of local government with the traditional titles
for the several offices were retained, except that the
financial system was reorganized.

**360. Changes in Provincial Government.** The governors of imperial provinces were appointed by the emperor,
administered their provinces under his supervision, and
looked to him for advancement, and one of the most
marked but natural changes of the provincial system,
during the period under consideration, is the tendency
to leave all important matters of administration to the
decision of the emperor. This practice comes out very
clearly some fifty years later in Pliny's letters to Trajan,
where matters of almost a trivial character were referred
to the emperor for settlement. The senate theoretically
maintained its right to reverse the decisions of its own
governors, and on occasion actually exercised the right,
as we may infer from Pliny's correspondence (X. 56;
X. 72); but the commanding influence of the emperor in
the senate, his exalted position as proconsul of a large part
of the Roman world, and the deference shown him by the
governors of imperial provinces could not fail to have an
effect on the governors of senatorial provinces also. We
are not surprised, therefore, to find them, too, appealing to
the emperor for advice in difficult matters of administration.
Governors in both the imperial and senatorial provinces
seem to have taken more and more into their own hands the
supervision of the administrative affairs of the communities
located in their provinces. In particular, as we see from
Pliny's letters, they concerned themselves with the economic
affairs of these communities and the questions involved in
the construction of public buildings and public works.

**361. The Provincial Assemblies.**    A new and most interesting political institution of the imperial period is the provincial assembly, made up of representatives from the communities lying within a given area.   As early as the time of Verres the commonwealth of Sicily (*commune Siciliae*, Cic. *in Verr.* ii. 2. 154) chose representatives to pay certain honors to its governor.   It was left for the imperial cult in the provinces, however, in its development to direct this movement toward representative government. The cult of the emperor appeared first in Augustus's own lifetime in the Greek cities of Asia, and spread rapidly through the western as well as the eastern provinces.   The imperial officials fostered it, because it knit the Roman world together and developed a spirit of loyalty toward the central government, as personified in the emperor. To construct temples to him and to the *Dea Roma*, and to celebrate festivals in honor of the new deities, a provincial assembly (*concilium provinciae*) met annually in the principal city of the province under the presidency of the *flamen provinciae*.   Its main duties were of a religious character.   They consisted in arranging the details of the imperial worship, and in imposing taxes for its proper maintenance on the cities of the province ; but these assemblies also took it on themselves to discuss certain matters of general interest to their respective provinces, and to send deputations to the emperor to lay the results of their deliberations before him.   A large body of inscriptions attests the activity of the *concilia* and shows the varied character of the business which came before them.   The institution acquired in time some political importance (cf. p. 372), and it is interesting because it is one of the earliest attempts to establish on a large scale our modern system of representative government.

## SELECTIONS FROM THE SOURCES

Tacitus, *Ann.* I. 5–VI; XI–XVI; *Hist.* I; II. 11–101; Suetonius, *Tiberius, Caligula, Claudius, Nero, Galba, Otho, Vitellius;* Dio Cassius, LVII–LXV; Josephus, *Antiq. Iud.* XVIII–XX; Strabo; Velleius Paterculus, II. 124 ff.; Plutarch, *Galba, Otho;* Eutropius, VII. 11–18.

**Recommendations of Augustus read in senate:** Dio, LVI. 33. — **Elections given to senate** (A.D. 14) : Tac. *Ann.* I. 15; Vell. II. 126. 2. — **Mutiny in Germany:** *Ann.* I. 31 ff.; Dio, LVII. 4 f. — **Minuta maiestas:** *Ann.* I. 72. — **Curatores riparum et alvei Tiberis:** Dio, LVII. 14. — **Recall of Germanicus** (A.D. 16): *Ann.* II. 26. — **Cappadocia, Roman province** (A.D. 17) : Dio, LVII. 17. — **Alliance with Parthia** (A.D. 18) : *Ann.* II. 58. — **Death of Germanicus** (A.D. 19): *Ann.* II. 69–73. — **Law governing price of grain** (A.D. 19) : *Ann.* II. 87. — **Death of Cn. Piso** (A.D. 20) : *Ann.* III. 15. — **Sumptuary laws:** *Ann.* II. 33; III. 52–5. — **Drusus, the tribunicia potestas** (A.D. 22): *Ann.* III. 56–7. — **L. Aelius Sejanus:** *Ann.* IV. 1–2. — **Sejanus is refused the hand of Livia** (A.D. 25) : *Ann.* IV. 39–40. — **Tiberius retires to Capri** (A.D. 27) : *Ann.* IV. 67. — **Overthrow of Sejanus** (A.D. 31): Dio, LVIII. 11; Suet. *Tib.* 65. — **Prosecutions:** *Ann.* VI. 3 ff. — **Financial legislation** (A.D. 33): *Ann.* VI. 17. — **Death of Tiberius** (A.D. 37) : *Ann.* VI. 50; Suet. *Tib.* 73. — **Gaius succeeds:** Suet. *Cal.* 14. — **Elections restored to comitia** (A.D. 38) : Dio, LIX. 9. — **Prosecutions:** Dio, LIX. 13, 16, 18. — **Cruelties of Gaius:** Dio, LIX. 25–6. — **Murder of Gaius** (A.D. 41): Suet. *Cal.* 58; Dio, LIX. 29. — **Claudius succeeds:** Suet. *Claud.* 10–11; Dio, LX. 1. — **Character:** Suet. *Claud.* 2 f., 29 ff.; Dio, LX. 2; Sen. *Apoc.* — **Reforms:** Dio, LX. 6. — **Provinces of Mauretania established** (A.D. 42) : Dio, LX. 9. — **Conspiracy of Vinicianus** (A.D. 42): Dio, LX. 15. — **Campaigns of Plautius and Ostorius in Britain** (A.D. 43 and 50): Dio, LX. 19–22, 30; *Ann.* XII. 31–40; *Agr.* 13 f. — **Achaea and Macedonia become senatorial provinces** (A.D. 44): Dio, LX. 24. — **Treasury under two quaestors:** Dio, LX. 24. — **Advocates' fees limited:** *Ann.* XI. 5–7. — **Census taken** (A.D. 48): *Ann.* XI. 25. — **Messalina killed** (A.D. 48) : *Ann.* XI. 26–38. — **Agrippina:** *Ann.* XII. 1–8. — **Seneca, tutor of Domitius, son of Agrippina:** *Ann.* XII. 8. — **Claudius adopts Domitius with name of Claudius Nero** (A.D. 50): *Ann.* XII. 25 f. — **Lake Fucinus:** *Ann.* XII. 56–7. — **Aqua Claudia and Anio Novus:** Frontin. *de Aquaed.* 13. — **Death of Claudius** (A.D. 54): *Ann.* XII.

66–8. — **Nero succeeds**: *Ann.* XII. 69; Dio, LXI. 3. — **Burrus and Seneca**: Dio, LXI. 4; *Ann.* XIII. 2. — **Nero poisons Britannicus** (A.D. 55): *Ann.* XIII. 16–17. — **Agrippina killed** (59 A.D.): *Ann.* XIV. 3–8; Suet. *Nero*, 34. — **Death of Burrus** (A.D. 62): *Ann.* XIV. 51. — **Tiridates accepts crown from Nero** (A.D. 63): *Ann.* XV. 29 ff.; Dio, LXIII. 2–7. — **Death of Seneca** (A.D. 65): *Ann.* XV. 60 ff. — **Vindex**: Dio, LXIII. 22. — **Galba proclaimed emperor by his troops**: Dio, LXIII. 23. — **Vindex defeated**: Dio, LXIII. 24. — **Death of Nero** (A.D. 68): Suet. *Nero*, 47–9. — **A. Vitellius proclaimed emperor by his troops** (A.D. 69): *Hist.* I. 56–7. — **Galba adopts Piso**: *Hist.* I. 14–19. — **Otho declared emperor by praetorian guard**: *Hist.* I. 27 f. — **Death of Galba**: *Hist.* I. 41. — **Bedriacum**: *Hist.* II. 40–45. — **Death of Otho**: *Hist.* II. 46 ff.; Dio, LXIV. 15. — **Vitellius recognized at Rome**: *Hist.* II. 55. — **Character**: *Hist.* II. 62, 73; Dio, LXV. 3.

## Selected Bibliography [1]

A. Stahr, Tiberius. Berlin, 1873.

G. Boissier, L'opposition sous les Césars. Paris, 1892.

H. Lehmann, Claudius und Nero und ihre Zeit, Vol. I. Gotha, 1877.

Sievers, Studien zur Geschichte der römischen Kaiser. Berlin, 1870.

R. Bompard, Le crime de lèse majesté. Paris, 1888.

Guiraud, Les assemblées provinciales dans l'empire romain. Paris, 1887.

Hirschfeld, Zur Geschichte des röm. Kaisercultus, in Sitzungsb. d. Akad. d. Wissensch. zu Berlin, 1888, 2ter Halbb. pp. 833 ff.

## Supplementary Literature, 1901–1910

Henderson, The Life and Principate of the Emperor Nero. London, 1903.

Ferrero, Characters and Events of Roman History. From Caesar to Nero. London, 1909.

Houdoy, Le droit municipal. Paris, 1876.

Tarver, Tiberius the Tyrant. London, 1902.

[1] See also p. 288.

# CHAPTER XIV

## THE FLAVIAN EMPERORS

**362. Vespasian proclaimed Emperor.** When the news of the battle of Bedriacum and of the death of Otho reached Rome, the soldiers took the oath of allegiance to Vitellius, and the senate accorded him imperial honors; but before he had reached the city a new aspirant for the throne had arisen — this time in the East, in the person of Vespasian. He was proclaimed emperor in Alexandria by the prefect of Egypt, July 1, 69, and from this date he subsequently counted the years of his reign. The legions in Judaea, Syria, Moesia, Pannonia, and Illyricum supported him, and Mucianus, governor of Syria, and his principal lieutenant was sent into Italy. Antonius Primus, who commanded seven legions in Illyricum, reached Italy in advance of Mucianus, however, defeated the army of Vitellius at Cremona in a bloody battle, marched rapidly toward Rome, and entered the city December 20. Vitellius, in attempting to escape, was seized and put to death. On the following day Vespasian was made consul, and received from the senate the title of Augustus and the tribunician power.

**363. Precarious Position of Vespasian.** The outlook for Vespasian, however, seemed anything but promising. He was a man of humble birth, and, therefore, apparently hampered by the same drawbacks which had prevented Verginius Rufus from yielding to the temptation held out to him by his soldiers (p. 297). He was a mere soldier, with no experience in civil affairs, and finally he followed a series of pretenders, who had been set on the throne by one army to be displaced by another. In fact, the uprising of the troops in Germany under Claudius Civilis, before he had ascended the throne, seemed to foreshadow the same fate for him also.

**364. The Character of Vespasian.** His sterling qualities, however, saved him from all these dangers. Indeed, from a knowledge of his antecedents and character, one could almost forecast the outcome of his reign and the political and social changes which he would strive to effect. We have noticed that he was of humble birth. His family came from the little town of Reate, in the Sabine territory. His grandfather had been engaged in collecting small debts; his father was a tax-collector. The family stock was not unlike that of the poet Horace, and the picture which Horace has drawn of his father may well serve to give us a fair impression of the grandfather and father of Vespasian. He was already advanced in life — he was sixty years old at this time — and he had received the hardy training of a soldier. Both of these facts must have emphasized the traits of character which he inherited from his immediate ancestors. Having been born outside the city, he had none of the narrow municipal prejudice of the native Roman. His humble surroundings in early life, and his experience as a soldier, had made his tastes simple and his methods direct. Then, too, if he had been brought up in Rome, he would have felt himself bound by the social and political traditions, which prevented several of his predecessors from aiming directly at the object which they wished to accomplish. The fact that he was born in a little country village left him free in this respect. His obscure birth saved him also from paying undue deference to aristocratic prejudice.  Finally, he inherited from his immediate ancestors shrewdness in dealing with the practical affairs of life, and especially in managing financial transactions.

**365. Administrative and Constitutional Reforms during his Reign.**  These traits of Vespasian's character found expression in the administrative and constitutional reforms which he introduced.  His methodical tendency and his sense of order led him to take immediate measures to suppress the insurrection under Civilis, to restore order in Germany, and to perfect the system of frontier defenses on the borders of Moesia, of Pannonia, and in the East. Most of the principalities and free states in the Orient were made provinces, and were governed as the adjoining countries.  His regard for system led to the formulation, though possibly not for the first time, of the constitutional powers and privileges of the emperor in the celebrated *lex de imperio Vespasiani* (cf. p. 407).  This trait in his character led him also to make early arrangements to take the census, and from the information which the census-lists gave him he was able to reorganize the senate and the equestrian order, to pick out men who were qualified to fill administrative positions, and to decide how and where to levy troops.  He gained exact information with reference to the resources of the state, information which was of inestimable value to him in determining the most equitable and profitable form and rate of taxation.  On the other hand, he learned the needs of the empire, in the way of public works and public buildings.  According to the emperor's own estimate, the reorganization of the financial system and the material needs of the empire called for forty billions of sesterces.  This enormous sum was raised without apparently crippling industry or exciting serious opposition. In some cases the rate of taxation was increased, new taxes were levied, or larger contributions from the provinces were required ; but the greatest gain was made by doing away with the exemption of favored classes, and by insisting on honesty and economy in raising the levy. Here Vespasian's clear insight into financial matters helped him greatly.

His freedom from native Roman and aristocratic prejudice allowed him to make important changes in the character of the senate and the senatorial order. Some of his predecessors had aimed at creating a new senatorial aristocracy dependent on the emperor for its position and honors, and Claudius had gone so far as to admit men from the provinces who had distinguished themselves, but in most cases those who received seats in the senate were natives of the city of Rome and ex-magistrates. Vespasian, however, freely gave the senatorial rank to provincials, and, with that directness of purpose which characterized him, he did not in all cases require a candidate for senatorial honors to hold a magistracy, but he conferred the dignity upon him directly. Vespasian's practice in this respect was followed by his successors, and from the time of Domitian this imperial prerogative was freely exercised. The senatorial order thus ceased to be a Roman aristocracy ; it was no longer based, even formally, on republican tradition. It was an aristocracy of the empire, whose privileges were within the gift of the emperor. This policy of conferring privileges and honors upon deserving persons throughout the Roman world was carried down into the lower strata of society also. The rights of Latin citizenship were given to all the hitherto subject communities in Spain, and to some among the Helvetii. The practice of bestowing the rights of citizenship and the privileges of senatorial rank on provincials is a definite part of the Flavian policy, and perhaps nothing did more to develop throughout the empire a unity of interests and a loyalty to the central government. Those who had received these honors were proud of them, and grateful to the ruler who gave them. Those who had not attained them were anxious to prove their fitness to receive them. The fruits of this generous policy toward the provincials are seen in the Spanish origin of Trajan, Hadrian, and M. Aurelius, and in the Gallic origin of Antoninus.

The power which Vespasian exercised in raising private citizens to senatorial rank took from the magistracies the greater part of the importance which they had had under the early emperors. It was no longer necessary to hold a magistracy in order to be admitted to the senate. The practice of holding the consulship for only two months also materially lessened the dignity of that office, which was still further diminished by the encroachment of various imperial offices.

**366. The Reign of Titus.** With all his care in defining the powers of the emperor, and in introducing system into the affairs of government, Vespasian had not settled the principle of the succession. At his death, however, in the summer of the year 79, it was rather a theoretical than a practical question. He had secured for his son Titus a point of vantage, by making him prefect of the praetorian guard, by granting him the tribunician power in the year 71, by allowing him to receive the title of *imperator* after his success in Judaea, and by making him his colleague in the censorship and the consulship. The reign of Titus, which extends through a period of only about two years, was scarcely long enough to enable us to estimate the character of his administration. He seems to have been an amiable and mild ruler.   His kindness to the people of Campania after the eruption of Vesuvius shows this plainly enough.   But this amiability of nature had its unfortunate side.   It led him to spend large sums of money to amuse the people, without counting the cost or considering the unfortunate precedent which he set for the future.   He held the power firmly in his own hands, however, neither recognizing the historic claims of the senate nor admitting his brother Domitian to a share in the government.

**367.  The Drift toward Monarchy under Domitian.**   The theory upon which the government of Augustus was based, that the Roman world was under the joint control of the *princeps* and the senate, had been seriously undermined by the reorganization of the senate under Vespasian, and the subordination of that body and of the whole senatorial order to him.   Domitian, who ascended the throne in September, 81, rejected completely the theory that the *princeps* and the senate jointly ruled the state, that the government was a dyarchy, as it has been called, and took a long step toward the establishment of the monarchy. He was an autocrat by instinct, and consistently followed the policy of keeping the supreme power entirely in his own hands.   In the fourth year of his reign he had himself made censor for life.   He did not take this office, as his father had done, for the sake of reorganizing the finances of the state, but solely, or mainly, for the purpose of controlling the appointment of senators.   In this way he was able to degrade his enemies and to fill the senate with his supporters.   He also formally claimed the right of sitting in judgment on senators charged with capital offenses.   In the year 84, in which he took the censorship for life, he had himself made consul for a period of ten years, a step which indicated his intention of taking from his colleagues in that office even an apparent equality with him. The same intention is obvious in his decision to reserve for himself the laurel wreath, and in his assumption of certain unusual insignia of office. His autocratic attitude shows itself also in the fact that he tolerated no favorites, and that he did not rule through ministers. In fact, constant changes were made in the personnel of the imperial household. In this respect his course is in contrast to the policy of the tyrants who had preceded him, like Tiberius and Nero. This theory of government puts on the ruler's shoulders the responsibility for the mistakes which may be made, as well as for the wise measures which may be taken, and Domitian seems to have felt the responsibility and to have tried in many respects to do his duty conscientiously. The same deliberate purpose to rule alone, reinforced perhaps by the dread of a military uprising, led him to divide the provincial armies in such a way that not more than one or two legions should be under the command of a single general. It was probably a desire to maintain his prestige in all fields of activity, and his knowledge of the fact that success in arms still offered the surest road to popularity, which led him to take charge in person of the military operations against the Chatti in 83, and in Moesia in 86, and to celebrate a triumph on his return from the first expedition.

**368. Social and Economic Reforms.** As has been said, Domitian accepted conscientiously the responsibility which his attempt to hold all the power in his own hands laid upon him. He worked faithfully, though not always wisely, to improve the moral, religious, and economic condition of the people in Italy and the provinces. The Julian laws, passed to protect the purity and integrity of family life, were vigorously enforced, and, like Augustus and Tiberius, Domitian strove to stimulate the religious life of the people by building temples and by restoring the dignity of the priesthoods. To combat the tendency towards luxurious living he adopted the eccentric policy of discouraging and, in some cases, of forbidding the cultivation of the vine. All these measures for the moral and religious improvement of the people naturally met with little success, but his reforms in the judicial system and in the army were of more importance. In particular, the administration of justice profited greatly by his watchful supervision of the courts. His management of the finances of the state, which seems to have been in the main wise and economical, enabled him to construct many important buildings and public works and to restore others which needed repair. The jealous watch which he kept on provincial governors in most cases fostered justice and economy in the government of the empire outside of Italy.

**369. Domitian's Jealousy and Tyranny.** In spite of all this, however, Domitian was a tyrant, and a tyrant with certain traits of character which always make autocracy odious. His inordinate ambition and unscrupulous selfishness, which had prevented his father and his brother from conferring on him the honors that he would otherwise have had, took the form, after he had ascended the throne, of a jealous suspicion of any one who opposed him or won any distinction. As in the case of several of the Julian emperors (cf. pp. 289 f., 295 f.), his life falls into two periods. Before the uprising under Saturninus in 88 his policy was reasonably mild. After that event he pursued those who opposed him, or excited his suspicion, with a vindictiveness which knew no bounds. The fact that he was childless, and hence that the way to the throne seemed open to any ambitious aspirant, probably increased still more his suspicion of any one whose ability raised him above the common level.

He fell by the hand of members of his own household in September of the year 96.

**370. Military Operations of the Flavian Period.** The disorder which had prevailed throughout the Roman world in the year preceding the accession of the Flavian emperors was repressed within a year or more after Vespasian ascended the throne. This spirit of unrest showed itself in Pontus, Britain, Moesia, and on the banks of the Rhine, and both native peoples and legionaries joined in several of the movements. The most serious of these uprisings was that of various German and Gallic tribes under Julius Civilis, which was also supported by the Roman legions in the vicinity. It seems to have been an expression of the nationalist feeling (cf. pp. 296–7), for the Remi, who were concerned in the movement, tried to convoke a Gallic national assembly to lay plans for the future; but at the approach of Petilius Cerialis, one of Vespasian's lieutenants, toward the close of the year 70, the various rebellious peoples submitted one after another, and the Roman troops returned to their allegiance. At about the same time the war in Judaea was brought to an end by Titus, and the city of Jerusalem was taken. For years religious teachers had been going up and down in the land prophesying the approaching triumph of the Jew over the Gentile, and the fierce religious and racial hostility which resulted found expression in wholesale massacres of Jews and their enemies in Judaea and outside of it. The Roman officials were incapable of dealing with the secret organizations which the Jews formed, and the supine governor of Syria, Cestius Gallus, allowed matters to drift until open war broke out in 66. Thereupon Nero intrusted the conduct of affairs in Judaea to Vespasian. For four years more the Jews held out against the Roman legions, but in 70 Titus took Jerusalem, and Judaea for the second time was made a separate province. Perhaps the greatest extension of Roman territory was made in Britain, as a result of the successful campaigns of Cerialis, Frontinus, and Agricola. At the close of Nero's reign, Roman authority was recognized as far north as Lincoln and Chester. Agricola pushed his conquests to a point considerably farther north and even carried on a successful campaign in Scotland. The most serious danger from without, which threatened the empire during the Flavian period, came from the Dacians, who crossed over into lower Moesia, under their leader, Decebalus, and defeated the governor, Oppius Sabinus, as well as the prefect of the guard, Cornelius Fuscus. The Romans seem at first to have underestimated the fighting qualities of the enemy and the size of the coalition formed against them, for they suffered repeated disasters. The result was that, after the Dacians had been joined by the Quadi, Sarmatians, Marcomanni, and other peoples in that region, Domitian was forced to make peace on the basis of certain annual gifts to the Dacian king, although the latter, on his side, probably acknowledged in some measure the suzerainty of the Roman emperor. The revolt in the year 88 of L. Antonius Saturninus, the governor of Upper Germany, excited a greater alarm in Domitian's mind than the more serious difficulty on the Danube, and although it was suppressed within a few months, it permanently affected the character of Domitian's reign (cf. p. 312).

**371. General Changes in Provincial Government.** The most important changes made in the division of the provinces between the emperor and the senate in the Flavian period were the assignment of Sardinia and Corsica to Vespasian, and the union of Achaea and Epirus, which

Nero had declared independent states, into a senatorial province. Moesia was divided into two provinces, Upper and Lower Moesia, by Domitian. Galatia was added to Cappadocia by Vespasian and put under a consular legate. But the most noteworthy administrative change in the provinces consisted in the movement to introduce a uniform system of government, by the reduction of principalities and suzerain states to the form of provinces. This change was made especially in the Orient, where several principalities, like Commagene and Judaea, were placed directly under a Roman governor. Egypt, however, still maintained its anomalous position as the personal domain of the emperor. It was ruled by a prefect of equestrian rank, and the administrative system of the Ptolemies was still retained.

**372. Improvement in the Condition of the Provincials.** Vespasian's skill as an organizer, and Domitian's jealous supervision of provincial governors, alike contributed to the prosperity of the provinces. By the elevation of their most distinguished citizens to the senatorial order (cf. pp. 308–9), and by the grant of Latin rights to native communities, they were made to feel themselves integral parts of the empire and not dependencies, and their material prosperity was promoted by the judicious construction of public roads and public works and the improved management of local finances. In Baetica alone 120 cities received the *ius Latii* under the Flavian emperors. The extant charters of Salpensa and Malaca, in this province, give us a clear idea of the nature of the government established in these communities. Paradoxical as it may seem, hand in hand with this extension of self-government there seems to have developed a tendency on the part of provincial governors to concern themselves more and more with local affairs (cf. p. 301).

## Selections from the Sources

Tacitus, *Hist.* II. 1–10; III–V, and *Agricola;* Josephus, *Bell.
Iud.* III ff.; Dio Cassius, LXVI–LXVII; Suetonius, *Vespasianus,
Titus,* and *Domitianus.*

Vespasian proclaimed emperor in the Orient (69): Tac. *Hist.* II.
80–81.—Battle of Cremona (Oct. 69): *Hist.* III. 22–33.—Disorders in
Rome (Dec. 69): *Hist.* III. 69–74.— Vespasian made emperor (Dec.
21, 69): *Hist.* IV. 3; Dio, LXVI. 1.— Revolt under Civilis (69–70):
*Hist.* IV. 14–37; 54–79; V. 14–26.— Titus takes Jerusalem (70):
Jos. *Bell. Iud.* VI. 8. 4–5.— Vespasian enters Rome (70): *Hist.* IV.
53.— Improvements in Rome: *C. I. L.* VI. 931; VI. 1238; VI. 1257.
— Latin rights to Spain (74): Plin. *N. H.* III. 30.— Death of Ves-
pasian and accession of Titus (79): Suet. *Vesp.* 24; Dio, LXVI. 17.
— Eruption of Vesuvius (79): Plin. *Ep.* VI. 16 and 20; Dio, LXVI.
21–3.— Relief for Campania: Dio, LXVI. 24.— Campaigns in
Britain: Tac. *Agr.* — Death of Titus: Suet. *Tit.* 11; Dio, LXVI.
26.—Charters of Salpensa and Malaca (82–4): *C. I. L.* II. 1963–4.
— Domitian consul for 10 yrs. (84): Dio, LXVII. 4.— War against
Dacians, etc.: Dio, LXVII. 6, 7, 10.— Death of Domitian (96): Dio,
LXVII. 15–17.

## Selected Bibliography [1]

J. Asbach, Römisches Kaisertum u. Verfassung bis auf Traian.
  Köln, 1896.
Chambalu, De magistratibus Flaviorum.  Bonn, 1882.
Chambalu, Flaviana, Philol. XLIV (1885), pp. 106 ff.; 502 ff., and
  XLV (1886), pp. 100 ff.
Hirschfeld, Untersuchungen auf dem Gebiete der römischen Ver-
  waltungsgeschichte, Bd. I.  Berlin, 1876.
Frz. Pichlmayr, T. Flavius Domitianus.  Erlangen, 1889.
Gsell, Essai sur le règne de l'empereur Domitien.  Paris, 1894.

[1] See also pp. 288, 304.

# CHAPTER XV

## FROM NERVA TO SEPTIMIUS SEVERUS

**373. Nerva.** It is not clear what influences led to the choice of M. Cocceius Nerva as emperor, but he was probably supported by the conspirators who had overthrown Domitian. His reign lasted only two years, and there were no important constitutional or administrative changes in it. He was able, however, to right many of the abuses which had grown up under his predecessor. Prosecutions for *lèse-majesté* were forbidden, and the impoverished condition of the people in Italy was somewhat relieved by loaning money to needy farmers, at a low rate of interest, for the purchase of land.

**374. Trajan.** On the death of Nerva in January, 98, M. Ulpius Trajanus, the governor of Upper Germany, whom Nerva had adopted the year before, succeeded to the throne without opposition. Trajan, like his predecessor, was punctilious in his treatment of the senate. He renounced the right to try senators on capital charges. He encouraged freedom of speech at the meetings of the senate, and in general carefully observed the fiction of the dual control of affairs by the emperor and the senate. In fact, during his prolonged absences from Rome, the senate acquired some importance as a legislative body in administrative matters. In his dealings with the magistrates he showed a similar regard for republican traditions by accepting the consulship only four times during the nineteen years of his reign, whereas Domitian had been consul ten times during his reign of fifteen years. He checked delation, as Nerva had done, and reformed the laws governing prosecution for treason. The result of his attempts to carry out Nerva's plans to improve the condition of the farmers, and to increase the free population of Italy and the outcome of his policy, and that of his successor, of remitting taxes, and of encouraging the construction of public buildings in the small towns, will be considered in another connection.

**375. Hadrian.** By far the most important administrative change which Hadrian made consisted in the introduction of a bureaucratic system into the civil service, with its fixed gradation of offices and corresponding order of promotion. The functions of each official were carefully marked out, and the government took into its own hands certain matters, like the collection of taxes, which before had been wholly or in part managed under private contract. Hadrian made some important changes in the judicial system also. He chose eminent jurists as members of his *consilium*, made it a permanent body, and increased its judicial functions. He took away from the republican magistrates the jurisdiction in civil cases which they had exercised throughout Italy and gave it to four imperial officials, later known as *iuridici*. In this connection may be mentioned the codification in a single edict by the jurist Salvius Julianus of the principles and forms published by praetors and curule aediles, in so far as such principles were still in force. The provinces received as careful attention from him as Italy did, and his long journeys, covering ten years of his reign, into all parts of the empire made him familiar with their condition and their needs. Having no children, he adopted in 136 L. Ceionius Commodus Verus, giving him the title of L. Aelius Verus. In 138, on the death of Aelius, Hadrian

named as his successor T. Aurelius Fulvus Boionius Arrius
Antoninus, who was known after his adoption as T. Aelius
Hadrianus Antoninus.   Hadrian died the same year.

376. **Antoninus Pius.**   Antoninus, or Antoninus Pius,
as he is commonly called, does not seem to have lacked
strength of character.   The energy with which he checked
the plans of the senate to pass certain measures reflecting
on the reign of his adoptive father would disprove such a
theory.   But he lacked the restless spirit of his predecessor, his breadth of view, and his power of initiative.   He
had no ambition to extend the limits of the empire, nor tò
introduce important administrative reforms.   To insure the
succession he had been required to adopt M. Annius Verus,
known later as M. Aurelius Antoninus, and also the son of
L. Aelius Verus, who was given the title of L. Aelius Aurelius
Commodus.   It does not seem to have been the purpose
of Hadrian to grant equal powers to the two heirs of Antoninus, but rather to insure a peaceful succession in case
M. Aurelius should die.   At all events, Antoninus Pius
chose the latter as his associate in the government, and,
just before his death in 161, plainly indicated him as his
successor.

377. **M. Aurelius.**   But, immediately after his accession to the throne, M. Aurelius raised L. Aelius to a
position of like power with himself, and the equal authority
of the latter was recognized up to the death of Aelius in
169.   Seven years later M. Aurelius made his own son,
L. Aurelius Commodus, his colleague, and father and son
held the imperial authority together until M. Aurelius died,
in 180.   This interesting reversion to the republican principle of collegiality had its administrative advantages.   The
Roman empire extended over so wide an area that a division of the territory between two rulers, acting in harmony,

would be to the advantage of both sections, and this was what the joint rule of M. Aurelius and L. Aelius amounted to. The supervision of M. Aurelius was largely confined to the West, that of his brother to the East. One may well question whether such an exercise of autocratic power by two emperors would be workable in ordinary cases, but in the two cases mentioned the family relations existing between the joint rulers made rivalry improbable and prevented a serious conflict of authority. The amiable disposition and the philosophic tastes of M. Aurelius had a good and a bad influence on the character of his reign. On the one hand, they made him strive to ameliorate the condition of the slaves, to interpret the law in accordance with its spirit rather than its letter, and to treat the senate with consideration. On the other hand, he showed an unwise generosity in giving largesses, in increasing the number of those who received help from the state, and in remitting taxes. His peaceful tastes also prevented him from giving necessary attention to the needs of the army and to the loyalty of his generals. The unwisdom of this neglect was made clear before his death by the uprising under Avidius Cassius, the governor of Syria.

**378. Commodus.** Commodus revived the evil memories of the later Julian emperors. During the greater part of his reign, which extended from 180 to 192, he was under the influence of favorites. The prefect Perennis held the reins of government from 180 to 185, and the freedman Cleander from the downfall of Perennis to 189. The overthrow of Perennis was due to the discontent which was excited in the army by his attempt to substitute knights for senators in important military commands. Cleander owed his downfall to his general unpopularity and to the machinations of his political enemies. Perennis had

executive ability and was in the main patriotic, but the loose
delegation of almost autocratic power to a single individual,
whose position was determined neither by law nor by tradition, and the encroachment of court favorites on the functions which belonged to established officials, could not fail
to result in disorder and maladministration and to under-
mine the official system which Hadrian and his successors
had so carefully elaborated. In the end Commodus, who
had given himself up completely to the pursuit of pleasure,
fell by the hands of the court favorites, to whom he had
intrusted the government.

**379. Pertinax and Didius Julianus.** P. Helvius Pertinax, whom the conspirators placed on the throne, was like
Vespasian a man of humble birth, and had Vespasian's
shrewd knowledge of affairs and his ability as an organizer.
Although he was emperor for only three months, his success
in reforming the finances was remarkable, but his economical and upright management of affairs displeased the court
officials and the soldiers in the city, who had been accustomed to the gratuities of Commodus, and he was murdered.
A senator named Didius Julianus, who surpassed all other
aspirants for the throne in his promises to the praetorian
guard, was invested with the purple. But the break in the
succession, and the unpopularity of Didius Julianus in
Rome, encouraged L. Septimius Severus in Pannonia, Pes-
cennius Niger in Syria, and Clodius Albinus in Britain, to
lay claim to the throne. Septimius Severus was nearer Italy
than his rivals, and, without meeting serious resistance, made
himself master of the peninsula and of Rome. The frightened senate condemned Julianus to death, and Septimius
Severus was proclaimed emperor in the summer of 193.

**380. The Senate during the Second Century.** The constitutional relations which the senate bore to the emperor

at the beginning of this period when Nerva ascended the throne were unchanged at the accession of Septimius Severus. All of the emperors of the second century, with the possible exception of Commodus, treated the senate, however, with consideration. They encouraged also the free discussion of matters brought before it, so that the senate practically reverted to the position which it had held under the monarchy and the early republic, and became the *consilium* of the chief-magistrate. Its failure to assert its independence seems to have been due in part to the fact that it was overawed by the comprehensive powers of the emperor, and in part to the bitter experiences which many of its members had suffered under some of the earlier emperors, — experiences which made individual senators more anxious to protect their lives and their personal privileges than to uphold the traditional powers of the senate as an independent branch of the government. The passage of the formal act creating a new emperor was still the prerogative of the senate, but there is no case during this period in which the selection of the emperor was left to its free choice.

**381. The Equestrian Order.** The members of the equestrian order gained greatly by Hadrian's reorganization of the civil service, since many of the important positions closely connected with the emperor's person were put into their hands. Hadrian also freely made knights members of his *consilium*, and Perennis, the favorite of Commodus, even tried the unsuccessful experiment of giving them important military commands. The senatorial order was deeply offended at these encroachments on its prerogatives. It is important to notice that all of these changes indicate the drift toward a leveling of the classes and foreshadow the coming absolutism.

**382. The People.** The people counted for little politically during this period, except so far as the popular
dislike of an emperor might encourage some rival to attempt his overthrow, as happened in the case of Didius
Julianus. The interest of the Italians in municipal politics was also dying out, and it was difficult to find candidates for the municipal offices. This state of things was
partly due to the heavy financial burdens imposed on
municipal magistrates and partly to the encroachment of
imperial officials on the traditional functions of the local
magistrates. Furthermore, the people of Italy were so dis-
inclined to military service that little attempt was made to
recruit the army from this quarter. As a consequence, the
great mass of the Italians had no share whatever in civil
or military affairs. They became incapable of governing
or of defending themselves, and their horizon was limited
by their own personal interests. This period is characterized, however, by an improvement in the condition of
freedmen, slaves, orphans, and the aged poor. Freedmen
were given a much larger share in municipal life, and the
position of slaves before the law was greatly ameliorated.
Slaves, for instance, could no longer be put to death without due process of law, nor could they be sold to a gladia-
torial trainer or a procurer at the pleasure of their owners.
These changes were largely due to the spread of the doc-
trine of the brotherhood of man, or to the recognition of
the *ius naturale*, as the Roman jurist styled it. The tendency toward a leveling of all classes, which was a social
and political result of the exalted position of the emperor,
also had something to do with the movement. The support which the government gave to orphans and to needy
parents was inspired, partly by humane considerations, and
partly by a desire to keep up the population of Italy. At

all events, the *alimentatio* became an important function of
the government from the time of Trajan.

**383. The Provinces.** The military operations of the
period under consideration fall mainly in the reigns of
Trajan and M. Aurelius. The former was a soldier by
nature. The latter had war forced on him. The most
important accession of territory during the period was
that of Dacia. The Romans must have chafed under the
humiliating peace which Domitian had made with the
Dacians (cf. p. 314), and the existence of a strong power
across the Danube under an able leader like Decebalus
certainly threatened Roman territory to the south. The
raids of the Dacians gave Trajan a reasonable pretext for
declaring war against them in the year 101. After two
campaigns the country was subdued, and in 107 it was
reduced to the form of a province. Colonies were planted
in the new territory, the frontier along the Danube was
strengthened, military roads were built, and Pannonia and
Moesia were provided with numerous camps and walled
towns. This whole section was so well protected that for
sixty years perfect quiet prevailed there. But in the reign
of M. Aurelius, the Marcomanni, Quadi, and other tribes
to the north, pushed southward by the pressure of the
peoples beyond them, crossed the Danube, and even
entered Italy, carrying back with them on their return thou-
sands of captives. This incursion came at a most inop-
portune moment for the Romans. The empire was in
great financial straits; a plague had made a serious reduction in the population, and many of the troops were
engaged in the Parthian war. M. Aurelius and his colleague, L. Verus, took charge in person of the military
operations, but it required thirteen years to restore perfect
order on the Danube.

In the East the only permanent acquisition of this period was Arabia, which was made a province in 106. Of the two provinces which Trajan acquired in his brilliant campaign against the Parthians in 114–5, Mesopotamia was given up by Hadrian, and Armenia was allowed to become a suzerain state.

In no period of imperial history did Roman civilization spread so rapidly and take such deep root as in the second century. The rapidity with which Dacia, for instance, adopted Roman ideas is almost incredible. Much of this improvement was due to the knowledge and administrative skill which Hadrian applied to provincial questions. The great civilizing agencies which he used with such effect were roads, colonies, public buildings, and the concession of Roman or Latin rights. In fact, the whole tendency of the period was to place the provinces on the same plane as Italy.

**384. Signs of Weakness in the Empire.** Signs of weakness, however, were visible in the empire, especially in Italy. Some of them have already been noticed. The loss of political interest and the disappearance of civic life in the peninsula, and the unwillingness of the Italians to serve in the army are symptoms of decline. An equally serious matter was the wretched financial condition of Italy during a great part of the period. Both Hadrian and M. Aurelius, when they ascended the throne, found it necessary to cancel large sums which were due the state in the form of taxes. In Hadrian's case the taxes which were remitted amounted to the enormous sum of 900,000,000 sesterces. The large amounts which were spent by Trajan and his successors in helping the needy also offer a striking proof of the widespread poverty. An explanation of the impoverished state of the people may be found in a variety of reasons. Perhaps a faulty system of taxation and an unfortunate industrial organization are partly responsible for it, but the real difficulty undoubtedly lay in the lack of energy and the incapacity of the people themselves, and in their tendency during times of prosperity to assume financial responsibilities which they could not maintain when unexpected demands were made on their resources. The first factor we have already had occasion to notice. The emperor Hadrian was largely responsible for the second evil. Under his encouragement, and following his example, the small towns all through Italy and the provinces during the period of peace, which lasted through his reign and that of his successor, erected costly baths, theatres, and other public buildings and works, whose construction exhausted their resources at the time, and whose maintenance became an intolerable burden, when supplemented by the financial demands made by the wars of the next two reigns. A clear indication of the way in which things were going is furnished by the debasement of the coinage under M. Aurelius. Thus, at the moment when Rome needed all of her resources to stem the tide of invasion, the state was almost bankrupt. The condition of affairs outside the empire also grew more and more threatening as the period drew to a close. The peoples from the north were pressing down toward Italy, and the pressure was so strong that many barbarian communities were allowed to settle in Roman territory, even in the peninsula itself. Yet the Roman army was not in a good condition to withstand this pressure, because Antoninus Pius and M. Aurelius, during the early part of his reign at least, gave little attention to its needs, and the questionable policy was adopted of filling its ranks with the newly conquered barbarians.

**385. The Drift toward Monarchy.** The formal courtesy with which almost all the emperors of this period treated the senate tends to conceal the fact that the theory of the joint control of the state had almost entirely lost its meaning. The contempt which Commodus showed for the senate, however, brought out clearly the true state of affairs. It showed plainly that the independent coöperation of the senate with the emperor was a fiction, which could take on the semblance of reality only under emperors like Antoninus Pius or M. Aurelius. The whole drift of the period was toward the elimination of the senate from the control of affairs. Neither in the choice of an emperor, nor in the management of affairs after he had ascended the throne, could it play an effective part. The theory of the succession rested on two irreconcilable things — heredity, or adoption, and the free choice of the senate. These two methods of selecting an emperor could not be followed at the same time. As a consequence, the weaker power, the senate, yielded, and accepted the candidate thrust on it. As for the control of the state during the reign of an emperor, Hadrian's bureaucratic system made such thorough and systematic provision for the administration of affairs that little or no place was left for the senate or for the old republican magistracies.

### SELECTIONS FROM THE SOURCES

Scriptores Historiae Augustae; Marius Maximus; Eutropius; Orosius; Herodianus; Sextus Aurelius Victor.

**Reforms of Nerva :** Dio, LXVIII. 2. — **Indigent children succored :** Aur. Victor, *Ep.* 12 ; Plin. *Panegyr.* 28. — **Election of magistrates in senate made secret** (100) : Plin. *Ep.* III. 20. — **The capital of Dacia taken by Trajan** (102) : Dio, LXVIII. 9. — **Second Dacian campaign** (105-7) : Dio, LXVIII. 10 ff. — **Parthian war** (114-117) :

Dio, LXVIII. 17–33; Eutr. VIII. 3. — Accession of Hadrian: Dio, LXIX. 1; Eutr. VIII. 6; Ael. Spart. *vita Hadr.* 4. — Territorial acquisitions of Trajan given up: Eutr. VIII. 6; *vita Hadr.* 5; Tac. *Ann.* II. 61. — Hadrian's travels: *vita Hadr.* 11–14; Dio, LXIX. 9–11. — His severity: *vita Hadr.* 22–3. — Antoninus Pius adopted: Iul. Capit. *vita Pii*, 4. — Antoninus adopts M. Aurelius and L. Verus: *ibid.* 4. — Faustina called Augusta: *ibid.* 5. — Parthian war (162–6): Iul. Capit. *Verus Imp.* 7. — War against Marcomanni, etc. (167–180): Dio, LXXI. 3; *ibid.* 7–21; Iul. Capit. *Ant. Phil.* 12–17; 21–7. — Reign of Commodus: Dio, LXXII; Herod. I; Lamprid. *vita Comm.* — Pertinax: Dio, LXXIII. 1–10; Herod. II. 1–5; Iul. Capit. *vita Pert.* — Didius Julianus: Dio, LXXIII. 11–17; Herod. II. 6–12; Ael. Spart. *vita Iul.* — Septimius Severus: Dio, LXXIV–LXXVI; Herod. II. 13–III; Ael. Spart. *vita Sev.*

### SELECTED BIBLIOGRAPHY [1]

M. Pelisson, Rome sous Trajan.   Paris, 1886.

De la Berge, Essai sur le règne de Trajan.   Paris, 1877.

H. F. Hitzig, Die Stellung Kaiser Hadrians in der römischen Rechtsgeschichte.   Zürich, 1892.

Ferd. v. Gregorovius, Der Kaiser Hadrian. 3te Aufl. Stuttgart, 1884.

Julius Dürr, Die Reisen des Kaisers Hadrian.   Wien, 1881.

Büdinger, Untersuchungen zur römischen Kaisergeschichte.   Leipzig, 1868.

E. C. Bryant, The Reign of Antoninus Pius.   (Cambridge Historical Essays, VIII.)

G. Lacour-Gayet, Antonin le Pieux et son temps (Diss.).   Paris, 1888.

W. W. Capes, The Age of the Antonines.   London, 1876.

G. Hassebrauk, Kaiser Septimius Severus.   Holzminden, 1890–91.

A. Wirth, Quaestiones Severianae.   Leipzig, 1888.

A. v. Brinz, Alimentenstiftungen der röm. Kaiser (Sitzungsber. d. k. bayr. Akad. d. Wiss., 1887, Hist. Klasse, pp. 209 ff.).

[1] See also pp. 288 and 304.

# CHAPTER XVI

## THE EMPIRE OF THE THIRD CENTURY AND THE REFORMS OF DIOCLETIAN

**386. The Third Century.** During the century which elapsed between the accession of Septimius Severus and the transformation of the government into a monarchy by Diocletian, there was no continuous forward movement in constitutional development, and no new political institutions of great importance were created, so that the condition of the empire may be described very briefly.

**387. The Emperor and the Senate.** The history of the period brings out clearly the fact that the position of the senate was what the emperor chose to make it. It is true that, during the reigns of Severus Alexander, Pupienus and Balbinus, Tacitus, and Probus, the prestige of the senate recalled the palmy days of that body under the republic, and at times during these periods it showed some of its former dignity and administrative capacity. The motives which led these emperors to grant to it some of its traditional powers were various. Thus, for instance, it was apparently the conservative policy of his mother, Julia Mamaea, and of Ulpian, his chief adviser, strengthened by a feeling that the influence of the senate might be used to offset that of the praetorian guard, which led Severus Alexander to delegate real power to that body. Pupienus and Balbinus and Tacitus were ex-consuls, who represented the free choice of the senate, and the consideration which they showed for that body was a natural result of the gratitude which they felt for their advancement. The case of Probus is different still. Under no emperor of the third century did the senate exercise so much real power as it did under him. The administration of civil affairs was left almost entirely to it. This arrangement, however, was not due to his respect for republican or Augustan tradition, but rather to the fact that he was a soldier, and was engaged in campaigns against the barbarians during his entire reign, and had no time to give to civil affairs. These apparent exceptions, therefore, merely confirm the truth of the statement that, during the third century, the emperor was master of the Roman world, and that the senate exercised only such powers as he chose to delegate to it. This fact comes out clearly enough, if we examine the policy of the better emperors, like Septimius Severus or Aurelian, or of the worse ones, like Caracalla and Gallienus, under all of whom the senate failed to secure any recognition of its authority.

**388. The Army as a Political Factor.** The real powers which made and unmade most of the emperors of this period, and largely influenced their policy, were the army and the praetorian guard, so that the condition of things during the three months' reign of Didius Julianus, when, besides the recognized emperor at Rome, there were claimants to the throne in Pannonia, Britain, and Syria, is a fair illustration of the course of events from the death of Septimius Severus in 211 to the accession of Diocletian in 284. During this period of seventy-three years there were twenty-three different emperors, almost all of whom owed their elevation to the throne to the force of arms, and kept their position only so long as they kept the favor of their armed supporters, or prevented some military rival from acquiring too much power.

**389. Administrative and Constitutional Changes.** Perhaps the most important administrative or constitutional changes of the third century were the transformation which the functions of the prefect of the praetorian guard underwent, the development of the *consilium*, and the separation of the civil and military administrations. The judicial *consilium*, which had been organized on a permanent basis by Hadrian (p. 318), became the most important civil and criminal court of the period. The emperor presided in person and associated with him his most eminent jurists. The members of this court even accompanied him when he left the city. The most influential member of it was the *praefectus praetorio*. The fact that the prefect of the praetorian guard held this important judicial position is indicative of a great change in his functions. Under the early empire the office was a purely military position. Even in the first century, however, as we noticed in the case of Burrus, the influence of this prefect, as commander of the strongest military force in the city, led the emperor to consult him in judicial and administrative affairs. It was natural for Hadrian, therefore, in organizing his *consilium*, to give the foremost position in it to the prefect, and for Severus Alexander to make the same official his minister also. Henceforth military experience was not so important a prerequisite for the prefect of the guard as administrative ability and knowledge of the law. The military duties of the position were largely delegated to subordinate officials. This change is in harmony with the tendency, which is noticeable under Severus Alexander and Gallienus especially, to separate the civil and military administrations in the provinces where large armies were required. The last-mentioned change is an anticipation of one of the reforms of Diocletian.

**390. The Incursions of the Barbarians during the Reign of Gallienus.** During the century which we are considering, the provinces were thrown into confusion by the incursions of the barbarians, and by the appearance of usurpers, who maintained for a longer or shorter time their sovereignty over one part or another of the empire. It is unnecessary for our purpose to follow the fortunes of these tyrants, or even of the emperors at Rome, through the century. The reign of Gallienus from 260 to 268 is in some respects typical, and a sketch of it will give one a clear, though perhaps an exaggerated, picture of the state of affairs during the entire period which is under consideration.

In these eight years no part of the Roman world, with the possible exception of Africa and the islands, escaped the devastating raids of the barbarians. In the East the Persians had made a prisoner of Valerian, the father of Gallienus, and his former colleague, and had overrun the province of Syria. On the Danube the Goths entered Roman territory from the north by land, and supplemented their land campaign by an attack from the sea on the east, ultimately pushing down as far as Achaea, and plundered Corinth and Athens. In the North the Alemanni broke through the barriers along the Rhine, and penetrated as far as Ravenna without meeting serious opposition. The Franks entered Gaul, pressed down into Spain, and even made their way across the Mediterranean to Africa. These incursions were essentially marauding expeditions, and when the lust for booty had been satisfied, the barbarians usually withdrew as speedily as they had come. No serious loss of territory, therefore, resulted from them, but cities were destroyed, the country was laid waste, and commerce in many cases was ruined. The result was that the resources of the people, already scarcely sufficient to support the burden of taxation laid upon them, were still further impaired.

**391. Usurpers during the Reign of Gallienus.** The appearance of usurpers both in the East and the West during the reign of Gallienus, and the recognition of their authority for a term of years over a well-defined territory, seemed to portend the speedy dismemberment of the empire. These nationalist movements, if we may so term them, were a very natural result of the existing situation. In their origin and character they were not unlike the successful attempt which Sertorius made in the first century B.C. to set up an independent government in Spain. The interests of the people within a given province or group of provinces were the same; their foes were the same, viz., the barbarians along their frontiers, and, since the central government could not protect them effectually, they felt it necessary to organize for their own defense. The provincials and soldiers, too, looked to the governors of the respective provinces for leadership. The sense of loyalty toward the emperor, far off in Rome, was seriously impaired. It was a very easy thing, therefore, for ambitious generals to usurp powers and titles which did not legitimately belong to them.

The most notable cases of the sort are those of Postumus in Gaul and Odaenathus in Palmyra. Postumus, after driving back the Franks, was saluted as emperor by his troops; but instead of marching against Rome, as other aspirants for imperial honors had done, he set up an independent government in Gaul, established a court, appointed his own generals, and took the titles of consul and *pontifex maximus*, like the emperors at Rome. He maintained his position from 258 to 268, and Tetricus, the governor of Aquitania, who succeeded him after a brief interval of confusion, seems to have added Spain to his empire. The vigorous measures of Aurelian, however, and the mutinous conduct of his own troops, forced him to resign his authority to the central government in the year 273.

Postumus and Tetricus were never formally recognized by Gallienus, but this cannot be said of Odaenathus in the East. The entire charge of Asia, with the power to appoint governors and generals, was given to him, and the titles of king and queen of Palmyra, which he and his widow Zenobia respectively took, do not seem to have been disputed in Rome. Odaenathus had recognized the authority of Gallienus, but Zenobia threw off Roman authority and invaded and subdued Egypt in 269. She took the title of Augusta, and her son that of Augustus. Her triumph, however, was of short duration. Her troops were driven out of Egypt by Probus, the future emperor, in 271, and the city of Palmyra was taken in the following year.

**392. The Restoration of Order.** The weakness of the central government and the state of confusion in the empire were at their worst during the reign of Gallienus. With the accession of Claudius in 268 an improvement set in. Although the raids of the barbarians continued intermittently for many years, they were more quickly checked than they had been before, so that when Diocletian ascended the throne in 284, the continuance of the empire and its unity were assured, at least for a time. The province of Dacia, however, was given up, and the Rhine and the Danube were henceforth taken as the limits of the empire to the north.

**393. The System of Diocletian.** With the accession of Diocletian in 284 a new epoch begins. He frankly broke away from republican tradition, substituted a monarchy for the nominal dyarchy of the three preceding centuries, and reorganized completely the civil and military administrative systems of the empire.

**394. The Augusti.** His scheme of government involved the appointment of two emperors who bore the title of *Augusti*. The republican principle of collegiality was fully recognized in the relations which they bore to each other. All laws and edicts were issued in the name of both, and all appointments to office were thought of as coming from them conjointly. In point of fact, however, Diocletian made Nicomedia his capital, or rather his headquarters, and confined his attention to the East, while his colleague, Maximian, ruled in the West, with Milan for his seat of government. This arrangement, therefore, involved a virtual division of the empire, although its unity was assumed in styling the territory of Diocletian *partes Orientis*, and that of Maximian *partes Occidentis*. Under the old régime the *princeps* exercised the right to issue edicts whose binding force was recognized during his reign, just as the proclamations of a republican magistrate were valid during his term of office. The theory of the monarchy was essentially different. The formally expressed will of the *Augusti* became the law of the land, and, like the actions of the senate and popular assemblies in the earlier period, continued in force unless it was annulled by a later emperor. The logical corollary of this principle was also unhesitatingly accepted, that the emperor could not be legally controlled or restrained by the action of any magistrate or legislative body. The exalted position of the *Augusti* was indicated to the eye by their imperial robes trimmed with precious stones, by the imperial diadem, and by the elaborate ceremonial required of all who approached them. Under the influence of the Oriental environment, within which the seat of Diocletian's government lay, the emperor was looked

upon as more than mortal, and received during his lifetime
many of the honors paid to the gods.

**395. The Caesares.** Nine years after the accession
of Diocletian he and his colleague, Maximian, chose two
*Caesares*, who stood just below the *Augusti* in point of
dignity. Their position was, however, a dependent one.
They had no authority except that which was conferred on
them by the *Augusti*. The fact that they received a fixed
salary indicates clearly enough that their powers were delegated to them. These powers consisted mainly in the right
to hear appeals, and to exercise a general supervision over
the governors whose provinces lay within their jurisdiction.
After the appointment of the two Caesars, the Roman world
was divided between them and the *Augusti* on the following
basis : Diocletian took Thrace, Egypt, Syria, and Asia Minor,
and assigned to Galerius, the Caesar whom he had personally nominated, the Danubian provinces, Illyricum, Greece,
and Crete, while Maximian governed Italy and Africa,
assigning Gaul, Spain, and Britain to Constantius.

The main purpose of the institution of the Caesars was
to provide for the succession, and it was a part of Diocletian's plan that, when one of the *Augusti* died or resigned,
his position should be filled at once by the advancement of
one of the Caesars, who, at the time of their elevation to
office, were adopted by the *Augusti*. In fact, Diocletian
intended to have the *Augusti* resign in favor of the *Caesares*
after a specified time, whereupon the latter were expected
to adopt two new *Caesares*.

**396. The Senate.** When Rome ceased to be the seat
of the central government, the Roman senate lost its
character as an imperial body. It became essentially an
organization with local powers. This state of things was
bluntly recognized by Constantine when he established a

senate with like functions at Constantinople. Furthermore, Diocletian did not ask the senate to confirm his
imperial powers, nor to approve his action in making Maximian his colleague. Now from the earliest times the senate
had maintained that the control of the state returned to it
whenever the chief-magistracy became vacant, and even
under the empire the choice of an emperor needed the
confirmation of the senate to be constitutional. Diocletian's neglect to secure its approval was, therefore, in
violation of the theory that the senate was the ultimate
depositary of supreme power (cf. pp. 13 f.), or that it represented the continuity of the government. It, of course, lost
its power to legislate for the empire, and, since under the
new bureaucratic system the old magistracies had been
robbed of almost all their functions, its electoral rights had
little meaning. Its duties consisted mainly in electing the
*consules suffecti*, the praetors, and the quaestors, in legislating with reference to the public games and matters affecting the senatorial order, and in sitting as a court on cases,
especially those of treason, referred to it by the emperor.

397. **The Republican Magistracies.** Under the later
empire the old magistrates had become in reality municipal officials. Their true political position was recognized
openly in Diocletian's constitution. The consul had no
other duty of importance than to preside at the meetings
of the senate; the functions of the praetor and quaestor were confined to the superintendence of the public
games, except that certain praetors exercised limited judicial powers. The other magistracies disappeared. The
*consules ordinarii*, whose term of office expired April 21,
were appointed by the emperor, while the *consules suffecti*,
the praetors, and the quaestors were chosen by the senate,
subject to the approval of the emperor.

**398. The Administrative System.** The system of Diocletian, as elaborated by Constantine, was based upon a
complete separation of the civil and military administrations and a carefully graded hierarchy of officials in each.
At the head of the civil administration were the four
*praefecti praetorio*, one of whom resided at Constantinople,
the second at Sirmium, the third at Milan, and the fourth
at Treves. They were styled, respectively, *praefectus praetorio Orientis*, *Illyrici*, *Italiae*, and *Galliarum*. The civil
governors of Rome and Constantinople were outside the general scheme, inasmuch as they were directly responsible to
the emperor and not to the *praefecti* within whose jurisdiction the cities in question lay. The powers of the *praefectus
praetorio* were varied and far-reaching. It was his privilege
to nominate the provincial governors to the emperor, to
supervise their conduct, and to suspend them from office, if
he thought it best to do so. He had the right to interpret
the law and to hear cases of appeal, and after 331 his judgment was accepted as final. In particular he had complete
control of imperial finances within the territory assigned to
him. Up to the reign of Constantine he exercised certain
military functions, but from that time on these functions
were lost altogether. The prefects had such extensive
powers that, as a rule, they were allowed to hold office for
a short time only.

The prefectures were divided into dioceses, and these
again into provinces. In the fifth century there were
twelve dioceses, and some of them were made up of as
many as seventeen provinces, so that the unit of government became a very small one. The governor of a diocese,
who bore the title of *vicarius*, and was named directly by
the emperor, exercised with the prefect a general supervision over the governors of the provinces and the financial

officers of his district. The governor of a province
(*praeses*, *consularis*, or *corrector*), like his superiors, the
*vicarius* and the *praefectus praetorio*, had charge of civil
administration only. At the head of the military administration there were from five to ten officials who bore such
titles as *magistri militum per Orientem* and *per Illyricum*,
and under them came the territorial commanders, who
were styled *duces* or *comites*. The *ducatus*, or unit of
military administration, did not in all cases correspond
exactly with the *provincia*.

**399. The Relation between the Old and the New.** In
discussing the history of the empire the gradual drift
toward monarchy has been mentioned (cf. pp. 310 f.,
327). In the first 150 years of our era the movement is
especially noticeable under Domitian and Hadrian. Perhaps the most important changes which prepared the way
for the reforms of Diocletian were the exercise of the censorial power by Domitian (cf. p. 310), the establishment
of a bureaucratic system of government by Hadrian (cf.
p. 318), and the gradual separation of the civil and military administrations. These are not, however, the only
distinctive features of the new system which are to be found
in the old one. In fact, almost all the important institutions of Diocletian's government existed in an undeveloped
or in a fully developed form in the empire of the third century. The principle of collegiality, carrying along with it
the practical division of the empire between two rulers, was
tried during the reign of M. Aurelius (cf. pp. 319 f.). The
practice of conferring the title of *Caesar* on the intended
successor to the throne goes back to the reign of Hadrian,
although it is true that under the empire a *Caesar* needed
the confirmation of the senate. The process of reducing
Italy to a level with the provinces, which became an

accomplished fact under the new régime and was an essential part of Diocletian's system, had been going on for centuries. The division of the larger provinces into smaller units of government, which is a noticeable feature of Diocletian's system, was carried out in many cases as early as the time of Domitian, and many of the honorary titles and insignia of office which Diocletian and his successors took go back to the reigns of Domitian or Aurelian.

It is clear, therefore, that many of the features of his system are to be found in the empire, so that, aside from reorganizing the administration, the most important changes which Diocletian effected consisted in breaking away from the theory of the dyarchy, in securing formal recognition thereby of the fact that the emperor was the sole source of authority, and in putting the succession on a new basis.

### SELECTIONS FROM THE SOURCES

**All freemen become citizens (212):** Dio, LXXVII. 9. — Diocletian: Eutr. IX. 19–28; Aur. Vict. *Caes.* 39; Lactant. *de Mort. Pers.* 7 ff.; Zonaras, XII. 31–2; Orosius, VII. 25.

### SELECTED BIBLIOGRAPHY [1]

Th. Preuss, Kaiser Diocletian.  Leipzig, 1868.

Büdinger, Untersuchungen, etc.

A. W. Hunzinger, Die diocletianische Staats-Reform.  Rostock, 1900.

Karlowa, Römische Rechtsgeschichte, Vol. I.  Leipzig, 1885.

Walter, Geschichte d. römischen Rechts, Vol. I.  Bonn, 1845.

[1] See also pp. 288 and 304.

# SECTION II — DESCRIPTIVE

## CHAPTER XVII

### THE EMPEROR

*(a) The Succession; conferring Imperial Powers, Titles, Insignia; Term of Office*

**400. Eligibility and the Succession.** In the case of the emperor there were no specified general conditions governing eligibility, as there were for the higher republican magistracies, but the principle was tacitly recognized that an emperor must be a patrician and a senator, and the successful candidates for the imperial purple, who did not satisfy these two traditional requirements, were made patricians or senators, as the case might be, at the time of their election. The senate was theoretically the ultimate source of authority in the state, so that, on the death of an emperor, the selection of his successor rested with it. However, most of the emperors indicated their choice for the succession by making certain persons heirs to their private fortunes, and by conferring on the chosen candidates the proconsular *imperium* and the tribunician power, and the nomination thus indirectly made by the emperor was invariably ratified by the senate. From the time of Hadrian the title of *Caesar* was given to the person designated by an emperor as his successor.

Spart. Did.
Iul. 3; Capit
Macr. 7.

Capit. Ver.
Imp. 1;
Vict. Caes. 14

**401. Method of granting Imperial Powers.** The essential acts in conferring the imperial power were the passage

341

Append. I.
no. 10;
Tac. Hist. 1.
47; Henz.
Act. Fr. Arv.
pp. 65 ff.

of the *lex de imperio* and of the *lex de tribunicia potestate.*
These measures were the joint action of the senate and the
popular assembly.   The coöperation of the popular assembly, however, was from the outset a mere matter of form.

**402. Imperial Titles.**   At the election of an emperor,
or shortly after his accession, various titles were conferred
upon him, some of which were purely honorary, while others
implied the grant of new powers.   An inscription from the
early part of the reign of Augustus (*C. I. L.* III. 6070), and
another from the reign of Hadrian (*C. I. L.* VI. 967), may
illustrate the names and titles of the emperors during the
two periods in question.   The first one reads *Imperator
Caesar Divi Filius Augustus Consul XII Tribunicia Potestate XVIII Pontifex Maximus.*   In the other Hadrian is
styled *Imperator Caesar Divi Traiani Parthici Filius
Divi Nervae Nepos Traianus Hadrianus Augustus Pontifex Maximus Tribunicia Potestate II Consul II.*   With
few exceptions, the emperors, at the time of their election,
substituted the title *Imperator* for their former *praenomina.*
The same word also appears again, in many cases as an
honorary title, in the latter part of the name.   *Caesar* was
the cognomen of the Julian house, and was transferred to
the members of the Claudian family.   From the time of
Hadrian its use was restricted to the emperor and his candidate for the succession.   In the first century it stood after
the praenomen or the nomen; but later it was usually
placed between *Imperator* and the *praenomen* or *nomen.*
After the indication of descent from the emperor's predecessor or predecessors, and the *nomina* or *cognomina*, came
the title *Augustus.*   This title was granted to Octavius in
27 B.C. (cf. p. 269), and was conferred by the senate on
all his successors when they ascended the throne.   The
position of *pontifex maximus* was held by all the emperors,

Tac. Hist.
1. 47; Suet.
Aug. 7.

as well as membership in the colleges of the augurs, the *epulones*, and the quindecemvirs. The tribunician power was granted for life, but it was renewed from year to year. It is, therefore, the surest indication in any document containing the emperor's name of the year to which the document belongs. The consulship was held from time to time by the emperor, at least for a part of the year, and during these periods *consul* appears among his titles, with an indication of the number of times he has taken the office. After Trajan's reign the title *proconsul* was assumed outside of Italy, while, from the time of Septimius Severus, it was borne even in Rome. Other titles like *pater patriae*, or epithets of distinction like *pius felix*, were conferred on some of the emperors. Special titles like *Parthicus* or *Germanicus* were taken after successful campaigns.

St. R. II. 795, n. 1.

St. R. II. 778, n. 1.

**403. Insignia of Office.** On formal occasions the emperor sat on the *subsellium* of the tribunes, or on a curule chair between the consuls. His robe of office in Italy was the *toga praetexta;* outside of Italy the *paludamentum*. From the time of Septimius Severus the latter was worn even in Italy. Up to Domitian's reign the emperor was attended by twelve lictors ; later by twenty-four.

Dio, 50. 2; Suet. Tib. 17, Claud. 23.

Lampr. Heliogab. 15.

**404. Induction into Office.** When the emperor ascended the throne, a sacrifice was made on the Capitol, and on the first of January of each year the senate, the magistrates, and the soldiers took the oath of allegiance. Augustus accepted his extraordinary powers for a limited period, but his successors held theirs without such limitation.

Tac. Ann. 1. 8; Hist. 1. 55.

Suet. Tib. 24

**405. The Memory of a Dead Emperor.** The office became vacant when the emperor died a natural death, or resigned, or was overthrown. In the last instance an act was usually passed, known as the *damnatio memoriae*, or a declaration was made by the newly chosen emperor, in accordance

with which the wearing of mourning garments was forbidden, the statues of the deceased were destroyed, his

name was erased from public monuments, and his *acta*
were annulled. In case the judgment of the senate on a
dead emperor was favorable, he received the title of *divus*
and a flamen was appointed in his honor.

### (b) The Powers of the Emperor

**406. Legal Basis of the Emperor's Power.** The powers
of the emperor, so far as they had a purely legal basis, rested
on the *imperium* and the *tribunicia potestas*. After the
year 23 B.C. Augustus ceased to hold the consulship regularly, and the *imperium* which he exercised he held *pro consule*. By special enactments, however, he was allowed to
retain this *imperium* within the city, and to rank with the
consul in the exercise of its powers. The measures which
thus interpreted and extended the *imperium* of the *princeps* and freed him from certain restrictions ordinarily put
on magistrates, were reënacted at the beginning of each
reign, and have come down to us in a fragmentary form in
the celebrated *lex de imperio Vespasiani*. To facilitate a
comparison of the position of the emperor with that of the
republican chief-magistrate, it will be convenient to restate
here the powers covered by the *imperium* under the republic, and to discuss the several functions of the emperor in
the same order in which the similar powers of the republican
magistrate were taken up (cf. pp. 157 ff.). The *imperium*
under the republic covered the right to supervise certain
matters of a politico-religious character, to represent the
state in its dealings with individuals and with other communities, to command the army and navy, to punish, to exercise civil and criminal jurisdiction, to issue proclamations

or edicts, to call and preside over the senate and the popular assemblies, and to supervise certain administrative matters.

**407. Authority in Politico-Religious Matters.** The emperor's magisterial right to supervise such religious matters as had a political side was strengthened by his election to the four great priesthoods and by his elevation to the position of *pontifex maximus* (cf. pp. 342 f.), and was formulated in the *lex de imperio*, which empowered him to do *quaecumque ex . . . maiestate divinarum . . . rerum esse censebit*. By virtue of this authority he had the right to name a certain number of priests, to control the temples, and to exercise a general supervision over religious affairs.

**408. Foreign Affairs.** In the management of foreign affairs the *princeps* was supreme. The senate, which under the later republic had taken such matters almost entirely into its own hands, became purely an advisory body. This change was merely a return to the early republican theory, under which only the people or their authorized representative, the magistrate, could carry on negotiations with a foreign power. The senate had usurped the functions which it exercised in such matters. The powers of the republican magistrate in this field were, however, limited by the rights of the popular assembly; those of the *princeps* were unlimited. This extension of the *imperium* was in all probability granted to him specifically by law. He was empowered on his own authority to declare war, to make peace, or to carry on negotiations with foreign nations. This did not, of course, prevent him from asking the senate for advice on such matters, or from complimenting it by allowing it to discuss them occasionally.

*Append. I no. 10.*

**409. Command of the Army and Navy.** Closely connected with the power just mentioned was the right of the

Dio, 53. 17.

*princeps* to command the army and navy. He had the exclusive right to levy and organize troops, and to direct the movements of troops in the imperial provinces, and, since the unsettled provinces were made imperial (cf. pp. 268, 283), practically the entire army and navy of the state were under his control. The officers were appointed by him; the soldiers took the oath of allegiance to him, and were paid by him. The senate retained the power to grant a triumph, or the *ornamenta triumphalia*. Even in

Tac. Ann. 2. 43.

the senatorial provinces the *princeps* had the *maius imperium* over the proconsuls, and they looked rather to him than to the senate for instructions. In this whole matter again the *princeps* resumed the power which the king and the chief-magistrate of the early republic had exercised, but which the senate, during the period of its ascendency, had in large part usurped.

**410. Judicial Powers of the Emperor as an Appellate Judge.** Perhaps the most important change which the empire made in the judicial powers of the executive was to introduce the principle of appeal. Under the republic this right was unknown. The nearest approach to it lay in

Cic. pro Quinct. 29.

the veto power which the tribune seems to have exercised on rare occasions even in judicial matters. The appellate power which the *princeps* freely used seems to have developed out of his magisterial right to exercise jurisdiction and his tribunician power.

**411. The Emperor's Jurisdiction in Civil Cases.** In this way he heard appeals in civil cases from the governors of provinces, and from Roman or Italian magistrates. Such

Suet. Claud. 14, 23; Dio, 71. 6.

appeals were sometimes heard by him in person. Sometimes they were heard before persons delegated by him for the purpose; in certain cases, before the consul or praetor at Rome, or the governor in a province. Appeals from the

decision of a magistrate in the city of Rome were usually
turned over to the *praetor urbanus,* or later to the *prae-*
*fectus urbi.*   Appeals from the provinces were usually taken
before ex-consuls appointed to hear such cases, but later
they came to the *praefectus praetorio.*   A final appeal to
the emperor from the decision of his representative was
not forbidden, but in all probability was rarely taken.
Appeals were ordinarily not allowed in jury trials except
when there was evidence of bribery, or when there was a
fundamental legal defect in the constitution of the court
or in the conduct of the suit.   The *princeps* could, of
course, hear a case in the first instance also.   He was
assisted by a *consilium* of jurists from the equestrian
and senatorial orders (cf. p. 331).   The members of this
body received salaries ranging from 60,000 to 100,000
sesterces.   The *princeps* presided; the *consiliarii* gave
their opinions in writing, and the *princeps* rendered his
decision.

**412. The Emperor's Jurisdiction in Criminal Cases.**   The
most interesting developments in the organization of the
system of criminal courts were the recognition of the right
of appeal, the gradual disappearance of the jury system,
and the assignment of judicial powers to the senate, and to
the emperor or imperial officials.   The first point has been
discussed in a preceding paragraph.   As for the senate, it
seems to have acquired its judicial functions first in the
case of senators charged with capital offenses.   This was a
very natural development.   It was the aristocratic interpretation of the principle that a man has a right to be
tried by his peers.   The recognition of the principle was a
matter of much dispute, however, between the senate and
various emperors.   The senate in criminal trials bore the
same theoretical relation to the presiding consul as a jury to

Suet. Aug.
33; Dio, 52.
22.

Dio, 52. 33.

Suet. Dom. 8.

Suet. Aug.
33; Nero, 15;
Tac. Ann.
3. 10; Dig.
36. 1. 76.

Dio, 52. 31;
67. 2; 74. 2;
Suet. Cal. 53

Dio, 67. 2;
74. 2.

the presiding judge, and the consul in conducting a court which exercised the right to inflict capital punishment without appeal was merely calling into existence again a prerogative which the king and the early consuls had enjoyed (p. 16). Hence the assumption of criminal jurisdiction in capital cases by the consul and senate was merely another case of reversion to the early theory of the constitution. Inasmuch as cases in which senators were concerned often involved men belonging to other classes, especially if the offense in question was political, the criminal jurisdiction of the senate was exercised over a greater number of persons than would appear at first thought. The consul presided, but of course the emperor exercised a controlling influence. The senate seems to have lost its judicial powers in the third or fourth century. From that time charges against senators were heard before the *praefectus urbi*, the *praefectus praetorio*, or the provincial governors.

The emperor himself heard only cases in which the persons concerned were prominent, or the matter at issue was important. The decision rested with him alone, but he consulted his *consiliarii*. Gradually the practice grew up of conferring on imperial officials the same right to exercise criminal jurisdiction which the emperor himself enjoyed. In this way persons charged with the commission of crimes in Rome or its vicinity were tried before the *praefectus urbi*, or in the case of minor offenses, or those of a special character, before the *praefectus vigilum* or the *praefectus annonae*. The *praefectus praetorio* heard such cases for Italy, and the governors in the provinces exercised the same right for the territory under their control. Appeal could be taken, in capital cases at least, to the emperor, but he usually delegated the *praefectus praetorio* to act in his stead, from whose decision appeal could indeed be taken,

St. R. II. 270.

Plin. ad Tra.
96. 4.
St. R. II.
972 f.

but rarely was taken, to the emperor. Thus the tribunal of the praetorian prefect became the court of last resort. In this way the *quaestiones perpetuae* were gradually crowded out, and disappeared, probably toward the close of the second century of our era. The emperor and the imperial officials reached their decisions without the help of a jury, so that the substitution of the new system for the old involved the disappearance of trial by jury.

**413. Edicta, Decreta, Rescripta, etc.** The emperor could influence legislation directly or indirectly. He seems to have had the power, for instance, to grant the rights of Roman or of Latin citizenship on his own authority to individuals or to communities (cf. pp. 308, 315), but his greatest influence over legislation lay in an interpretation and amplification of existing law by issuing *edicta*, *decreta*, or *rescripta*, which were not only applicable to the cases immediately concerned, but furnished precedents for similar cases in the future. The *edicta* were imperial proclamations addressed to citizens or *peregrini*, and dealt particularly with matters affecting the army, the treasury, or the food supply. The *decreta* were judicial decisions of the emperor. The *rescripta*, of which we hear frequently from the time of Trajan, were replies made by the emperor to important questions submitted to him for decision by imperial officers or private individuals.

Dig. 28. 2. 26; 47. 11. 6; C. I. L. X. 4842. C. I. L. VI. 1016; VIII. 10570; Eph. Epigr. IV. 787. C. I. L. III. 781; Plin. ad Tra. 71, 80.

*Mandata* and *epistulae* contained official instructions from the emperor. To all these classes of official documents the generic term *constitutiones principis* was applied, although the same term was used in a more restricted sense of documents in which a general legal principle was stated. In this way, by interpreting authoritatively existing laws, and by supplementing them when necessary, the emperors preceding Diocletian, although they did not have the general power to legislate directly, exerted a controlling influence on the development of the law.

**414. The Ius cum Patribus Agendi.** The *princeps* had the right to convoke the senate, to preside over it, to lay matters before it for consideration, or to take part in its deliberations, when it met under the presidency of another magistrate. Even when the *princeps* did not preside, the business brought up by him took precedence of all other matters. In the second century of our era, in such cases, as many as five propositions could be submitted by him before the senate took up other business. Toward the end of his reign, when Augustus was unable to attend all the meetings of the senate, he sent propositions to it in written form. Propositions of this sort, whether presented orally or in writing, were out of courtesy adopted without change, so that in the course of time these *orationes principis*, as they were called, were thought of as forming an essential part of the law of the empire. When the emperor presided over the senate, his practice differed in one important particular from that of the republican presiding officer, in that he could propose, and ordinarily did propose, a definite motion for adoption, whereas in important matters the consul was expected merely to make a statement of the business in hand (cf. p. 228); but whether he presided or merely exercised the rights of a senator, whether he was present or absent, the influence of the *princeps* controlled the decisions of the senate. The authority which Augustus received in his later years to establish a political *consilium* has already (p. 277) been mentioned.

**415. The Ius cum Populo Agendi.** Augustus took into his own hands the control of foreign affairs. Tiberius transferred the election of magistrates to the senate (p. 291), and there was a tendency to submit matters for legislation

*Margin notes:*

Tac. Ann. 2. 50.

Capit. Macr. 6.

Tac. Ann. 11. 24–5; Boissieu, Inscr. de Lyon, p. 136.

to the same body, so that the meetings of the popular assemblies were few in number, and of little importance. Thus the emperor's *ius cum populo agendi* did not amount to much.

**416. The Nomination of Magistrates and the Appointment of Officials.** In this connection it is convenient to mention the emperor's practice of passing on the eligibility of candidates for the magistracies, and of recommending certain names to the electors (cf. pp. 275 f.). This privilege of commending candidates was legally recognized by the *lex de imperio Vespasiani* in these words : *utique quos magistratum potestatem imperium curationemve cuius rei petentes senatui populoque Romano commendaverit, quibusque suffragationem suam dederit promiserit, eorum comitis quibusque extra ordinem ratio habeatur.* Under Augustus the recommendation was made to the popular assemblies ; under later emperors, to the senate. The number of candidates recommended under this law seems to have varied from reign to reign, according to the degree of respect which the *princeps* showed for the senate. The men thus recommended for office were known as *candidati Caesaris* or *Augusti*. When the *princeps* himself wished the consulship he could inform the senate of that fact. The emperor, of course, had the right to appoint imperial officials without even consulting the senate. Such officials were, for instance, the various procurators in the department of finance, the prefects in the city, and the *legati* in the provinces.

Append I no. 10.

**417. The Finances.** Under the republic the effective control of the finances rested with the senate. In the early period that body exercised the right to impose a *tributum* or special taxes on citizens. It fixed the contributions to be made by the provinces, and although the control of the *ager publicus* was often a matter of dispute

Liv. 23. 31. 1; 24. 11. 7–9.

between the senate and the popular assemblies, the former, during the period of its ascendency, legislated with reference to its rental or sale, as the case might be. In the matter of expenditure it adopted a budget every five years covering the amount to be expended by the censor on public works, and annual appropriations were made by it for the provinces.

Cic. in Pis. 5;
Sall. Iug. 27.

**418. Division of the Treasury.** Under the dyarchy these functions were divided between the *princeps* and the senate. This fact was recognized by the organization of three separate treasuries, known as the *aerarium Saturni*, the *fiscus Caesaris*, and the *aerarium militare*.

**419. The Aerarium Saturni.** The control of the funds in the *aerarium Saturni* rested with the senate, but when in the year 44 Claudius took from that body the right to appoint the officials in charge of this treasury, its authority in the matter became purely nominal. An appropriation bill was necessary before money could be paid out, but the passage of such a measure was merely a matter of form. Little by little the revenues paid into the *aerarium Saturni* were diverted to the *fiscus*, and although the distinction between these two departments was kept up until the reign of Diocletian, the funds in the former grew smaller steadily, and in the third century it became simply a municipal treasury. After 44 the administrative officers in charge of it were regularly appointed by the emperor.

Tac. Ann.
13. 29; Suet.
Claud. 24.
Dio, 71. 33.

**420. The Fiscus Caesaris.** The revenues of the *fiscus Caesaris* came mainly from the rental or sale of the *ager publicus* in the provinces, from mines, from the *vectigalia* or *stipendia* paid by the imperial provinces and in some measure by the senatorial provinces, from legacies left to the emperor, from the *aurum coronarium*, and from customs duties and other indirect taxes. The funds in the *fiscus*

Dio, 52. 28;
Madv. II.
431 ff.
Dio, 53. 15;
Suet. Aug.
66; Dom. 9.

were used to support the army and navy, to meet the expenses of provincial administration, to build roads and maintain a post system, to cover the expenditure of the emperor for charitable purposes, and to provide the city of Rome with grain and water.

**421. The Emperor's Private Fortune.** Out of the private fortune of the emperor his personal expenses and the outlay necessary in maintaining the imperial household were probably met, although a careful distinction does not seem to have been made between the *res privata* and the *fiscus*.

**422. The Aerarium Militare.** The *aerarium militare* was established by Augustus in A.D. 6. It continued in existence up to the third century of our era. He assigned to it a large sum from his private fortune, and gave it a permanent income from the tax on inheritances (*vicesima hereditatium et legatorum*) and on auction sales (*centesima rerum venalium*). Its funds were not expected to cover the main expenses for military purposes, but were used especially to provide for the veterans.

Suet. Aug. 49; Mon. Ancyr. 3. 36 f

**423. Taxation and Adjudication.** It is doubtful if the *princeps* had the right to impose new taxes. He could, however, rate the property of citizens, and in the later period at least he could raise or lower the rate of taxation. In the collection of taxes the contract system was gradually given up. In some cases collections were made by subordinate officials attached to the office of the *procuratores;* in other cases, where communities were required to pay a fixed sum, the local officials made their payments directly into the treasury. Similarly, the construction of public works was no longer let out by private contract. Questions arising between the *aerarium Saturni* and citizens were heard by the officials in charge of the *aerarium*, with the right of appeal to the senate. Matters at issue between

Suet. Dom. 9 Dio, 77. 9.

the *fiscus* and individuals, after some variation in the method of procedure, were also adjudicated by the treasury officials.

**424. Coinage.** Under the republic the senate had the entire control of the coinage of money. By legislation of the year 15 B.C., however, the minting of gold and silver coins was intrusted to the emperor; that of copper coins was retained by the senate.

**425. The Censorial Power and Adlectio.** Much of the financial business of which the emperor took charge, such as the collection of the taxes and the construction of public works, had been managed in the earlier period by the censor. Another function also of the censor, that of drawing up the list of senators, was exercised by many of the emperors. In the first century Augustus, Claudius, Vespasian, and Domitian held the censorship, the latter taking it for life. By virtue of this office they not only drew up a formal list of senators, but men who had held no magistracy they advanced to senatorial rank by the *adlectio inter quaestorios* or *inter tribunicios, inter praetorios, inter consulares,* as the case might be. By a somewhat similar exercise of power senators of quaestorian rank were promoted *inter tribunicios,* and so on. The earlier emperors who took the censorial power, and after Domitian all the emperors, exercised the right of removing members from the senate.

C. I. L. V. 1812;
V. 3117;
VI. 1359.
C. I. L. VIII. 7062;
Tac. Ann. 2. 32.
Tac. Ann. 11. 25.

**426. The Government of Rome.** The management of the city of Rome passed over in time entirely into the hands of the emperor. The principal branches of the municipal government were the police and fire departments, the *cura annonae,* and the bureaus which had charge of the aqueducts, of the construction of public buildings, and of the banks of the Tiber and the city sewers. Augustus, early in his reign, took to himself the right to maintain public order in Rome, the *cura urbis*, and delegated this power to his representative, the *praefectus urbi*, during his absence from the city. The organization of the *praefectura vigilum*, to put out fires and protect the city at night, was effected in A.D. 6. A famine in 22 B.C. led the same emperor to make extraordinary arrangements for keeping Rome supplied with grain, but he did not organize an imperial bureau to take charge of the grain supply until late in his reign. Augustus took the *cura aquarum* in 11 B.C., and at about the same time the *cura operum tuendorum*. In the first year of his reign Tiberius assigned the duty of protecting the city against inundations to commissioners, who after Trajan took charge of the sewers also, and were known as *curatores alvei et riparum Tiberis et cloacarum urbis*. The details of the organization of these bureaus will be considered in another connection. Only the emperor, from the time of Claudius, had the right to extend the *pomerium*.

**427. The Government of Italy.** The process of reducing Italy to the level of the provinces, and of making it, like the rest of the empire, subject to the will of the emperor, was completed in the third century of our era, when a governor called a *corrector* was placed over it. The movement in this direction had been continuous from the beginning. Augustus had stationed a fleet at Ravenna, and another at Misenum, under officers of his own appointment. Troops for the maintenance of public order were also quartered by him at various convenient points. His commissioners, the *curatores viarum*, took charge of the public roads. In the reigns of Trajan and Hadrian the administrative supervision of the emperor over Italy was extended still further by the establishment of the *praefecturae*

*Marginal notes:*
Tac. Ann. 6. 11;
Suet. Aug. 37
Dio, 55. 26;
Suet. Aug. 30
Dio, 54. 1;
Tac. Ann. 1. 7.

Frontin. de Aq. 99 ff.

Dio, 57. 14;
Tac. Ann. 1. 76.
C. I. L. V. 5262;
VI. 1242.

Suet. Aug. 49.

Suet. Aug. 32; Tib. 37.

*alimentorum* (cf. pp. 323 f.), and by the usurpation, on the part of the emperor, of the right to exercise a control over the finances of Italian municipalities. The civil jurisdiction of the officials in these towns was restricted by Hadrian, and in the third century criminal jurisdiction throughout Italy was divided between the *praefectus praetorio* and the *praefectus urbi* (cf. p. 364).

Spart. Hadr. 22.

**428. The Government of the Provinces.** The *ius proconsulare* of the emperor made him master of the imperial provinces, and the *maius imperium* gave him control over the governors of senatorial provinces. In the imperial provinces not only the governors but the officers in command of the legions were appointed by him. The close surveillance which he exercised over the details of administration in his own provinces, and the tendency which senatorial governors showed to defer to his judgment and wishes and to follow the precedents established by him in imperial provinces, have been noted in another connection (p. 301). Roman citizens could appeal from the judicial decisions of imperial governors in criminal cases to the emperor or to his representative at Rome (cf. p. 348). Appeals from the governors of senatorial provinces were heard by the emperor or senate, and of course in these cases the judgment of the emperor, or of his counsellors, was the decisive factor.

**429. The Tribunician Power.** The possession of the tribunician power had for the emperor more of a sentimental or traditional than legal value. Many of the constitutional powers which it conferred, like the right to convoke the senate, came to him in another way, but it did invest his person with a sacrosanct character, and made him the recognized champion of popular rights (cf. pp. 201 f.). Since the sanctity of the tribune's person could be violated by offensive or threatening language, as well as by deeds of violence, it is easy to see how prosecutions for *minuta maiestas* under the empire (cf. p. 291) could be legally based on this interpretation of the sacrosanct character of the tribune's office. It is not probable that the emperor found it necessary to use the *ius auxilii* or the *ius intercessionis* directly in legislative or executive matters. The prestige which his position gave him was so great that a failure to conform to his wishes on the part of the senate or of a magistrate is hardly conceivable. We have had occasion to notice (pp. 346–7), however, that certain important judicial functions of the emperor perhaps rested on the *ius intercessionis*. There is a subtle distinction under the imperial constitution between holding the position of tribune and having the tribunician power. The emperor, by virtue of his tribunician power, could veto the action of a tribune, but he was not himself a tribune, and his action could not be vetoed by a tribune. This distinction was probably of little practical importance, however, since no tribune would dare to oppose him. The tribunician power was given to the emperor for life. Augustus received it in 36 B.C., Tiberius in 6 B.C., the other emperors from the time when they were associated in the government by their predecessors, or, if they were not so associated, on the day of their accession, or shortly after it.

St. R. II. 880, n. 5.

**430. Exemption from Certain Laws.** In connection with the tribunician power the fact may be mentioned that the emperor was exempted from observing certain laws. Although the laws in question are not specified in the *lex de imperio Vespasiani*, the principle is distinctly stated: *utique quibus legibus plebeive scitis scriptum fuit, ne divus Aug., Tiberiusve Iulius Caesar Aug., Tiberiusque Claudius Caesar Aug. Germanicus tenerentur, iis legibus plebisque*

Append. I. no. 10.

*scitis Imp. Caesar Vespasianus solutus sit, quaeque ex quaque lege rogatione divum Aug., Tiberiumve, etc., facere oportuit, ea omnia Imp. Caesari Vespasiano Aug. facere liceat.*

## SELECTED BIBLIOGRAPHY [1]

F. B. R. Hellems, The lex de imperio Vespasiani. Chicago (in press).

J. Kromayer, Die rechtliche Begründung des Prinzipats. Strassburg, 1888.

H. Pelham, On some disputed points connected with the imperium of Augustus and his successors, Journ. of Philol. XVII (1888), pp. 27–52.

H. Pelham, Princeps or princeps senatus, *ibid.* VIII (1879), pp. 323–333.

## SUPPLEMENTARY LITERATURE, 1901–1910

Hardy, Studies in Roman History: Second Series.    London, 1909.

Homo, Le domaine impérial à Rome.    Mélanges d'arch. et d'hist. XIX (1899), 101–129.

Stobbe, Die Candidati Caesaris.    Philologus, XXVII.

[1] See also bibliography on pp. 173, 288, 304, 316, 328.

# CHAPTER XVIII

## IMPERIAL OFFICIALS

### (a) Officials Attached to the Imperial Household

**431. Imperial Officials.** The organization of the different bureaus of civil administration under the empire was effected gradually, and the functions of many officials changed somewhat from one period to another, so that a description of the powers and duties of an imperial officer in one reign may not be strictly accurate for another reign. Some officials even pass over from the military to the civil side of the administration, as happens in the case of the *praefectus praetorio;* or the opposite change takes place. In view of this development and these changes, it will be convenient to have in mind especially the imperial system in the period subsequent to Hadrian, since that emperor did so much to organize the several bureaus of administration (cf. p. 318). No classification of imperial officials seems satisfactory in all respects, but it will serve our purpose best to group them as follows : (a) *those attached to the imperial household,* (b) *judges,* (c) *financial officials; those charged with the government* (d) *of Rome,* (e) *of Italy,* and (f) *of the provinces.*

**432. The Imperial Family and the Caesar.** Most closely attached to the person of the emperor were the members of his own family. Since the principate was not an hereditary office, they had no extraordinary powers, titles, or honors, except as these were conferred on them by the

senate at the request, or with the approval, of the emperor.
The empress usually received the title of *Augusta*, and the
princes of the imperial household bore the title of *Caesar*
until the time of Hadrian, who restricted it to the person
whom the emperor had picked out as his successor (cf.
p. 341). Upon the person selected for the succession the
*imperium proconsulare* and the *potestas tribunicia* were
conferred. He was thus made in a sense a colleague of
the emperor, and is designated by Tacitus (*Ann.* I. 3) as
*collega imperii, consors tribuniciae potestatis*. The relation
was one of imperfect collegiality, however, for, although
the prospective successor had the *maius imperium* over all
magistrates and imperial officials, in the exercise of both
his *imperium* and his tribunician power he must have been
subject to the emperor. The significance of the title of
*Caesar* and the passage of the two acts above mentioned
lay in the fact that they designated a certain person for
the succession (cf. p. 341). To the Caesar such honors
were ordinarily granted as the title of *imperator*, and the
right to participate in a triumph and to have his likeness
stamped on coins. He usually held the magistracies also
with the emperor. In the relation existing between Marcus
Aurelius and Lucius Aelius (cf. pp. 319 f.), the collegiate
principle in an almost pure form was recognized, the title
of *pontifex maximus* being the only one reserved by Marcus
Aurelius.

**433. The Praefectus Praetorio.** To the *praefectus praetorio* was committed the protection of the emperor's person,
so that, although in time his authority extended far beyond
the limits of the court, he may properly be considered as a
member of the emperor's household. Intrusted at first
only with the charge of the three praetorian cohorts at
Rome, he acquired the command in the course of time

Tac. Ann.
12. 26.

Tac. Ann.
1. 3; 1. 14;
3. 56.

of all the troops stationed in Italy, with the exception of Dio. 52. 24 the *cohortes urbanae* and one legion outside the city. The control of this armed force in and near Rome, and the power which it gave him to influence the succession, gave the praetorian prefect the position which he held next in importance to the emperor. The execution of imperial decrees and a general supervision of imperial officials were, therefore, naturally turned over to him.

His jurisdiction in civil and criminal cases has already been noticed (cf. pp. 347 ff.). These functions were a natural development of the original powers of his office. His position as commander-in-chief of the forces in Italy carried along with it the right to exercise military jurisdiction over the troops under his command. This duty called for judicial qualities, and when the principle of appeal was introduced it was a not unnatural thing to place him in charge of the appellate court. In this way the office of praetorian prefect became in the later empire more of a judicial than of a military position, and was held by the most distinguished jurists of the period. The legal attainments of the prefect naturally gave him also the leading place in the judicial *consilium* of the emperor (p. 331). The office was restricted to knights under the early empire.

**434. The Amici and Comites Augusti.** The *amici Augusti* held a semi-official position at court. They enjoyed the personal favor of the emperor, and were employed by him in various administrative matters. From their number he made up in large measure his *consilium,* and by men chosen from among them he was accompanied on his journeys to Wilm. Ex Inscr. II. p. 555. the provinces. In fact, *comes Augusti* was essentially an official title, and those who were honored with it were steadily employed on imperial business. Only senators became *comites*.

**435. The Officials a Rationibus.** The principal bureaus attached to the imperial household were those *a rationibus, ab epistulis, a libellis, a cognitionibus,* and *a memoria.* The imperial fiscus (cf. p. 352) was managed at first by a freed-

C. I. L.
VIII. 1641.

man, but after Hadrian by a *procurator Augusti a rationibus,* or a *rationalis,* chosen from the equestrian order. The *tabularii* and other assistants in this department were freedmen or slaves.

**436. The Officials ab Epistulis.** The officials designated as *ab epistulis* had charge of the official correspondence of the emperor. They received despatches from governors, generals, towns, and embassies, and put into final form the emperor's replies. Documents intended for Greek-speaking peoples were written in Greek, so that the bureau was

Dio, 71. 12;
C. I. L.
VI. 8606.

divided into the two sections, *ab epistulis Latinis* and *ab epistulis Graecis.*

**437. The Officials a Libellis.** The bureau *a libellis* received the petitions and memorials addressed by individuals to the emperor, and drew up decisions or replies for the emperor's signature.

**438. The Officials a Cognitionibus.** The officials *a cognitionibus* were charged with collecting information and preparing opinions for the emperor on judicial questions submitted to him for settlement. A legal training was very important for those who held this office. In the early period its incumbents were freedmen; later it was filled by members of the equestrian order.

**439. The Officials a Memoria.** Those who held the office *a memoria,* which was established in the second century, were employed in collecting materials for the emperor's public utterances, or in putting the emperor's decisions in a suitable form for public presentation.

## (b) Imperial Judicial Officers

**440. Criminal Jurisdiction of the Senate and the Quaestiones Perpetuae.** A few words must be said about the different criminal courts before the judicial functions of certain imperial officers will be understood. By the close of the republican period the popular assemblies were no longer called together as judicial bodies, so that all criminal cases came before the *quaestiones perpetuae* (cf. pp. 74, 105 f.). From 70 to 46 B.C. the juries in these courts were composed of senators, knights, and *tribuni aerarii*. The *tribuni aerarii* were not represented on them after 46, and Augustus excused the senators from jury duty, but he added a certain number of men having property amounting to 200,000 sesterces (*ducenarii*). They served, however, only on juries in civil cases of minor importance. The *quaestiones perpetuae* disappeared in the third century. The criminal jurisdiction of the senate, which came in with the empire (cf. p. 277), was exercised over serious political offenses, especially if senators were concerned (cf. pp. 347 f.). The penalties of banishment, deportation, or death could be imposed. No appeal could be taken to the emperor, but he could interpose his veto, if he wished. The senate lost its judicial powers in the third or fourth century.

**441. Criminal Jurisdiction of Imperial Officials.** The emperor exercised his criminal jurisdiction in person, or delegated it. When he sat in person he generally observed the procedure of the criminal law, and was assisted by the members of the bureau *a cognitionibus* (cf. p. 362), and by such members of his *consilium* (cf. p. 347) as he had chosen for the case in hand. For special cases he delegated his power to a *iudex datus*, but for cases belonging to certain categories the *praefectus praetorio*, the *praefectus urbi*, the *praefectus vigilum*, and the *praefectus annonae* were competent without special authorization from him. The praetorian prefect exercised criminal jurisdiction over the soldiers in Italy, and in capital cases over civilians in Italy outside of a radius of one hundred miles from Rome, and in the later period on appeal from the governors of provinces (cf. pp. 348 f., 361). In a similar way the city prefect tried persons charged with capital offenses committed in Rome or within one hundred miles of the city. He could even delegate his judicial power to others. The *praefectus vigilum* exercised jurisdiction over minor crimes. An appeal could be taken from his decision to the emperor or the praetorian prefect. The *praefectus annonae* heard criminal cases coming within his special province, such as attempts to create a corner in grain. The governors of provinces had criminal jurisdiction, even in capital cases, over all Roman citizens in their provinces, except that senators, officers of a certain rank, and members of the municipal senates had a right to be tried in Rome.

**442. Civil Jurisdiction of Republican Courts.** For the adjudication of civil cases the empire inherited from the republic the courts of the praetors (cf. p. 189), the curule aediles, the *X viri stlitibus iudicandis* (cf. p. 210), and the *centum viri*. The judicial functions of the curule aediles were of little importance (cf. p. 206). The centumviral court was increased in membership from 105 to 180. Sometimes it sat as a unit, but more frequently it was divided into four sections. Under the empire its members were probably chosen from among the regular *iudices*. From the time of Augustus the *X viri stlitibus iudicandis* acted as presiding officers in the several sections of the centumviral court. The business which came before the court was essentially the same as under the republic.

Plin. Ep. 4. 24. 1; 6. 33. 3 ff.; Quint. 5. 2. 1.

Suet. Aug. 36.

The civil jurisdiction of the praetors was somewhat extended by the assignment to them of new classes of cases, notably those arising between the fiscus and individuals.

**443. Civil Jurisdiction of Imperial Officials.** To the several civil courts mentioned above we must add for the empire the court presided over by the emperor or by some one exercising authority delegated by him. The emperor himself heard cases in the first instance or on appeal. Special cases were assigned to a *iudex*. Cases falling within certain categories were heard in the emperor's name by praetors, consuls, or provincial governors, while questions of appeal came before the *praefectus urbi* or the *praefectus praetorio* (cf. p. 347). Civil and criminal jurisdiction in the municipalities will be considered in another connection.

### (c) Imperial Financial Officers

**444. Census Officials.** The valuation of property and the levying of taxes were based on the census books (*libri censuales*) prepared under the supervision of the *censitores* appointed by the emperor, one for each province or smaller unit of territory. The method of procedure which they adopted was similar to that followed by the censor at Rome (cf. pp. 192 f.). Wilm. Ex. Inscr. 1249 b, 1609.

**445. Officials of the Aerarium Saturni.** At the beginning of the imperial period the *aerarium Saturni* was in charge of the city quaestors (cf. p. 208), but Augustus transferred it to two *praefecti aerarii* elected by the senate from the list of praetorian senators. Later it was placed in charge of praetors, and still later it was restored to the quaestors, but the system finally established by Nero in 56, in accordance with which prefects appointed by the emperor had control of it, was retained down to the time of Diocletian. Tac. Ann. 13. 29; Suet Aug. 36.

Wilm. Ex. Inscr. 1150, 1152, 1188.

**446. Officials of the Fiscus.**   The management of the fiscus was intrusted to an official known successively as the *patronus* or *procurator fisci*, the *procurator a rationibus*, and, toward the close of the second century, as the *rationalis*.   From the time of Hadrian this position was filled by a knight.   A subordinate officer, called a *procurator*, was appointed to collect the taxes in each province, or to take charge of taxes of a particular sort, so that one hears, for instance, of a *procurator Asiae* and a *procurator vicesimae hereditatium*.   The procurators sat in judgment on questions arising between the state and an individual, just as the censors had done under the republic (p. 194).

**447. Officials of the Aerarium Militare.**   The *aerarium militare* was managed by three *praefecti aerarii militaris* chosen for a period of three years from senators of praetorian rank.   Under Augustus they were selected by lot, but later the emperor appointed them, and this change constitutes one of the earliest instances of the encroachment of the emperor on the traditional rights of the senate in financial matters.

**448. Officials of the Res Privata.**   To the *res privata* or *patrimonium* of the emperor belonged the estates of the imperial family and the additions made by legacies, presents, or by confiscation.   This property was in charge of officials appointed by the emperor, and we hear, for instance, of a *procurator saltus Domitiani*.   A sharp distinction between the *fiscus* and the *res privata* of the emperor was not made until the reign of Septimius Severus, when we find mention of a *procurator rerum privatarum*, under whom in the various parts of the empire were officials who bore such titles as *procurator provinciarum Bithyniae Ponti Paphlagoniae tam patrimoni quam rationum privatarum.*

Wilm. Ex.
Inscr. 638,
1271, 2809 b.

Wilm. Ex.
Inscr. 1253.

Wilm. Ex.
Inscr. 1155,
1162 b;
Dio, 55. 25.

Wilm. Ex.
Inscr. 1292.

Wilm. Ex.
Inscr. 1293.

## (d) Imperial Officers Charged with the Government of Rome

**449. The Praefectus Urbi.** The *praefectura urbis* was established by Augustus to provide for the government of the city during his absence. The creation of this office involved an open recognition by him of the fact that he was at the head of the state, and that when he left the city it was without a chief-magistrate, because under the constitutional republic the *praefectura urbis* was only called into existence when both the consuls were absent (cf. p. 212). Tiberius went a step farther than his predecessor, by appointing a *praefectus urbi* to hold office whether he himself was in Rome or not. The incumbent of the office was named by the emperor for an undetermined period from the senators of consular rank. He was intrusted with the maintenance of order in the city, and his duties required him to take charge in particular of public gatherings at the markets, in the theatres, or the circus. For this purpose he had under his command at the outset three, and later as many as six, *cohortes urbanae*, comprising from 1000 to 1500 men each. Along with his functions as a police official in preventing disorder, he naturally acquired criminal jurisdiction, at first in cases where the lower classes only were concerned ; but in time these judicial functions developed to such an extent that his court became the most important criminal court in Rome, and even extended its jurisdiction far beyond the limits of the city.

**450. The Praefectus Vigilum.** The provision which had been made under the republic for the extinction of fires having proved utterly inadequate, in A.D. 6 Augustus organized seven cohorts of 1000 to 1200 men each, charged with this duty. This body of men was also used as a police force to protect the city at night, and, therefore, coöperated with the *cohortes urbanae* in maintaining order. It was in charge of the *praefectus vigilum*, who, like the city prefect, acquired criminal jurisdiction, but in his judicial capacity he was subordinate to the *praefectus urbi*. Since the *vigiles* were usually freedmen, and were commanded by an officer who held only the equestrian rank, they exercised far less political influence than the praetorian or urban cohorts.

**451. The Praefectus Annonae.** To supply grain to the city without interruption was a matter of so great economical and political importance that a special department of the government with numerous officials was established to arrange for it (cf. p. 355). Upon this bureau, which was in charge of an official known as the *praefectus annonae*, devolved the duty of maintaining a general supervision of the sources of supply in the provinces, of the transportation of grain to Rome, and of its distribution to the needy. Incidental to its duties also were the maintenance of suitable ports of entry and the control of the provision markets in Rome. The prefect in charge had civil and criminal jurisdiction over certain cases arising in commercial transactions.

Suet. Aug. 42; Tac. Ann. 6. 13.

**452. The Commissioners Having Charge of Aqueducts, Buildings, and Sewers.** The three boards which supervised the aqueducts, public buildings, and sewers formed, with the commission to which Italian roads were intrusted, a college whose members were of senatorial rank and were appointed by the emperor for an indefinite period. The *curatores aquarum* were three in number, and took over the aqueduct system as Agrippa left it at his death. From the time of Claudius they were assisted by a freedman or knight appointed by the emperor and bearing the title of

Frontin. de Aq. 98 ff.

Frontin. de Aq. 105.

*procurator aquarum.* The *curatores operum publicorum* had nothing to do with the construction of new buildings. The emperor took charge of that matter himself, and met the attendant expenses from the spoils of war, from private contributions, and from sums appropriated by the senate for the purpose. The commissioners mentioned above took upon themselves only the function, which the aediles had formerly exercised, of keeping public buildings in repair. The duties of the *curatores alvei et riparum Tiberis et cloacarum urbis* have been mentioned already (cf. p. 355).

Mon. Ancyr 4, ll. 9–23

### (e) Imperial Officers in Italy

**453. Imperial Administration of Italy.** The system of local government adopted in the *municipia* throughout Italy has been briefly discussed in another connection (cf. pp. 299 f.), so that we are concerned here only with the administrative officials appointed to represent the central government. Augustus divided Italy outside of Rome into eleven *regiones*, although these territorial sections do not seem to have been the units adopted for administrative purposes in all cases, as we should expect them to have been. The principal matters of business of which the central government took partial or complete charge were the management of the roads, the control of the *alimentatio*, the supervision of local finances and of the civil and criminal courts.

**454. The Cura Viarum.** The *cura viarum* came into the hands of imperial officers in 20 B.C. Each of the great roads was put in charge for an indefinite period of a *curator* of senatorial rank, selected by the emperor. It was his duty to keep the road in good condition and to protect public property connected with it from the

Tac. Ann. 3. 31; Dio, 59. 15; 60. 17

encroachment of individuals. Branch roads were in the care of *procuratores* of equestrian rank.

Asbach,
Röm. Kaiser-
tum, etc.
188 ff.

**455. The Cura Alimentorum.** Possibly Domitian established the *cura alimentorum*, but more probably it dates from the reigns of Nerva and Trajan (cf. pp. 323 f.), who established foundations, from the interest of which

Wilm. Ex.
Inscr. 2844–8;
Plin. Pan.
26 ff.;
Dio, 68. 5.

gratuities in the form of money or grain were given each month to a selected number of children of free birth. The immediate management of the funds set aside for the purpose, and the distribution of the monthly allowance, were in the hands of municipal officials; but a general supervision of the matter was confided to a *praefectus* or a *procu-*

Wilm. Ex.
Inscr. 1179,
1194.

*rator* for each district, with perhaps a single *praefectus alimentorum* in charge of the whole department. The money which the state appropriated was in many cases supplemented by the gifts of public-spirited citizens.

**456. Supervision of Municipal Finances.** It was Trajan also who introduced the practice of bringing municipal finances under imperial supervision. He and his successors

Wilm. Ex.
Inscr. 2167,
2479.

appointed for the municipalities *curatores* of senatorial or equestrian rank, whose duty it was to audit the town accounts, and whose consent must be obtained before a town could contract a new debt or sell public property. It is not clear whether one of these officials was appointed for each Italian town or only when imperial supervision seemed desirable.

**457. Iuridici.** The establishment of district courts, to use a modern term, dates from the reign of Hadrian (cf. p. 318). The institution was not kept up by Antoninus Pius, but was restored by M. Aurelius. The judges were of

Spart. Hadr.
22; Appian,
B. C. I. 38;
Wilm Ex.
Inscr. 1195,
1197.

senatorial rank and bore the title of *iuridici*. Ultimately, as we have already seen (p. 355), Italy lost entirely its exceptional position and sank to the level of the provinces.

### (f) Imperial Officers in the Provinces

**458. Imperial Control of the Provinces.** The control which the emperor exercised over imperial provinces was supreme. The senate nominally supervised the government of senatorial provinces, but the *maius imperium* of the emperor, and his exalted position, led senatorial governors to turn to him for advice and instructions. Furthermore, even in the senatorial provinces certain administrative departments, for instance those which had to do with public roads, the post, and some branches of the financial system, were managed in the name of the emperor. Only in the case of the finances, however, did the emperor have a personal representative, styled a *procurator*, in the senatorial provinces. Dio, 53. 15

**459. Limitations and Extensions of the Power of Imperial Officers.** The general system of government in the provinces, and the limits put on the jurisdiction of governors in civil and criminal cases, have been discussed elsewhere (cf. pp. 284 f., 346 f., 348 f.), so that it only remains for us to mention certain factors which tended to curtail in some respects, and to extend in other ways, the power of the emperor's representatives. In general it may be said that, as time went on, the cause of local self-government lost, while the rights of a province as a province increased. The towns and cities lost their independence in some measure, because they, like the municipalities in Italy (cf. p. 370), were required from an early period to submit to the supervision of imperial *curatores* in financial matters. On the other hand, the autocratic power of the governor was lessened, and the province gained to some extent, by the more direct control which the emperor assumed, and by the development of provincial assemblies. The strict

accountability to which governors were held naturally made
them hesitate about taking responsibility in important matters, and, when the practice of referring questions to the
emperor was once adopted (cf. p. 301), it must have developed rapidly. The inevitable result of it, however, was to
take from a governor the right of initiative in important
matters. The development of the provincial assemblies
(cf. p. 302) must have restricted the power of governors
still further. All, or almost all, the provinces had *concilia*
whose right to send deputations or petitions to the emperor,
without consulting the governor, came to be freely recognized. The independent existence of the assembly was
recognized by the emperor in the fact also that his reply
was sent directly to it. The possibility which every governor had to face, of seeing a document criticising his conduct sent to the emperor at the close of his term of office,
must have exercised a wholesome restraining influence on
his administration.

Marq. St.<br>Verw. I.<br>503 ff.<br>Tac. Ann.<br>15. 20; Plin.<br>Ep. 3. 4. 2.<br>Dig. 47. 14. 1.

### SELECTED BIBLIOGRAPHY [1]

W. T. Arnold, The Roman System of Provincial Administration.
London, 1879.

Cagnat, Les impôts indirects.   Paris, 1882.

Carette, Les assemblées provinciales de la Gaule romaine.   Paris,
1895.

E. Cuq, Le conseil des empereurs d'Auguste à Dioclétien.   Paris,
1884.

P. Guiraud, Les assemblées prov. dans l'empire rom.   Paris, 1887.

Cyprien Halgan, Essai sur l'administration des provinces sénato-
riales.   Paris, 1898.

O. Hirschfeld, Untersuchungen auf dem Gebiete d. röm. Verwaltungsgeschichte, Bd. I.   Berlin, 1877.

O. Hirschfeld, Das aerarium militare, N. Jahrb. f. Philol. XCVII
(1868), pp. 683–697.

[1] See also bibliography on pp. 173, 288, 304, 316, 328, 358.

O. Hirschfeld, Die Getreideverwaltung der röm. Kaiserzeit, Philol. XXIX, pp. 1–96.

E. Klebs, Zur Entwicklung d. kaiserl. Stadtpräfektur, Rhein. Mus. (N.F.), XLII, pp. 164–178.

Klein, Die Verwaltungsbeamten der Provinzen des röm. Reichs bis auf Diocletian. Bonn, 1878.

G. Kretschmar, Das Beamtentum der röm. Kaiserzeit. Giessen, 1879.

W. Liebenam, Forschungen zur Verwaltungsgeschichte des röm. Kaiserreichs, Bd. I. Leipzig, 1888.

W. Liebenam, Die Laufbahn der Prokuratoren. Jena, 1886.

W. Liebenam, Beiträge zur Verwaltungsgeschichte d. röm. Kaiserreichs. Jena, 1886.

W. Liebenam, Städteverwaltung im römischen Kaiserreiche. Leipzig, 1900.

J. Marquardt, Römische Staatsverwaltung, 2te Aufl., 3 vols. Leipzig, 1881–5.

Th. Mommsen, Die diocletianische Reichspräfectur, Hermes, XXXVI (1901), pp. 201–218.

W. Schurz, De mutationibus in imp. Rom. ordinando ab imp. Hadr. factis. Bonn, 1883.

SUPPLEMENTARY LITERATURE, 1901–1910

Arnold-Shuckburgh, The Roman System of Provincial Administration. Oxford, 1906.

Hirschfeld, Die kaiserlichen Verwaltungsbeamten bis auf Diocletian. Berlin, 1905.

Borghesi, Œuvres complètes, Tome dixième: Les préfets du prétoire. Paris, 1897.

Heisterbergk, Provincia. Philologus, LI (1890), 629–644.

Arnold, Studies of Roman Imperialism. London, 1906.

Rostowzew, Geschichte der Staatspacht in der römischen Kaiserzeit bis Diocletian. Leipzig, 1902.

Vigneaux, Essai sur l'histoire de la praefectura urbis à Rome. Paris, 1896.

Graham, Roman Africa. London, 1902.

Chapot, La province romaine proconsulaire d'Asie. Paris, 1904.

# CHAPTER XIX

**THE MAGISTRACIES**

### (a) The Magistracies in General

**460. The Cursus Honorum.** In the election and appointment of citizens to official positions under the empire, the division of society into the senatorial order, the equestrian order, and the plebs was strictly observed, and corresponding to these three classes there were three careers of official service, known as the *cursus honorum*. To citizens of senatorial rank were assigned, along with certain important imperial offices, all the old republican magistracies. The full *cursus honorum* for men of this class, leaving out of consideration the appointive offices, comprised membership in the college of the *XX viri*, the position of *tribunus militum*, the quaestorship, the aedileship, the tribunate of the plebs, the praetorship, and the consulship. Before the Flavian period the military tribunate could be held before or after the vigintivirate, but after that time it took invariably the second place.

**461. Conditions of Eligibility.** The conditions of eligibility to the vigintivirate were senatorial rank and the attainment of manhood, as indicated by the assumption of the *toga virilis*. The office was, therefore, open to the sons of senators, and to those whom the emperor had raised to the senatorial rank. The senatorial census (cf. p. 381) was of course required in both cases. For the quaestorship a candidate was required to have completed his

Tac. Ann.
3. 29; 15. 28;
Quint.
12. 6. 1;
Dio, 52. 20.

twenty-fourth year and to have held the offices mentioned. An interval of a year must elapse between the quaestorship and the tribunate of the plebs or the aedileship, and another year before the praetorship could be held. Patricians could pass directly from the quaestorship to the praetorship, although the minimum age requirement of thirty years for the praetorship took away the advantage which they would otherwise have had over the plebeians. An interval of two years was required between the praetorship and the consulship, which practically fixed the age requirement for the consulship at thirty-three. Candidates were eligible to the same office again after a short interval, and it was not illegal to hold a magistracy and an imperial office at the same time. From the restrictions mentioned above candidates for office could be relieved by the emperor, and fathers of families were regularly given precedence over others.

St. R. I. 535.

St. R. I. 555, n. 3.

Dio, 52. 20.

St. R. I. 528, n. 1.

Plin. Ep. 7. 16. 2.

**462. Nomination; Election; Term of Office.** The formalities attending nomination were like those under the republic, except that the emperor exercised the right of nomination (cf. pp. 275 f., 351). From the reign of Tiberius magistrates were elected in the senate. The term of office continued to be a year, except in the case of the consulship.

**463. Loss of Dignity and Power.** The magistracies suffered, of course, a serious loss of dignity and real power. Since the emperor's power to nominate candidates for office counted for so much, a citizen's political future depended on imperial favor, and when he was elected he could not hope to exercise freely the traditional functions of his office with the emperor, or an appointee of the emperor, as his colleague. Furthermore, the powers of the several magistrates were seriously curtailed by law, as we have already seen, and by the assignment of magisterial functions to imperial procurators and prefects.

## (b) *The Several Magistracies*

**464. The Consul.** The most significant formal change which the consulship experienced under the empire was the shortening of the term of office. Up to the death of Nero the term was usually one of six months; after that date ordinarily of two or four months. The purpose of the change was to lessen the importance of the office. The election of the first pair of consuls for a given year, known as *consules ordinarii*, usually took place in the autumn of the preceding year. The *consules suffecti* were commonly chosen at the beginning of the year during which they were to serve. Official documents were still dated by mentioning the consuls of the year in question, but the names of the *consules ordinarii* were usually selected for the purpose. This gave them a certain prestige over the *consules suffecti*.

The principal functions of the consul consisted in presiding over the senate, in exercising judicial powers in certain cases, and in taking charge of the *ludi circenses* and other public games. The senate under the early empire had nominal charge of Rome, Italy, and the senatorial provinces, and the importance of the consulship depended largely on the success which the senate had in making good its constitutional rights within these limits — and its success in this matter varied from reign to reign. The criminal jurisdiction and, to some extent, the civil jurisdiction of the consul were exercised by him in conjunction with the senate. Apart from that body, however, he heard certain important classes of civil cases, assigned to him by the emperor.

**465. The Praetor.** Julius Caesar had raised the number of praetors to sixteen (cf. p. 137). Augustus reduced it to

---

*Marginal notes (left column):*

Herz. II. 828, n. 3.

St. R. I. 588 f.

Suet. Claud. 23; Instit. Iust. 2. 23. 1.

twelve, but under succeeding emperors it was raised until it reached its maximum, eighteen, under Claudius. The *praetor urbanus* still took precedence over his colleagues. Next him came the *praetor peregrinus*. The encroachment of the emperor and of his officials, however, on the prerogatives of the city praetor greatly diminished the importance of his position. The significance of the office of the *praetor peregrinus* was taken away in large measure by Caracalla's edict. The powers of the whole college of praetors were seriously abridged also by the publication of Hadrian's *edictum perpetuum* (cf. p. 318), which robbed them of the right to issue their annual edicts, by the assignment of certain civil cases to the consuls (cf. p. 376), and by the appointment of district judges for Italy (cf. p. 318). A partial compensation for these losses may be found in the fact that the supervision of certain public games was given to them, and, for a time, the administration of the *aerarium Saturni* (cf. p. 365). Their principal function, that of presiding over the *quaestio perpetua*, was lost when that court disappeared in the second or third century (cf. p. 349).

*Dio, 54. 2; Tac. Ann. I. 15; I. 77.*

**466. The Censor.** The censorship, as a republican institution, came to an end in 22 B.C. In that year the office was held by P. Aemilius Lepidus and L. Munatius Plancus, although the census was not completed. Claudius, with his fondness for tradition, attempted to revive the office by having himself and L. Vitellius made censors in the year 47; but the precedent was not followed. This seems to have been the last effort made to treat the office as a separate magistracy. In all other cases its functions were apparently exercised by the emperor alone, or by the emperor in conjunction with some other member of the imperial family. Thus, in 8 B.C. Augustus took the census alone, in A.D. 14

*Vell. 2. 95.*

*Nipperdey on Tac. Ann. II. 13.*

with Tiberius, while in A.D. 73–4 Vespasian and Titus coöperated in taking it. In the year 84 Domitian took the censorial power for life (p. 310). The duties of the office (cf. pp. 191 f.), as exercised by the emperors, consisted in the assessment of property and in drawing up the lists of senators and knights. The management of finances was, in large measure, assigned to certain commissions and imperial officers, as we have already seen (cf. pp. 354, 365 f., 369).

**467. The Aedile.** Julius Caesar had increased the number of aediles to six, assigning to the new members of the college supervision of the grain supply (cf. p. 137), but during the reign of Augustus this function was turned over to a board of commissioners (cf. pp. 355, 368). The aediles lost the *cura ludorum* also (cf. p. 377), and their right to maintain order in the city was in large measure relinquished in favor of the *praefectus vigilum* and the *praefectus urbi* (cf. pp. 367–8). There is no mention of the office later than the middle of the third century.

**468. The Tribune.** The tribune retained under the empire his sacrosanct character, his *ius auxilii* and *ius intercessionis*, his right to summon the senate and probably the popular assembly also. But these were formal powers with little meaning. Thus, for instance, his action could be vetoed by the emperor, but he could not interfere with the emperor (cf. p. 357). His right to summon the popular assembly was of little importance because of the decadence of that body. What little significance the office had lay in the fact that the tribune could veto the action of the senate, protect citizens in the courts, and impose fines in certain cases.

Tac. Ann. 1. 13; 6. 47.

**469. The Quaestor.** Augustus seems to have reduced the number of quaestors from forty to twenty. The college was divided into two sections, one consisting of the provincial

St. R. II. 528, n. 2.

quaestors, and the other of those whose functions kept them in Rome. A quaestor was assigned to each one of the eleven senatorial provinces, except that two were sent to Sicily. Of the eight remaining members of the college, two were *quaestores urbani* and two were assigned to each of the consuls and to the emperor. In the provinces the quaestor, who bore the title *quaestor pro praetore*, represented the *aerarium Saturni*, and exercised the jurisdiction which had traditionally belonged to his office (pp. 208–209). The *quaestores urbani* had charge of the *aerarium* for a time, but this was taken from them in the year 56 (cf. p. 365). Thereafter their principal duty consisted in caring for the decrees of the senate. The two quaestors selected by the emperor acted as his secretaries in laying matters before the senate. The four quaestors assigned to the consuls were subordinates in the service of those officials.

Dio, 54. 36.
Tac. Ann.
16. 27.

**470. The XX Viri and Extraordinary Magistrates.** The college of *IIII praefecti Capuam Cumas* (cf. p. 210), and that made up of the *II viri viis extra urbem purgandis*, were abolished under the empire, and the four remaining groups were consolidated into a single college known as the vigintivirate. The *X viri stlitibus iudicandis*, from the time of Augustus, presided in the centumviral court (cf. p. 364). The *III viri monetales* had charge of senatorial coinage only (cf. p. 354). The functions of the *III viri capitales* were seriously abridged by the establishment of the *praefectura vigilum*. Otherwise the duties of the members of these groups of officials were unchanged. Some significance was given to these offices, however, by the fact that they were made the first step in the *cursus honorum* (cf. p. 374). Of the extraordinary republican magistracies (cf. pp. 211 ff.), we hear of the *praefectus*

Tac. Ann.
6. 11; Wilm.
Ex. Inscr.
1132.

*urbi feriarum Latinarum*, of *praefecti frumenti dandi ex s. c.*, and occasionally of special commissioners sent out by the senate.

## SELECTED BIBLIOGRAPHY [1]

Julius Asbach, Zur Geschichte des Konsulats in d. röm. Kaiserzeit, Histor. Untersuchungen, etc., pp. 190–217. Bonn, 1882.

J. Centerwall, Quae publica officia ante quaesturam geri solita sint temporibus imperatorum. Upsala, 1874.

Chambalu, De magistratibus Flaviorum. Bonn, 1882.

Göll, Ueber d. röm. Censur zur Zeit ihres Untergangs. Schleiz, 1859.

Göll, Das Volkstribunat in d. Kaiserzeit, Rhein. Mus. (N.F.), XIII. 111 ff.

Henzen, De nundinis consularibus aetatis imperatoriae, Ephem. Epig. I. 187–199.

Lenel, Das Edictum perpetuum. Leipzig, 1883.

[1] See also bibliography on pp. 173, 219, 288, 304, 316, 328, 358.

# CHAPTER XX

## THE SENATE

### (a) Composition of the Senate

**471. Size of the Senate.** On at least three different occasions, as he himself tells us (*Mon. Ancyr.* II, l. 2), Augustus revised the list of senators. As a result of these revisions, the membership was reduced from 900 (cf. p. 137) to 600, which was accepted as the normal number under the empire. In drawing up his lists Augustus also took occasion to exclude many men of low birth, whom Julius Caesar had admitted. In this way he restored the aristocratic character of the senate.

Dio, 54. 13 f

Suet. Aug. 35
Dio, 52. 42.

**472. Admission to the Senate.** The conditions of eligibility to membership in the senate included citizenship and free birth, an acceptable reputation, and property rated at 1,000,000 sesterces. By those who fulfilled these conditions admission to the senate could be had by securing election to the quaestorship. Inasmuch as the magistracies were open only to those of senatorial rank, that is, to the sons of senators (cf. p. 374), the senate became a close corporation. The emperor could, however, at his discretion grant to men not of senatorial rank, who had the necessary property, the right to wear the *latus clavus*, or broad purple stripe on the tunic. This entitled them to become candidates for a magistracy with the prospect later of entering the senate. Furthermore, citizens with a fortune of 1,000,000 sesterces, who had not held a magistracy,

Dio, 54. 17;
Tac. Ann. 2
37; Suet.
Aug. 41.

381

were from time to time admitted to the senate by *adlectio* (cf. p. 354).

**473. The Album Senatorium.**   From 9 B.C. on, the *album senatorium*, or official list of senators, was revised each year. The names of those who had held a magistracy since the last revision, and of those chosen by the method of *adlectio*, were added to the old list, while those whose property had fallen below the required minimum, and those who had been convicted of an offense against the laws, were excluded from the senate.   In the list the names were arranged in the order of official rank.   After the emperor's name came those of the *consulares*, then the *praetorii*, etc.   Those who had held a given magistracy more than once ranked higher in dignity than those who had held it once only.   No distinction was made between ex-consuls who had been *consules ordinarii* and those who had been *suffecti*.   Up to the time of Pertinax those who were assigned to a given group by *adlectio* were of equal rank with those who had attained the position in question by virtue of having held a magistracy.

### (b) Meetings of the Senate

**474. The Presidency of the Senate.**   The magistrates who had the *ius cum patribus agendi* under the republic (cf. p. 225) exercised that right under the empire also. Of course the offices of dictator, master of the horse, and interrex had disappeared, so that they do not come into consideration.   Whether the city prefect had the theoretical right to convoke the senate or not is a matter of no moment.   He would scarcely have exercised it, except during the absence of the other qualified officials, and such a contingency could not arise.   It is also probably true that the tribune rarely made use of this privilege.   The *princeps* took precedence of all the magistrates in calling the senate together, and even when that body had been convoked by a magistrate, a place of honor was given to him between the two consuls, or on the tribunes' bench.

**475. The Place and Time of Meeting.** The ordinary place of meeting was the *curia Iulia*. Except during the months of September and October, stated meetings were held on the Kalends and Ides of each month. Otherwise the senate met at the call of the qualified official.

Suet. Aug. 35; Dio, 55. 3.

**476. A Quorum.** The attendance of senators was required, but the efforts made to enforce this regulation were not effective. In the early part of the reign of Augustus a quorum was fixed at 400 members, but later it was found necessary to reduce this number and not to require a quorum for action on unimportant matters.

Dio, 54. 18; Tac. Ann. 16. 22.

Dio, 54. 35; 55. 3.

**477. The Transaction of Business.** The purpose for which the senate was convoked was indicated only in a general way in the call which was issued. The subjects to be considered were laid before the meeting by the presiding officer. Individual senators still lacked theoretically the right to introduce new business, but in discussing a matter laid before them they were allowed, as under the republic, to introduce extraneous questions, and to ask for action by the senate. Senators were asked their opinions in the traditional order (cf. p. 224), except that the emperor gave his views first, or, if he chose, last. During some reigns at least, when the emperor presided, the magistrates in office were also called upon in the group to which they belonged. As we have already had occasion to notice (p. 350), the business of the emperor, whether he was present or not, took precedence, within certain limits, of all other matters. In any case the *princeps* controlled the discussion and the action of the senate, and a

Tac. Ann. 1. 7.

Tac. Ann. 4. 74.

Tac. Ann. 1. 74.

Tac. Ann 3. 17.

senator could indicate his disapproval of a measure only by staying away from the meeting when the bill in question was to be presented. The *discessio* was the accepted method of voting, even upon candidates for the magistracies. Trajan introduced the secret ballot for the latter purpose, but the new arrangement did not become permanent. It was the duty of the presiding officer to appoint a committee for the formulation of each motion, and decrees which were intended for the public eye were engraved on bronze tablets. One of the quaestors, appointed for the purpose by the emperor, and known as *ab actis senatus*, prepared for the archives the *acta senatus*, or proceedings of the senate, which comprised the *senatus consulta*, official documents submitted to the senate, and the speeches made by leading senators. From these records such extracts as the senate selected were published in the *acta diurna*.

Tac. Ann.
5. 4; 15. 74;
Wilm. Ex.
Inscr. 636,
1154.

Plin. Pan. 75.

### (c) The Powers of the Senate

478. **The Senate and the Princeps.** In the last years of the republic, and in the period of transition from the republic to the dyarchy, the senate had been reduced to the position which it theoretically held under the constitution, viz., that of an advisory body. Under the new régime its formal powers were much greater and more explicitly recognized. It became a legislative, a judicial, and an electoral body. Its real influence over affairs had always depended, however, not on the powers which it had received when the state was organized, but on the measure of control which it was able to exercise over the magistrates and over the resources of the commonwealth. This was still the case under the empire. Bearing this fact in mind, it is easy to understand how a formal extension

of the powers of the senate by Augustus and Tiberius could take place simultaneously with a real loss of influence. The fact that the *princeps* held his position for life freed him from the influences which had made the consul amenable to it (cf. pp. 67 f.). Furthermore, it lost outright the management of foreign affairs, the control of the army and navy (pp. 237 ff., 345 f.), the government of the important provinces (pp. 283 ff.), and consequently in large measure the management of the finances.

**479. The Senate as a Legislative Body.** The decadence of the *comitia* made the senate the sole legislative body in the state. *Senatus consulta* had the force of law, and touched every field of public activity, subject to the limitations mentioned in the preceding paragraph. The business which required the greatest share of its attention was the financial management and the administration of Rome, Italy, and the senatorial provinces. Upon all these matters it heard reports, and took the necessary action. It exercised the right to raise or lower the rate of taxation, but only on the imperial initiative. The control of the *ager publicus* was, however, transferred to the emperor. It took action with reference to the introduction of foreign cults, managed the temples, and provided for extraordinary festivals; but in all religious matters its action must have been perfunctory, since the emperor was *pontifex maximus* and a member of all the important priesthoods. Furthermore, it passed measures imposing penalties on those convicted of certain offenses, and granting honors, privileges, and dispensation from certain laws to favored individuals or classes.

Suet. Tib. 30.

Dio, 55. 25.

Tac. Ann. 3. 71; 15. 74.

Plin. Ep. 5. 4. 1.

**480. The Senate as a Judicial Body.** The criminal jurisdiction of the senate was exercised mainly in the case of serious offenses, particularly those of a political nature (cf. p. 347), where senators were concerned. Perhaps those charged with such offenses were at the outset allowed to have their cases heard either before a *quaestio* or before the senate. Senators would naturally choose the latter tribunal. When the practice was once established it developed rapidly. The procedure, as can be seen from the well-known case of Piso, seems to have been modeled on that followed in the *quaestiones*. The consul presided, and the senate delivered its verdict in the form of a *senatus consultum*. Even the penalty of death could be imposed, and no appeal could be taken from the senate's decision, although the emperor could virtually grant a pardon by using his veto power. Appeals could also be taken to the senate by senators and members of certain other favored classes from the decisions of senatorial governors in capital cases. In civil cases also appeals came to the senate from the senatorial provinces, but they were usually referred by it to the consuls.

**481. The Senate as an Electoral Body.** The most important function of the senate as an electoral body consisted in choosing the emperor (cf. p. 341), and in joining with the popular assembly in conferring on him his constitutional powers (cf. pp. 341 f.). The right to deify a deceased emperor, or to pass the act known as the *damnatio memoriae*, was its exclusive prerogative (cf. pp. 343 f.). Tiberius transferred the election of magistrates to the senate, but its freedom of choice was in large measure restricted by the emperor's right to name candidates for the several offices (p. 351). Notwithstanding this fact, there was a lively competition for the several magistracies, and candidates for office gave costly presents and elaborate dinners to their senatorial colleagues in the hope of winning their suffrages.

Tac. Ann.
3. 10 ff.

Tac. Ann.
3. 17; 3. 37.
Tac. Ann.
2. 32.

Tac. Ann.
14. 48.

Plin. Ep.
6. 19. 1.

## Selected Bibliography[1]

Caduzac, Décadence du sénat rom. depuis César jusqu'à Constantin. Limoges, 1847.

E. Cuq, Le conseil des empereurs, d'Auguste à Dioclétien. Paris, 1884.

Duméril, De senatu romano sub imp. Augusto Tiberioque. Paris, 1856.

Dürr, Die Majestätsprozesse unter dem Kaiser Tiberius. Heilbronn Progr., 1880.

Rotter, Ueber d. Verhältniss zwischen Kaisertum u. Senat unter Aug. u. Tib. Prague, 1875.


### Supplementary Literature, 1901–1910

Abele, Der Senat unter Augustus. Paderborn, 1907.

[1] See also bibliography on pp. 243, 288, 304, 316, 328, 358.

# CHAPTER XXI

## THE PEOPLE

### (a) Citizenship

**482. The Methods of Acquiring Citizenship.** Citizenship could be acquired, as under the republic, by birth, by adoption, by manumission, and by a special grant. The son of a Roman citizen inherited the rights of citizenship. The son of a Latin acquired them when he was adopted by a Roman citizen. The other two methods of acquiring them call for a fuller statement.

**483. Citizenship Acquired by Special Grant or by Manumission.** Various classes of persons acquired the rights of citizenship by virtue of having conformed to certain specified conditions. Thus, for instance, those who received an honorable discharge, after having served twenty-five years in the auxiliary force, or twenty-six years in the navy, became Roman citizens. Latins gained the same privilege when they were enrolled in the legions, and magistrates in towns enjoying the Latin rights were honored with Roman citizenship. Freedmen also, after serving a certain number of years as *vigiles*, gained full civic rights. The conditions on which citizenship was granted to individuals or particular communities cannot be so exactly stated. Personal favor, or political considerations, or a desire to reward those who had rendered a noteworthy service to the community, were usually the deciding factors in these cases. Augustus gave the rights of Roman citizenship to few communities,

C. I. L. II.
1945; V. 532.

Suet. Aug.
40, 47;
Dio, 60. 17;
Tac. Hist.
1. 8.

but his successors bestowed them upon towns in all parts
of the empire.  The *imperium proconsulare* of the emperor
entitled him to make these grants in the imperial provinces
(cf. p. 245), but, although Augustus may have consulted
the senate and popular assembly in cases outside the
imperial provinces, it is plain that his successors felt free, on
their own authority, to grant Roman citizenship to any individual or community.  The greatest addition to the number
of citizens, however, came by way of manumission, and
the rapid increase in the number of freedmen which resulted
seemed so serious a matter to Augustus that he caused a
series of laws to be passed to restrict it (cf. p. 390).

Dio, 57. 17;
Suet. Nero,
12; Galba,
14; Tac.
Ann. 1. 58.

**484.  The Loss of Citizenship.**  As under the republic
(cf. p. 245), those who had been captured in war, turned
over to the enemy, or sold into slavery suffered *capitis
deminutio maxima.*  The third provision just mentioned
underwent a strange interpretation or extension in the case
of those known as *servi poenae.*  The legal fiction involved
in the matter is clearly indicated by Pliny (*ad Traianum*,
XXXI. 2): *in plerisque civitatibus, maxime Nicomediae et
Nicaeae, quidam vel in opus damnati vel in ludum similiaque
his genera poenarum publicorum servorum officio ministerio-
que funguntur atque etiam ut publici servi annua accipiunt.*
Those became *servi poenae, qui ad ferrum aut ad bestias
aut in metallum damnantur* (Dig. XXVIII. 1. 8. 4).  *Capitis
deminutio media* was visited on those who suffered *deportatio*,
or transportation to an island.  *Relegatio*, or the penalty of
being obliged to live within a certain section of the empire,
did not bring with it a loss of citizenship.

**485.  The Rights of Roman Citizens.**  All Roman citizens, except freedmen, had the full enjoyment of the traditional *iura commercii, conubii, provocationis, legis actionis,
suffragii*, and the *ius honorum.*  In respect to their private

rights freedmen stood essentially on the same plane as freemen, except that they were forbidden to marry with members of the senatorial order and were liable to the punishment of being obliged to live at least one hundred miles from Rome for certain offenses against their patrons. Freedmen thus punished were known as *peregrini dediticii*. All freedmen were still restricted to four of the city tribes (p. 247), but this restriction was of little moment because of the decadence of the popular assemblies. The most important limitations put on them were in the matter of the *ius honorum*, and of admission to the equestrian order. Not only freedmen, but their sons and grandsons, were excluded from the equestrian order and from the magistracies, and consequently from the senatorial order. It was within the power of the emperor, however, by a *natalium restitutio* to remove this disability. Reference has been made above to the attempt which Augustus made to restrict indiscriminate manumission. The most important step which he took in this direction consisted in securing the passage in A.D. 4 of the *lex Aelia Sentia*, which provided, among other things, that slaves under thirty years of age who were declared free, and those who were declared free in the will of a deceased owner, did not become technically free. Their legal status was more clearly defined by the *lex Iunia Norbana* of A.D. 19, which rendered them incapable of making a will, and gave them the rights, with certain limitations, of *Latini Iuniani*.

**486. The Obligations of Citizenship.** The two principal obligations resting on Roman citizens were the payment of taxes and service in the army. Roman citizens in Italy paid no direct taxes. Those in the provinces were subject to the *tributum soli* and the *tributum capitis*. This exemption of Roman citizens in Italy was the peculiar privilege

*Margin notes:*

Plin. N. H. 33. 32.

Herz. II. 915 ff.

Nipperdey on Tac. Ann. 2. 59 and 13. 27.

St. R. III. 806 f.

going with the *ius Italicum*. Military service was incumbent on every freeman, but, since a sufficient number of soldiers was usually to be had by voluntary enlistment, it was rarely necessary to resort to a draft. In fact, after the time of the Flavian emperors, the legions were never recruited from Italy. The legions and the praetorian guard were made up exclusively of free-born Roman citizens and of Latins or *peregrini* belonging to *oppida*. Freedmen served in the navy and in the *cohortes vigilum*.

Herz. II. 349 f.

### (b) The Plebeians

**487. The Legal Status of the Plebeians.** The old distinction between the plebeians and patricians is lost sight of under the empire, but by a strange turn of the wheel of fortune the term *plebs* came to indicate, just as it had done in the early republic, those who were outside the privileged classes. It comprised, in fact, all those who were below the senatorial and equestrian orders. And just as had been the case under the early republic, the plebeians under the empire were essentially without political rights, and were shut out of the classes above them by legal restrictions. There was, however, this important difference between the two cases. The barrier was not an insurmountable one. By acquiring the fortune required of a knight or senator a plebeian freeman could rise into one of the higher orders. The most important legal difference, then, between the plebeians on the one hand and the members of the equestrian and senatorial orders on the other, was in the matter of political rights. In one respect their private rights were less, since for a given offense they were liable to a severer punishment than were those who belonged to the two upper classes.

Dig. 48. 8. 3 5.

**488. The Plebs Urbana.** The massing of property in the hands of the few had practically blotted out the independent middle class, and the great body of freemen outside the two orders were partly or entirely dependent on the state for support. The term *plebs urbana* was practically applied to the 200,000 or more whose names made up the list of recipients of grain.

Mon. Ancyr. 3, l. 7; Dio, 55. 10.

**489. The Plebeians outside Rome.** The population in the Italian municipal towns reproduced in miniature the state of things in Rome. A freeman who had a rating of 100,000 sesterces, and was eligible in other respects, could by election to one of the local offices secure admission to the municipal senate. Those who did not have the requisite property were not eligible, so that these small towns also had their senatorial order and their plebeians, although the minimum sum which made one eligible to the senatorial order in the municipalities was so small that the members of that order constituted a middle class in Italy.

### (c) The Equestrian Order

**490. Admission to the Equestrian Order.** The conditions of eligibility to the equestrian order were the possession of property valued at 400,000 sesterces, free birth, and a respectable standing in the community. It was, however, in the power of the emperor to pass over the condition of free birth, and to elevate freedmen to the equestrian rank. Admission to the order rested with the emperor, who established a bureau, known as *a censibus equestribus*, to receive applications and collect the necessary information. If the property of a member of the order fell below the required minimum, or if his mode of life was objectionable, his name was dropped from the list.

Plin. Ep. 1. 19.

Suet. Aug. 27; Tac. Hist. 1. 13.

**491. Limits put on the Order.** Although up to the reign of Tiberius the term *ordo equester* technically included only the *equites equo publico*, it seems probable, while still a matter of dispute, that there was a body of men, who perhaps may be called *equites equo privato*, who satisfied the requirements of the equestrian order, but had not technically been admitted to it. The members of this group did not have certain privileges conceded to the *equites equo publico*, but they received some official recognition until they were formally excluded from the order by the legislation of Tiberius.

St. R. III. 481 ff.; Herz II. 961, n. 1; II. 966, n. 3; Will. Dr. 385.

**492. Seviri Equitum Romanorum.** The way in which the *equites* were organized into *turmae* is not clear. Mention is made of six *turmae* of thirty men each under *seviri*. Possibly only six of the *turmae* had special leaders. The *seviri* were usually the sons of senators or the younger members of the imperial family.

**493. Insignia and Titles.** The members of the equestrian order were distinguished by the *anulus aureus*, the *tunica angusticlavia*, and by the right to reserved seats in the theatre and at the circus. From the time of M. Aurelius the members of the order who were procurators bore the title of *viri egregii*, the equestrian prefects were styled *viri perfectissimi*, with the exception of the prefect of the praetorian guard, who was called *vir eminentissimus*. The title *vir splendidus* was probably applied to the knights living outside Rome who had held no office.

Tac. Hist. I. 13; Suet. Galba, 14; Plin. N. H. 33. 29; Liv. Ep. 99.

Wilm. Ex. Inscr. 132, 1058, 1639, 2857.

**494. The Equestrian Cursus Honorum.** The members of the equestrian order were especially employed by the emperor as his representatives in the imperial service, and in the first century of our era a fixed equestrian *cursus honorum* developed. At the bottom of the series were the *militiae equestres*, including the *praefectura cohortis*, the

C. I. L. V. 8659; VI. 1625 b; IX. 5439.

*tribunatus legionis*, the *tribunatus cohortis vigilum*, or *cohortis urbanae* or *cohortis praetoriae*, the *praefectura alae*, and the *praefectura castrorum*. An aspirant for higher honors served in the early period in three, later in four of these positions. After the bureaucratic system of government had been fully developed by Hadrian, a preliminary civil career could be substituted for the military service just mentioned. After these preliminary military or civil positions came the various procuratorships, which may be classified according to the salaries received as *sexagenarii* (*i.e.*, recipients of 60,000 sesterces), *centenarii* (100,000 sesterces), *ducenarii* (200,000 sesterces), and *trecenarii* (300,000 sesterces). The highest official positions of the equestrian career were the prefectures, such, for instance, as the *praefectura vigilum* or the *praefectura annonae*. The knights gained in prestige under Gallienus, who transferred to the equestrian order all the important military positions. Membership in certain priesthoods was also reserved for the knights, and the most distinguished *equites* were from time to time admitted to the senate. In the nature of things, the *ordo equester* could not be an hereditary aristocracy, but the sons of knights who satisfied the conditions governing admission to the order were naturally preferred to others.

### (d) The Senatorial Order

**495. Admission to the Senatorial Order.** The privileges of the *nobilitas* under the republic had depended on the organization of society (cf. pp. 47 f.). The exclusive rights of the senatorial order under the empire had a legal basis. The conditions governing admission to the order were the same as in the case of the knights (cf. p. 392), except that the property requirement was 1,000,000 sesterces. For those who satisfied these conditions admission was to be had by birth, or through an imperial grant of the *latus clavus* to those who were not the sons of senators. Exclusion from the senatorial order was governed by the same principles as those which led to exclusion from the equestrian order (p. 392).

**496. Insignia and Titles.** The insignia of the order were the *anulus aureus*, the *calceus senatorius*, and the *latus clavus*. Like the knights, members of the senatorial order were entitled to reserved seats at the theatre and at the circus. From the close of the first century of our era they bore the title *viri clarissimi*, and even the younger members of a senator's family were styled *clarissimi pueri* or *clarissimae puellae*.

Suet. Aug. 38; Stat. Silv 5. 2. 27 f.; Will. I. 135.

**497. The Senatorial Cursus Honorum.** The main privilege which they enjoyed, however, was the exclusive right to become candidates for the republican magistracies (cf. p. 374), and thereby to gain admission to the senate. Certain important imperial offices also were open only to members of the order. The republican magistracies and the imperial offices open only to senators constituted the senatorial *cursus honorum*, which is illustrated in so many inscriptions.

C. I. L. V. 5262; X. 6006.

### (e) *Latinitas and Peregrinitas*

**498. Latinitas.** As a result of the Social war the rights of Roman citizenship had been granted to the people of Italy living south of the river Po (cf. p. 102). Julius Caesar extended the same rights to the communities of Transpadane Gaul (p. 122), so that there were no communities with Latin rights in the peninsula at the beginning of the imperial period. The *ius Latii* was, however,

conferred by Vespasian, Domitian, and other emperors
upon many cities in the provinces (p. 315). The citizens
of the *municipia* or *oppida civium Latinorum* or *coloniae
civium Latinorum*, as these Latin communities were vari-
ously called, had the *ius commercii*, and the prospect of
acquiring the rights of Roman citizenship, in case they
were elected to a local magistracy or admitted to the
local senate. They acquired Roman citizenship also if
they were enrolled in a legion, and individuals who had
rendered a noteworthy service to the state were rewarded
in the same way. Their right to vote in one of the
tribes at Rome (cf. p. 248) amounted to little under the
empire. In general they were subject to taxes and to military service. Mention has already been made (p. 390) of
the *Latini Iuniani*.

**499. The Peregrini.** Even those with Latin rights are
Liv. 8. 5. 8.    sometimes spoken of as *peregrini*, but the term is usually
applied only to freemen who had neither Roman nor Latin
citizenship. Into this category fell citizens of independent
states, and members of communities which Rome had conquered. Such legal rights as the *peregrini* had they gained
by treaties between their own states and Rome, or in the
court of the praetor, or through the charter of the province
in which they lived.

They were allowed to acquire property, to buy and to
sell, but they did not have the *ius conubii*, nor the right
to wear the toga, except as a specially granted privilege.
The *peregrini dediticii* (cf. p. 390) belonged to a special
category. A large addition was made by Marcus Aurelius
and some of his successors (p. 326) to the number of
the *peregrini dediticii* by the settlement of barbarian
colonists, especially on the banks of the Rhine and the
Danube.

**500. The Edict of Caracalla.** The edict of Caracalla in the year 212 granted Roman citizenship to all freemen living in the Roman empire. This measure did not affect the *Latini Iuniani* or the *peregrini dediticii*, nor did it preclude the possibility of establishing new colonies of *peregrini*. In point of fact, the first two classes are found after Caracalla's time, but probably no new colonies of *peregrini* were established.

### (f) *Political Divisions and Popular Assemblies*

**501. Tribes, Centuries, and Classes.** The division of the people into thirty-five tribes continued under the empire, but, since citizens were no longer subject to the *tributum* or to military service, it served no other political purpose than to indicate the citizenship of those whose names appeared in the list. The one practical purpose which the tribal list did serve was to give the names of those who were entitled to gratuities of grain, or to such other largesses as the state saw fit to dispense. Membership in a tribe was usually hereditary. Almost all freemen were assigned to the thirty-one country tribes; freedmen to the St. R. III. four urban tribes. Up to a late period the tribes were still 447 f. divided into centuries of *seniores* and *iuniores*. Even the C. I. L. VI. division of the people into classes continued for a time, 10215. but it ultimately disappeared before the new property rating on which the equestrian and senatorial orders were based.

**502. The Comitia Curiata.** After the fall of the republic we hear nothing of the *lex curiata de imperio* (p. 14), the one political measure upon which the *comitia curiata* had the right to act. That body still met, however, to pass on Suet. Aug. 65. family affairs which required formal action.

**503. The Comitia Centuriata.** The machinery of the *comitia centuriata* was still in existence, and the external forms were still observed, such as the taking of auspices and the displaying of a red flag on the Janiculum while the assembly was in session; but the centuriate *comitia* had lost its meaning, and for the sake of convenience almost all the measures which were submitted to a popular assembly were brought before the *comitia tributa*. The one legislative matter over which it had held exclusive control under the republic, viz., the declaration of an offensive war, was now within the competence of the emperor; the elections were transferred to the senate by Tiberius, and, although the assembly was called together a few days after the senate had elected the magistrates, to hear the *renuntiatio*, that ceremony was a simple act of confirmation by the multitude. The *quaestiones* had already supplanted the centuriate *comitia* in judicial matters.

Plin. Pan. 63;
Dio, 37. 28.

**504. The Comitia Tributa.** The *comitia tributa* assembled for the *renuntiatio* in the case of the curule aediles, the quaestors, and the *XX viri*, just as the centuriate assembly met to hear the announcement made of the newly elected consuls and praetors. In the field of legislation it played a more important part for a time than the centuriate *comitia*. Several of the important laws of Augustus were passed in this body, and ever in the reign of Domitian there is evidence of its activity, although, since most of the bills brought before it were probably drawn up by the *princeps*, its action can hardly have been free.

Dio, 58. 20.

Herz. II.
909, n. 3.

**505. The Concilium Plebis.** A similar state of things robbed the *concilium plebis* of all significance. It was still in existence under the early empire, but the measures which it passed were submitted to it by the *princeps* by virtue of his tribunician power.

## Selected Bibliography [1]

A. v. Brinz, Alimentenstiftungen d. röm. Kaiser, Sitzungsber. d. k. bayr. Akad. d. Wiss. 1887, Hist. Klasse, pp. 209 ff.

L. Cantarelli, I latini Iuniani. Bologna, 1883.

G. Cothénet, De la condition des pérégrins. Dijon, 1885.

L. M. Hartmann, De exilio apud Romanos usque ad Severi Alexandri principatum. Berlin, 1887.

H. Lemonnier, Étude hist. sur la condition privée des affranchis, etc. Paris, 1887.

F. Lindet, De l'acquisition et de la perte du droit de cité rom. Paris, 1880.

N. H. Michel, Droit de cité rom. Paris, 1885.

Stobbe, Ueber die Komitien unter den Kaisern, Philol. XXXI. 288–295.

[1] See also bibliography on pp. 265, 288, 304, 316, 328, 358.

# SUPPLEMENT

## THE ROMAN JUDICIAL SYSTEM

**506. Administration of Justice by the State.** Among primitive peoples the individual who has suffered an injury at the hands of another relies largely upon his own efforts, or those of his kindred, to regain his rights or to punish the offender. But this method of securing justice disturbs the peace, and often leads to excesses. Many offenses too, like theft or dishonesty, are a menace to the community. It is in the interest of the community, therefore, to compose differences between citizens, and to assist them in securing their rights. These considerations lead the state to take upon itself the administration of justice.

**507. The Roman Judicial System under the King.** The function is of course exercised by some official or officials representing the state. Since in the earliest period of Rome of which we have any positive knowledge the supreme power lay in the hands of the king, it was he, or some one delegated by him, who acted as judge in both civil and criminal cases. He was assisted by the *quaestores parricidi* (sec. 18), the *duumviri perduellionis*, and the pontiffs, and a decision was rendered in accordance with the ancestral customs. The pontiffs played an important part in such matters, because they alone knew the exact methods of procedure, and they were more familiar than any one else with the *mores maiorum*. They held this exceptional position until the Twelve Tables were published in 450 B.C., and the "forms of action" in 304 B.C. (cf. sec. 51). So far as procedure in

400

the regal period was concerned, probably the case was instituted before the king, and the finding of facts delegated to the duumvirs or the quaestors. If a capital sentence was imposed, an appeal to the people could be asked, but a citizen does not seem to have had the right to it.

508. **Division into Civil and Criminal Actions.** All civilized peoples think of wrongful acts as directed primarily either against the state or against the individual. Acts of the first kind constitute crimes; those of the second kind give rise to civil cases. Under the republic they were carefully distinguished, and courts were established for both classes of cases. In discussing the Roman judicial system, therefore, it will be our object to find out how these civil and criminal courts were organized and to study their method of procedure.

## (a) Criminal Courts

509. **Jurisdiction of the Family, the Church, and the State.** In the early period there were three classes of criminal offenses, of which the family, the church, and the state respectively took cognizance. The father of a family had the right to inflict a punishment, even that of death, upon any member of his household; the pontiff sat in judgment on such offenses against the gods as the lapse from chastity of a vestal virgin, and these two kinds of jurisdiction continued throughout republican history. But we are concerned here only with the administration of justice by the state.

510. **Officials who had Criminal Jurisdiction.** In its development the history of the Roman criminal courts of the republic falls into two periods, that of the early and middle republic, and that of the late republic. The dividing line is 149 B.C., when the first standing court, or *quaestio perpetua*, was established. The right to sit in judgment was

inherent in the imperium, and consequently all the republican magistrates with the imperium enjoyed it. Besides officials who had the imperium, quaestors, aediles, tribunes, and *triumviri capitales* had criminal jurisdiction in certain classes of cases. In the early period the conduct of criminal cases which would have been heard by the consul was usually delegated by him to the quaestor. The aediles prosecuted for usury and similar offenses. The tribunes brought charges against those who had violated the rights of the plebeians or had committed political offenses. The *triumviri capitales* were police magistrates, and especially heard charges of disorderly conduct. They also inquired into serious offenses committed by slaves or foreigners.

**511. The Popular Assemblies acquire Judicial Power.** The laws which gave citizens the right of appealing to a popular assembly in case the death sentence or a fine of 3020 *asses* was involved (cf. secs. 27, 30) brought about a great change in the conduct of criminal cases. These measures made the popular assemblies judicial bodies, and persons sentenced to either of the penalties mentioned were brought before them for trial. After the passage of the laws of the Twelve Tables all cases involving the death penalty were heard by the centuriate comitia ; but this penalty was rarely inflicted because an accused person could avoid the imposition of it by going into exile before the final vote was taken. Cases involving fines above the maximum mentioned were brought before the tribal assemblies. On occasions the assembly, at the request of the senate, passed a measure establishing a special court, or *quaestio extraordinaria*, to hear a given case.

**512. The Quaestiones perpetuae and their Composition.** It was probably the advantage which such a small judicial body of picked men had over a large assembly, which led the

Romans in 149 B.C. to establish a permanent court, or *quaestio perpetua* (*de repetundis*). This court, as its title indicates, was intended to try magistrates charged with extortion. On the analogy of it seven or eight others were established, each by a special law, to investigate such charges as those of treason (*maiestas*), corrupt practices at elections (*ambitus*), and peculation in office (*peculatus*). The system was rounded out by Sulla (cf. sec. 96), and after his day it was only in exceptional cases that criminal prosecutions were brought before a popular assembly or a *quaestio extraordinaria*. The presidency of these courts was held by praetors and ex-aediles, who bore the title of *iudices quaestionis*. Each year a list of several hundred jurors was drawn up by the praetor and the quaestor, and from this list (*album iudicum*) the panel for a particular trial was chosen by lot. From this panel both the prosecution and the defense could reject a certain number of unacceptable jurors, and the remaining number constituted the jury, whose size was fixed within certain limits by the laws establishing the several courts. The smallest jury of which we have any record numbered thirty-two, the largest seventy-five. Down to 123 B.C. the jurors were taken from the senatorial order; from that date to 70 B.C. they were all knights, but the *lex Aurelia* of 70 B.C. introduced a compromise under which juries were composed of senators, knights, and *tribuni aerarii*.

**513. Procedure in Criminal Courts.** We do not know how criminal cases were conducted before a magistrate or in a special court, but probably the magistrate compelled the attendance of the accused person and examined him, although before the special tribunals the practice of allowing private citizens to prosecute doubtless developed.

The method of procedure before a popular assembly has already been described (cf. sec. 309). The meetings of the standing courts were held in the Forum, with the praetor on his raised tribunal and the jurors seated on benches. The principal prosecutor (*accusator*), who was always a private citizen, might be supported by others (*subscriptores*). The accused (*reus*) was commonly represented by advocates (*patroni*) and attended by prominent friends (*advocati*), who assisted him by their presence and advice. The personnel of the court also included messengers, heralds, clerks (*viatores, praecones, scribae*), lictors, and a *consilium* of three or more jurists to give legal advice to the praetor. If several persons claimed the right to prosecute the accused man, as was not infrequently the case, the praetor selected the prosecutor in a preliminary proceeding (*divinatio*). The charge and the names of the accuser and the accused were then made a matter of record, and ten days or more were allowed the prosecutor to prepare his case. In the meantime the accused person was imprisoned or given his freedom on bail. At the next meeting the jury was constituted, and speeches were made by counsel for the prosecution and the defense. After the pleadings came the evidence, followed by brief questions and answers (*altercatio*) by *patroni* of the two parties to the case. The proceedings up to this point were *in iure;* with the active participation of the *iudices* they became *in iudicio*. An oath was administered to the jurors, and they retired to deliberate on their verdict. Each member of the jury was provided with a wooden tablet, covered on both sides with wax. In the wax on one side stood *c* (*ondemno*), on the other *a* (*bsolvo*). The juror erased the one or the other of these letters and deposited the tablet in an urn, or he could erase both letters, if the evidence had not convinced him of the guilt or the innocence of the accused person, and scratch the two letters n(*on*) l(*iquet*) on his tablet. A majority of the votes decided the case. Probably in the later period the tablets upon which *n. l.* had been written by jurors were counted for acquittal, but if these tablets were in the majority, the case could be instituted anew by a new prosecutor. The vote was counted and the verdict announced by the presiding magistrate, who also fixed the penalty under the law. The severest penalty was *aquae et ignis interdictio.* This meant that no one in Italy, for instance, was allowed to offer fire or water to a person upon whom this sentence had been passed, and was therefore equivalent to a decree of exile. From the decision of a *quaestio perpetua* there was no appeal. In case of acquittal the prosecutor was liable to the charge of *calumnia*, i.e. of having made a groundless accusation ; or of *praevaricatio*, i.e. of having conspired with the defense to secure an acquittal. In case of conviction he received a *praemium*, fixed by the magistrate and jury. The decisions of the civil as well as the criminal courts were based on statutes and judge-made laws. The Twelve Tables and the actions of the senate and of the popular assemblies made up the former ; the edicts of the magistrates, notably of the praetor (cf. sec. 204), gave rise to the latter.

**514. Ancient and Modern Procedure.** There are some interesting points of resemblance and of difference between the procedure adopted in the Roman court and that followed in our own criminal trials. The law in both cases is the secular law, uninfluenced by any ecclesiastical principles or religious observances save the administration of an oath. The case is adjudicated by a magistrate, who confines himself in the main to an interpretation of the law, and a jury which considers the facts and renders a verdict. The panel is chosen by lot and unacceptable jurors may be challenged.

Both oral and written testimony is admissible. The differences between the ancient and modern practices are of a comparatively minor character, but still they are important. A magistrate in modern times has no board of legal advisers, but the advice of such a body was necessary to a praetor who held office for a year only, and had no extended legal experience. The bringing of the action by a private citizen is not in accordance with our practice. A Roman trial was much shorter than one in modern times, being often concluded within a day. Under Anglo-Saxon law a majority vote of the jury does not settle a case as it did in Rome. The Romans, under the republic, had no graded series of courts from one to another of which an appeal could be taken. The point in the Roman procedure most remarkable to us lay in the presentation of the main arguments by counsel before the evidence had been heard, although, of course, use was made, by anticipation, of the testimony to be given. The same looseness of procedure which characterized the meetings of Roman legislative bodies (cf. sec. 276) is noticeable in the courts. Thus, for instance, the jury was not under careful surveillance ; prominent political friends of the accused occupied conspicuous places in the court, demonstrations of approval or disapproval occurred, and the rules of evidence were less strict than with us, so that even hearsay evidence was admitted.

**515. Criminal Trials under the Empire.** Under the empire the popular assemblies ceased to exercise their criminal jurisdiction. The *quaestiones perpetuae* continued to exist up to the third century of our era, but their importance was lessened even under the early empire by the establishment of the criminal jurisdiction of the senate and of the emperor. Under Augustus the *album iudicum* contained about four thousand names, under Caligula five thousand. Jurors were chosen for life from the knights and the *ducenarii*, or citizens who had a fortune of 200,000 sesterces. The procedure in the *quaestiones* continued without essential change, except that in case there was a majority of one only for conviction, the emperor, if he were present in court, could deposit the *calculus Minervae* and secure the acquittal of the accused person.

The criminal jurisdiction of the senate and the emperor has already been discussed (cf. secs. 412, 480). Of the more severe penalties the commonest were *relegatio*, which involved exile for life, often to a specified place, and *deportatio*, which included *relegatio* as well as the loss of citizenship and confiscation of property. The sources of criminal and of civil law under the empire were in part *senatus consulta*, but more particularly the edicts of magistrates and the *constitutiones principis* (cf. sec. 413).

### (b) Civil Courts

**516. Officials who had Civil Jurisdiction.** Since the quaestor had general supervision of the state treasury (cf. sec. 239), and since the censor had charge of farming the taxes and constructing public works (cf. sec. 213), almost all civil cases to which the state was a party came under the jurisdiction of these two officials. Such cases would include particularly the collection of money due the state and the enforcement of state contracts. The aediles had charge of the markets (cf. sec. 234), and consequently disputes with reference to mercantile transactions were naturally referred to them. Civil cases other than those mentioned came before the praetor.

**517. Organization of Civil Courts under the Republic.** Under the developed judicial system of the republic the division of the procedure in civil cases into the proceedings *in iure* and *in iudicio* was carefully observed. The magistrate conducted the former in person ; the latter were referred by him to a *iudex* or to *iudices*. The reference was made either to *iudices*, to *recuperatores*, to *arbitri*, to the *decemviri stlitibus iudicandis*, or to the *centumviri*. The method of making out the *album iudicum*, and of choosing a jury for a particular case has already been discussed (cf. sec. 512). The *recuperatores* were chosen, in accordance with treaties with foreign nations, for the trial of civil cases in which both citizens and *peregrini* were concerned. They made their appearance, therefore, in the court of the *praetor peregrinus*, but the procedure before them was so much more simple than that in other courts that they were not infrequently employed when citizens only were concerned. Such a number was selected by lot that after the prosecution and defense had exhausted their right of challenging, the board still numbered three or five. When it was necessary to use a large measure of discretion *arbitri* were called in. The difference between cases assigned to *iudices* and to *arbitri* has been clearly illustrated by Cicero (*pro Rosc. Com.* 4): *aliud est iudicium, aliud arbitrium. Iudicium est pecuniae certae ; arbitrium incertae. Ad iudicium hoc modo venimus, ut totam litem aut obtineamus, aut amittamus ; ad arbitrium hoc animo adimus, ut neque nihil, neque tantum quantum postulavimus, consequamur.* The decemviral and centumviral courts were permanent courts of great antiquity. The members were chosen for a year, those of the former court being elected in the tribal comitia, those of the latter being appointed by the praetor. Under the republic the centumviral court contained three representatives from each tribe, which gave it a total of one hundred and five members. The decemvirs considered cases affecting the civil status of citizens; the centumvirs dealt with such questions of ownership as those involved in inheritances and the transfer of land.

**518. Procedure by the Legis Actiones.** In the early period of the republic a claim was prosecuted in a civil court by one of the five *legis actiones*. These bore the following technical names : *per sacramentum*, *per iudicis postulationem*, *per condictionem*, *per manus iniectionem*, and *per pignoris capionem*. It will be sufficient for our purpose to consider the method *per sacramentum*, which was the commonest and is the one best known to us. Under it each party to the action deposited a guarantee, which was forfeited to the state by the losing party. The exact words of the law had to be followed, and any deviation from them caused the loss of the case. After this preliminary step had been taken before the magistrate, the case was usually referred to a *iudex*, who followed the procedure, borrowed by the *quaestiones*, which has already been described (cf. sec. 513).

**519. Procedure by the Formulary Method.** The technical difficulties of the old system and its failure to meet the needs of a more complex civilization led to the gradual introduction, in the second and first centuries before our era, of the formulary method, although the old system was retained in the decemviral and centumviral courts. The necessary flexibility to meet the growing industrial needs of the community was obtained through the use of the praetor's edict. In this document each praetor, at the beginning of the year, incorporated those maxims of law and forms of procedure which he would follow during his term of office (cf. sec. 204). It represented the edict of his predecessor with such modifications and additions as his own judgment and the needs of the times required. The growth of legal

principles and *formulae* which were thus embodied in the
praetor's edict kept pace with the development of society,
and the *formulae* of the praetor gradually supplanted the
*legis actiones* in the civil courts. When the formulary
method was followed the plaintiff summoned the defendant to appear before the magistrate on a certain day,
when the case at issue was presented by the two parties,
and the plaintiff requested the praetor to instruct the *iudex*
under a certain formula of the edict which he (the plaintiff)
had already picked out. The praetor either refused to
allow the suit to proceed, or he instructed the *iudex* under
the desired formula. A formula was made up of three
important parts : (1) the *demonstratio*, or grounds of action
on the part of the plaintiff ; (2) the *intentio*, or claim of the
plaintiff ; and (3) the sentence, which took the form of a
*condemnatio* or an *adiudicatio*. These three parts are well
illustrated by a typical case in Gaius (IV. 40 ff.) : (1) *quod
Aulus Agerius Numerio Negidio hominem vendidit*, (2) *si
paret Numerium Negidium Aulo Agerio sestertium X milia
dare oportere*, (3) *iudex Numerium Negidium Aulo Agerio
sestertium X milia condemna ; si non paret, absolve*. The
third part of the formula just given applies to a sum already
fixed, and is a *condemnatio*. If the sum was to be fixed by
a *iudex*, as when property was to be divided between
several litigants, the third part of the formula was an *adiudicatio*, and took some such form as this : *quantum adiudi-
cari oportet, iudex Titio adiudicato*. The essential portion of
the formula was the *intentio*, and it could even stand alone
when the *iudex* was called upon to pass judgment on the
truth or falsity of the statement embodied in it. The formula was presented to the *iudex* by the two parties to the
action. He fixed a day for the hearing, and with that the
proceedings *in iudicio* began. After the pleas of both sides

had been made, the evidence heard, and the *altercatio* finished, the *iudex* with his legal advisers, or with the jurors, retired to consider the verdict. The plaintiff was assisted by the magistrates in recovering from the defendant the award of the court. Under the *legis actiones* the plaintiff must plead his own cause, but under the formulary method advocates could be employed.

**520. Civil Courts under the Empire.** Under the empire the praetors and curule aediles and the *decemviri* and *centumviri* retained their functions, and to these officials and bodies are to be added the consul, who heard certain cases of appeal assigned to him by the senate, and the emperor, who in person or through a delegate heard cases in the first instance and on appeal. The centumviral court, which still kept the procedure by *legis actiones*, now numbered one hundred and eighty members and was divided into four chambers. Some cases in this court were heard successively before two chambers, others before the four chambers sitting together. The decemvirs acted as presidents of the chambers, with a praetor as first president. (Upon the judicial functions of the consul and emperor cf. secs. 464, 410, 411.) The formulary procedure continued in common use, except that decisions of the emperor and his delegates were made without calling in *iudices*. The practice of having a small board of legal advisers sit with the magistrate continued in force, and in course of time these *assessores*, as they were called, received a salary from the state. The parties to a civil case could also consult certain designated jurists; the advice of these specialists was binding on the *iudex*, and thus the *responsa prudentium* furnished a new and important source of law.

**521. Courts in the Provinces.** The governor of a province held court at convenient points, to which cases from the surrounding country were brought. In course of time regular " circuits " were established. From his jurisdiction free towns were exempt, and probably in other communities also the less important civil and criminal cases were settled in the local courts in accordance with local law. In the courts held by the governor or his delegate the Roman official conducted the proceedings *in iure*, but the examination into facts was made by *iudices*. Under the empire civil cases heard by the *legati* in senatorial provinces could be appealed to the proconsul and to the senate or emperor ; those which arose in imperial provinces could be appealed to the emperor. A governor had the right of life and death over *peregrini*, but capital cases where Roman citizens were concerned were referred to Rome.

### General Bibliography

Girard, Histoire de l'organisation judiciaire des Romains, I.   Paris, 1901.

Cuq, Les institutions juridiques des Romains, etc.   Paris, 1902.

Roby, Roman Private Law in the Times of Cicero and of the Antonines, 2 vols.   Cambridge (England), 1902.

Lenel, Essai de reconstitution de l'édit perpétuel.   Paris, 1901.

Greenidge, Legal Procedure of Cicero's Time.   New York, 1901.

# APPENDIX I

## (a) *Senatorial Documents*

**1.** Motion made by Caesar with reference to the Catilinarian conspirators (Sall. *Cat.* 51. 43). Cf. pp. 228 f.

Sed ita censeo, publicandas eorum pecunias, ipsos in vinculis habendos per municipia, quae maxume opibus valent, neu quis de eis postea ad senatum referat neve cum populo agat; qui aliter fecerit, senatum existumare eum contra rem publicam et salutem omnium facturum.

**2.** Motion made by Cicero in 43 B.C. with reference to Antony's soldiers (Cic. *Phil.* 8. 33).

Quas ob res ita censeo : eorum, qui cum M. Antonio sunt, qui ab armis discesserint et aut ad C. Pansam aut ad A. Hirtium consules aut ad Decimum Brutum imperatorem, consulem designatum, aut ad C. Caesarem pro praetore ante Idus Martias primas adierint, eis fraudi ne sit, quod cum M. Antonio fuerint. Si quis eorum, qui cum M. Antonio sunt, fecerit quod honore praemiove dignum esse videatur, uti C. Pansa, A. Hirtius consules, alter ambove, si eis videbitur, de eius honore praemiove primo quoque die ad senatum referant. Si quis post hoc senatus consultum ad Antonium profectus esset praeter L. Varium, senatum existimaturum eum contra rem publicam fecisse.

**3.** The *senatus consultum de Bacchanalibus*, so-called, of the year 186 B.C. (*C. I. L.* I. 196 = X. 104).[1] In reality

---

[1] In most of the epigraphical documents which follow, the text of Bruns, *Fontes Iuris Romani Antiqui* (6th edition, 1893), has been adopted.

it is a letter from the consuls embodying the decree, and addressed to certain municipal magistrates.

[*Q.*] Marcius L. f., S(p.) Postumius L. f. cos. senatum con-soluerunt n(onis) Octob. apud aedem Duelonai.

Sc(ribendo) arf(uerunt) M. Claudi(us) M. f., L. Valeri(us) P. f., Q. Minuci(us) C. f.

De Bacanalibus quei foideratei esent ita exdeicendum censuere :

Neiquis eorum *B*acanal habuise velet; sei ques esent, quei sibei deicerent necesus ese Bacanal habere, eeis utei ad pr(aitorem) urbanum Romam venirent, deque eeis rebus, ubei eorum ve*rb*a audita esent, utei senatus noster decerneret, dum ne minus senatorbus C adesent [*q̃uom e*]a res cosoleretur.

Bacas vir nequis adiese velet ceivis Romanus neve nominus Latini neve socium quisquam, nisei pr. urbanum adiesent, isque [*d*]e senatuos sententiad, dum ne minus senatoribus C adesent quom ea res cosoloretur, iousis*et*. Ce[*n*]suere.

Sacerdos nequis vir eset; magister neque vir neque mulier quisquam eset. Neve pecuniam quisquam eorum comoine[*m h*]abuise ve[*l*]et; neve magistratum, neve pro magistratu*d*, neque virum [*neque mul*]ierem quiquam fecise velet. Neve post hac inter sed conioura[*se nev*]e comvovise neve conspon-dise neve conpromesise velet, neve quisquam fidem inter sed dedise velet. Sacra in *o*quoltod ne quisquam fecise velet; neve in poplicod neve in preivatod neve exstrad urbem sacra quis-quam fecise velet, nisei pr. urbanum adieset, isque de senatuos sententiad, dum ne minus senatoribus C adesent quom ea res cosoleretur, iousis*et*. Censuere.

Homines plous V oinvorsei virei atque mulieres sacra ne quisquam fecise velet, neve interibei virei plous duobus, mulieri bus plous tribus arfuise velent, nisei de pr. urbani senatuosque sententiad, utei suprad scriptum est.

Haice utei in coventionid exdeicatis ne minus trinum noun-dinum, senatuosque sententiam utei scientes esetis eorum sen-tentia ita fuit : ' sei ques esent, quei avorsum ead fecisent, quam

suprad scriptum est, eeis rem caputalem faciendam censuere'
atque utei hoce in tabolam ahenam inceideretis, ita senatus
aiquom censuit, uteique eam figier ioubeatis, ubei facilumed
gnoscier potisit; atque utei ea Bacanalia, sei qua sunt, exstrad
quam sei quid ibei sacri est, ita utei suprad scriptum est, in
diebus X, quibus vobeis tabelai datai erunt, faciatis utei dismota
sient.— IN AGRO TEURANO.

4. An extract from the *senatus consultum de Thisbaeis*,
of the year 170 B.C., preserved on a marble tablet found in
Boeotia (Eph. Epigr. I, p. 278).

(*a*) Κόιντος Μαίνιος Τίτου υἱὸς στρατηγὸς τῆι συνκλήτωι συνε-
βουλεύσατο ἐν κομετίωι πρὸ ἡμερ[ῶ]ν ἑπτὰ εἰδυῶν Ὀκτωμβρίων.

Γραφομένωι παρῆσαν Μάνιος Ἀκίλιος Μανίου υἱὸς Ὀλτε[ινί]α,
Τίτος Νομίσιος Τίτου υἱός.

Περὶ ὧν Θισ[β]εῖς λόγους ἐποιήσαντο περὶ τῶν καθ' αὑ[τ]οὺς
πραγμάτων, οἵτινες ἐν τῆι φιλίαι τῆ· ἡμετέραι ἐνέμειναν, ὅπως
αὐτοῖς δοθῶσιν, [ο]ῖς τὰ καθ' αὑτοὺς πράγματα ἐξηγήσωνται.

περὶ τούτου τοῦ πράγματος οὕτως ἔδοξεν· ὅπως Κόιντος
Μαίνιος στρατηγὸς τῶν ἐκ τῆς συνκλήτου [π]έντε ἀποτάξηι, οἳ
ἂν αὐτῶι ἐκ τῶν δημοσίων πρα[γμ]άτων καὶ τῆς ἰδίας πίστεως
φαίνωνται. Ἔδοξε.

(*b*) Q. Maenius T. f. praetor senatum consuluit in comitio
a. d. VII idus Octobres.

Scribendo adfuerunt M'. Acilius M'. f. Vol(tinia), T. Numi-
sius T. f.

Quod Thisbaei verba fecerunt de rebus ad se pertinentibus
ii qui in amicitia nostra permanserunt, ut sibi darentur, quibus
res ad se pertinentes exponerent,

de ea re ita censuerunt: ut Q. Maenius praetor ex senatu
quinque delegaret, qui sibi e re publica fideque sua viderentur.
Censuere.

5. A *senatus consultum*, passed in 51 B.C. with reference
to Caesar's provinces (Cic. *ad Fam.* 8. 8. 5).

Pr. Kal. Octobris in aede Apollinis scrib. adfuerunt L. Domitius Cn. f. Fab. Ahenobarbus, Q. Caecilius Q. f. Fab. Metellus Pius Scipio, L. Villius L. f. Pom. Annalis, C. Septimius T. f. Quir., C. Lucilius C. f. Pup. Hirrus, C. Scribonius C. f. Pop. Curio, L. Ateius L. f. An. Capito, M. Eppius M. f. Ter. Quod M. Marcellus cos. v(erba) f(ecit) de provinciis consularibus, d(e) e(a) r(e) i(ta) c(ensuere), uti L. Paulus, C. Marcellus coss., cum magistratum inissent, ex Kal. Mart., quae in suo magistratu futurae essent, de consularibus provinciis ad senatum referrent, neve quid prius ex Kal. Mart. ad senatum referrent, neve quid coniunctim, utique eius rei causa per dies comitialis senatum haberent senatique consultum facerent, et, cum de ea re ad senatum referretur, a consiliis, qui eorum in CCC. iudicibus essent, s(ine) f(raude) s(ua) adducere liceret; si quid de ea re ad populum plebemve lato opus esset, uti Ser. Sulpicius, M. Marcellus coss., praetores tribunique pl., quibus eorum videretur, ad populum plebemve ferrent; quod si ii non tulissent, uti, quicumque deinceps essent, ad populum plebemve ferrent. C(ensuere).

**6.** A *senatus auctoritas* (cf. pp. 198 f., 229 f.) of the year 51. Four tribunes interposed their vetoes (Cic. *ad Fam*. 8. 8. 6).

Pr. Kal. Octobris in aede Apollinis scrib. adfuerunt L. Domitius Cn. f. Fab. Ahenobarbus, Q. *Caecilius* Q. f. *Fab*. Metellus Pius Scipio, L. Villius L. f. Pom. Annalis, C. Septimius T. f. Quir., C. Lucilius C. f. Pup. Hirrus, C. Scribonius C. f. Pop. Curio, L. Ateius L. f. An. Capito, M. Eppius M. f. Ter. Quod M. Marcellus cos. v(erba) f(ecit) de provinciis, d(e) e(a) r(e) i(ta) c(ensuere), senatum existimare neminem eorum, qui potestatem habent intercedendi, impediendi, moram adferre oportere, quo minus de r(e) p(ublica) p(opuli) R(omani) q(uam) p(rimum) ad senatum referri senatique consultum fieri possit: qui impedierit, prohibuerit, eum senatum existimare contra rem publicam fecisse. Si quis huic s. c. intercesserit, senatui placere auctoritatem prescribi et de ea

re ad senatum p(rimo) q(uoque) t(empore) referri. Huic s. c.
intercessit C. Caelius, L. Vinicius, P. Cornelius, C. Vibius
Pansa, tribuni pl.

7. The *senatus consultum de nundinis saltus Beguensis,*
found at Henschir Begar in Africa. Its date is A.D. 138
(*C. I. L.* VIII. 270 and Suppl. 11451).

SC. de nundinis saltus Beguensis in t(erritorio) Casensi,
descriptum et recognitum ex libro sententiarum in senatu
dic[*ta*]rum k(apite) VI T. Iuni Nigri, C. Pomponi Camerini
co(n)s(ulum), in quo scripta erant A[*frica*]ni iura et id quod
i(nfra) s(criptum) est.

In comitio in curia . . . . .

[*Scr*]ibundo adfuerunt Q. Sa[*l*]onius Q. f. Ouf. [*Lo*]ngus,
. . .·[*A*]ni Quar[*t*]inus, C. Oppius C. f. Vel. Severus, C.
For(?) . . C. f. . . . [*Sex. Eru*]ciu[*s*], M. f. Quir. Clarus, P.
Cassius L. f. Aem. Dexter q(uaestor), P. Nonius M. f. Ou[*f*].
Macrinus q(uaestor). In senatu fuerunt C.

SC. per discessionem factum.

Quod P. Cassius Secundus, P. Delphius Peregrinus Aleius
Alennius Maximus Curtius Valerianus Proculus M. Nonius
Mucianus coss. verba fecerunt de desiderio amicorum Lucili
Africani c(larissimi) v(iri), qui petunt: ut ei permittatur in
provincia Afric(a), regione Beguensi, territorio Musulamiorum,
ad Casas, nundinas IIII nonas Novemb. et XII k. Dec., ex eo
omnibus mensibus IIII non. et XII k. sui cuiusq(ue) mensis
instituere habere, quid fieri placeret,

de ea re ita censuerunt: permittendum Lucilio Africano,
c. v., in provincia Afric(a), regione Beguensi, territorio Musulamiorum, ad Casas, nundinas IIII non. Novemb. et XII k.
Decembr. et ex eo omnibus mensibus IIII non. et XII k. sui
cuiusq(ue) mensis instituere et habere, eoque vicinis adve-
nisq(ue) nundinandi dumtaxat causa coire convenire sine iniuria
et incommodo cuiusquam liceat.

Actum idibus Octobr. P. Cassio Secundo, M. Nonio Muci-
ano. Eodem exemplo de eadem re duae tabellae signatae

sunt. Signatores: T. Fl. Comini scrib(ae), C. Iuli Fortunati scrib(ae), M. Caesi Helvi Euhelpisti, Q. Metili Onesimi, C. Iuli Periblepti, L. Verani Philerotis, T. Flavi Crescentis.

## (b) *Actions of the Popular Assemblies*

8. Selections from the fragments preserved in literature of the Laws of the Twelve Tables, dating from 451–450 B.C. Cf. pp. 30 f.

### Tabula I

1. Si in ius vocat, ito. Ni it, antestamino: igitur em capito. Si calvitur pedemve struit, manum endo iacito. Si morbus aevitasve vitium escit, iumentum dato. Si nolet, arceram ne sternito.

2. Assiduo vindex assiduus esto; proletario iam civi quis volet vindex esto.

3. Rem ubi pacunt, orato. Ni pacunt, in comitio aut in foro ante meridiem caussam coiciunto. Com peroranto ambo praesentes. Post meridiem praesenti litem addicito. Si ambo praesentes, solis occasus suprema tempestas esto.

### Tabula II

1. ... Morbus sonticus .. aut status dies cum hoste .. quid horum fuit unum iudici arbitrove reove, eo dies diffissus esto.

2. Cui testimonium defuerit, is tertiis diebus ob portum obvagulatum ito.

### Tabula III

1. Aeris confessi rebusque iure iudicatis xxx dies iusti sunto. Post deinde manus iniectio esto. In ius ducito. Ni iudicatum facit aut quis endo eo in iure vindicit, secum ducito, vincito aut nervo aut compedibus xv pondo, ne minore, aut si volet maiore vincito. Si volet suo vivito. Ni suo vivit, qui eum vinctum habebit, libras farris endo dies dato. Si volet, plus dato.

2. Tertiis nundinis partis secanto.  Si plus minusve secue-
runt, se fraude esto.

3. Adversus hostem aeterna auctoritas [esto].

9. The first paragraph of the *lex Quinctia de aquaeduc-*
*tibus* of 9 B.C. (Frontin. *de Aq.* 129).  This is a *plebisci-*
*tum*.  On the method of voting in the two tribal assemblies,
cf. pp. 262 f.

T. Quinctius Crispinus consul populum iure rogavit populusque iure scivit in foro pro rostris aedis divi Iulii pr(idie)
[k.] Iulias.  Tribus Sergia principium fuit, pro tribu Sex......
L. f. Virro [primus scivit].

10. The *lex de imperio Vespasiani* (cf. pp. 270, 307,
341 f., 345).  It is of the year 69, and was found on a
bronze tablet at Rome (*C. I. L.* VI. 930).

.... foedusve cum quibus volet facere liceat ita, uti licuit
divo Aug(usto), Ti. Iulio Caesari Aug(usto), Tiberioque
Claudio Caesari Aug(usto) Germanico;

utique ei senatum habere, relationem facere, remittere, senatus consulta per relationem discessionemque facere liceat ita,
uti licuit divo Aug(usto), Ti. Iulio Caesari Aug(usto), Ti.
Claudio Caesari Augusto Germanico;

utique cum ex voluntate auctoritateve iussu mandatuve eius
praesenteve eo senatus habebitur, omnium rerum ius perinde
habeatur servetur, ac si e lege senatus edictus esset habe-
returque;

utique quos magistratum potestatem imperium curationemve
cuius rei petentes senatui populoque Romano commendaverit
quibusque suffragationem suam dederit promiserit, eorum
comitis quibusque extra ordinem ratio habeatur;

utique ei fines pomerii proferre promovere cum **ex re**
publica censebit esse, liceat ita, uti licuit Ti. Claudio Caesari
Aug(usto) Germanico;

utique quaecunque ex usu rei publicae maiestate*que* divinarum huma*na*rum publicarum privatarumque rerum esse censebit,

ei agere facere ius potestasque sit, ita uti divo Aug(usto), Tiberioque Iulio Caesari Aug(usto), Tiberioque Claudio Caesari Aug(usto) Germanico fuit;

utique quibus legibus plebeive scitis scriptum fuit, ne divus Aug(ustus), Tiberiusve Iulius Caesar Aug(ustus), Tiberiusque Claudius Caesar Aug(ustus) Germanicus tenerentur, iis legibus plebisque scitis imp(erator) Caesar Vespasianus solutus sit; quaeque ex quaque lege rogatione divum Aug(ustum), Tiberiumve Iulium Caesarem Aug(ustum), Tiberiumve Claudium Caesarem Aug(ustum) Germanicum facere oportuit, ea omnia imp(eratori) Caesari Vespasiano Aug(usto) facere liceat; —

utique quae ante hanc legem rogatam acta gesta decreta imperata ab imperatore Caesare Vespasiano Aug(usto) iussu mandatuve eius a quoque sunt ea perinde iusta rataq(ue) sint, ac si populi plebisve iussu acta essent.

Sanctio.

ʽSi quis huiusce legis ergo adversus leges rogationes plebisve scita senatusve consulta fecit fecerit, sive quod eum ex lege rogatione plebisve scito s(enatus)ve c(onsulto) facere oportebit, non fecerit huius legis ergo, id ei ne fraudi esto, neve quit ob eam rem populo dare debeto, neve cui de ea re actio neve iudicatio esto, neve quis de ea re apud [s]e agi sinito.

## (c) Edicts

11. Two sections from the *edictum perpetuum praetoris urbani*, entitled respectively (A) *De vi turba incendio rel.*, and (B) *De iniuriis.* Cf. pp. 190, 318.

### A. *De vi turba incendio rel.*

1. Vi bonorum raptorum et de turba. Si cui dolo malo hominibus coactis damni quid factum esse dicetur sive cuius bona rapta esse dicentur, in eum, qui id fecisse dicetur, iudicium dabo. Item si servus fecisse dicetur, in dominum iudicium noxale dabo. Cuius dolo malo in turba damni quid factum esse dicetur, in eum in anno, quo primum de ea

re experiundi potestas fuerit, in duplum, post annum in simplum iudicium dabo.

2. De incendio ruina naufragio rate nave expugnata. In
eum, qui ex incendio ruina naufragio rate nave expugnata
quid rapuisse recepisse dolo malo damnive quid in his rebus
dedisse dicetur: in quadruplum in anno, quo primum de ea re
experiundi potestas fuerit, post annum in simplum iudicium
dabo. Item in servum et in familiam iudicium dabo.

B. De iniuriis. 1....... Qui autem iniuriarum agit,
certum dicat, quid iniuriae factum sit, et taxationem ponat non
ma*i*orem quam quanti vadimonium fuerit.

2. Qui adversus bonos mores convicium cui fecisse cuiusve
opera factum esse dicetur, quo adversus bonos mores convicium
fieret; in eum iudicium dabo.

3. Ne quid infamandi causa fiat. Si quis adversus ea fecerit, prout quaeque res erit, animadvertam.

4. Qui servum alienum adversus bonos mores verberavisse
deve eo iniussu domini quaestionem habuisse dicetur, in eum
iudicium dabo. Item si quid aliud factum esse dicetur, causa
cognita iudicium dabo.

5. Si ei, qui in alterius potestate erit, iniuria facta esse
dicetur et neque is, cuius in potestate est, praesens erit neque
procurator quisquam existat, qui eo nomine agat: causa cognita
ipsi, qui iniuriam accepisse dicetur, iudicium dabo.

12. An extract from an edict of the curule aediles. Cf.
pp. 204 ff.

1. De mancipiis vendundis. Qui mancipia vendunt,
certiores faciant emptores, quid morbi vitiive cuique sit, quis
fugitivus errove sit noxave solutus non sit: eademque omnia,
cum ea mancipia venibunt, palam recte pronuntianto. Quod si
mancipium adversus ea venisset sive adversus quod dictum
promissumve fuerit, cum veniret, fuisset, quod eius praestari
oportere dicetur: emptori omnibusque, ad quos ea res pertinet,
(*in sex mensibus, quibus primum de ea re experiundi potestas
fuerit*) iudicium dabimus, ut id mancipium redhibeatur, si

quid autem post venditionem traditionemque deterius emptoris
opera familiae procuratorisve eius factum erit, sive quid ex eo
post venditionem natum adquisitum fuerit, et si quid aliud in
venditione ei accesserit, sive quid ex ea re fructus pervenerit
ad emptorem, ut ea omnia restituat, item, si quas accessiones
ipse praestiterit, ut recipiat. Item si quod mancipium capi-
talem fraudem admiserit, mortis consciscendae sibi causa quid
fecerit, inve harenam depugnandi causa ad bestias intromissus
fuerit, ea omnia in venditione pronuntianto : ex his enim causis
iudicium dabimus. Hoc amplius, si quis adversus ea sciens
dolo malo vendidisse dicetur, iudicium dabimus.

**13.** An edict of the censors of the year 92 B.C.
(Gell. 15. 11). Cf. pp. 192 ff.

Renuntiatum est nobis esse homines, qui novum genus
disciplinae instituerunt, ad quos iuventus in ludum conveniat;
eos sibi nomen imposuisse Latinos rhetoras ; ibi homines adu-
lescentulos dies totos desidere. Maiores nostri, quae liberos
suos discere et quos in ludos itare vellent, instituerunt. Haec
nova, quae praeter consuetudinem ac morum maiorum fiunt,
neque placent neque recta videntur. Quapropter et iis, qui eos
ludos habent, et iis, qui eo venire consuerunt, videtur faciundum,
ut ostenderemus nostram sententiam, nobis non placere.

**14.** A proclamation of the proconsul of Farther Spain
of the year 189 B.C. (*C. I. L.* II. 5041).

L. Aimilius L. f. inpeirator decreivit, utei quei Hastensium
servei in turri Lascutana habitarent, leiberei essent; agrum
oppidumqu(e), quod ea tempestate posedisent, item possidere
habereque iousit, dum poplus senatusque Romanus vellet.
Act(um) irr castreis a. d. XII k. Febr.

**15.** The *praescriptio* of a proclamation of the proconsul
of Sardinia of the year 69 (*C. I. L.* X. 7852).

Imp. Othone Caesare Aug. cos. XV k. Apriles descriptum
et recognitum ex codice ansato L. Helvi Agrippae procons(ulis),

quem protulit Cn. Egnatius Fuscus scriba quaestorius, in quo
scriptum fuit it quod infra scriptum est tabula V c . . . . . . VIII
et VIIII et X, etc.

16. An extract from an edict of the Emperor Claudius
of the year 46, bearing the title *de civitate Anaunorum*
(*C. I. L.* V. 5050). Cf. p. 349.

M. Iunio Silano Q. Sulpicio Camerino cos. idibus Martis
Bais in praetorio edictum Ti. Claudi Caesaris Augusti Ger-
manici propositum fuit id quod infra scriptum est:

Ti. Claudius Caesar Augustus Germanicus, pont(ifex) maxi-
m(us), trib(unicia) potest(ate) VI, imp(erator) XI, p(ater)
p(atriae), co(n)s(ul) designatus IIII, dicit:

Cum ex veteribus controversis pen*d*entibus aliquamdiu
etiam temporibus Ti. Caesaris patrui mei, ad quas ordinandas
Pinarium Apollinarem miserat, quae tantum modo inter
Comenses essent, quantum memoria refero, et Bergaleos,
isque primum apsentia pertinaci patrui mei, deinde etiam
Gai principatu quod ab eo non exigebatur referre, non stulte
quidem, neglexserit, et posteac detulerit Camurius Statutus ad
me, agros plerosque et saltus mei iuris esse: in rem praesentem
misi Plantam Iulium amicum et comitem meum, qui cum
adhibitis procuratoribus meis qu*i*que in alia regione quique in
vicinia erant, summa cura inquisierit et cognoverit, cetera
quidem, ut mihi demonstrata commentario facto ab ipso sunt,
statuat pronuntietque ipsi permitto.

17. An oath of allegiance to the Emperor Gaius, on a
bronze tablet found in Lusitania (*C. I. L.* II. 172).

C. Ummidio Durmio Quadrato, leg(ato) C. Caesaris Ger-
manici imp(eratoris) pro pr(aetore).

Ius iurandum Aritiensium.

Ex mei animi sententia, ut ego iis inimicus ero, quos
C. Caesari Germanico inimicos esse cognovero, et si quis
periculum ei salutiq(ue) eius in*f*er*t* in*f*er*et*que armis bello
internicivo terra mariq(ue) persequi non desinam, quoad

poenas ei persolverit: neq(ue) me [*neque*] liberos meos eius
salute cariores habebo, eosq(ue), qui in eum hostili animo
fuerint, mihi hostes esse ducam: si sciens fallo fefellerove,
tum me liberosq(ue) meos Iuppiter optimus maximus ac divus
Augustus ceteriq(ue) omnes di immortales expertem patria
incolumitate fortunisque omnibus faxint.

[*A. d.*] V idus Mai[*as*] in Aritiense oppido veteri Cn. Acer-
ronio Proculo, C. Petronio Pontio Nigrino cos., mag(istris)
Vegeto Tallici, . . . ibio . . . arioni.

18. A *tabula patronatus* by which the *pagus Gurzen-
sium* in Africa makes L. Domitius Ahenobarbus, the grandfather of Nero, its patron (*C. I. L.* VIII. 68).

P. Sulpicio Quirinio, C. Valgio cos. senatus populusque
civitatium stipendiariorum pago Gurzenses hospitium fecerunt
quom L. Domitio Cn. f. L. n. Ahenobarbo procos., eumque et
postereis eius sibi posterisque sueis patronum coptaverunt,
isque eos posterosque eorum in fidem clientelamque suam
recepit.

Faciundum coeraverunt: Ammicar Milchatonis f., Cynasyn-
(ensis); Boncar Azzrubalis f., Aethogursensis, Muthunbal
Saphonis f., Cui. Nas. Uzitensis.

### (d) *Inscriptions illustrating the Cursus Honorum*

19. Two inscriptions illustrating the *cursus honorum*
of a member of the senatorial order under the empire
(*C. I. L.* VI. 1333 and VI. 332). Cf. pp. 374, 395.

L. Aemilio L. f. Cam. Karo cos., leg. Aug. pr. pr. provinciae
Cappadociae, leg. Aug. pr. pr. censitori provinciae Lugdunensis, leg. Aug. pr. pr. provinciae Arabiae, curatori viae Flami-
niae, leg. leg. XXX U. V., praet., trib. pleb., quaest. Aug.,
trib. militum leg. VIII Aug., trib. militum leg. VIIII His-
panae, X viro stlitib. iudic., sodali Flaviali, XV viro s. f.,
C. Iulius Erucianus Crispus praef. alae primae Ulpiae Daco-
rum amico optimo.

[*Her*]cul[i] Victori P. Plotius Romanus cos., sod. Aug. Cl.,
leg. Aug. pr. pr. prov. Arab. item Gal., praef. aer. Sat., leg.
Aug. cens. acc. Hisp. Cit., iur. per Aem. Lig., cur. viae Labic.,
cur. Verc., pr. urb., trib. pl., q̄. kand., VI vir eq. R. tur. II̅,
trib. mil. legg. I Min. et II Adiut., IIII v. v. cur., aedem cum
omni cultu consecravit.

20. An inscription illustrating the *cursus honorum* of a
member of the equestrian order under the empire (*C. I. L.*
VIII. 9990). Cf. pp. 393 f.

P. Besio P. f. Quir. Betuiniano C. Mario Memmio Sabino
praef. coh. I Raetorum, trib. leg. X G. p. f., praef. alae
Dardanorum, procuratori imp. Caesaris Nervae Traiani Aug.
Germ. Dacici monetae, proc. provinc. Baeticae, proc. X̅X̅
hered., proc. pro leg. provinc. Mauretaniae Tingitanae, donis
donato ab imp. Traiano Aug. bello Dacico corona murali
vallari hastis pur. vexillo argent., exacti exercitus.

21. An inscription illustrating the official career of a
member of the third class (*C. I. L.* VI. 1808). Cf. pp.
391 f.

Sex. Caecilio Epagatho scrib. libr. tribunicio, apparitori
Caesarum, scrib. libr. q. III decur., viat. III vir. et IIII vir.,
scrib. libr. aed. cur., patri optimo, Sex. Caecilius Sex. f. Quir.
Birronianus et M. Caecilius Sex. f. Quir. Statianus.

# APPENDIX II

**SOME PASSAGES, DEALING WITH POLITICAL INSTITUTIONS,
FOUND IN LATIN WRITERS**

## (a) The Magistracies

### 1. The aediles, censors, praetors, and consuls.

Sunto aediles curatores urbis, annonae ludorumque sollem-
nium ; ollisque ad honoris amplioris gradum is primus ascensus
esto. — Censores populi aevitates, suboles, familias pecuniasque
censento ; urbis tecta templa, vias, aquas, aerarium, vectigalia
tuento ; populique partes in tribus discribunto ; exin pecunias,
aevitates, ordines partiunto ; equitum peditumque prolem descri-
bunto ; caelibes esse prohibento ; mores populi regunto ; probrum
in senatu ne relinquunto. Bini sunto ; magistratum quinquen-
nium habento [reliqui magistratus annui sunto] eaque potestas
semper esto. — Iuris disceptator, qui privata iudicet iudicarive
iubeat, praetor esto. Is iuris civilis custos esto. Huic potestate pari quotcumque senatus creverit populusve iusserit, tot
sunto. — Regio imperio duo sunto ; iique praeeundo, iudicando,
consulendo praetores, iudices, consules appellamino ; militiae
summum ius habento ; nemini parento ; ollis salus populi
suprema lex esto. Eumdem magistratum, ni interfuerint decem
anni, ne quis capito. Cic. *de Legg*. 3. 7–9.

### 2. Collegiality; magistratus maiores and minores. Cf. pp. 154 ff.

In edicto consulum, quo edicunt, quis dies comitiis centuriatis futurus sit, scribitur ex vetere forma perpetua : ne quis
magistratus minor de caelo servasse velit. Quaeri igitur solet,
qui sint magistratus minores. Super hac re meis verbis nil

ɒpus fuit, quoniam liber M. Messalae auguris de auspiciis
primus, cum hoc scriberemus, forte adfuit. Propterea ex eo
libro verba ipsius Messalae subscripsimus : Patriciorum auspicia in duas sunt divisa potestates. Maxima sunt consulum,
praetorum, censorum. Neque tamen eorum omnium inter se
eadem aut eiusdem potestatis, ideo quod conlegae non sunt
censores consulum aut praetorum, praetores consulum sunt.
Ideo neque consules aut praetores censoribus neque censores
consulibus aut praetoribus turbant aut retinent auspicia; at
censores inter se, rursus praetores consulesque inter se et vitiant
et obtinent. Praetor, etsi conlega consulis est, neque praetorem neque consulem iure rogare potest, ut quidem nos a
superioribus accepimus aut ante haec tempora servatum est et ut
in Commentario tertio decimo C. Tuditani patet, quia imperium
minus praetor, maius habet consul, et a minore imperio maius
aut maior [a minore] conlega rogari iure non potest. Nos
his temporibus praetore praetores creante veterum auctoritatem
sumus secuti neque his comitiis in auspicio fuimus. Censores
aeque non eodem rogantur auspicio atque consules et praetores.
Reliquorum magistratuum minora sunt auspicia. Ideo illi
' minores,' hi ' maiores ' magistratus appellantur. Minoribus
creatis magistratibus tributis comitiis magistratus, sed iustus
curiata datur lege ; maiores centuriatis comitiis fiunt.

Ex his omnibus verbis Messalae manifestum fit, et qui sint
magistratus minores et quamobrem ' minores ' appellentur. Sed
et conlegam esse praetorem consuli docet, quod eodem auspicio
creantur. Maiora autem dicuntur auspicia habere, quia eorum
auspicia magis rata sunt quam aliorum. Gell. *N. A.* 13. 15.

### 3. The right of appeal. Cf. pp. 27, 31, 98, 240 ff.

(P. Valerius Publicola) legem ad populum tulit eam, quae
centuriatis comitiis prima lata est, ne quis magistratus civem
Romanum adversus provocationem necaret neve verberaret.
Provocationem autem etiam a regibus fuisse declarant ponti-
ficii libri, significant nostri etiam augurales, itemque ab
omni iudicio poenaque provocari licere indicant XII Tabulae

compluribus legibus, et, quod proditum memoria est, decem viros, qui leges scripserint, sine provocatione creatos, satis ostenderit reliquos sine provocatione magistratus non fuisse; Luciique Valerii Potiti et M. Horatii Barbati, hominum concordiae causa sapienter popularium, consularis lex sanxit ne quis magistratus sine provocatione crearetur. Neque vero leges Porciae, quae tres sunt trium Porciorum, ut scitis, quidquam praeter sanctionem attulerunt novi. Itaque Publicola, lege illa de provocatione perlata, statim secures de fascibus demi iussit postridieque sibi collegam Sp. Lucretium subrogavit, suosque ad eum, quod erat maior natu, lictores transire iussit, instituitque primus ut singulis consulibus alternis mensibus lictores praeirent, ne plura insignia essent imperii in libero populo quam in regno fuissent. Cic. *de Re Publ.* 2. 53-5.

### 4. History of the quaestorship. Cf. pp. 206 f.

P. Dolabella censuit spectaculum gladiatorum per omnes annos celebrandum pecunia eorum qui quaesturam adipiscerentur. Apud maiores virtutis id praemium fuerat, cunctisque civium, si bonis artibus fiderent, licitum petere magistratus; ac ne aetas quidem distinguebatur, quin prima iuventa consulatum et dictaturas inirent. Sed quaestores regibus etiam tum imperantibus instituti sunt: quod lex curiata ostendit, a L. Bruto repetita. Mansitque consulibus potestas deligendi, donec eum quoque honorem populus mandaret. Creatique primum Valerius Potitus et Aemilius Mamercus, sexagesimo tertio anno post Tarquinios exactos, ut rem militarem comitarentur. Dein, gliscentibus negotiis, duo additi, qui Romae curarent. Mox duplicatus numerus, stipendiaria iam Italia, et accedentibus provinciarum vectigalibus. Post lege Sullae viginti creati supplendo senatui, cui iudicia tradiderat. Et, quamquam equites iudicia recuperavissent, quaestura tamen ex dignitate candidatorum aut facilitate tribuentium gratuito concedebatur, donec sententia Dolabellae velut venundaretur. Tac. *Ann.* 11. 22.

## (b) *The Senate*

**5. Rules governing meetings of the senate.** Cf. pp. 225 ff.

Gnaeo Pompeio consulatus primus cum M. Crasso designatus est. Eum magistratum Pompeius cum initurus foret, quoniam per militiae tempora senatus habendi consulendique, rerum expers urbanarum fuit, M. Varronem, familiarem suum rogavit, uti commentarium faceret εἰσαγωγικόν — sic enim Varro ipse appellat—, ex quo disceret, quid facere dicereque deberet, cum senatum consuleret. Eum librum commentarium, quem super ea re Pompeio fecerat, perisse Varro ait in litteris, quas ad Oppianum dedit, quae sunt in libro Epistolicarum Quaestionum quarto, in quibus litteris, quoniam quae ante scripserat non comparebant, docet rursum multa ad eam rem ducentia.

Primum ibi ponit, qui fuerint, per quos more maiorum senatus haberi soleret eosque nominat: ' dictatorem, consules, praetores, tribunos plebi, interregem, praefectum urbi,' neque alii praeter hos ius fuisse dixit facere senatusconsultum, quotiensque usus venisset, ut omnes isti magistratus eodem tempore Romae essent, tum quo supra ordine scripti essent, qui eorum prior aliis esset, ei potissimum senatus consulendi ius fuisse ait, deinde extraordinario iure tribunos quoque militares, qui pro consulibus fuissent, item decemviros, quibus imperium consulare tum esset, item triumviros rei publicae constituendae causa creatos ius consulendi senatum habuisse.

Postea scripsit de intercessionibus dixitque, intercedendi, ne senatusconsultum fieret, ius fuisse iis solis, qui eadem potestate, qua ii, qui senatusconsultum facere vellent, maioreve essent.

Tum adscripsit de locis, in quibus senatusconsultum fieri iure posset, docuitque confirmavitque, nisi in loco per augurem constituto, quod ' templum' appellaretur, senatusconsultum factum esset, iustum id non fuisse. Propterea et in curia Hostilia et in Pompeia et post in Iulia, cum profana ea loca

fuissent, templa esse per augures constituta, ut in iis senatus-
consulta more maiorum iusta fieri possent. Inter quae id
quoque scriptum reliquit, non omnes aedes sacras templa esse
ac ne aedem quidem Vestae templum esse.

Post haec deinceps dicit, senatusconsultum ante exortum
aut post occasum solem factum ratum non fuisse, opus etiam
censorium fecisse existimatos, per quos eo tempore senatusconsultum factum esset.

Docet deinde inibi multa : quibus diebus habere senatum
ius non sit; immolareque hostiam prius auspicarique debere,
qui senatum habiturus esset, de rebusque divinis prius quam
humanis ad senatum referendum esse ; tum porro referri oportere aut infinite de re publica aut de singulis rebus finite; senatusque consultum fieri duobus modis : aut per discessionem, si
consentiretur, aut, si res dubia esset, per singulorum sententias
exquisitas; singulos autem debere consuli gradatim incipique
a consulari gradu. Ex quo gradu semper quidem antea primum
rogari solitum, qui princeps in senatum lectus esset; tum
autem, cum haec scriberet, novum morem institutum refert
per ambitionem gratiamque, ut is primus rogaretur, quem
rogare vellet qui haberet senatum, dum is tamen ex gradu
consulari esset. Praeter haec de pignore quoque capiendo
disserit deque multa dicenda senatori, qui, cum in senatum
venire deberet, non adesset. Haec et alia quaedam id genus
in libro, quo supra dixi, M. Varro epistula ad Oppianum scripta
executus est.

Sed quod ait, senatusconsultum duobus modis fieri solere,
aut conquisitis sententiis aut per discessionem, parum convenire
videtur cum eo, quod Ateius Capito in Coniectaneis scriptum
reliquit. Nam in libro IX. Tuberonem dicere ait, nullum
senatusconsultum fieri posse non discessione facta, quia in
omnibus senatusconsultis, etiam in iis, quae per relationem
fierent, discessio esset necessaria, idque ipse Capito verum esse
adfirmat. Sed de hac omni re alio in loco plenius accuratius-
que nos memini scribere. Gell. *N. A.* 14. 7.

## 6. The expression of opinion and obstructive methods in the senate. Cf. pp. 227 ff.

Ante legem, quae nunc de senatu habendo observatur, ordo rogandi sententias varius fuit. Alias primus rogabatur qui princeps a censoribus in senatum lectus fuerat, alias qui designati consules erant; quidam e consulibus, studio aut necessitudine aliqua adducti, quem is visum erat honoris gratia extra ordinem sententiam primum rogabant. Observatum tamen est, cum extra ordinem fieret, ne quis quemquam ex alio quam ex consulari loco sententiam primum rogaret. C. Caesar in consulatu, quem cum M. Bibulo gessit, quattuor solos extra ordinem rogasse sententiam dicitur. Ex his quattuor principem rogabat M. Crassum; sed, postquam filiam Cn. Pompeio desponderat, primum coeperat Pompeium rogare.

Eius rei rationem reddidisse eum senatui Tiro Tullius, M. Ciceronis libertus, refert, itaque se ex patrono suo audisse scribit. Id ipsum Capito Ateius in libro, quem De Officio Senatorio composuit, scriptum reliquit.

In eodem libro Capitonis id quoque scriptum est: C., inquit, Caesar consul M. Catonem sententiam rogavit. Cato rem, quae consulebatur, quoniam non e re publica videbatur, perfici nolebat. Eius rei ducendae gratia longa oratione utebatur eximebatque dicendo diem. Erat enim ius senatori, ut sententiam rogatus diceret ante quicquid vellet aliae rei et quoad vellet. Caesar consul viatorem vocavit eumque, cum finem non faceret, prendi loquentem et in carcerem duci iussit. Senatus consurrexit et prosequebatur Catonem in carcerem. Hac, inquit, invidia facta Caesar destitit et mitti Catonem iussit. Gell. *N. A.* 4. 10.

## 7. Pedarii senatores. Cf. pp. 223 f.

Non pauci sunt, qui opinantur, 'pedarios senatores' appellatos, qui sententiam in senatu non verbis dicerent, sed in alienam sententiam pedibus irent. Quid igitur? cum senatusconsultum per discessionem fiebat, nonne universi senatores

sententiam pedibus ferebant? Atque haec etiam vocabuli istius
ratio dicitur, quam Gavius Bassus in Commentariis suis scriptam
reliquit. Senatores enim dicit in veterum aetate, qui curulem
magistratum gessissent, curru solitos honoris gratia in curiam
vehi, in quo curru sella esset, super quam considerent, quae
ob eam causam ' curulis' appellaretur; sed eos senatores, qui
magistratum curulem nondum ceperant, pedibus itavisse in
curiam; propterea senatores nondum maioribus honoribus
' pedarios' nominatos. M. autem Varro in satira Menippea,
quae Ἱπποκύων inscripta est, equites quosdam dicit ' pedarios'
appellatos, videturque eos significare, qui nondum a censoribus
in senatum lecti senatores quidem non erant, sed, quia honoribus populi usi erant, in senatum veniebant et sententiae ius
habebant. Nam et curulibus magistratibus functi, si nondum
a censoribus in senatum lecti erant, senatores non erant et, quia
in postremis scripti erant, non rogabantur sententias, sed, quas
principes dixerant, in eas discedebant. Gell. *N. A.* 3. 18. 1–6.

### 8. The praefectus urbi and the tribune as presiding officers in the senate. Cf. pp. 225 f.

Praefectum urbi Latinarum causa relictum senatum habere
posse Iunius negat, quoniam ne senator quidem sit neque ius
habeat sententiae dicendae, cum ex ea aetate praefectus fiat,
quae non sit senatoria. M. autem Varro in quarto Epistolicarum Quaestionum et Ateius Capito in Coniectaneorum IX.,
ius esse praefecto senatus habendi dicunt; deque ea re adsen-
sum esse Capito [Varro]nem Tuberoni contra sententiam Iunii
refert: Nam et tribunis, inquit, plebis senatus habendi ius erat,
quamquam senatores non essent, ante Atinium plebiscitum.
Gell. *N. A.* 14. 8.

### 9. Secret voting in the senate. Cf. p. 384.

Excesseramus sane manifestis illis apertisque suffragiis
licentiam contionum. Non tempus loquendi, non tacendi
modestia, non denique sedendi dignitas custodiebatur. Magni
undique dissonique clamores, procurrebant omnes cum suis

candidatis, multa agmina in medio, multique circuli ct indecora
confusio : adeo desciveramus a consuetudine parentum, apud
quos omnia disposita, moderata, tranquilla, maiestatem loci
pudoremque retinebant! Supersunt senes, ex quibus audire
soleo hunc ordinem comitiorum. Citato nomine candidati
silentium summum. Dicebat ipse pro se, explicabat vitam
suam, testes et laudatores dabat, vel eum sub quo militaverat,
vel eum cui quaestor fuerat, vel utrumque, si poterat; addebat
quosdam ex suffragatoribus; illi graviter et paucis loquebantur.
Plus hoc quam preces proderat. Nonnumquam candidatus aut
natales competitoris, aut annos, aut etiam mores arguebat.
Audiebat senatus gravitate censoria. Ita saepius digni quam
gratiosi praevalebant. Quae nunc immodico favore corrupta,
ad tacita suffragia quasi ad remedium decucurrerunt. Plin.
*Ep.* 3. 20. 3–7.

### 10. The frivolity of certain senators.

Scripseram tibi verendum esse ne ex tacitis suffragiis vitium
aliquod exsisteret. Factum est. Proximis comitiis in qui-
busdam tabellis multa iocularia atque etiam foeda dictu, in
una vero pro candidatorum nominibus suffragatorum nomina
inventa sunt. Excanduit senatus, magnoque clamore ei qui
scripsisset iratum principem est comprecatus. Ille tamen
fefellit et latuit, fortasse etiam inter indignantes fuit. Quid
hunc putamus domi facere, qui in tanta re, tam serio tempore,
tam scurriliter ludat? qui denique omnino in senatu dicax et
urbanus et bellus est? Tantum licentiae pravis ingeniis adicit
illa fiducia: "Quis enim sciet?" Poposcit tabellam, stilum
accepit, demisit caput: neminem veretur, se contemnit. Inde
ista ludibria, scaena et pulpito digna. Quo te vertas? quae
remedia conquiras? Ubique vitia remediis fortiora. Ἀλλὰ
ταῦτα τῷ ὑπὲρ ἡμᾶς μελήσει, cui multum cotidie vigiliarum,
multum laboris adicit haec nostra iners et tamen effrenata petu-
lantia. Plin. *Ep.* 4. 25.

## (c) *Popular Assemblies*

### 11. Popular assemblies in Athens and Rome.

O morem praeclarum, disciplinamque, quam a maioribus accepimus, si quidem teneremus! sed nescio quo pacto iam de manibus elabitur. Nullam enim illi nostri sapientissimi et sanctissimi viri vim contionis esse voluerunt. Quae sisceret plebes, aut quae populus iuberet, summota contione, distributis partibus, tributim et centuriatim discriptis ordinibus, classibus, aetatibus, auditis auctoribus, re multos dies promulgata et cognita, iuberi vetarique voluerunt. Graecorum autem totae res publicae sedentis contionis temeritate administrantur. Itaque, ut hanc Graeciam, quae iam diu suis consiliis perculsa et adflicta est, omittam, illa vetus, quae quondam opibus, imperio, gloria floruit, hoc uno malo concidit, libertate immoderata ac licentia contionum. Cum in theatro imperiti homines, rerum omnium rudes ignarique, consederant, tum bella inutilia suscipiebant, tum seditiosos homines rei publicae praeficiebant, tum optime meritos cives e civitate eiciebant. Cic. *pro Flacco*, 15 f.

### 12. The ius cum populo agendi. Cf. p. 164.

Idem Messala in eodem libro de minoribus magistratibus ita scripsit : Consul ab omnibus magistratibus et comitiatum et contionem avocare potest. Praetor et comitiatum et contionem usquequaque avocare potest, nisi a consule. Minores magistratus nusquam nec comitiatum nec contionem avocare possunt. Ea re, qui eorum primus vocat ad comitiatum, is recte agit, quia bifariam cum populo agi non potest nec avocare alius alii potest. Set, si contionem habere volunt, uti ne cum populo agant, quàmvis multi magistratus simul contionem habere possunt. Ex his verbis Messalae manifestum est, aliud esse 'cum populo agere,' aliud 'contionem habere.' Nam 'cum populo agere' est rogare quid populum, quod suffragiis suis aut iubeat aut vetet, 'contionem' autem 'habere' est verba facere ad populum sine ulla rogatione. Gell. *N. A.* 13. 16.

### 13. Some points concerning the comitia and the concilium. Cf. pp. 251 ff.

In libro Laelii Felicis ad Q. Mucium primo scriptum est, Labeonem scribere, 'calata' comitia esse, quae pro conlegio pontificum habentur aut regis aut flaminum inaugurandorum causa. Eorum autem alia esse 'curiata,' alia 'centuriata'; 'curiata' per lictorem curiatum 'calari,' id est 'convocari,' 'centuriata' per cornicinem.

Isdem comitiis, quae 'calata' appellari diximus, et sacrorum detestatio et testamenta fieri solebant. Tria enim genera testamentorum fuisse accepimus: unum, quod calatis comitiis in populi contione fieret, alterum in procinctu, cum viri ad proelium faciendum in aciem vocabantur, tertium per familiae emancipationem, cui aes et libra adhiberetur.

In eodem Laelii Felicis libro haec scripta sunt: Is qui non ut universum populum, sed partem aliquam adesse iubet, non 'comitia,' sed 'concilium' edicere debet. Tribuni autem neque advocant patricios neque ad eos referre ulla de re possunt. Ita ne 'leges' quidem proprie, sed 'plebiscita' appellantur, quae tribunis plebis ferentibus accepta sunt, quibus rogationibus ante patricii non tenebantur, donec Q. Hortensius dictator legem tulit, ut eo iure, quod plebs statuisset, omnes Quirites tenerentur. Item in eodem libro hoc scriptum est: Cum ex generibus hominum suffragium feratur, 'curiata' comitia esse, cum ex censu et aetate 'centuriata,' cum ex regionibus et locis, 'tributa'; centuriata autem comitia intra pomerium fieri nefas esse, quia exercitum extra urbem imperari oporteat, intra urbem imperari ius non sit. Propterea centuriata in campo Martio haberi exercitumque imperari praesidii causa solitum, quoniam populus esset in suffragiis ferendis occupatus. Gell. *N. A.* 15. 27.

### 14. Definition of a rogatio, a lex, and similar technical terms. Cf. pp. 255 ff.

Quaeri audio, quid 'lex' sit, quid 'plebiscitum,' quid 'rogatio,' quid 'privilegium.' Ateius Capito, publici privatique

iuris peritissimus, quid 'lex' esset, hisce verbis definivit:
Lex, inquit, est generale iussum populi aut plebis, rogante
magistratu. Ea definitio si probe facta est, neque de imperio
Cn. Pompei neque de reditu M. Ciceronis neque de caede
P. Clodi quaestio neque alia id genus populi plebisve iussa
'leges' vocari possunt. Non sunt enim generalia iussa neque
de universis civibus, sed de singulis concepta; quocirca 'privilegia' potius vocari debent, quia veteres 'priva' dixerunt, quae
nos 'singula' dicimus. Quo verbo Lucilius in primo Satira-
rum libro usus est:

abdomina thynni
Advenientibus priva dabo cephalaeaque acarnae.

'Plebem' autem Capito in eadem definitione seorsum a
populo divisit, quoniam in populo omnis pars civitatis omnes-
que eius ordines contineantur, 'plebes' vero ea dicatur, in qua
gentes civium patriciae non insunt. 'Plebiscitum' igitur est
secundum eum Capitonem lex, quam plebes, non populus,
accipit.

Sed totius huius rei iurisque, sive cum populus sive cum
plebs rogatur, sive quod ad [singulos sive quod ad] universos
pertinet, caput ipsum et origo et quasi frons 'rogatio' est. Ista
enim omnia vocabula censentur continenturque 'rogationis'
principali genere et nomine; nam, nisi populus aut plebs
rogetur, nullum plebis aut populi iussum fieri potest.

Sed quamquam haec ita sunt, in veteribus tamen scriptis
non magnam vocabulorum istorum differentiam esse animad-
vertimus. Nam et 'plebiscita' et 'privilegia' translaticio
nomine 'legis' appellaverunt eademque omnia confuso et
indistincto vocabulo 'rogationes' dixerunt. Sallustius quoque, proprietatum in verbis retinentissimus, consuetudini con-
cessit et privilegium, quod de Cn. Pompei reditu ferebatur,
'legem' appellavit. Verba ex secunda eius Historia haec sunt:
Nam Sullam consulem de reditu eius legem ferentem ex con-
posito tr. pl. C. Herennius prohibuerat. Gell. *N. A.* 10. 20.

## (d) Miscellaneous

### 15. Origin of Roman law.

Necessarium nobis videtur ipsius iuris originem atque processum demonstrare.  Et quidem initio civitatis nostrae populus sine lege certa, sine iure certo primum agere instituit, omniaque manu a regibus gubernabantur.  Postea, aucta ad aliquem modum civitate, ipsum Romulum traditur populum in triginta partes divisisse, quas partes curias appellavit propterea, quod tunc rei publicae curam per sententias partium earum expediebat, et ita leges quasdam et ipse curiatas ad populum tulit ; tulerunt et sequentes reges, quae omnes conscriptae exstant in libro Sexti Papirii. . . .  Is liber appellatur Ius Civile Papirianum, non quia Papirius de suo quidquam ibi adiecit, sed quod leges sine ordine latas in unum composuit.  Exactis deinde regibus lege tribunicia omnes leges hae exoleverunt iterumque coepit populus Romanus incerto magis iure et consuetudine aliqua uti quam per latam legem, idque prope viginti annis passus est.  Postea, ne diutius hoc fieret, placuit publica auctoritate decem constitui viros per quos peterentur leges a Graecis civitatibus et civitas fundaretur legibus ; quas in tabulas eboreas perscriptas pro rostris composuerunt. *Digest*, I. 2. 2.

### 16. The laws of the twelve tables.   Cf. pp. 30 f.

Fremant omnes licet, dicam quod sentio : bibliothecas mehercule omnium philosophorum unus mihi videtur XII Tabularum libellus, si quis legum fontes et capita viderit, et auctoritatis pondere et utilitatis ubertate superare.  Ac si nos, id quod maxime debet, nostra patria delectat, cuius rei tanta est vis ac tanta natura ut Ithacam illam in asperrimis saxulis, tamquam nidulum affixam, sapientissimus vir immortalitati anteponeret ; quo amore tandem inflammati esse debemus in eius modi patriam, quae una in omnibus terris domus est virtutis, imperii, dignitatis.  Cuius primum nobis mens, mos, disciplina nota

esse debet, vel quia est patria parens omnium nostrum, vel quia
tanta sapientia fuisse in iure constituendo putanda est, quanta
fuit in his tantis opibus imperii comparandis. Percipietis etiam
illam ex cognitione iuris laetitiam et voluptatem, quod quantum
praestiterint nostri maiores prudentia ceteris gentibus tum
facillime intellegetis, si cum illorum nostras leges conferre
volueritis. Incredibile est enim quam sit omne ius civile,
praeter hoc nostrum, inconditum ac paene ridiculum; de quo
multa soleo in sermonibus cotidianis dicere, cum hominum
nostrorum prudentiam ceteris omnibus et maxime Graecis
antepono. Cic. *de Or.* 1. 195-7.

### 17. The optimates and the populares.

Duo genera semper in hac civitate fuerunt eorum qui versari
in re publica atque in ea se excellentius gerere studuerunt;
quibus ex generibus alteri se populares, alteri optimates et
haberi et esse voluerunt. Qui ea quae faciebant quaeque
dicebant multitudini iucunda volebant esse, populares; qui
autem ita se gerebant, ut sua consilia optimo cuique pro-
barent, optimates habebantur. Quis ergo iste optimus quis-
que? Numero si quaeris, innumerabiles: neque enim aliter
stare possemus. Sunt principes consilii publici; sunt qui
eorum sectam sequuntur; sunt maximorum ordinum homines,
quibus patet curia; sunt municipales rusticique Romani; sunt
negotia gerentes, sunt etiam libertini optimates. Numerus, ut
dixi, huius generis late et varie diffusus est; sed genus universum, ut tollatur error, brevi circumscribi et definiri potest.
Omnes optimates sunt, qui neque nocentes sunt, nec natura
improbi, nec furiosi, nec malis domesticis impediti. Est igitur
ut ei sint, quam tu nationem appellasti, qui integri sunt, et
sani, et bene de rebus domesticis constituti. Horum qui
voluntati, commodis, opinionibus in gubernanda re publica
serviunt, defensores optimatium ipsique optimates gravissimi
et clarissimi cives numerantur, et principes civitatis. Cic. *pro
Sest.* 96.

**18. Municipia and coloniae.** Cf. pp. 59 f., 90 f., 281 f., 299 f.

'Municipes' et 'municipia' verba sunt dictu facilia et usu obvia, et neutiquam reperias qui haec dicit, quin scire se plane putet, quid dicat. Sed profecto aliud est, atque aliter dicitur. Quotus enim fere nostrum est, qui, cum ex colonia populi Romani sit, non se 'municipem' esse et populares suos 'municipes' esse dicat, quod est a ratione et a veritate longe aversum? Sic adeo et 'municipia' quid et quo iure sint quantumque a 'colonia' differant, ignoramus existimamusque meliore condicione esse 'colonias' quam 'municipia.'

De cuius opinationis tam promiscae erroribus divus Hadrianus in oratione, quam de Italicensibus, unde ipse ortus fuit, in senatu habuit, peritissime disseruit mirarique se ostendit, quod et ipsi Italicenses et quaedam item alia municipia antiqua, in quibus Vticenses nominat, cum suis moribus legibusque uti possent, in ius coloniarum mutari gestiverint. Praenestinos autem refert maximo opere a Tiberio imperatore petisse orasseque, ut ex colonia in municipii statum redigerentur, idque illis Tiberium pro ferenda gratia tribuisse, quod in eorum finibus sub ipso oppido ex capitali morbo revaluisset.

'Municipes' ergo sunt cives Romani ex municipiis, legibus suis et suo iure utentes, muneris tantum cum populo Romano honorari participes, a quo munere capessendo appellati videntur, nullis aliis necessitatibus neque ulla populi Romani lege adstricti, nisi in quam populus eorum fundus factus est. Primos autem municipes sine suffragii iure Caerites esse factos accepimus concessumque illis, ut civitatis Romanae honorem quidem caperent, sed negotiis tamen atque oneribus vacarent pro sacris bello Gallico receptis custoditisque. Hinc 'tabulae Caerites' appellatae versa vice, in quas censores referri iubebant, quos notae causa suffragiis privabant.

Sed 'coloniarum' alia necessitudo est; non enim veniunt extrinsecus in civitatem nec suis radicibus nituntur, sed ex civitate quasi propagatae sunt et iura institutaque omnia populi

Romani, non sui arbitrii, habent. Quae tamen condicio, cum sit magis obnoxia et minus libera, potior tamen et praestabilior existimatur propter amplitudinem maiestatemque populi Romani, cuius istae coloniae quasi effigies parvae simulacraque esse quaedam videntur, et simul quia obscura oblitterataque sunt municipiorum iura, quibus uti iam per innotitiam non queunt. Gell. *N. A.* 16. 13.

# INDEX[1]

Ab actis senatus 477

Ab epistulis 436

Accensus 170

A censibus equestribus 490

A cognitionibus 438

Acta diurna 477

Acta senatus 477

Actium 142

Adiudicatio, the 519

Adlectio 22, 425, 473

Adrogatio 22

Advocati 513

Aediles ceriales, instituted 127

Aediles curules, instituted 38, 230; plebeians eligible 43; relation to plebeian aediles 231; powers 232–236; division of duties 237; under the empire 467

Aediles plebei, instituted 27; early functions 228; development of office 229; relation to curule aediles 231; powers 232–236; division of duties 237; under the empire 467

Aelius, L., emperor 377

Aelius Sejanus, L. 347

Aemilius Lepidus, M. 135, 139

Aerarium militare, the 422, 447

Aerarium Saturni, the 419, 445

Ager publicus, the 9, 29, 36, 85–86; control of 184

Agrippina, the younger 351–352

Album iudicum, the 512, 515

Album senatorium, the 473

A libellis 437

A memoria 439

Amici Augusti, the 434

Antiochus 77

Antoninus Pius 376

Antonius, M., Caesar's lieutenant 109; consul in 44 B.C. 131, relations with Octavius 134–142

Apparitores 170

Appeals, under king 507; under the republic 27, 30, 31, 87, 159, 287, 511, 513; under the empire 515, 520, 521

A rationibus 435

Arbitri 517

Army, the, reformed by Servius Tullius 23; its officers 159, 186; as a political factor 117, 388; reformed by Augustus 345; under the empire 388, 409

Asia 77, 110–112, 114

Assemblies, the popular, as criminal courts 511; procedure 513. See also *comitia centuriata* and *tributa*, and *concilium plebis*

Assessores 520

Auctoritas patrum, the, and legislation 50, 94. See also the *senate*

Augusti, the, of the system of Diocletian 394

---

[1] The numbers refer to the sections.

The numbers refer to the sections.

The numbers refer to the sections.

The numbers refer to the sections.